Freud

An Introduction to his Life and Work

J. N. Isbister

Polity Press

© J. N. Isbister, 1985

First published 1985 by
Polity Press, Cambridge, in association with Basil Blackwell, Oxford. Reprinted 1985.

Editorial Office: Polity Press
                    Dales Brewery, Gwydir Street, Cambridge, CB1 2LJ, UK.

Basil Blackwell Ltd
108, Cowley Road, Oxford, OX4 1JF, UK.

Basil Blackwell Inc.
432 Park Avenue South, Suite 1505, New York, NY 10016, USA.

British Library Cataloguing in Publication Data

Isbister, J. N.
   Freud: an introduction to his life and work.
   1. Freud, Sigmund   2. Psychoanalysts,
   Austria – Biography
   I. Title
   150.19'52   BF173.F85

   ISBN 0-7456-0013-1
   ISBN 0-7456-0014-X Pbk

Library of Congress Cataloging in Publication Data

Isbister, J. H.
   Freud, an introduction to his life and work.

   Bibliography: p.
   Includes index.
   1. Freud, Sigmund, 1856–1939. 2. Psychoanalysts –
   Austria – Biography. I. Title.
   BF173.F85183   1984   150.19'52[B]   84-18229
   ISBN 0-7456-0013-1
   ISBN 0-7456-0014-X (pbk.)

Phototypeset by Dobbie Typesetting Service, Plymouth, Devon.
Printed and Bound in Great Britain by T.J. Press (Padstow) Ltd, Padstow, Cornwall

For Judy, in gratitude for all we have shared:
When we can share – that is poetry in the prose of life. (Freud)

and for Sam and Joe, for the future:
The world is still there for them to conquer, so far as may be in their power. I leave them only a foothold; I have not led them to a mountain-peak from which they could climb no higher. (Freud)

Freud

Fools, visionaries, sufferers from delusions, neurotics and lunatics have played great roles at all times in the history of mankind and not merely when the accident of birth had bequeathed them sovereignty. Usually they have wreaked havoc; but not always. Such persons have exercised far-reaching influence upon their own and have made great discoveries. They have been able to accomplish such achievements on the one hand through the help of the intact portion of their personalities, that is to say in spite of their abnormalities; but on the other hand it is often precisely the pathological traits of their characters, the one-sidedness of their development, the abnormal strengthening of certain desires, the uncritical and unrestrained abandonment to a single aim, which give them the power to drag others after them and to overcome the resistance of the world . . . We cannot . . . deny that, in this case as in all cases, a more intimate knowledge of a man may lead to a more exact estimate of his achievements. (Sigmund Freud, 1932)

Contents

List of Plates

Acknowledgements

I should like to record my gratitude to Peter Swales, as Janet Malcolm has recently described him 'perhaps *the* leading authority . . . on the early life of Freud and on the early history of psychoanalysis'. Had it not been for his encouragement, both in direct communication, and through his sending me his many essays on Freud (most of which are only privately published) I doubt whether this book would have been written. His insight into Freud has provided many of the central themes of this work. Again, I should like to record my debt also to the standard, major 'biographical' treatments of Freud. Though my interpretation is often at variance with these 'biographies' I doubt if any biographical work on Freud can fail to be impressed by, indebted to, reliant upon the work of Ernest Jones, Frank Sulloway and Ronald Clark.

I should further like to thank Elaine Iles of Sigmund Freud Copyrights Ltd for her encouragement; Robin Keely and Simon Jenkins of Lion Publishing for theirs; and Tony Giddens for the final impetus he provided to produce the book.

I have made extensive use of the facilities of the following institutions: the Ipswich Hospital Medical Library; the Department of Psychology MacCurdy Library, Cambridge University; and the University Libraries at Cambridge and Leicester. I am grateful to the forbearance of the librarians in each of these libraries.

In terms of the production of the final manuscript I should like to thank: John Forrester for his incisive comments on an earlier draft; Malcolm Elliman for his skill in checking grammar and sense in my prose; Lorraine Evans and Susan Chandler for their typing skills; Helen Pilgrim at Basil Blackwell for her patience.

This book would not have been possible but for the generous help of my parents and my parents-in-law – I offer them my thanks for creating the opportunity for me to write.

Finally, to an extent that defies description, my wife and family have given so much to this book that my dedication can only be to them.

The author and publishers are also indebted to a large number of individuals, institutions and organizations for granting permission to reprint material in this book. Full details are given in the permissions acknowledgements on p. 304.

Introduction

The world is the world through its theorists. Their function is to conceive of the whole and, from the centre of their immense perspectives, to tell us about it. (Wallace Stevens)

Throughout the history of humankind there have been thinkers whose theories have quite literally dominated the thoughts and perceptions of those who followed after them. In the West our minds spring quite naturally to the names of Plato and Aristotle, to Isaac Newton and Albert Einstein, to Charles Darwin and Karl Marx. In the East the names of Lao Tzu or Mao-Tse-Tung might spring more readily to mind. Of all such men, who have told us about the world from their 'immense perspectives', one, Sigmund Freud, would probably have pride of place in any discussion about those who have theorized about the mind. To many, the name of Sigmund Freud is synonymous with the science of the mind, with psychology, and they would find it difficult to name any comparable figure of equal stature from the field. This identification of his name with the science of psychology would have pleased Freud greatly for he certainly conceived himself to be the instigator of a new science 'depth psychology' or psychoanalysis.

However, nowadays, Freud is not just heralded as a great psychologist, or as the instigator of a new discipline for his influence and ideas have spread far wider than the narrow confines of a specialized scientific discourse. They have affected our culture in many and varied ways and they pervade society. We may illustrate this by posing a number of questions, the answers to which most probably would contain some element of Freudian thought. Many parents, for example, as they watched their young children grow and develop, must have asked themselves questions about what is going on in the minds of their children, particularly in relation to sexuality. Most people too, will have come across the problem of mental illness, whether through painful personal experience, or as a result of some less direct contact, and have asked themselves the questions about the causes or the meanings behind it. Similarly, in the sphere of our own behaviour how many of us have not wondered about whether seemingly innocent blunders, or strange dreams, or aspects of our own idiosyncrasies, are not some sign or symbol of hidden motives or desires, or an indication of emotional immaturity or impoverishment? Or how many people have not been faced with questions concerning their beliefs and ideals, and have not wondered about the relationship between these and the views of their parents and society? Students, from social workers to philosophers, are frequently confronted during the course of their studies with psychoanalytic theories (often presented in a barrage of other theories and ideologies), and have to face the important methodological questions psychoanalysis raises. In all these questions, our perception of the phenomena under scrutiny has been subtly and persuasively coloured by Freudian thinking. Many of the very terms we use in our explanations of human behaviour – repression, suppression, projection, sublimation, the unconscious, the complex, the ego, the libido – though not necessarily invented by Freud, received an indelible stamp upon them by his theorizing. As such, Freud contributed to something much wider than merely the growth of a scientific discipline. He has contributed to the whole cultural milieu of the twentieth century in that he has given us a way of seeing things. In doing so he has established no more than those other great figures of Newton, Marx, Darwin or Einstein who equally framed the perceptions of their contemporaries, and of subsequent generations.

The fact that Freud has effected this would have pleased him as much as the fact that he is remembered as a great psychologist. Throughout his life he longed to fulfil a destiny. He once wrote to his fiancée that he 'could gladly sacrifice [his] life for one great moment in history'.[1] He saw that 'great moment' as one that transcended the realms of science, that reached out to affect the very way that men conceive of themselves. He set out to conquer mankind's self-perception. With the skill and ingenuity of his great childhood heroes – Hannibal, Oliver Cromwell, Napoleon – Freud set out to take on the powers of traditions, science, and religion to fashion a new image of what it is to be human.

He began his career as a man of science, and as a physician hoping to cure individuals with emotional problems, but he was led inexorably to consider wider questions of a more philosophical or religious nature. He felt he had an answer (a scientific answer) to the age-old question posed by the psalmist 'What is man that thou art mindful of him?' Freud's answer to that question was straightforward and uncompromising: humanity was an imperfect product of nature; a battleground of irrational forces; a creature driven by barely controllable impulses and drives. To Freud, we can, at best, convert these impulses into creative channels, but at worst we can indulge ourselves in selfishness and destruction. Accordingly, even our most noble creations – science, art, literature, religion – were products of a dark continent of unconscious forces, and our highest ideals were irremediably held captive by infantile desires. He felt it was his task to complete the revolution begun when Copernicus ousted the earth from the centre of the universe, and when Darwin succeeded in closing the gap between humankind and the rest of creation. He felt that his mission was to effect the final blow to any vestiges of self-pretension to divinity that humanity might still possess. He did this by showing that human beings were nothing but products of nature, minds or souls equally being nature's products. Our human characteristics thus became merely transformed animal desires, and our 'higher powers' – our rationality, morality, self-consciousness – were only superficial epiphenomena resting uneasily upon their ultimate sources – irrationality, biological necessity, and the unconscious.

It is not possible to assess Freud's claim for 'a place beside Copernicus and Darwin' without standing back and establishing the grounds for his claim. We cannot discover whether he has in fact delivered the final death-blow to what he called 'the naïve self-love of man' and our 'megalomania' in believing that we have any other significance apart from being a part of nature. These wider claims have to be seen within the whole context of his life and thought – in isolation they remain stark assertions the validity of which we remain at a loss to grasp. Once his ideas are seen within their proper biographical and intellectual context it becomes much easier to weigh and evaluate them; in his own words 'a more intimate knowledge of a man may lead to a more exact estimate of his achievements'.[2]

This book, therefore, has a threefold aim: I intend first, to provide a brief account of the life of Sigmund Freud; secondly, to sketch the details of the evolution of his ideas pointing out some of their origins and some of the transformations Freud wrought on them; finally, I attempt to assess those ideas, in relation to his life, and our contemporary understanding of man, and in the light of those wider philosophical or religious questions that he himself claimed to have answered. Freud stressed the negative aspects of humanity and dwelt upon the darker aspects of his soul, yielding to pessimism and nihilism. No one, I am sure, would deny that we do have dark, hidden, destructive, irrational elements in our natures (who, in our world where wars and atrocities are daily displayed on our television screens could deny it?). Freud's emphasis on these as ultimate sources of our behaviour is, I believe, an oversimplification. Human behaviour, indeed, what it is to be human, is far more complex than Freud would have had us believe. The answer to the age-old question concerning the nature of man requires a psychology and an anthropology which is far richer than Freud's reductive model. The human sciences, while they need to work through the insights Freud developed, require an understanding of human beings that is far more complex than psychoanalysis posits; in particular, they require models that maintain a balance or poise between the dark elements and the light.

We may say that these sciences require an adequate 'image of what it is to be human' in order to remain *human* sciences.[3]

Freud himself would have hated a book such as this, quite apart from any redress I might uphold to his one-sided model of humankind, for he had a jaundiced view of biography in general; and an aversion to biographies about himself in particular. He detested and feared the prospect of his own life being made the subject of a biography. He was always less than candid about the origins and evolution of his thought. Concerning biography in general he once wrote: 'Anyone turning biographer commits himself to lies, to concealment, to hypocrisy, to flattery, and even to hiding his own lack of understanding, for biographical truth is not to be had, and even if it were couldn't be used. Truth is unobtainable: humanity does not deserve it. . . .'[4] Concerning his own biography specifically, he was emphatic that 'the public has no concern with my personality, and can learn nothing from an account of it, so long as my case (for manifold reasons) cannot be expounded without any reserves whatever'.[5] Moreover, he felt that he had actually revealed enough of himself in his works to provide a sufficient biographical context: 'The public has no claim to learn anymore of my personal affairs . . . I have . . . been more open and frank in some of my writings . . . than people usually are who describe their lives for their contemporaries or for posterity.'[6]

Perhaps the most revealing passage we have from Freud's pen, however, about biography and his own development, comes from one of his letters to his fiancée in 1885. In that letter he described how he had made a bonfire of all his 'letters, scientific excerpts, and the manuscripts of [his] papers'. There is a sense of glee in Freud as he confessed 'all my thoughts and feelings about the world in general and about myself in particular have been found unworthy of further existence'. Freud was particularly concerned lest any of these early thoughts and papers escape destruction: 'I couldn't have matured or died without worrying about who would get hold of those old papers.' It is ironic that this man who claimed to be so frank and open about his own life should have left such a revealing hint of his own fundamental fear of self-disclosure, and of his own desire to obscure his origins. He closed his account of his feast of destruction with the ultimate challenge to any biographer: 'As for the biographers, let them worry, we have no desire to make it too easy for them. Each one of them will be right in his opinion of "The Development of the Hero" and I am already looking forward to seeing them go astray.'[7] Freud, many years later, said of yet another of his heroes, Goethe, 'not only was he a great revealer, but he was also, in spite of the wealth of autobiographical hints, a careful concealer'.[8] The assessment is eminently applicable to Freud himself, who used to like to quote from Goethe's *Faust* 'the best that you know you must not tell to the boys'.[9]

The incident reported to his fiancée was the first of two occasions when Freud totally destroyed any evidence which might have put his ideas in context (the second time was in 1907). In addition, when in 1938 he was forced to flee Austria following the Nazi take over of the country he also had to destroy many of his papers lest they fall into Nazi hands. Many, including Freud himself, have attempted to chronicle 'the development of the hero', and many, as Freud predicted, have gone palpably wrong in their interpretations. Though wrong, they should not necessarily be blamed, for these three premature funeral pyres have created two vast lacunae in Freud studies. Biographical work on Freud is further hampered by an embargo on many of his letters (some of which have been published – but in bowdlerized form with passages deleted); and by the fact that Freud had a propensity for remembering and recording history in a particularly one-sided way. In the absence of the evidence available from the missing documents and the unpublished letters, Freud's life has taken on a mythological character. Myths abound around his life, many having been self-generated. One Freud scholar, writing recently, has suggested that there are twenty-six recognizable and refutable myths surrounding Freud and his life.[10]

Freud: An Introduction to his Life and Work offers one account of 'the development of the hero'. For many it will be an introductory text to the man and his ideas. I have attempted to steer a precarious path between exposition and criticism in the body of the book. I have, in general, preferred to let Freud speak for himself, where possible; however, it is important when reading Freud's own words to bear in mind the date when they were written, for he was the master of *double entendre* – words which purport to be about one situation frequently refer to many others. Accordingly, I have adopted a slightly unusual form of referencing which gives either the date when the words were written (in the case of letters and unpublished material), or when they were published (in the case of material that Freud actually had published) immediately after any quotation. In fact this is not an absolute guide to the precise timing of his words and thoughts as there were a number of occasions when material he had completed was held back from publication for various reasons. The presence of these dates in the text, though at times obtrusive to the narrative, is intended to serve as a reminder to the reader that often *when* Freud said something is as important as *what* he said.

1

Beginnings
Early Days and Early Influences

In my beginning is my end. (T. S. Eliot)

It is a truism, oft repeated by poets and philosophers, that the child is father of the man. Biographers are particularly prone to the tendency to uphold this principle. They constantly seek to find in the early lives of their subjects the pointers to their future destinies. In the absence of firm biographical material about a person this desire can degenerate into a fixation upon the few isolated incidents available for biographical attention. Freud himself was prone to this kind of error in his later years interpreting the whole life of a person, and building an entire psychological portrait of a person, around the one recorded childhood memory of that person (cf. chapter 5). With respect to Freud's own beginnings we are fortunate in that there is a fair deal of material available about his early life. Interest in Freud and his beginnings has been a legitimate field of study ever since he began to become famous in the 1920s and 1930s. One might even say that there is a veritable 'Freud Industry', thriving, despite the recession, on the search for yet more detail of his life.

For all that we have already, when we come to order that material we are faced immediately with a problem, indeed a problem that resides at the very heart of the whole of Freud's psychoanalysis. The problem arises because much of the biographical material that we have comes from Freud himself. Not only that, Freud produces this biographical detail within the context of the exposition of his theories; in fact, frequently, the biographical material is produced as *evidence* to support them. So, right at the very outset, a biographer of Freud is faced with the task of evaluating the reliability of early biographical material, but in order to do that he has to have some awareness of the role and function of that material when it was produced. This is no mere pedantry for in the papers and books which contain biographical detail reported memories are seen to be a function of the contemporary context of the person reporting them. Psychoanalysis, the 'science of the mind' which Freud was later to develop, puts great stress on the importance of early infantile relationships and on the period from birth to puberty. Early infantile desires and experiences become, in this system, the determinants of all subsequent behaviour. The fact that we do not remember these experiences or desires is proof enough for Freud that they are the hidden springs of human action. Relationships and feelings in adulthood and adolescence are then determined by infantile relationships and feeling. Thus, when Freud introduced biographical material into his thoughts it was in confirmation of this central thesis of causality. This renders all the material we have available from Freud about his own childhood as potentially infused with elements which are, dare we say it, suspect (because they are products of later periods). Consequently such early biographical data must be used with caution.

HOME AND FAMILY BACKGROUND: FREIBERG AND JUDAISM

> Of one thing I am certain: deep within me, although overlaid, there continues to live the happy child from Freiberg, the first-born son of a youthful mother, the boy who received from this air, from this soil, the first indelible impressions. (1931)[1]

Sigismund Freud (it was not until he was aged 22 that he changed his name to Sigmund) was born on 6 May 1856, in a small Moravian town called Freiberg. Freiberg, now named Pribor and part of modern Czechoslovakia, was then a minor provincial centre, of the Austro-Hungarian Empire. It had a population of some 5000 inhabitants the majority of whom were Roman Catholics. Sigismund was born into the family of Kallman Jacob Freud, a wool merchant, and member of a Jewish minority within the town. Jacob Freud had moved to the town in 1852 and, by all accounts, appears to have been a well-respected, if not-too-well-off, trader in the town. The Freud family lived like many other similar families in a small, one-roomed flat a mere 10 metres square. Sigmund was later to recall: 'I was the child of people who were originally well-to-do and who, I fancy, lived comfortably enough in that little corner of the provinces' (1899).[2]

Sigismund's mother, Amalie Freud, was a young, attractive woman from Vienna who was under 20 years old when she married Jacob, and barely 21 when her first child, Sigismund was born. Jacob, twice Amalie's age, had been married twice before and had already produced two sons: Emmanuel, born in 1832, and Philip born in 1836. These sons had been born to Jacob's first wife, Sally Kanner, whom he married in 1831. It is not known what happened to this first wife, presumably she died prior to his move to Freiberg. Jacob married again, for in 1852, on moving to Freiberg, he is recorded as being married to a 32-year-old woman named

Rebecca. Again, as with Sally Kanner, nothing is known of what happened to Rebecca, since, on marrying Amalie, Jacob is described as being a widower since 1852 – but there are no records extant of her death, and no mention was ever made of her name by any of the Freud family. Whatever the truth behind these family mysteries – and there is a variety of explanations to account for them – Sigmund never referred to a second woman in his father's life called Rebecca, and always asserted that Amalie was the *second* wife of Jacob.

Whatever the validity of Freud's later views on infantile material it is important to realize that the bond between Sigismund and Amalie was very strong (see plate 3). Amalie's first-born son, Sigismund, was the apple of her eye – his name, in German, has associations with the idea of 'victory' (*Sieg*) – and he was born in a caul – a sign which, by tradition, is taken to be a portent of good fortune. There is a story, often told by Freud, though undoubtedly suspect, of a woman (a midwife or a shopkeeper) who, on Sigismund's birth, announced to Amalie that she had brought a great man into the world. When Freud was reflecting upon this incident some 40 years later he remarked how common such encouraging prophecies must be. He also mused in keeping with his views on causality whether it could have been 'the source of my thirst for grandeur?' (1900).[3] The story is apocryphal, but the interpretation of the event by Freud gives us an indication of themes which will emerge throughout his life: of all development being determined; of a desire to transcend merely living and dying; and of a desire to impose his mark upon history.

Whether or not a midwife pronounced upon the greatness of the newly born Sigismund is immaterial. What is true is that Amalie herself believed her son to be great and actively supported him throughout his life. Freud himself was to state of one of his heroes, Goethe: 'if a man has been his mother's undisputed darling he retains throughout life the triumphant feeling, the confidence in success, which not seldom brings actual success along with it' (1917).[4] The autobiographical allusion here is plain. Many years later, Ernest Jones commentated on the strangeness of hearing the then old lady, Amalie, referring to '*mein goldener Sigi*'.[5] Some indication of the way in which this closeness and mutual regard was maintained throughout their lives may be seen from Freud's reactions to his mother's death in 1930. To a fellow psychoanalyst he wrote:

It has affected me in a peculiar way, this great event. No pain, no grief, which probably can be explained by the special circumstances – her great age, my pity for her helplessness towards the end; at the same time a feeling of liberation, of release, which I think I also understand. I was not free to die as long as she was alive, and now I am. The values of life will somehow have changed noticeably in the deeper layers. (1930)[6]

In Freud's memories of his early years, which may, as I have said, be as much a reflection of his later years, it was relationships and reactions to relationships which form the focus of his attention. Freud apparently recalled intense feelings of love and hate toward the people around him, indeed it is to one of Freud's admirer's, Bleuler, that we owe our contemporary characterization of such mixed feelings – we call them ambivalent. With his parents he says he recalled feelings of sexual love and jealousy and sexual curiosity. With his brother, who was born when Freud was 1 year old, he remembered, 'I welcomed [him] with ill wishes and real infantile jealousy.' When that brother died as an infant Freud noted 'his death left the germ of guilt in me' (1897).[7]

Freud's account of his first friendship with his nephew, John, provides an illustration of the complexity of interpreting these early, infantile relationships, and of the danger of taking Freud's descriptions of them at face value. Freud first mentioned John to his close friend and confidant, Wilhelm Fliess, in 1897. There he described John as 'my companion in crime', and made the observation that 'my nephew and younger brother determined, not only the neurotic side of all my friendships, but also their depth' (1897).[8] Later in his book on *The Interpretation of Dreams* Freud provided more information about John, but this time he linked his relationship to John with his subsequent relationships: 'we loved each other and fought with each other, and this childhood relationship . . . had a determining influence on all my subsequent relations with contemporaries. Since that time my nephew John has had many reincarnations . . . unalterably fixed as it was in my unconscious memory' (1900).[9] He elaborated this theme yet further:

> My emotional life has always insisted that I should have an intimate friend and a hated enemy. I have always been able to provide myself afresh with both, and it has not infrequently happened that the ideal situation of childhood has been so completely reproduced that friend and enemy have come together in a single individual – though not, of course, both at once or with constant oscillations, as may have been the case in my early childhood. (1900) [10]

The passages about John must be viewed in the light of the fact that Freud was attempting to account for his *contemporary* relationships, notably with Fliess; and that he had also developed a theory of memories that stated that 'phantasies are products of late periods which project themselves back from the present into earliest childhood' (1899).[11] The account of the young Sigismund's ambivalent relationship to John was specifically introduced to explain why it was that Freud had had a dream expressing a desire for the death of his friend Fliess. The infantile relationship was thus said to be the source of wish, and Freud was thus exonerated from any guilt about having such desires for his contemporary friend. In the words of Freud's physician, himself a psychoanalyst: 'the emphasis on infantile material can be used successfully as a defence against recent conflicts in particular those which arise in the transference relationship [meaning in a loving relationship]'.[12]

A similar account may be made of all of the figures of Freud's early childhood – we learn of them, by and large, within the context of an analagous argument. Freud had a 'Nannie' for instance, that he alleged was the 'primary originator' of his neuroses, and that was 'my instructress in sexual matters, and [that] chided me for being clumsy and not being able to do anything' (1897)[13] – a reference usually taken to refer to aspects of Freud's toilet training. This 'Nannie', in reality merely a maid-servant who worked for Freud's half-brother, was dismissed from service when Sigismund was about 2½ years old for stealing money and encouraging her charge to steal. She was a Catholic Czech who introduced Freud to Catholicism – an experience to which he reacted most unfavourably. Freud later recalled her as 'the prehistoric old woman', and as 'an ugly, elderly but clever woman' (1897).[14] As with John though, Freud's recollections of her were produced within the specific context of attempting to account for his feelings for someone in his contemporary context. Freud felt that relationships in later life were determined by these infantile encounters. Contemporaries were thus only *revenants* or reincarnations (in a psychological sense) of earlier significant people. Memories about those earlier people were thus 'masks or symbols' to express feelings about contemporaries.

The suggestion that we should treat with scepticism Freud's accounts of his early relationships – with his nephew John, and his Nannie – runs counter to the whole weight of psychoanalytic tradition. That tradition suggests that the breakthrough Freud effected in his 'self-analysis' was precisely to reach back to that early childhood material, and to see its determining influences. The logic of this psychoanalytic position is that in analysing contemporary conflicts one is led inevitably to the childhood memories which themselves provide the key to understanding the dynamics of the present situation. When Freud first reported the 'discovery' of childhood memories – in his letter to Fliess – he himself was uncertain about its relevance. Thus, in October 1897, at the height of his self-analysis, when he first mentions his nephew, his younger brother, and his Nannie, he appends to his letter an account of a dream. Freud's interpretation of the dream contains a mixture of contemporary and childhood references – the Nannie who encouraged him to steal, concern over his wife's housekeeping money, his 'present uselessness as a therapist' – the unifying theme Freud suggested was 'bad treatment'. At the end of the account Freud adds a characteristic objection:

> A severe critic might say that all this was phantasy projected into the past instead of being determined by the past. The *experimenta crucis* would decide the matter against him . . . Where do all patients derive the horrible perverse details which are often as alien to their experiences as to their knowledge? (1897)[15]

Freud was not able to answer this question adequately for himself until his introduction of Lamarckian biological theorizing in the twentieth century. The objection of the 'severe critic' that our perception of the past is determined by our contemporary context is still valid; accordingly there is much to commend the approach to Freud's life and work which recontextualizes his memories, dreams, slips, and theories into their contemporary setting.

It was not just the relationships which left their mark on the impressionable Sigi, the physical environment of Freiberg itself left its impression on him. Freiberg is situated within half a mile of rolling pine forests. It was here as a young child that Sigismund was taken for long walks by his father. Something about the enclosed security of these woods imprinted itself upon this young boy such that, years later, in 1899, he was to contrast his adopted town, Vienna (itself a city with an abundance of woods), unfavourably with Freiberg: 'I never felt really comfortable in the town. I believe now that I was never free from a longing for the beautiful woods near our home' (1899).[16] That longing may even have departed from a normal desire, and have been a manifestation of a neurotic complaint: agoraphobia (a fear of open spaces). Many years later, when seen hesitating to cross a wide street by a young colleague he remarked, 'You see, there is a survival of my old agoraphobia which troubled me much in younger years' (c.1927).[17] However, that 'survival of . . . agoraphobia' did not prevent him from becoming an indefatigable traveller – throughout his life he loved walking particularly in the mountains (see plate 10).

The Freiberg period was all too short for the young Sigi. It was curtailed by a change in the circumstances of Freud's father. Freud, recalling what happened later, wrote, 'When I was about three, the branch of industry in which my father was concerned met with catastrophe. He lost all his means and we were forced to leave the place and move to a large town' (1899).[18] This family crisis necessitated the move of the entire Freud family, with Freud's older half-brothers moving to Manchester, England,

and Jacob taking his wife, Amalie, and their two children, Sigismund and Anna, to settle in Vienna, perhaps by way of Leipzig. The move was to bring Sigismund to the city which was to remain his home until he was forced into exile by the Nazis in 1938.

Yet another aspect of Freud's background may well have been significant for his development, his religious background. This is a subject of some controversy, with different commentators differing in their assessment of its importance. I favour the interpretation which regards his religious background as crucial to his whole life, indeed as a *Leitmotif* that runs through all his work. Certainly at significant points in his life we find him reaffirming his Jewish identity. Thus, when courting his future wife he wrote: 'And as for us, this is what I believe: even if the form wherein the old Jews were happy no longer offers us any shelter, something of the core, of the essence of this meaningful and life-affirming, Judaism will not be absent from our home' (1882).[19]

The influence of Judaism is by no means external to the development and course of his scientific work. Indeed in his later years he turned his attention specifically to the problems of religion (see chapter 5). In some senses this influence is a coda of the Freiberg period, for Freud received from his parents not only a psychological legacy of memories and feelings, but also a spiritual legacy. Ernest Jones, as Freud's biographer, and as a man unsympathetic to religion, was content to minimize this legacy maintaining that 'of Freud's religious background not a great deal is known'.[20] Freud himself, on the other hand, was proud to affirm his Jewish roots, and the continuing effect of them upon his work: 'My parents were Jews, and I have remained a Jew myself' (1925).[21] he boldly stated in his autobiography. Similarly, towards the end of his life, he was to assert that the problem of the Jewish character 'has pursued me throughout the whole of my life' (1935).[22]

In fact both of Freud's parents came from devout Jewish families, and Freud numbered in his relations two rabbis. Not surprisingly the Jewish Bible (in later years, Jones was to note his knowledge of both the Old and New Testaments) became an important book for him. This he revealed in his autobiography: 'My deep engrossment in the Bible Story (almost as soon as I had learnt the art of reading) had, as I recognised much later, an enduring effect upon the direction of my interest' (1935).[23] On his thirty-fifth birthday, his father presented him with a copy of the Bible with the inscription (in Hebrew):

My dear Son,
It was in the seventh year of your age that the spirit of God began to move you to learning. I would say the spirit of God speaketh to you: 'Read in My book; there will be opened to thee sources of knowledge of the intellect'. It

is the Book of Books; it is the well that wise men have digged and from which law givers have drawn the waters of their knowledge.

Thou hast seen in this Book the vision of the Almighty, thou hast heard willingly, thou hast done and has tried to fly high upon the wings of the Holy Spirit. Since then I have preserved the same Bible. Now, on your thirty-fifth birthday I have brought it out from its retirement and send it to you as a token of love from your old father. (Jacob Freud, 1891)[24]

Despite his father's positively eulogistic account of Freud's path to learning Sigmund himself was to lament his neglect of the more formal aspects of studying the Bible. It was the most important source of his Jewish heritage yet he recalled:

In the time of my youth our free-thinking religious instructors set no store by their pupils acquiring a knowledge of the Hebrew language and literature. My education in this field was, therefore, extremely behindhand, as I have since often regretted. (1925)[25]

Jones, as I have indicated, was concerned to play down even this influence and wrote: 'when Freud spoke of his having been greatly influenced by his early reading of the Bible he can only have meant in an ethical sense, in addition to his historical interest'. The legacy of Freud's Jewish background and upbringing is, however, more subtle than Jones could concede.

If we are to understand the religious context which formed the background to Freud's development we need to abandon any ideas we may have which holds being a Jew as being a well-defined idea, for Jews throughout the world were in a precarious position in society, and their position was in constant flux. We may see the changes in social status, and in identity, in an incident which Freud recorded in his self-analysis of the 1890s, an incident reported to him by his father when he was about 12. Jacob, prior to moving to Freiberg had lived in Galicia, a town now part of Poland One day Jacob was walking down the street wearing a new fur hat; 'A Christian came up to me,' he said 'and with a single blow knocked off my cap into the mud and shouted: "Jew! get off the pavement!"' Asked what happened next Jacob replied: 'I went into the roadway and picked up my cap.' When Freud was recounting the incident at the age of 43 he still recalled the shame he had felt for his father, and wrote: 'I contrasted this situation with another which fitted my feelings better: the scene in which Hannibal's father . . . made his boy swear before the household altar to take vengeance upon the Romans. Ever since that time Hannibal had had a place in my phantasies' (1900).[27]

Quite apart from any psychological significance this incident concerning his father may have had upon Freud's development (and there are grounds, given that psychoanalysis considers that children's feeling of hatred to their fathers are crucial in development, for wondering about this aspect of the story for Freud himself) this incident gives us an indication of the changing role and status of the Jew in society at that time. For Jacob, nurtured as he had been in the Ghetto, with all the concomitant isolation and social disadvantage, there was no other response for him to make; for Sigismund, the child of a much more socially integrated experience of Jewry, overt anger and outrage were more appropriate. The incident, with its disgraceful anti-semitism perpetrated by a supposed Christian may also help to shed some light on Freud's eventual attacks upon Christianity.

If the social position and the nature of Jewry were changing at this time – fewer Jews were having to become baptized and 'Christianized' in order to gain acceptance in society, ideas about the possibility of a Zionist state were beginning to be mooted – we have to be even more circumspect in our identification of Freud as a Jew in this fluid period for he himself did not adopt any of the standard alternative options – he did not become a Zionist or an overtly religious Jew. Thus, he was able to write to a Jewish learned society of which he was an active member and contributor, 'what bound me to Jewry was (I am ashamed to admit) neither faith nor national pride, for I have always been an unbeliever and was brought up without any religion' (1926).[28] Despite the perfunctory admission of shame, Freud was generally pleased to admit his being 'alienated from the religion of my forebears' (1926),[29] and declared himself 'glad that I have no religion' (1926) and 'a completely Godless Jew' (1918)[30] possessing only a 'feeling of solidarity with my people' (1926).[31] However, Freud's Jewish identity and concerns went beyond that rather bland description and were more extensive and enduring – on another occasion he described being a Jew as giving him a 'clear consciousness of inner identity [founded upon] many obscure emotional forces, which were the more powerful the less they could be expressed in words' (1926).[32]

This 'clear consciousness' Freud maintained gave him a number of benefits:

> [it was] to my Jewish nature alone . . . that I owed two characteristics that had become indispensable to me in the difficult course of my life. Because I was a Jew I found myself free from many prejudices which restricted others in the use of their intellect; and as a Jew I was prepared to join the Opposition and to do without agreement with the compact majority. (1926)[33]

A third benefit Freud derived from his being a Jew was a kindred with a number of other Jews which throughout his life sustained and supported him in his work – the majority of his disciples were Jews with whom he formed deep attachments. Freud wished, then, both to deny certain aspects of being a Jew – the need for a religious faith or for nationalism – while at the same time to affirm some aspects – intellectual clarity and boldness and even a sense of being chosen. He did not, however, adhere to any stereotypical expression of that identity. Freud described his position in the following way:

> If the question were put to him [Freud]: 'Since you have abandoned all these common characteristics of your countrymen what is there left to you that is Jewish?' He would reply: 'A very great deal, and probably its very essence.' He could not now express that essence clearly in words; but some day, no doubt it will become accessible to the scientific mind. (1930)[34]

Freud's religious roots are not confined to his being a Jew, for, as I indicated briefly earlier, at an early age Freud encountered a form of Christianity which was to have an enduring effect upon him – the Catholicism of 'that prehistoric old woman', the maid-servant, Therese Wittek. The effect of this exposure to Catholic ritual may well have radically imprinted itself upon the mind of this impressionable young child – when, in 1907, he wrote his first essay on religion it was entitled 'obsessive actions and religious practices' (1907). In that same paper he described religion as a 'universal obsessional neurosis' (1907).[35] Freud remembered this 'ugly, elderly but clever woman' as telling him 'a great deal about God and hell' (1897),[36] and when he asked his mother about her she replied that she was 'an elderly woman, very shrewd indeed. She was always taking you to church. When you came home you used to preach, and tell us how God conducted His affairs'.[37] It is clear that all this talk of 'God and hell' made a lasting impression on him at the time, for on the journey away from Freiberg Freud recalled passing through the town of Breslau, there he recounted he saw: 'gas jets . . . the first I had seen [they] reminded me of souls burning in hell' (1897).[38]

These early experiences of Catholic ritual, and of a religion with a preoccupation with hell and damnation, together with a lifelong experience of anti-semitism, particularly by the Catholic establishment, gave Freud an enduring aversion to Christianity. Many years later, when one of his disciples was trying to persuade him to leave Vienna in the face of a possible Nazi invasion of Austria he answered: 'The Nazis? I am not afraid of them. Help me rather to combat my true enemy.' When asked who that enemy was he replied. 'Religion, the Roman Catholic Church' (1937).[39] Indeed he was to suffer for many years from what he jokingly called his 'Rome neurosis', a desire to go to see Rome and a hatred of it as the source of Christianity. Freud frequently identified himself, with those who opposed Rome. Hannibal was one such hero:

> Hannibal, whom I had come to resemble in these respects, had been the favourite hero of my later school days . . . and when in the higher classes I began to understand for the first time what it meant to belong to an alien race . . . the figure of the semitic general rose still higher in my esteem. To my youthful mind Hannibal and Rome symbolised the conflict between the tenacity of Jewry and the organisation of the Catholic Church. (1900)[40]

I shall be returning to the development of Freud's views on religion in chapter 5; for the present I wish merely to emphasize their rootedness in Freud's beginnings.

EDUCATION AND EARLY CAREER:
THE GYMNASIUM AND THE UNIVERSITY

> The years between ten and eighteen would rise from the corners of my memory, with all their guises and illusions, their painful distortions and heartening successes – my first glimpses of an extinct civilization (which in my case was to bring me as much consolation as anything else in the struggles of life), my first contacts with the sciences, among which it seemed open to me to choose to which of them I should dedicate what were no doubt my inestimable services. And I seem to remember that through the whole of this time there ran a premonition of a task ahead, till it found open expression in my school-leaving essay as a wish that I might during the course of my life contribute something to our human knowledge. (1914)[41]

The downturn in the fortunes of his father precipitated the move of the Freud family to Vienna in 1860. The family was very poor, and Freud talked of those early years as 'long and difficult years, of which, as it seems to me, nothing was worth remembering' (1899).[42] To his friend Wilhelm Fliess he wrote that he had known 'helpless poverty and have a constant fear of it' (1899)[43] an obvious reference to this time. It is clear from a study of the Archives in Vienna that his father did not register in the city as a trader. This indicates that whatever financial support they had must have come from a source other than Jacob's work. It probably came from his two older sons who were now established in England. Freud's sister suggested that 'father had business interests' in England,[44] while Sigmund himself recalled that his father was always waiting for his boat to come in – 'he is the greatest optimist of all us young people' (1882).[45] Jacob's inability to provide adequately for his family may well

Plate 2. Freud with his father Jacob c.1864

have contributed to Sigmund's feeling of hatred for his father which was to provide a key to Freud's whole psychological system. In one of his essays he generalizes about the father/son relationship in such a way as to indicate his own feelings:

> In the second half of childhood a change sets in in the boy's relation to his father – a change whose importance cannot be exaggerated. From his nursery the boy begins to cast his eyes upon the world outside. And he cannot fail now to make discoveries which undermine his original high opinion of his father and which expedite his detachment from his first ideal. He finds that this father is no longer the mightiest, wisest and richest of beings; he grows dissatisfied with him, he learns to criticize him and to estimate his place in society. (1914)[46]

The city to which Jacob had brought his young family was the capital of a vast empire, the Austro-Hungarian Empire. It stretched from what is now part of Italy to the Carpathians, and from the Rhine to the Dniester. Franz Joseph, the last of the Hapsburgs, had presided over this Empire for 12 years when Sigismund arrived in Vienna. He was to continue to do this for a further 50 years. That period was, though, one of decline, for under the pressure of nationalism the Empire gradually began breaking up. But in 1860, when the Freuds arrived, the Empire was in its hey-day. Vienna was its pulsating heart where Germans, Hungarians, Poles, Czechs, Slovaks, Serbo-Croats, Slovenes, Rumanians and Italians all met and lived (so cosmopolitan was it that each of these groups had their own newspapers published in Vienna). The Freud family were just one family of a whole influx to the city. That influx resulted in an increase in population of 200 000 within 20 years during this period.

They joined a growing Jewish community in the city. In 1857, the year after Sigi had been born, Jews formed 1.3 per cent of the total population of Vienna; in 1869 this percentage was 6.3; and by 1890 it had risen to 12 per cent. The Jews consisted of two relatively distinct groups: an exclusive community of upper-middle-class Jews many of whom had been ennobled by the Emperor; and a group of lower-middle-class Jews and eastern European Jews who enjoyed few privileges and endured considerable anti-Semitism. During the course of the century this second group began to establish itself as professionals and as intellectuals. In 1867 their official position was much enhanced by the granting of a new constitution which gave them equal status as citizens – but anti-Semitism continued to predominate throughout the society.

In Vienna, Freud embarked upon his education. At first this was at the hand of his father, then at a private primary school and then, beginning in 1865 at the 'Gymnasium' (the Grammar School). The family, by now growing rapidly following the births in Vienna of Rosa (in 1860), Marie (1861), Adolphine (in 1862), Pauline (in 1863), and Alexander (in 1866), was now in a position to move to larger accommodation in the Leopoldstradt which one biographer called 'another Jewish quarter one step removed from a slum'.[47] Here Sigismund was to live with his family until he took up a post in the General City Hospital in 1882.

As the favoured son he received preferential treatment in the home. His younger sister Anna recounted: 'no matter how crowded our quarters, Sigmund always had a room to himself. There were a parlor, a dining room, three bedrooms which the rest of us shared, and a so-called cabinet, a single room separated from the rest of the apartment'.[48] With similar preference, only Sigi was allowed one of the new, expensive, gas lamps that appeared at the time, the rest of the family had to be content with older, cheaper candles. The household, in large measure, revolved around him. His sister Anna recalled that he was allowed the privilege of eating alone – he had his meals 'alone in the room where he pored endlessly over his books' (ibid). Likewise when she began practising piano at the age of 8 Sigi complained to his mother that the sound disturbed him and asked her 'to remove the piano if she did not wish him to leave the house altogether' (ibid). The piano was duly removed 'and with it all opportunities for his sisters to become musicians' (ibid). Sigi even 'exercised definite control' over the reading matter of his sister, declaring books too advanced for her to read. In short, we may note the conclusion of his sister that 'though he was not spoiled [words which have a hollow air about them] . . . Sigmund's words and wish were respected by everyone in the family' (ibid).

There is no doubt that the young Sigismund was an exceptional pupil. In his autobiography he recounted that: 'at the "gymnasium" I was at the top of my class for seven years; I enjoyed special privileges there, and had scarcely ever to be examined in class' (1925).[49] His sister recalled that 'the household became familiar with the fact that Sigi constantly won prizes for excellent school work'.[50] Here at school, as is clear from the quotation which opens this section, he gained his first experiences of the world of learning. Here, too, he developed, of necessity (given the continuing anti-Semitism of Vienna), an ability to cope with antagonism and to survive being in a minority. He was later to write to his fiancée, Martha Bernays, that: 'even at school I was always the bold oppositionist, always on hand when an extreme had to be defended and usually ready to atone for it' (1886).[51] He took his studies at the Gymnasium seriously though, for all his brilliance, so much so that his sister was to observe that 'his friends were not play- but study-mates'.[51] The young Sigi was being drawn slowly towards an academic life, again as his sister observed: 'All through the years of his school and university life, the only thing that changed in [his] room was the increasing number of crowded bookcases added'.[52]

Freud was a person of intellect even at this time and yet, in addition, he was a man who could forge deep and intense friendships. Of these friendships we may note three relationships in particular which were of importance to him at this time. The first was with a young man named Heinrich Braun. Braun was a contemporary from school who was subsequently to become a leading social democrat politician in Vienna. Freud, on being asked by Braun's biographer to recount his friendship, wrote:

> We became inseparable friends. I spent every hour not taken up by school with him, mostly at his place . . . we . . . got along very well. I can hardly remember any quarrels between us or periods when we were 'cross' with each other . . . he encouraged me in my aversion to school and what was taught there, and aroused a number of revolutionary feelings within me, and we encouraged each other in overestimating our critical powers and superior judgement. (1927)

Under Heinrich's influence Sigismund 'decided at that time to study law at the university' (ibid).[53] Another of Freud's schoolmates, a young Roumanian called Eduard Silberstein, became not just a friend at school, but also the first of Freud's important correspondents. Later Freud described his relationship with Silberstein to his fiancée:

> Silberstein was here again today, he is as devoted to me as ever. We became friends at a time when one doesn't look upon friendship as a sport or an asset, but when one needs a friend with whom to share things. We used to be together literally every hour of the day that was not spent on the school bench. We learned Spanish together, had our own mythology and secret names which we took from some dialogue of the great Cervantes . . . Together we founded a strange scholarly society, the *Academia Castellana* (AC), compiled a great mass of humorous work . . . shared our frugal suppers and were never bored in each other's company. (1884)[54]

Heinrich Braun and Eduard Silberstein were but two of the most important of a group of young men calling themselves the *Bund* (Union). The *Bund* used to congregate in a local cafe for conversation and games of cards and chess. Freud was close to them all, but Silberstein was to be the most intimate of his friends over this period. He even wrote of his friend 'I honestly believe that we shall never be rid of each other, although we became friends by free choice, we are now as attached to one another as if nature had put us on this earth as blood relatives'

(1875).[55] The group also numbered in its company three brothers, the Fluss brothers, who were part of a family that the Freuds had known in Freiberg. Unlike the Freuds the Fluss family had remained in Freiberg, they were relatively well off, and in 1872 Sigismund, together with two companions from school, spent a summer holiday at their home.

During the holiday Sigismund experienced a relationship which I take to be the third significant relationship of this period of his life. The details of this relationship have long been shrouded in mystery, since, as I have indicated in the introduction, Freud destroyed all of his papers, notes and letters in 1885. He told Martha about the affair soon after they had met and begun corresponding. 'Did I ever tell you that Gisela [Fluss] was my first love when I was but 16 years old?' he asked her rhetorically 'No? Well then you can have a good laugh at me, firstly on account of my taste and also because I never spoke a meaningful, much less an amiable word to the child. Looking back, I would say that seeing my old home-town again had made me feel sentimental' (1883).[56] The incident, is also described, in disguised form, as a case history in which he refers to it as 'my first calf-love' (1899).[57] He also reported it to Gisela's brother Emil Fluss, one of the *Bund*. In a letter to Emil he described his relationship to Ichthyosaura (Freud's nickname for Gisela derived from the Greek word for a fluvia creature) and noted 'there was more irony, yes, mockery, than seriousness in this whole flirtation' (1872). Sigismund, it seems, had fallen in love with the beautiful sister of his friend, he had become a member of 'a large group whose star was "Ichthyosaura"' (1873).[58]

In itself such an infatuation is hardly significant, the young Sigismund was growing up, and beginning, as were his companions, to experience desires and passions. The incident becomes more interesting on examination of yet another account he gave of it, which has only recently come to light. In a set of letters to his friend Eduard Silberstein there are more detailed references to the incident. Having described the emergence of his interest and desire for Gisela as something that had come over him in a manner akin to experiencing a spring day, he went on to explain that actually there were two aspects to his '*Leidenschaft*'.[59] The word Freud used here means a 'vehement, commanding, or overpowering emotion', a passion (though not necessarily a sexual one). Freud continued saying that he had misinterpreted his emotions and had confused a love for Gisela's mother for a love of Gisela. Frau Fluss, Gisela's mother, was then also an object of his affections: he had a 'crush' on this older woman. His descriptions of her to Silberstein were glowing. Freud recounted to him that she treated him with the care normally reserved for a child of her own after he had rendered himself unconscious by drinking in order to take away the pain of a tooth-ache. Frau Fluss, to judge from Freud's description of her, became perfection personified as Freud catalogued her merits to Silberstein. Compared even to his own mother Frau Fluss had taken an interest in Sigi so caring and so diverse — not merely in his physical needs but his intellectual too – that he had fallen hopelessly in love with her. So profound was this acceptance and encouragement that Sigi confessed to Silberstein that he thought he would remember it always. He had continued:

> She fully appreciates that I need encouragement before I speak or bestir myself and she never fails to give it. That's how her superiority shows itself: as she directs so I speak, and come out of my shell. (ibid)

During his adolescence Sigismund was forced to re-evaluate his father; so too, in the presence of Frau Fluss a similar evaluation occurred of his mother — in Frau Fluss he found ideals for motherhood and for marriage which were to remain with him possibly throughout his life.

It is not unusual for adolescent boys to develop strong passions both for their contemporaries and for older women. In that respect Freud's '*Leidenschaft*' for Gisela, and that for her 'esteemed mother' (1872)[60] may not be particularly significant. Jones, the official biographer, speculated that 'one must suppose that in Freud's earliest years there had been extremely strong motives for concealing some important phases of his development – perhaps even from himself'.[61] Jones conceded that Freud was most concerned to hide these early experiences in sexuality noting that 'what he revealed of his life was far more carefully selected and censored than is generally supposed'.[62] Indeed, when Jones discovered that Freud had engaged in masturbation in connection with the '*Leidenschaft*' he noted that 'his secrecy was certainly neurotic (not only in such matters)'.[63] Despite his revelation to Silberstein of his '*Leidenschaft*', and of his retaining her memory, he never mentioned Frau Fluss (although he did again mention Gisela), either in his work or in any of his letters. For one who declared 'the theory of repression is the cornerstone on which the whole structure of psychoanalysis rests' (1914)[64] we may note this absence with interest.

Freud returned to Vienna in mid-September and settled down having 'calmed my surging thoughts' (1872)[65] to study for his final-year exams, the *Matura* as it was known. Naturally, he viewed the approach of these impending exams with trepidation. However, he did not have sufficient fear to stop him from allowing himself to be distracted by the World Exhibition in Vienna — he wrote to Emil Fluss 'when my "martyrdom" (this is what we call the *Matura* among ourselves) is over, I intend to go there every day. It is entertaining and distracting. One can be gloriously alone there in all that crowd' (1873).[66] During the course of this year, he began to change his ideas about the future direction of his career. In his autobiography he attributed this change to a sudden and dramatic event: 'it was hearing Goethe's beautiful essay on Nature read aloud at a popular lecture . . . just before I left school that decided me to become a medical student' (1925).[67] It is clear from his letters to Emil Fluss that his conversion to the natural sciences from law was not as dramatic as he later suggested. In a letter dated 17 March 1873, Freud reported cryptically that he '[could] report what is perhaps the most important bit of news in my miserable life . . . But the matter is as yet undecided' (1873).[68] In response to Emil's probings about that which 'I, in your opinion, speak so meekly and dejectedly' Sigismund replied, on 1 May, that:

> Today it is as certain and as fixed as any human plan can be (any being can turn into a Tower of Babel) . . . I have decided to be a Natural Scientist and herewith release you from the promise to let me conduct all your law-suits. It is no longer needed. I shall gain insight into the age old dossiers of Nature, perhaps even eavesdrop on her eternal processes and, share my findings with anyone who wants to learn. (1873).[69]

Whatever the reasons for this change in intentions, and there may be many contributing factors – from a genuine change of interests even to a desire to seek financial security – one thing is apparent in this transformation: Sigismund's interests were primarily scientific not therapeutic. He recalled this in his autobiography 'neither at that time, nor indeed in my later life, did I feel any particular predilection for the career of a doctor' (1925).[70] His studies paid off, and he passed the *Matura*, and was even complimented on the classical German style of his prose. He graduated from the Gymnasium *summa cum laude*, top of his year.

Having graduated, the University of Vienna was his next testing ground. The tests he faced there were not solely academic, as his autobiographical reflections years later recalled:

> When in 1873, I first joined the University, I experienced some appreciable disappointments. Above all, I found that I was expected to feel myself inferior and an alien because I was a Jew. I refused absolutely to do the first of these things. I have never been able to see why I should feel ashamed of my descent or, as my people were beginning to say, of my 'race'. I put up, without much regret, with my non-acceptance into the community; for it seemed to me that in spite of this exclusion an active fellow-worker could not fail to find some nook or cranny in the framework of humanity. These first impressions at the university, however, had one consequence which

was afterwards to prove important, for at an early age I was made familiar with the fate of being in the Opposition and of being put under the ban of the 'compact majority'. The foundations were thus laid for a certain degree of independence of judgement. (1925)[71]

Sigismund began his studies at the University of Vienna in the autumn of 1873. He enrolled at the medical department but intended to study as widely as possible 'I shall spend [my first year] entirely in studying humanistic subjects' he wrote to Silberstein 'which have nothing at all to do with my future profession, but not unprofitable for all that' (1873).[72] He kept Silberstein fully informed of his progress at the University. His letters are full of the intellectual challenges he was facing – philosophical questions, political issues, religious arguments abound in the letters. He was like most students of his day interested in the intractable concerns of the period – in short, with man's place in the order of things. In his autobiography he mentions the influence of Charles Darwin (who had published his famous book *The Origin of Species* in 1859): 'the theories of Darwin, which were then of topical interest, strongly attracted me', he wrote later, 'for they held out hopes of an extraordinary advance in our understanding of the world' (1925).[73] In the summer of 1874 Freud attended a lecture series specifically on Darwinism. Many years later, after the founding of psychoanalysis, Freud was to compare his achievements to those of Darwin (and those of Copernicus) – these men submitted 'the naïve self-love of men . . . to two major blows at the hands of science' (1917).[74] Freud believed that with psychoanalysis he had delivered the third, and final blow.

Darwinian evolutionary thought, with its implicit reductionism and naturalism, was, as Freud admits, a subject of general and widespread interest; it was not the only philosophy that Freud was interested in: he was at this time courting other forms of naturalism notably materialism. He described himself at that time as 'a green youngster, full of materialistic theories' (1900),[75] and as 'the godless physician and empiricist' (1874).[76] Not surprisingly for one who later confessed 'when I was young, the only thing I longed for was philosophical knowledge' (1896),[77] in keeping with his earlier prediction to Silberstein, he attended philosophy lectures at the University. He also read widely in the philosophical field including works by Aristotle and Feuerbach – the German philosopher whose critique of religion had had such a pronounced effect upon the young Karl Marx. Later, in 1879, he even translated into German a volume of the English philosopher, John Stuart Mill's, collected works. Freud considered Mill as 'very possibly . . . the man of the century most capable of freeing himself from the domination of the usual prejudices' (1883).[78] His teacher in philosophy, Franz Brentano, had been a Catholic priest but had left the church in 1873 because he could not accept the doctrine

of papal infallibility. He exerted a marked influence upon young
Sigismund (he it was who put forward Freud's name as a translator for
Mill). To Silberstein Freud described Brentano as 'this remarkable man
(a believer, a teleologist, a Darwinian and a darned clever fellow, a genius,
in fact) who is, in many respects, ideal' (1875). Again to Silberstein he
confided 'under Brentano's fruitful influence I have arrived at the decision
to take my Ph.D. in philosophy and zoology' (1875).[79]

Brentano's influence was to spread beyond Freud, he is the direct
antecedent of two important movements in philosophy: phenomenology
and existentialism. Brentano's concerns at this time are reflected in the
title of his most famous work of the period 'Psychology from the
Empirical Standpoint'. This work includes two detailed discussions of
the notion of 'the unconscious' – admittedly, ultimately, to deny the need
for the term in psychology. The historian of ideas, L. L. Whyte, in a
detailed study of 'the unconscious before Freud' has pointed out that
far from Freud having simply invented this term, as it were, *ex nihilo*,
he formulated his concept in the context of a widespread general concern
and interest in the topic. Whyte considers that: 'the unconscious was
conceivable around 1700, topical around 1800, fashionable around 1870–
1880'.[80] Freud was later to suggest that it was only 'poets and philosophers' who discussed 'the unconscious' whereas *he* was a scientist.[81]

Freud continued to maintain his interest in the natural sciences – in his
curriculum vitae written in 1885 he recorded 'in the first years of my
university life I attended lectures mainly in physics and natural history'
(1885).[82] In 1874 he planned to make a trip to Berlin to study for
a term under three of the most famous natural scientists of the day –
Du Bois-Reymond, Helmholtz and Virchow – the first two being
physiologists and the third a pathologist. It would have been a momentous
trip for Sigismund who was later to write to his fiancée of 'the great
Helmholtz . . . one of my idols' (1883).[83] For some reason, possibly
financial, he was unable to go. Instead, as a treat promised for passing
his *Matura*, he was able, in 1875, to make a trip to Manchester, England
to stay with his half-brothers who had emigrated there on leaving Freiberg.
Just prior to this trip, his letters to Silberstein reveal a significant
change – the young man who had regularly signed himself 'Sigismund'
now began to sign himself 'Sigmund' – a small change perhaps but not
without significance when it is considered that the name 'Sigismund' was
used in Vienna as the most common form of abuse in anti-Semitic jokes
(as inappropriate for a sensitive person in those circumstances, as Paddy
or Mick might be today in some circumstances).

Sigmund loved England, and England, or at least his relations in
England, loved him. His half-brother Emmanuel wrote back to Vienna:
'You have given us great pleasure by sending us Sigmund. He is a splendid

specimen of a fine human being'.[84] Sigmund, in turn, confessed to Silberstein that he would rather live in England than Austria, despite the prevalence of 'rain, fog, drunkenness and conservatism' in England.[85] In England he consolidated his earlier scientific interests studying the writings of, amongst others, Huxley, Lyle and Darwin. But while the trip consolidated his interest it also significantly changed it. To Silberstein he revealed what was to be the most significant change in his interests, namely that he was becoming interested in medicine. In a letter he explained that whereas hitherto, had he been asked what his greatest desire was, he would have responded that it was to be a scientist with the resources to work, now, however he would admit that his greatest desire was 'to mitigate or eradicate some of the ills that ravage man's body' (ibid.). He also pointed out to Silberstein that if one wanted to make an impact on society one could work wonders with appropriate backing from the press and patrons with money 'if only [one] is enough of an explorer to enter new curative paths' (ibid.). At this point in time such ideas were, as he admitted to Silberstein 'still vague ideas' (ibid.).

Vague they may have been but they marked the beginning of a turning point for Sigmund. His sister Anna was later to recall:

> It was in England that Sigmund resolved to study medicine on his return to Vienna, and so informed my father. Not satisfied with this decision, father stated his objections, claiming that Sigmund was much too soft-hearted for the task. But Sigmund's mind was made up, though at first he planned to do only research. 'I want to help people who suffer' was his reply.[86]

Having returned to Vienna after his summer trip to England he began to devote more time to those basic sciences which were the bedrock of medicine – physiology, anatomy and practical zoology. This latter science he studied under Carl Claus at the Institute of Comparative Anatomy in Vienna. On two occasions he also studied at the Zoological Experimental Station which Claus had just established on the Adriatic coast at Trieste. Freud must have been an industrious student for Claus to endorse these two vacation study trips, for both trips required special funding. On his return from the second of these trips, Freud prepared his research material – on the gonads of the mature male eel. Claus presented the paper to the Academy of Science in March 1877. It was Freud's very first scientific success. Rather than further developing his career with Claus, however, Freud changed departments, and moved over to Ernst Brücke's Institute of Physiology.

Ernst Brücke, whom later in his autobiography Freud was to describe as the man 'who carried more weight with me than anyone else in my whole life' (1925),[87] had been part of the Berlin group of physiologists whose leaders were Du Bois-Reymond and Helmholtz (the same pair that in 1874 Freud had wished to study with). Brücke, described by his Berlin colleagues as 'our ambassador to the Far East', had earlier been at the heart of a concerted attempt to found a science of biology on thoroughly materialistic grounds. Du Bois-Reymond has succinctly summarized their philosophy:

> Brücke and I pledged a solemn oath to put into effect this truth: 'No forces other than the common physical and chemical ones are active in the organism. In those cases which cannot at the time be explained by these forces, one has either to find the specific way or form of their action by using the physical – mathematical method or to assume new forces equal in dignity to the chemical–physical forces inherent in matter reducible to the force of attraction and repulsion.[88]

In his autobiography Freud recounted this period in the following terms: 'At length, in Ernst Brücke's physiological laboratory I found rest and full satisfaction – and men, too, whom I could respect and take as my models . . . I worked at this institute, with short interruptions, from 1876 to 1882' (1925).[89] At the Institute Freud began to specialize in the study of nerve tissues, a subject at the centre of controversy over Darwinian theory as it concerned the relationships between the higher animals and the lower. At that time Freud was a strange mixture of the dedicated scientist, concerned to have his results published and acknowledged, and a rather happy-go-lucky individual. In the 1890s he recalled of that period that 'I went quietly on with my work . . . and in my circle of acquaintances I was regarded as an idler and it was doubted whether I should ever get through [my exams]' (1900).[90] Or again, in his autobiography he confessed 'the various branches of medicine proper, apart from psychiatry, had no attraction for me. I was decidedly negligent in pursuing my medical studies, and it was not until 1881 that I took my somewhat belated degree as a Doctor of Medicine' (1925).[91]

Having qualified as a doctor in the spring of 1881, Sigmund then became eligible for a career in medical research. In May 1881 he was appointed Demonstrator in the Institute of Physiology. The promotion gave him an official title but little else, he remained very poor dependent partly upon loans made to him by his wealthier friends. There was little prospect of advancement within the Institute, as Brücke had two younger assistants already primed to continue his work – a change of direction was imminent. Freud himself described what happened next:

> The turning point came in 1882, when my teacher [E. Brücke], for whom I felt the highest possible esteem, corrected my father's generous improvidence by strongly advising me, in view of my bad financial position,

Plate 3. Freud with his mother Amalie in 1872

to abandon my theoretical career. I followed his advice, left the
physiological laboratory and entered the General Hospital as an *Aspirant*
(clinical assistant) . . . In complete contrast to the diffuse character of my
studies during my earlier years at the university, I was now developing an
inclination to concentrate my work exclusively upon a single subject or
problem. (1925)[92]

However, Freud was less than candid about his motivation, as he
reflected upon 'the turning point' from the distance of 40 odd years, for
this account fails to mention that in April 1882, Sigmund had met, and
fallen in love with, Martha Bernays, a 21-year-old friend of his sister.
In a very real sense the 'inclination to concentrate . . . exclusively upon
a single subject' is an apt description of his state having met Martha – his
sole desire became to marry her. The couple became engaged on 17 June
1882 without the knowledge of either family; they did not get married
until 1886 – in the intervening years, often spent miles apart for long
periods, Sigmund had to create a career which could support him
sufficiently to get married.

PROLEGOMENA TO PSYCHOANALYSIS:
NEUROLOGY, COCAINE AND PARIS

After all, you know the key to my life, that I can work only when spurred
on by great hopes for things uppermost in my mind. Before I met you I
didn't know the joy of living, and now that 'in principle' you are mine,
to have you completely is the one condition I make to life, which I otherwise
don't set any great store by. I am very stubborn and very reckless and need
great challenges; I have done a number of things which any sensible person
would be bound to consider very rash. For example, to take up science
as a poverty-stricken man, then as a poverty-stricken man to capture a poor
girl – but this must continue to be my way of life: risking a lot, hoping
a lot, working a lot. To average bourgeois common sense I have been lost
long ago. (1884)[93]

In July 1882 Freud began work at the Vienna General Hospital, initially
in the department of surgery. The General Hospital, as the main hospital
of the capital of such a great empire, was a huge and prestigious place –
a 25 acre site accommodated over 3000 patients, not just from the city
but also from the Empire and from further abroad. Despite its imperial
significance, the conditions there, even by the standards of the day, were
very poor – Freud was to describe some of them to Martha in one of his
letters: 'Would you believe it?' he asked her incredulously 'there is no
gas installed in any of the non-clinical rooms in the hospital, so that in
the long winter evenings the patients have to lie in the dark, and the doctor

makes his rounds . . . and even operates in utter darkness, lit by a wax candle' (1884). Similarly, he described how, in the wards with ten out of every twenty patients having serious lung diseases, 'the place is swept out once a day, and the whole room is then enveloped in clouds of dust' (ibid).[94] Not surprisingly, given these conditions, Freud found himself tired and disliking his work. He soon applied to join a more congenial department, that of Professor Herman Nothnagel of the Department of Internal Medicine. Nothnagel was an imposing man of whom Freud wrote (to Martha) 'it gives one quite a turn to be in the presence of a man who has so much power over us, and over whom we have none . . . [He is] a Germanic cave-man' (1882).[95] Nothnagel decided to give Freud an opportunity to join his department, which he duly did until May 1883 when he made yet another move to the Department of Psychiatry, then under the control of Professor Theodore Meynert.

Theodore Meynert, described by Freud to his fiancée as 'severe' (1884)[96] was one of Europe's leading psychiatrists, and a passionate advocate of the importance of pathological anatomy for the study of mental illness. Early in the nineteenth century medicine had been transformed from a vague, clinical, art, into something more resembling a science by the introduction of the study of pathological anatomy – the study of the anatomical changes which were observed in the *post-mortem* examination of corpses. Following these successes in general medicine, Meynert and others had begun to apply the same methods to the study of mental illness. Under Meynert's influence Vienna had become, during the second half of the nineteenth century, one of the most prestigious centres for the study of psychiatry. Meynert insisted that the study of anatomy is 'indispensable to an understanding of the clinical manifestations of mental diseases' (Meynert 1884), and that accordingly 'anatomical changes are of the essence'[97] in the origin of *all* mental illnesses. The problem was that they had not *yet* been observed in *any* cases.

Freud had encountered Meynert as a medical student, and from May 1883 until October served as an assistant in his psychiatric clinic. In October he moved to the department of dermatology, and as is clear from his letters to Martha, had to work extremely hard. He wrote in October 1883:

What am I doing now? I am more industrious than ever and feel better than ever . . . [I am] busy learning, writing, and occasionally acting as a surgeon. The whole situation, my darling, had something heavy about it, akin to a dream or delerium; these are the right conditions to help me survive a long separation, whether they are pleasant it is hard to say; personal feelings don't get much chance of a hearing. Continually having so much to do acts as a kind of narcotic, but as you know I have lately been looking for something to rescue me from any great emotional and excitable state. Now I have it. It seems as though the waves of the great world do not lap against my door, at other times I have to fight against the sensation of being a monk in his cell. (1883)

Junior doctors, in whatever period, always have a hard time, and have to bear the brunt of long, tedious, hours of work. Freud, working in Vienna in the 1880s was no exception to this rule – as he described in the same letter to Martha 'one is not allowed to be a human being for an hour unless one has been a machine or a workhorse for eleven hours" (1883).[98]

Much to Freud's distress, his future mother-in-law 'at the behest of some extraordinary whim' (1883) decided to move with Martha and her family to Hamburg – a move which Freud remarked 'isn't very noble-minded . . . [and] an expression of the external conflict between age and youth which exists in every family' (ibid).[99] Having been separated from his intended Freud then redoubled his efforts to forge some sort of reputation for himself in order to enable him to marry. Prospects could only be secured by obtaining a reputation. 'A man must get himself talked about' he wrote to Martha in February 1884.[100] Publication of scientific papers was the sure way to achieve this, thus his letters to Martha in this period are peppered with references to his 'hope to be able to find some material for publication' (1884).[101] In January 1884 he complained to Martha that 'it is hard to find material for publication, and it infuriates me to see how everyone is making straight for the unexploited legacy of nervous disease' (1884).[102] Freud's infuriation arose from his own desire to contribute to this field. For, on advice from a friend, he had left the department of dermatology and had joined the department of nervous diseases. A week after joining the new department he wrote to Martha: 'today I put my case histories in order at last and started on the study of a nervous case; thus begins a new era' (1884).[103]

By all accounts Freud was an extremely good neurologist, finding favour with Meynert in the department. Freud talked later of 'the great Meynert, in whose footsteps I had trodden with such deep veneration' (1900).[104] He recalled an incident in his autobiography, when he considered himself to have been specially singled out by Meynert: 'One day Meynert, who had given me access to the laboratory even during the times when I was not actually working under him, proposed that I should definitely devote myself to the anatomy of the brain, and promised to hand over his lecturing work to me, as he felt too old to manage the newer methods' (1925).[105] Those newer methods included a system of staining brain tissue for examination by microscope which Freud himself had developed and of which Brücke had commented 'I see your methods alone will make you famous yet'.[106] The method required considerable development, and although he was able to marshal the help of friends to do some of this work, Freud ultimately had to abandon the technique. But in brain anatomy he was developing quite a reputation – as he recalled in his autobiography 'the fame of my diagnoses and of their *post-mortem* confirmation brought me an influx of American physicians, to whom I lectured upon the patients in my department in a sort of pidgin-English' (1925).[107] He was even to confess to his fiancée, to whom he wrote virtually every other day, 'I am at the moment tempted by the desire to solve the riddle of the structure of the brain; I think brain anatomy is the only legitimate rival you have or ever will have' (1885).[108]

Freud's work on neuro-anatomy was opening up an avenue for him to advance himself – as an academic. He discussed his options with Professor Nothnagel, who considered that his papers were rather too theoretical to develop a successful practice. 'The papers you have done up to now won't be of any use to you' Freud reported Nothnagel as saying. 'General practitioners, on whom everything depends, are prosaic people who'll think to themselves: "What's the good of Freud's knowledge of brain anatomy? That won't help him to treat a radialis paralysis [a common complaint]!"' (1884).[109] So with an 'eye to pecuniary considerations' (1925) he 'formed a plan of . . . obtaining an appointment as university lecturer [*Dozent*] on nervous diseases in Vienna' (ibid.) since there were at that time 'few specialists in that branch of medicine in Vienna' (ibid.).[110]

Before he was able to obtain that post Freud began to explore another avenue which seemed to offer him a route to success, and to his desired goal of having a suitably secure position such that he could marry. The first hint of this route came in a letter to Martha in April 1884:

> I am also toying with a project and a hope which I will tell you about, perhaps nothing will come of this, either. It is a therapeutic experiment. I have been reading about cocaine . . . There may be any number of people experimenting on it already, perhaps it won't work. But I am certainly going to try it and, as you know, if one tries something often enough and goes on wanting it, one day it may succeed. We need no more than one stroke of luck of this kind to consider setting up house. But my little woman, do not be too convinced that this will come off this time. As you know, an explorer's temperament requires two basic qualities: optimism in attempt, criticism in work. (1884)[111]

Freud's interest in cocaine had been stimulated by a report he had read of cocaine being administered to exhausted German soldiers who had miraculously revived and were able to carry out their manoeuvres. Freud ordered some of the substance and began taking it. To one himself exhausted from overwork, the effects were dramatic, and confirmed the earlier study. Freud began to administer the drug on himself, his friends and his patients, and then test the effects of it upon different (quantifiable) bodily functions such as muscle performance. His interest was further stimulated by the connection, manifest in the literature he had been studying, between cocaine and sexuality. Jones described his interest as 'libidinous', a psychoanalytic word referring to a sexual component. In some respects 'cocaine' seemed to Freud an *entrée* into the mysterious world of sexuality – a world he was longing passionately to enter throughout his engagement. The connection in his mind is very clear from his letters to his fiancée:

> Woe to you, my Princess, when I come. I will kiss you quite red and feed you till you are plump. And if you are forward, you shall see who is stronger, a gentle little girl who doesn't eat enough or a big wild man *who has cocaine in his body*. In my last severe depression I took coca again and a small dose lifted me to the heights in a wonderful fashion. I am just now busy collecting the literature for a song of praise to this magical substance. (1884)[112]

Freud's 'Song of praise' to cocaine was published as a paper entitled 'Über Coca', in 1884. As the last quotation indicates Freud wrote it just prior to his paying a visit to Martha whom he had not seen for over a year. In his eagerness to see Martha he was not able to fully explore all the effects of the drug that he had noticed, in particular he was not able to develop the discovery that the drug 'seemed to have powerful qualities for relieving pain'.[113] He had mentioned this property to a friend, Königstein. Königstein was an ophthalmologist and Freud suggested 'that he should investigate the question of how far the anaesthetizing properties of cocaine were applicable in diseases of the eye' (1925).[114] Another friend, Carl Koller, who had been one of those with whom Freud had experimented on cocaine, visited Freud, and chanced upon a sample of cocaine on his desk; he too had noted its anaesthetizing effects. Koller was an ophthalmologist as well and quickly began to think of the applications such a drug might have in his work. Accordingly he tried it on himself and discovered that if a solution of the drug was applied to the eye it became numb – this was the discovery of local anaesthesia in ophthalmology. Koller published his results with an acknowledgement that Dr Sigmund Freud had brought cocaine to the attention of 'us Viennese physicians', but Freud had missed a golden opportunity for advancement and fame because he had visited his fiancée – as he recalled in his autobiography 'Koller is . . . rightly regarded as the discoverer of local anaesthesia [of the eye] by cocaine, which has become so important in minor surgery: but I bore my fiancée no grudge for the interruption' (1925).[115]

Unfortunately for Freud the use of cocaine as an anaesthetic is about the only safe use of this powerful drug. Many of the supposed benefits of the drug soon proved illusory, and, most damagingly from Freud's point of view, one use even proved dangerous. In his paper 'Über Coca', and in a subsequent paper, Freud has recommended the use of the drug as a safe (non-addictive) substitute for morphine addicts. He had done this on the strength of a report he had found in an American medical publication, and on the strength of an initial partial success with a colleague von Fleischl who, due to an accident in the laboratory had begun to take morphine to relieve the pain. This friend subsequently died, in distressing circumstances, addicted to cocaine. However, early in the 1880s this serious problem with cocaine was not apparent, and people could only see its possibilities. 'Über Coca' became an important source of information on the subject being translated into English in 1884, and with the addition of supplementary material it was brought out as a booklet in Vienna early in 1885. Freud lectured on the use of cocaine to the Vienna Psychiatric Association in March 1885. His name was inextricably linked to the drug.

Freud himself continued to administer cocaine to himself even, perhaps, well into the 1890s. Jones, who had studied all of Freud's surviving letters, reported to a collaborator: 'I'm afraid that Freud took more cocaine than he should though I'm not mentioning that [in my biography]'.[116] It has even recently been suggested that many of the symptoms which Freud took to be signs of his own neurosis (notably paranoia) – which he attempted to tackle in his self-analysis – were indeed indications of cocaine dependency.[117] Freud's involvement with cocaine was a terribly sensitive subject with his family, who sought to minimize his enthusiasm for it. Despite their suppression of the evidence about Freud's cocaine involvement, it is increasingly being realized that the whole cocaine saga has an inextricable link to all of Freud's theories.[118] The link between cocaine and sexuality may be one of the keys to understanding the development of psychoanalysis with its stress on the power of sex. Throughout his career Freud stressed the similarities between the neuroses and the effects of certain psychoactive chemical agents. Thus in a case study which was written up in 1901 but published in 1905 (the Dora Case – see chapter 4) Freud defended his theory of hysteria in the following way:

No one, probably, will be inclined to deny the sexual function the character of an organic factor, and it is the sexual function that I look upon as the foundation of hysteria and of the psychoneuroses in general. No theory of sexual life will, I suspect, be able to avoid assuming the existence of some definite sexual substance having an excitant action. Indeed, of all the clinical pictures which we meet with in clinical medicine, it is the phenomena of intoxification and abstinence in connection with the use of certain chronic, poisons that most closely resemble the genuine psychoneuroses. (1905)[119]

In the light of Freud's involvement with cocaine it is hard not to draw the conclusion that the principal 'chronic poison' he had in mind here was cocaine – indeed in a similar defence he marshalled in his famous *Three Essays* of 1905 he asserted that 'the greatest clinical similarity' was to 'phenomena of intoxication and abstinence that arise from the habitual use of toxic, pleasure-producing substances (alkaloids)' (1905).[120] With such an organic conception of sexuality and the libido it is little wonder then that in 1908 he wrote to Jung maintaining: 'I am rather annoyed with Bleuler for his willingness to accept a psychology without sexuality, which leaves everything hanging in mid-air. In the sexual processes we have an indispensable 'organic foundation' without which a medical man can only feel ill at ease in the life of the psychic' (1908).[121] Freud never fully articulated precisely what he believed that organic foundation to be – in his *Introductory Lectures* he confessed: 'the edifice of psychoanalytic theory which we have erected is in truth but a superstructure which will one day have to be set on its organic foundation; but of this foundation we are still in ignorance' (1916/17).[122] Despite that profession of ignorance, it is most probable that he did actually believe that in reality his theory of sexuality was grounded upon the 'organic foundation' of a model of sexual chemistry which owed a good deal to his theories on cocaine.

But Freud, in his eagerness to exploit this 'stroke of luck' had abandoned one of those basic qualities of the explorer's temperament which he had spoken of to Martha – 'criticism in work' – and he had not noted its addictive properties. It soon became apparent to all that the 'magical substance' had a 'sting-in-the-tail' – it was impossible to be free of its grip once it had been taken for a long time. Medical and public opinion swung against the drug dramatically with men calling it 'the third scourge of humanity' (alcohol and morphine being the first two). Freud, who had staked so much on this work, became identified as someone who had unleashed a terror upon the world, and who was professionally discredited. He was very distressed, and tried for the rest of his life to blot out the memory of it – even leaving out the damaging reference from his bibliography of writings.

Meanwhile, the other route to advancement – the route of academic advancement in the university – was beginning to pay off. On 2 January 1885, he applied for a post as *Dozent* in neuropathology – he explained what this meant to Martha in a letter in March of the previous year:

One more word about the *Dozentur*. There is no salary attached to it, but two advantages. First the right (actually the only duty) to give lectures on which, if they are well attended . . . – I could manage to live . . . Secondly, one rises to a higher social level in the medical world and in the eyes of the public, has more prospects not only of getting patients but of better paying ones – in short, it helps one to build up a certain reputation. Admittedly, there is also *Dozenten* without patients and in spite of the fair success of my labours our whole future does indeed still look rather dark. (1884)[123]

His application for the post was supported by his former professors, Ernst Brücke, Hermann Nothnagel, and Theodore Meynert. Brücke himself composed a testimonial in support of the application which was glowing in its praise for the young doctor:

Dr Freud is a man of good general education and quiet serious character, an excellent worker in the field of neuroanatomy, finely skilled, clear sighted, with a wide knowledge of medical literature and a well-balanced capacity for logical deduction, together with a gift for elegant literary presentation. His findings enjoy recognition and confirmation. As a lecturer his manner is clear and confident. He combines the qualities of a scientific researcher with those of a competent teacher.[124]

The young doctor had clearly impressed his teachers, and accordingly, given this 'song of praise' he was duly appointed in September, once all the requisite formalities with the application had been attended to.

While his application to become a *Dozent* was being processed Freud determined to go 'to Paris to continue my studies' (1925).[125] It was in Paris that the greatest living psychiatrist, Dr Jean-Martin Charcot, was practising and gaining great notoriety for his work on nervous diseases – 'in the distance shone the great name of Charcot' (ibid.) he was to recall later. 1885 was the year in which a university travel scholarship, which was allocated to a different faculty each year, became available to the medical faculty. It was not a great sum but sufficient to (just) support a research trip of about 6 months. Freud applied for the grant in March 1885, and despite there being two other candidates for it, was successful. He learned of his success in June and thus prepared to travel to Paris – on his way he decided to visit Martha and spent 6 weeks with her. Rather than accept the customary 6-month leave of absence from the Vienna General Hospital to make the trip, he resigned his post determined, on his return, to begin a new life.

The prospect of a trip to Paris, and a visit to Martha was inducement indeed for Freud to be happy:

Oh, how wonderful it will be! I am coming with money and staying a long time and bringing something beautiful for you and then go on to Paris and become a great scholar and then come back to Vienna with a huge, enormous halo, and then we will soon get married, and I will cure all the incurable nervous cases and through you I shall be healthy and I will go on kissing you till you are strong and gay and happy . . . With 100,000 kisses, all of which are to be cashed. (1885)[126]

Earlier in the year Freud had written to Martha about his intentions in applying to travel: 'What I want, as you know, is to go on to Paris . . . have enough leisure to finish my work on the brain, and then the independence to find out what chances there are for us here' (1885).[127] During his visit to Martha, Freud's relationship with his future mother-in-law and her family which had been strained became much more cordial, and Freud moved on to Paris far more reassured about his personal life.

He arrived in Paris on 13 October 1885 and spent the first few days looking round the sights visiting the Place de la Concorde and the Louvre where he was fascinated by the Egyptian antiquities (years later he was to collect Egyptian figurines). After becoming conversant with the city he paid his first visit to Charcot's hospital, the Salpêtrière, but because he forgot the letter of introduction he had been given by a Viennese colleague he decided to wait before meeting the great man himself. On his return from this first visit he was frankly depressed – missing Vienna, desperate for Martha – he wrote to her: 'Apart from some subjective and scientific profit I expect so little from my stay here that in this respect I cannot be disappointed' (1885).[128] He regretted not going to study at Berlin, where, with some ingenuity, he could have visited Martha once a week.

Within a few more days his mood had changed – 'you may miss the note of melancholy to which you will have grown accustomed in my letters from Paris' (1885) he wrote to Martha.[129] The reason for this change in mood was that he had been introduced to Charcot and received a warm welcome; 'everything went off better than I had expected' (ibid.). From the start the great Charcot gripped his attention: 'I was very much impressed by his brilliant diagnosis and the lively interest he took in everything, so unlike what we are accustomed to from our great men with their veneer of distinguished superficiality' (ibid.). Charcot made the necessary arrangements for Freud to begin his anatomical investigations in the hospital, and thus continue his earlier work. But Freud, who attended Charcot's demonstrations and ward rounds, was finding his interest being directed away from his earlier concern to 'solve the riddle of the structure of the brain'. He described the effects of his encounters with Charcot in a letter to Martha in November:

I am really very comfortably installed now and I think I am changing a great deal. I will tell you in detail what is affecting me. Charcot, who is one of the greatest physicians and a man whose common sense borders on genius, is simply wrecking all my aims and opinions. I sometimes come out of his lectures as from out of Notre-Dame, with an entirely new idea about perfection. But he exhausts me; when I come away from him I no longer have any desire to work at my own silly things; it is three whole days since I have done any work, and I have no feelings of guilt. My brain is sated as after an evening in the theatre. Whether the seed will ever bear any fruit, I don't know; but what I do know is that no other human being has ever affected me in the same way. (1885)[130]

In particular Freud's desire to study brain anatomy was being replaced by a desire to emulate Charcot and explore the new, and hitherto unexplored, field of the neuroses. On his return to Vienna, in a report of his trip submitted to the Faculty of Medicine, he was to suggest that he was forced to make this move by the circumstances in Paris. In that report he wrote 'I arrived with the intention of making one single question the subject of a thorough investigation . . . my chosen concern [was] with anatomical problems' (1886). [131] But, Freud continued – perhaps with a fair degree of rationalizing – 'I found conditions for making use of [the material made available] were most unfavourable. The laboratory was not at all adapted to the reception of an extraneous worker' (ibid.). Freud concluded that he was forced to give up anatomical work (although he did visit the Paris morgue and watch the post-mortem examinations there and, he did also in fact subsequently return to it briefly in Vienna). It may well have been difficult for him in the lab where we might suggest there could have been anti-Semitism and anti-German feelings in the workers there (it had not been long after France's defeat in the Franco–Prussian war). But who would not consider the opportunity to go and watch Charcot's demonstrations of dramatic events occurring with hysterical women worth taking, and who would not leave the laboratory bench for the spectacles Charcot was staging when that same man was declaring 'the work of anatomy was finished and . . . the theory of the organic [that is disease where there is a demonstrable anatomical lesion] disease of the nervous system might be said to be complete'?[132]

Freud may have already had an interest in the neuroses prior to his visit to Paris, as a result of his friendship with a prominent Viennese physician, Josef Breuer. It was whilst Freud was still at Brücke's laboratory that he had first met Breuer. Breuer had become a close friend, a professional confidant, and a benefactor to Freud, indeed this older, general practitioner had acted as a sort of father figure for Freud during the 1880s. Freud wrote to him 'I realize that I owe you thanks especially for your good opinion of me which raises me high above my present situation; in giving it, you will either be moving out ahead of others, or even remaining a lone voice' (1884).[133] In 1880 Breuer began to treat a hysterical young woman – later described as 'Anna O' – her symptoms included sporadic and re-occurring paralysis of the limbs, severe speech disturbances and visual problems. Breuer found, by chance, that if she described in detail the circumstances a symptom first appeared in, it was relieved temporarily – he called this process 'catharsis'. 'Anna O' referred to this process as 'the talking cure' or 'chimney-sweeping'. Freud first learned of this remarkable case in November 1882. In July 1883 he had 'a lengthy medical conversation [with Breuer] on moral insanity and nervous diseases and strange case histories' (1883)[134] during which the case 'cropped up'. So interested was Freud in the case that he tried to discuss it with Charcot in Paris 2 years later – Charcot was not particularly interested. For Freud though, it formed part of the soil within which Charcot's 'seed' could begin to bear fruit. Breuer later described the case as 'the germ cell of the whole of psychoanalysis'.[135] Freud was later to claim 'if it is a merit to have brought psychoanalysis into being, that merit is not mine . . . [it belongs] to another physician, Dr. Josef Breuer' (1910).[136]

Now, under Charcot's influence, Freud began to consider that the neuroses represented his future field of study. Hysteria was the most pressing and challenging problem in the field to tackle. Long believed to be caused by a malfunctioning of the uterus (Greek name: *hysteron*) and thus a disease of women, it had a bad reputation to live down, being variously associated with excitable French actresses and with celebrated court cases involving the payments of compensation for accidents. Charcot, himself already assured of a lasting reputation for his early work in pathological anatomy, brought a degree of respectability to the field, and brought, it was thought, scientific order to the chaotic field. After his death Freud wrote in his obituary that Charcot was 'assured . . . for all time . . . of having been the first to explain hysteria' (1893).[137] Likewise in his own first publication on hysteria, Freud wrote of Charcot: 'in a series of researches he . . . succeeded in proving the presence of regularity and law where the inadequate or half-hearted clinical observation of other people saw only malingering or a puzzling lack of conformity to rule'.[138] The idea, derived from Breuer, that physical symptoms could be relieved by a mental (non-physical) solution, was supplemented now, before his very eyes, by Charcot, as he saw non-hysterical patients under hypnosis, on suggestion from Charcot develop (physical) symptoms – paralyses, tremors and the like. The mind could produce physical changes – this was a new departure for Freud. It is ironic that for all that Freud believed that Charcot was unfolding before his very eyes the inexorable pattern of a disease, it is clear that in the atmosphere of suggestibility and with the inevitable rewards of attention for the right symptoms Charcot was frequently the victim of gross deceptions. One of his patients, nicknamed, 'Queen of the Hysterics', is later reported to have been able to produce a perfect hysterical attack at will, and to have remained conscious throughout. Charcot's demonstration room even included a painting on the wall of the typical case – a sort of visual do-it-yourself portrait for his hysterics.[139]

Freud continued to drink in the city, and the new ideas he was being witness to. He became entranced by the city, reading Victor Hugo's *Notre-Dame*, and visiting its many cultural riches – to the point whereby he was convinced that you could not understand Paris *without* understanding Hugo's version of the city. He even began to move in Charcot's social circle. At one of Charcot's parties Freud suggested to his host that he translate into German a volume of Charcot's lectures, a move which had the double benefit of ingratiating him to Charcot, and of: '[making] me known to doctors and patients in Germany . . . it will be of great advantage to my practice and moreover will pave the way for my own book when that is ready for publication' (1885).[140] He wrote to Martha of his new-found importance in Charcot's eyes, and having described the latest party he had attended at the Charcot's home wrote: 'these were my achievements (or rather the achievements of cocaine) which left me very satisfied (1886).[141] The heady whirl of his life even led him to suggest to Martha 'given favourable conditions I could achieve more than Nothnagel, to whom I consider myself superior, and might possibly reach the level of Charcot' (1886).[142] This euphoria, inevitably, was punctured by hard realities, as Freud began to run out of money; 'what an ass I am to be leaving Paris now that spring is coming' he wrote to Martha just before leaving. He regretted his departure bitterly as he seemed to have such an advantageous position at the Salpêtrière: 'I have only to say one word to Charcot and I can do whatever I like with the patients' he wrote in the same letter.[143] To his friend Koller he was at least honest about why he was leaving:

> You are right in thinking that Paris meant the beginning of a new existence for me. I found Charcot there, a teacher such as I had always imagined. I learned to observe clinically as much as I am able to and I brought back with me a lot of information. I only committed the folly of not having enough money to last for more than five months. (1886)[144]

Freud returned to Vienna, on his way making a brief stop in Berlin where he conducted some further research on children's brain diseases. He was not impressed with Berlin: he wrote to his sister Rosa 'I am . . . very lonely here, and in the evenings, when I can't work, I'm bored stiff. The city doesn't really make an impression on me. Slightly more lively and a little less attractive than Vienna. Life much cheaper, and the people work hard for their living; many police and many soldiers' (1886).[145] Nowhere could quite compare, for Freud at this time, with Paris and the Salpêtrière with its sense of literally being at the forefront of a new battleground: the riddle of the neuroses.

Freud had departed from Vienna as a competent neurologist with an assured, albeit slow, future in the academic world of Vienna with the support of the city's leading professors in the field. He returned from Paris 'as Charcot's unqualified admirer' (1886)[146] and as such he became distinctly dubious in the eyes of the establishment. Not only did he have the stigma of being a Jew in a 'Catholic country' where anti-Semitism was rife but his name was becoming associated with a number of controversial topics. On top of his already tarnished scientific reputation over cocaine, he had become identified with a despised *French* psychiatry, a questionable technique (hypnosis), and a suspect disease (hysteria). He was not going to find it easy to gain acceptance in his new-found role as a 'pupil of Charcot' (1899).[147] He did not make things easier for himself when, shortly after his return, he submitted a report of his visit replete with veiled criticisms of 'scientific workers in Germany and Austria' for meeting the findings of Charcot, 'with more doubt than recognition and belief' (1886).[148] Having submitted this report, Dr Sigmund Freud, *Dozent* in Neuropathology at the University of Vienna, set up a practice – he now considered that he had the experience and expertise to run a private practice in neurology of sufficient size and quality to sustain himself. He was 30, had little financial backing, Jewish, and a bad name thanks to 'cocaine', and was dabbling in a controversial field – yet he was to maintain a practice, at first as a neurologist but soon increasingly as a psychoanalyst, through thick and thin until he was forced to leave Vienna in 1938. If the synthesis of the ideas of Breuer and those of Charcot can be said to represent the beginning of the science of psychoanalysis, this may be said to represent the beginning of a *profession* of psychoanalysis. Freud was the first professional analyst.

2

The Birth of Psychoanalysis
Hypnosis, Symptoms and Sexuality

*Man can stretch himself as he may with his knowledge and appear
to himself as objective as he may; in the last analysis he gives nothing
but his own biography.* (F. Nietzsche)

Historians tell us that if we consider the nineteenth century as a whole
we may discern trends and turns in the culture of Western Europe, which
are discernible throughout the sciences and the arts. Following the
publication of Darwin's *Origin of Species* in 1859 the predominant mood
of all academic disciplines was decidedly naturalistic – materialism and
mechanism prevailed in the sciences; Social Darwinism and Utilitarianism
dominated the human sciences; and in literature Romanticism was out
of vogue under the naturalistic impulses of Flaubert, Maupassant and
Zola. But, sometime around 1885, a new trend became discernible with
writers such as Friedrich Nietzsche emerging as representatives. Optimism
over humanity's future became replaced by pessimism. Reason failed and
despair began to enter the analysis of the human situation. Nietzsche
heralded the death of God and the consequent liberation of humanity
to be its own arbiter. 'The most important of more recent events – "God
is dead", that the belief in the Christian God has become unworthy of
belief – already begins to cast its first shadows over Europe' he declared.
One aspect of that shadow was the creation of a new morality of nihilism –
'nothing is true, everything is allowed' he proclaimed.

This new liberation, however, did not, as might be suspected, create a
new sense of humanity becoming at last an understandable subject. The
fact that humanity had become free of the influence of theological
prejudices and religious dogma, and that it had become accessible to
science did not, for these new writers, make it any more understandable but
rather less. Far from humanity having been rendered transparent to a new
objective gaze Nietzsche stressed its opacity. He grappled with the question
of how one can really know the true nature of being human – 'with all
that which a person allows to appear, one may ask: what is it meant to
hide? What should it divert the eyes from? What prejudice should it
conceive? How far goes the subtlety of this dissimulation? How far does

he deceive himself in this action?' Humankind became a duplicitous creature. A creature with hidden springs of actions, and covert reasons behind its behaviour – in short, a mask behind which hidden, ignoble yet true, instincts seethed. 'Good actions are sublimated evil ones' declared Nietzsche, and even our highest aspirations are infused with the baser, more fundamental instincts: 'the degree of quality of a person's sexuality finds its way into the topmost reaches of his spirit.'

Freud was deeply sympathetic to this mood and to Nietzsche in particular, although in his autobiography he wrote that he put off reading him for a long time to keep his mind 'unembarrassed'. Nevertheless, he declared 'Nietzsche [is] . . . a philosopher whose guesses and intuitions often agree in the most astonishing way with the laborious findings of psychoanalysis' (1925).[1] He was also happy to concede, on another occasion, that he had not discovered that our behaviour was governed by unconscious motives, that had been done previously: 'The poets and philosophers before me discovered the unconscious. What I discovered was the scientific method by which the unconscious can be studied'.[2]

If naturalism may be said to characterize the predominant mood of the 1860s, 1870s and early 1880s neo-Romanticism may be said to be the word to describe the reaction it evoked. Strictly speaking the term belongs only to a particular set of German poets writing at the time, but the general trends in society throughout Europe embody and exemplify remarkably similar values – a sense of the abandonment of God; an awareness not of the 'progress' of civilization but of 'decay' in all systems and processes; a love of decadence; a search for meaningful myths; an almost self-indulgent sense of the importance of the individual; a love of, and interest in, all the irrational, sensual, sexual and occult aspects of life. The artist Pissarro wrote, in 1883, 'everything the bourgeoisie has admired for the past fifty years falls into oblivion, becomes outdated and ridiculous'.

All of this came to a head in the notion of the *fin de siècle* spirit. The idea of the *fin de siècle*, the 'end of the era', was first postulated in Paris in 1886. Artists, novelists and journalists all began to discern in the decay of the old era the imminent culmination of it. Vincent Van Gogh exclaimed in 1886 'we are in the last quarter of a century which will end in a colossal revolution', while in 1890 Gauguin despaired 'a terrible ordeal awaits the next generation in Europe: the Kingdom of gold. Everything is rotten, both men and the arts.' The belief in the *fin de siècle* was nowhere more prominent than in Vienna where the Austro-Hungarian Empire – an unlikely conglomeration of nations and peoples – was beginning to show signs of death. The aging Franz Joseph was no longer able to hold together the disparate forces within the Empire. In Vienna on May Day 1890, for instance, there was the first-ever march of workers through the streets – an event which prompted the appearance of troops in the city. The city also elected a new mayor in 1895, Karl Luegar, who had already suggested that Jews should be crammed into ships to be sunk with all aboard. His appointment as mayor was not ratified by the Emperor for a further 2 years. The cracks in society were widening, it was a time when change was imminent. Thus in 1897, the Austrian Parliament passed the Czech ordinances granting the Czechs the right to speak their own language – a crisis was precipitated rendering the unity of the empire questionable. The Viennese journalist and writer Karl Kraus captured the mood of the moment in his play the 'Last Days of Mankind'. Many people reacted to the prevailing pessimism of the period with a flight into frivolity, triviality, mysticism, eroticism and hedonism – the *fin de siècle* spirit embodied these values.

Freud set up his first private practice at the beginning of this period (in 1886). He went on to write his first book on the neuroses at the height of the period (*Studies on Hysteria*, 1895); to formulate the basic principles of a new system of therapy for the neuroses, psychoanalysis, during this period; to conduct his own 'self-analysis'; and to culminate his creative work over the period with the book which is arguably his most enduring classic, *The Interpretation of Dreams*, in 1900. It goes without saying then that the period from 1885 to 1900 is of crucial significance for an understanding of the man universally recognized as having created the climate of opinion of the twentieth century. Freud's ideas were born out of this period; in the words of one of his close disciples (later a renegade): 'like Nietzsche, like the Great War so too Freud . . . is an answer to the sickness of the nineteenth century. This is certainly his chief significance'.[3]

PRELUDE TO HYSTERIA:
EARLY DAYS IN PRACTICE AND HYPNOSIS

> But if today were to be my last on earth and someone asked me how I had fared, he would be told by me that in spite of everything – poverty, long struggle for success, little favour amongst men, over-sensitiveness, nervousness and worries – I have nevertheless been happy simply because of the anticipation of one day having you to myself and of the certainty that you love me . . . For a long, long time I have criticized you and picked you to pieces, and the result of it all is that I want nothing but to have you and have you just as you are. (Freud to Martha Bernays, 1886)[4]

With a characteristic swipe at Catholic conventions Freud opened his private practice on Easter Day 1886 – a day traditionally regarded as a religious and public holiday. He then had to complete a brief period of military service as Regimental Chief Physician in Moravia where he gained 'great confidence among military and civilians' (to cite his military report). He then got married. That which he had desired for so long became possible after Martha had received a small legacy. So on 14 September 1886 Martha Bernays became Frau Martha Freud following a civil service on 13 September. Despite Freud's dislike of the religious rituals of a Jewish wedding ceremony he went through the service in order to fulfil the requirements of Austrian law for a religious wedding. The couple took a two-week honeymoon, first on the Baltic coast and then travelling through Germany. They returned to Vienna on 1 October.

If the 4 years of Freud's engagement, conducted as they were in such difficult circumstances (familial opposition, geographical separation), had been characterized by Freud's fervent desire to make sufficient name for himself in Vienna to become established enough to get married; then once having got married his efforts redoubled just to survive with his wife (and inevitably, children). In his autobiography, he recalled, somewhat misleadingly as it turns out, 'during the period from 1886–1891 I did little scientific work, and published scarcely anything. I was occupied with establishing myself in my new profession and with assuring my own material existence as well as that of a rapidly increasing family' (1925).[5] The historian of psychoanalysis, Ernst Kris, commenting upon Freud's early days in practice reports: 'In Vienna medical practice, "right to the very top of the tree" was severely affected by every economic recession, every one of which, in addition to the ups and downs in Freud's reputation with his colleagues and the public, was reflected in his household's welfare'.[6] Freud's correspondence throughout the period was thus replete with his financial anxieties.

Freud's recollection of that period as being one of scientific sterility is misleading as, he did, in fact, continue his studies in various fields. He worked: in neuropaediatrics (between 1886 and 1887 he was director of the neurological department of a children's clinic – a post without remuneration); on cocaine (in 1887 he published a further paper on the drug; in May 1886 Freud had been publicly criticized by a Viennese physician for his work on cocaine); on hypnotism (in May 1886 he twice lectured on the subject in defence of Charcot's views); and on brain anatomy (in 1887 he was complaining to a friend that he was 'busy writing three papers at the same time, including one on brain anatomy' (1887)[7] which he hoped to bring out as a book). None of these activities kept the wolf from the door, though: his private practice and the little money that Martha had brought with her were the means whereby he was able to do that. He described his situation to his friend Carl Koller: 'my little wife, with the help of her dowry and the wedding presents, has made a charming home . . . Only one thing has not up to now gone as I would have wished: the practice. It's a completely new beginning, and a much harder one than the first however perhaps things will soon begin to look up for us' (1886).[8] Following on from his success at translating Charcot's lectures (which he began in Paris and finished in Vienna) he was also able to supplement his income further by translating two volumes of another famous French physician's works, the works of Bernheim on hypnotism.

Despite this varied interest Freud was able, too, in the light of his recent 'conversion' to the views of Charcot, to devote much of his attention to two closely related subjects, hypnotism and hysteria – they were both subjects of the utmost controversy in Vienna at the time with protagonists for differing positions already clearly delineated. After delivering a lecture to the Physiological Club on hypnotism Freud wrote to Martha that 'the battle of Vienna is in full swing' (1886).[9] Freud as a proselyte of Charcot was prepared to take on all comers. The opening skirmish began as soon as 15 October 1886 when Freud delivered a paper to the Imperial Society of Physicians of Vienna (a group which included all the leading neurologists in Vienna) – the paper was entitled 'On Male Hysteria'. Some idea of the controversial nature of the subject can be gained from a passage Freud wrote a little later:

> [Hysteria] the most enigmatic of all nervous diseases, for the evaluation of which medicine had not yet found a serviceable angle of approach, had just then fallen into thorough discredit; and this discredit extended not only to the patients but to the physicians who concerned themselves with the neurosis. It was held that in hysteria anything was possible, and no credence was given to the hysteric about anything. (1893)[10]

Charcot's work in Paris had been directed at establishing some sort of order out of the confused ideas about hysteria which were prevalent at the time. In his obituary of Charcot, Freud was later to suggest that in doing this Charcot's name should be placed within the ranks of those most honoured in the history of psychiatry, specifically that he should rank with that other famous French physician Philippe Pinel who at the close of the eighteenth century had 'liberated' the insane from their chains and instigated the modern *medical* approach to insanity. Freud may well have regarded himself as completing the triumvirate of liberators: Pinel, Charcot, Freud. Freud wrote:

> The first thing that Charcot's work did was to restore its dignity to the topic. Little by little, people gave up the scornful smile with which the patient could at that time feel certain of being met. She was no longer necessarily a malingerer, for Charcot had thrown the whole weight of his own authority on the side of the genuineness and objectivity of hysterical phenomena. (1893)[11]

Dignity was not the only thing which Freud considered Charcot brought to hysteria – he suggested that Charcot brought three specific clinical insights to the problem. The first insight Charcot provided was that identical symptoms could be induced artificially by suggestion during hypnosis. Similarly Charcot demonstrated that 'hysterically prone' individuals could be hypnotized and, without any suggestion, be induced to exhibit hysterical paralyses by means of a light blow to the arm or to the leg – Charcot suggested this was the power of *auto*suggestion. Freud summed up this insight by saying that Charcot 'succeeded in proving, by an unbroken chain of argument, that these paralyses were the result of ideas which had dominated the patient's brain at moments of a special disposition' (1893).[12] This insight has a corollary, namely the second major contribution of Charcot. In Freud's words he 'was the first to teach us that to explain hysterical neurosis we must apply to psychology' (1893).[13] To Freud, a young Austrian neurologist trained within the traditions of brain anatomy and physiology this was a profound change in perspective. Admittedly, given his earlier interest in philosophy in general, it was a change which he was able to make by virtue of his deeper predilections, but none the less it went against the whole tide of academic opinion in Vienna. Charcot's third insight, though by no means original to him, was his rejection of the widespread belief that hysteria was caused by *female* patients' disturbed sexual organization (a disturbance in her *hysteria* or womb). Since the disease was no longer associated with the womb it became possible to talk of the existence of hysteria in men. It was this subject which Freud chose to discuss at the Imperial Society of Physicians.

Before describing that meeting, however, it is worth pointing out that Freud supplemented these insights of Charcot with an observation which was dramatic in its implications. As a neurologist he was in a good position to study the relationship between hysterical paralyses and those paralyses caused by a known anatomical (organic) lesion. Under Charcot's tutelage, and with material supplied to him at the Salpêtrière, Freud made the comparison and discovered that the two sorts of paralyses reflected two differing patterns. From his studies Freud found that the organic paralyses always conformed to the underlying anatomical structures – quite specific areas of hands or legs were affected by quite specific lesions in the nervous tissue such that it was possible to predict which nerves were the problem from observation of the particular paralysis. Hysterical paralyses, on the other hand, reflected not the logic of anatomy, but the logic of common sense: in Freud's words hysteria 'behaves as though anatomy did not exist or as though it had no knowledge of it' (1893).[14] This is a remarkable observation and quite startling to a neurologist. We can perhaps get some sense of the novelty of this insight by considering an analogy. When a car breaks down, the would-be mechanic knows in which system to look for the fault by the effects – if there is something wrong with the electrical system the ignition will not work or the lights do not come on. The logic of the breakdown reflects an underlying, understandable logic of the basic components. If you were to present our would-be mechanic with a car which had, say, broken down totally on its left side such that every part and system on the left-hand side of the car was not working while the corresponding parts on the right were then our mechanic would be baffled. The logic of the breakdown goes against the known logic of the components. Freud's observation that hysterical paralyses effect common sense parts and regions – legs and arms – not anatomically defined regions is akin to our left-side breakdown of the car – inexplicable without the introduction of a new order of explanation: in Freud's case without the introduction of psychological causation.

At the meeting of the Imperial Society of Physicians on 15 October 1886 Freud chose to present his paper 'On Male Hysteria'. The text of the lecture had been lost, though it seems reasonable to assume that the content of the paper was very similar to his 'Report on My Studies in Paris and Berlin' written in April of that year. One of Freud's contemporaries, a psychiatrist, has recorded in his memoires his impression of the meeting: '[Freud] spoke of nothing but Charcot and praised him in superlatives. This, however, the Viennese bigwigs could not tolerate well. Bamberger and Meynert had rejected Freud harshly and with this he had fallen into disgrace, so to speak, with the faculty. He was thus a practitioner in neurology without patients'.[15] It may well have been acceptable for a young neurologist to criticize his teachers in a private report to the faculty but to criticize them openly, and in public, is another matter – even Ernest Jones, generally Freud's most sympathetic biographer, commented on this meeting that it showed the 'naïveté of the youthful mentor'.[16]

Freud's naïveté may well be compounded by the fact that not only did he lecture his lecturers on their lack of understanding but he also failed to play the game according to their rules. One of the rules of the society was that the speaker should present *new* material. Freud failed to do this on two counts: first in his presentation of the views of Charcot on hysteria and secondly on his case material. In relation to the first failure Charcot's views were well known even to these Viennese professors – one had even given Freud his letter of introduction to Charcot – and the subject of male hysteria had received considerable attention in medical circles. The chairman of the meeting, Bamberger (who had, incidentally, been on the committee that had awarded Freud's travel scholarship) is reported to have responded to Freud's paper with the following words: 'in spite of my great admiration for Charcot and my high interest for the subject I was unable to find anything new in the report of Dr. Freud because all that had been said has already long been known'.[17] With regard to Freud's second failure, Freud used as his case material a patient whom he had seen at the Salpêtrière, but who was one of Charcot's cases. The presentation of such 'secondary' material prompted the Society (or perhaps Professor Meynert)[18] to demand some more original evidence.

At this point in the story we may pick up Freud's account of the meeting and its effects. Freud's account, written in his autobiography just under 40 years later is both revealing and misleading, but it is misleading in such a way as to illustrate a general point about these early days of psychoanalysis. One of the leading expositors of Freud's early work, Frank Sulloway, describes Freud's account as 'largely a myth'.[19] Just as we have to exercise care over our handling of the early infantile material in Freud's life, so too a similar *caveat* must be entered for his reflections on his early scientific work. Careful investigation of Freud's historical context reveals a situation of far more complexity than Freud usually presents. Freud's account of the first meeting, and of a second subsequent one are as follows:

> The duty devolved upon me of giving a report . . . upon what I had seen and learnt with Charcot. But I met with a bad reception. Persons of authority, such as the chairman (Bamberger, the physician), declared that what I said was incredible. Meynert challenged me to find some cases in Vienna similar to those which I had described and to present them before the Society. I tried to do so; but the senior physicians in whose departments I found any such cases refused to allow me to observe them or to work at them . . . I objected in vain that what I wanted was not to have my diagnosis approved, but to have the case put at my disposal. At length, outside the hospital, I came upon a case . . . and demonstrated it [to the Society]. This time I was applauded, but no further interest was taken in me. The impression that the high authorities had rejected my innovations remained unshaken; and with my hysteria in men and my production of hysterical paralyses by suggestion, I found myself forced into the opposition. As I was soon afterwards excluded from the laboratory of cerebral anatomy [by Professor Meynert] and for terms on end had nowhere to deliver my lectures, I withdrew from academic life and ceased to attend the learned societies. (1925)[20]

Freud's account clearly shows that there had begun to be a polarization between himself and his senior colleagues – but Freud interpreted this as an opposition to his radical views. A more balanced appraisal of the growing opposition might be to suggest that the 'medical establishment' objected to his tone and style and not to the content of his ideas. It is true that there developed a feud between Meynert and Freud over the coming years but this feud centred more around Freud's views on hypnotism than on his views on hysteria. Evidence for this more balanced assessment of Freud's standing in the academic community is provided by the text of a report submitted 10 years later by two professors in support of Freud gaining a promotion. The report includes the following assessment of Freud:

> Freud's stay at the Salpêtrière awakened his interest in the psychic side of the clinical picture of hysteria and in research into hypnotism and the use of suggestion therapy in neuroses . . . The novelty of this research, and the difficulty of verifying it, makes it impossible at present to reach a definite judgement as to its importance. It is possible that Freud overestimates it and generalizes too much on the results obtained. At all events his research in this field shows unusual talent and the ability to find new directions for scientific research.[21]

As we will see, this assessment of Freud's work is one that can be levelled at him throughout his career. Perhaps such passion and single-mindedness is necessary in a pioneer. Perhaps, in order to wrest a secret out of nature, Freud had to become prone to 'overestimation and generalization'. Pioneers have a notoriously difficult path to tread particularly when their sphere of interests touches upon concerns so fundamental to humanity; however, Freud does not appear to have helped himself very much by his manner and his passion.

Freud's recollections of those days have also been shown to be false in another respect – he continued to attend meetings of various learned societies including the supposedly antagonistic (or apathetic) Imperial Society of Physicians. Indeed, in 1897 his name was forwarded, and he was duly elected to membership of the Society. It was not until 1904 that he ceased to go to, and even contribute to, various Viennese medical societies – by which time he had begun his own weekly meetings in his home (meetings of a group of people who were to become the Vienna Psychoanalytic Society). Jones has suggested (by way of excuse for these errors in perception) that Freud's recollections of this period reflected his 'sensitiveness' to rejection and opposition. However, as Sulloway has shown such errors invariably serve the function in the history of psychoanalysis of perpetuating myths about Freud, in particular the myth that he was a lonely pioneer hero who forged his way single-handedly against all opposition to found a new science. Such myths usually serve to legitimate some aspect of Freudian doctrine. They are, in the light of more careful scrutiny, often plainly onesided.[22]

Opposition to Freud, and Meynert's withdrawal of his support centred not so much upon his views on hysteria (galling though they may have been to many) but rather on his views on hypnotism – in medical circles, another hot-potato of the period. It was not that Freud abandoned his interest in hysteria and the neuroses, for as we shall see in the next section they were to become areas of his special concern. It was just that Freud began to conduct the 'battle of Vienna' over the vexed question of hypnosis. Hypnosis became one of his main interests as is clear from a letter to Fliess, written in 1887: 'during the last few weeks I have plunged into hypnotism, and have had all sorts of small but peculiar successes' (1887).[23]

To have 'plunged into hypnotism' at such a time was a risky business, for there were a number of conflicting schools of thought about hypnosis. In particular, the prevalent view in Vienna was at variance with Freud's position, and with those other perspectives which were beginning to gain credence. Freud had not only recently translated some of Charcot's views on hypnosis but, had also set about translating a text of one of the leading alternative perspectives. He declared to Fliess in the same letter as he announced his recent plunge into hypnotism 'I am going to translate Bernheim's book on suggestion. Do not advise me not to, because I am already under contract' (1887).[24] Bernheim was a French physician working in Nancy in France who had developed a method of hypnotic cure, the theory of which was in conflict with Charcot's theories.

In the preface to his translation, Freud criticized Meynert for a 'general confusion' over the relationship between hysteria and hypnosis. Meynert had recently been opposing what he called the 'psychical epidemic among doctors'[25] which had become 'the favourite speciality of unmedical charlatans',[26] and, with a characteristic nationalistic dig at the origins of the movement declared 'we may predict, not without self-assurance, that in Germany this plague will come to an end before it does so anywhere else – and soon'.[27] Meynert also, in response to the ascription of 'confusion' to his views noted his astonishment that Freud who 'had left Vienna as a physician exactly trained in physiology . . . is now active here as a trained practitioner in hypnosis'.[28] In Meynert's eyes, his former pupil, a trained scientist, had abandoned his (German) heritage in favour of a disreputable, unscientific, foreign heresy.[29]

Charcot had suggested that hypnotism was a physiological phenomenon identical at core to certain of the phenomena in hysteria. Freud remarked that 'the great weight of Charcot . . . supports [an] exclusively somatic view of hypnosis' (1889).[30] Bernheim, on the other hand, maintained that far from there being strong similarities between hypnotism and hysteria as a result of their having a common physiological explanation, rather they were similar because they had a common psychological explanation – that all human beings were suggestible. At the end of the 1880s Freud was an advocate of the former position. He was a devotee of Charcot. In translating Bernheim Freud was confronted with an alternative position, much of which seemed cogent. To his friend, Wilhelm Fliess, he commented:

As for *Suggestion* [the shorthand title Freud gave Bernheim's book], you know all about it. I undertook the work very reluctantly, only to have a hand in something which is certainly going to have a big influence on the practice of nerve specialists in the next few years. I do not share Bernheim's views, which seem to me one sided, and I have tried to stand up for Charcot in the introduction – I do not know how skilfully, but I am sure unsuccessfully. (1888)[31]

By the time that he had translated Bernheim though, the primary focus of Freud's dissensions over hypnosis was not in France – Bernheim and Charcot were at least working in the field, albeit in different schools. Freud was out to forge a name for himself *in Vienna* and that meant taking on the might of his former professor, Meynert. The Viennese medical establishment, it seems, was more amenable to Bernheim, for his theory of suggestion could be seen as a special case of their own theories – that hypnosis was just a con-trick. Freud set out to counter such a dismissal. To Fliess he was frank about his target:

. . . because the attitude of all my friends demanded it, I had to be moderate in my criticism of Meynert [in his introduction to Bernheim], who in his usual impudent-malicious manner had delivered himself authoritatively on a subject of which he knew nothing. Even so, they think I have gone too far. I have belled the cat. (1888)[32]

In order to supplement his understanding of hypnosis Freud decided to go and study at Nancy for a brief period. The effects of this short stay, were to remain with him for the rest of his life, although in a way that he little realized. Freud recalled the visit in his autobiography:

With the idea of perfecting my hypnotic technique, I made a journey to Nancy in the summer of 1889 and spent several weeks there. I witnessed the moving spectacle of old Liebeault [Bernheim's teacher at Nancy] working among the poor women and children of the laboring classes. I was a spectator of Bernheim's astonishing experiments upon his hospital patients, and I received the profoundest impression of the possibility that there could be powerful mental processes which nevertheless remained hidden from the consciousness of men. (1925)[33]

The immediate effect of this visit, together with his own limited experience from his practice was that he began to reject Charcot's understanding of hypnosis. Indeed, by the time that Freud was called upon to publish an obituary for Charcot he admitted 'the exclusively nosological approach adopted at the School of the Salpêtrière was not suitable for a purely psychological subject . . . [Charcot's view] sank in the estimation of [his] contemporaries with Liebeault's pupil, Bernheim, set about constructing the theory of hypnotism on a more comprehensive psychological function and making suggestion the central point of hypnosis' (1893).[34] The less obvious effect of the visit, was to strengthen Freud's belief in the power of the unconscious – it was this which was to be the lasting legacy as Freud subsequently came to abandon using hypnosis as a therapeutic tool.

Freud was always to claim that psychoanalysis, i.e. his own particular system of psychological therapy 'was born out of medical necessity' (1919).[35] It was Freud's eventual disillusionment with hypnosis which was to provide the stepping stone to the development of a new approach. In his autobiography he recalled, of the period, that 'my therapeutic arsenal contained only two weapons, electrotherapy and hypnotism' (1925).[36] In fact he also made fairly extensive use of drugs, including cocaine. No therapy though proved adequate to cope with the patients who were beginning to come to him. Beginning in the summer of 1889 and again in 1890 one of his patients began to be treated 'to a large extent' by a 'new method' (1924).[37] Freud was later to say that psychoanalysts were the 'legitimate heirs' of hypnosis (1916)[38] but that the new system proper 'begins only with the new technique that dispenses with hypnosis' (1914).[39] It is to this new technique, and the context of its introduction that we must turn now.

STUDIES ON HYSTERIA: 'ANNA O' AND COMPANY

> From the very first I made use of hypnosis in *another* manner, apart from hypnotic suggestion. (1925)[40]

If it was indeed the case that psychoanalysis was born out of the inadequacies of hypnosis as a method of treatment then the quotation cited here may give us a clue to the alternative therapy that was in the process of being born. You will recall that for some years Freud had been in contact with a Viennese physician, Josef Breuer, who in 1880 had begun the treatment of a young woman suffering from severe, hysterical problems – the famous 'Anna O' case (her real name was, in fact, Bertha Pappenheim a woman who, subsequently, was to become a pioneer feminist and social worker in Germany). Freud had learnt about this case in 1882. So impressed was he by the story that he mentioned it to Charcot when he was in Paris. However, 'the great man' he recalled in his autobiography, 'showed no interest in my first outline of the subject, so that I never returned to it and allowed it to pass from my mind' (1925).[41]

Plate 4. Freud with Martha Bernays in 1885

Freud was able to put the case of 'Anna O' out of his mind for only a short period, for, as his autobiography continued: 'when I was back in Vienna I turned once more to Breuer's observation and made him tell me more about it' (1925).[42] Actually, Freud's return to Vienna from Paris threw these two men together in many important ways. Breuer, the well-established, well-respected, general practitioner who had stumbled upon a novel means of relieving the symptoms of a distressed neurotic ('the talking cure' or 'chimney sweeping'), and Freud a young man, increasingly out of favour with the academic community, with a newly established practice, the success of which depended upon his acquiring the right kind of (paying) patients. Freud was later to recall of Breuer 'he was a man of striking intelligence and fourteen years older than myself. Our relations soon became more intimate and he became my friend and helper in my difficult circumstances. We grew accustomed to share all our scientific interests with each other. In this relationship the gain was naturally mine' (1925).[43] Breuer's help extended to providing Freud with regular monthly loans (throughout 1881) and, importantly for Freud, to his recommending patients to Freud. This was by no means a minor matter for Breuer counted among his patients many of the Viennese scientific community including the families of Brücke and Exner (successor to the professorship on Brücke's death in 1892). Indeed, so important was Breuer to Freud at the time that he named his first child, Mathilde, born in 1887, after Breuer's wife.

Josef Breuer was a Jew whose father had been a respected religious teacher within the Jewish community of Vienna. He studied under Brücke, becoming a doctor in 1867. He acquired an impressive reputation as a scientist for two pieces of original research he undertook in the late 1860s and the 1870s – he discovered the self-regulating mechanism of breathing (the Hering–Breuer reflex), and the function and purpose of the semicircular canals of the inner-ear in maintaining posture, and equilibrium. During the 1880s he and Freud developed a deep friendship and collaboration – in his letters to his fiancée Freud referred to Breuer as 'the ever-loyal Breuer' (1884).[44] Although Freud was subsequently to stress *his* gain from the relationship, Breuer himself gained two things: intellectual stimulation and a practical outlet for some of his more difficult (more time-consuming) patients. The case of 'Anna O' had been extremely demanding and exacting for Breuer, necessitating harrowing, exhausting, evening visits where Anna would recount her hallucinations (she recounted 303 separate causal scenes which were associated with her hysterical hearing loss alone!). To a busy general practitioner with a successful and lucrative private practice it would have been folly to devote so much time and effort to every patient even if he had come to the conclusion that they all needed that sort of intensity. This practical consideration may have been reinforced once it became clear that sexuality was involved in the affair – Breuer later confessed 'that plunging into sexuality in theory and practice is not to my taste'.[45] Some time later, in a letter written by Breuer in response to a request for clarification on their collaboration, Breuer wrote this about his work with Freud:

> At that time I learned a very great deal: much that was of scientific value, but something of practical importance as well – namely, that it was impossible for a 'general practitioner' to treat a case of that kind [Anna O] without bringing his activities and mode of life completely to an end. I vowed at that time that I would *not* go through such an ordeal again. When cases came to me, therefore, which I thought would benefit much from analytic treatment, but which I could not treat myself, I referred them to Dr. Freud, who had returned from Paris and the Salpêtrière and with whom I had the most intimate friendly and scientific relations. These cases, their course, their treatment, and whatever contributions to theory arose from them, were naturally constantly discussed between us. In this way our theoretical views grew up – not, of course, without divergencies, but nevertheless in work that was so much carried out in common that it is really hard to say, what came from one and what from the other.[46]

In one sense Breuer's new 'cathartic method' slipped into Freud's therapeutic armamentarium very easily as he found a patient, Frau Emmy von N who 'was a hysteric and could be put into a state of somnambulism with the greatest of ease' (1895).[47]

Frau Emmy von N, now known to have been one Fanny Moser, was aged 40 when Freud began treating her in May 1889. She was the thirteenth child of a family (including half-siblings) of fourteen whose mother had been institutionalized for being insane. At the age of 23 she married a Swiss widower, Heinrich Moser aged 65. Four years later he died leaving her reputedly the richest woman in Europe. The children of Heinrich Moser's first wife contested the inheritance alleging that she had poisoned their father. The body of her husband was exhumed and an autopsy performed. Fanny was cleared of any suspicion. Despite Freud's comment that 'we shall scarcely be able to dispute that the case of Frau Emmy von N was one of hysteria' (1895)[48] her clinical picture was extremely complicated. From the evidence available other diagnoses are possible although three other physicians of the period concurred with Freud's diagnosis. She had a tic of the face and neck (apparently since the age of 5), and, for the previous 5 years, had made a periodic 'clicking' noise in the midst of her speech. She had a stammer, and her hands kept writhing with athetoid movements. She was coherent in her speech, but every few minutes would stretch out her hand, her face contorted with horror and exclaim in a changed voice 'be quiet – don't talk – don't touch me'. She explained this by hallucinations of gruesome animals that attacked her if anyone moved or made a noise.

Frau Emmy von N was Freud's first real opportunity to explore the new 'cathartic method' that Breuer had used so 'successfully' with 'Anna O'. In combination with other therapies (e.g. twice-daily, whole-body massage) Freud was able to uncover the memories which he believed (following Breuer) were responsible for the symptoms. Each symptom seemed to be related to a specific ('forgotten' or 'hidden') memory – the fainting spells and spasms being related to incidents at the age of 5 when her brothers had thrown dead animals at her; her cry of 'don't touch me' was related to three separate incidents when sick relatives had grabbed her and almost choked her. It was Freud's belief, based upon the insight of Breuer, that 'hysterics suffer mainly from reminiscences'.[49] That is to say, frightening or traumatic events happen to a person at an early age, the memory of those events together with all the emotional energy that is associated with the event remains in the mind – it does not go away. The mind is a system which seeks to release nervous energy in order to maintain the energy of the psychical apparatus at its lowest possible level (this principle Freud had borrowed and applied from contemporary electrical theory). The process whereby the mind seeks to reduce nervous tension, or minimize unpleasure was called by Freud 'the pleasure principle' – it was the one cardinal principle of mental functioning (he later changed this to recognize a second governing principle – 'the reality principle' cf. chapter 4). Since these events were painful and traumatic, hysterics could not face the memory of them and so they constantly pushed down or *repressed* the memory. This Freud called a *defence* mechanism. Repression of 'incompatible' ideas is only a partial solution:

> That idea is not annihilated by a repudiation of this kind, but merely repressed into the unconscious . . . the actual outcome is something different from what the subject intended. What he wanted was to do away with an idea, as though it had never appeared, but all he succeeds in doing is to isolate it psychically.[50]

Those highly charged memories, repressed from the consciousness of the person must find expression somehow and thus they are 'converted' into less obvious ways of expressing themselves – paralyses, stammers, tics and the like. They become pathological because they 'have been deprived the normal-wearing away processes' (Breuer and Freud 1893).[51] The energy (or affect) is thus used to produce symptoms and thereby partially dissipated. What Breuer and Freud succeeded in doing with the 'cathartic method' was discover the primary cause of the symptom, the distressing idea or memory, and then let the patient 'talk out' the memory.

The memory with its associated energy (affect) having in this way been removed, the 'hysterical' symptoms had no source to maintain them. Breuer and Freud wrote:

> We found, to our great surprise at first, that each individual hysterical symptom immediately and permanently disappeared when we had succeeded in bringing clearly to light the memory of the event by which it was provoked and in arousing its accompanying affect, and when the patient had described that event in the greatest possible detail and had put that affect into words.[52]

Freud was later to explain that in his own mind he 'often compared cathartic psychotherapy with surgical intervention' describing his treatments as 'psychotherapeutic operations' equivalent to 'the opening up of a cavity filled with pus, the scraping out of a carious region'. The value of this analogy Freud asserted was 'not so much in the removal of what is pathological as in the establishment of conditions that are more likely to lead the course of the process in the direction of recovery'. Or, as he described it in a memorable phrase 'transforming . . . hysterical misery into common unhappiness' (1895).[53]

However, these are the *conclusions* that Freud and Breuer presented. In our story we have but two cases, 'Anna O' and 'Frau Emmy von N', the first treated by Breuer over the period from 1880 to 1882, the second by Freud, once for 8 weeks, in May 1889 and, once for the same period in June 1890. By the time that Freud and Breuer were to publish their conclusions (in 1893 they published a 'Preliminary Communication' and in 1895 their *Studies on Hysteria*) they were able to draw upon some other case material – all of which was supplied by Freud himself from his practice. Although they collaborated on the work, Breuer's interests were not the same as Freud's and tensions were developing in their relationship. By the time that they published their joint findings in 1893 it had only been after 'a long battle with my collaborator' (1893).[54] Similarly it was only after Freud had felt obliged to 'dissociate' himself from the theoretical chapter which Breuer had been assigned to write (1894).[55] Freud, in his autobiography recollects both the areas they had in common and those where they diverged:

> In 1895 there followed our book, *Studies on Hysteria* . . . As regards the *theory* put forward in the book, I was partly responsible, but to an extent which it is today no longer possible to determine. That theory was in any case unpretentious and hardly went beyond the direct description of the observations. It did not seek to establish the nature of hysteria but merely to throw light upon the origins of its symptoms. Thus it laid great stress upon the significance of the life of the emotions and upon the importance

of distinguishing between mental acts which are unconscious and those which are conscious (or rather capable of being conscious); it introduces a dynamic factor, by supposing that a symptom arises through the damming-up of an affect, and an economic factor, by regarding that same symptom as the product of the transformation of an amount of energy which would otherwise have been employed in some other way (this latter process was described as conversion.) Breuer spoke of our method as *cathartic*; its therapeutic aim was explained as being to provide that the quota of affect used for maintaining the symptom, which had got onto the wrong lines and had, as it were, become strangulated there, should be directed on to the normal path along which it could obtain discharge (or *abreaction*) . . . In answering the question of when it is that a mental process becomes pathogenic – that is, when it is that it becomes impossible for it to be dealt with normally – Breuer preferred what might be called a physiological theory . . . I, on the other hand was inclined to suspect the existence of an interplay of forces and the operation of intentions and purposes such as are to be observed in normal life. (1925)[56]

There was then, a theoretical division between the two men but a difference in theoretical emphasis is not enough to account for the *depth* of division which was manifestly developing. The depth of the breach between them is shown by the events surrounding the publication of Freud's great neurological monograph, *On Aphasia*, which was published in 1891. Aphasia is a complex neurological complaint in which the person suffering from the problem involuntarily garbles speech or cannot understand the speech of others – indeed, there are specific types of aphasia. The aphasias had been subjected to much study during the nineteenth century. They seemed to provide a clue to how the brain worked since if it were possible to correlate specific speech disorders with specific brain lesions this should provide the beginning of an account of the relationship of mind and brain. Many neurologists including Meynert had made significant discoveries using the aphasias to study the localization of cerebral functions. Freud subjected their work to critical scrutiny. To Fliess he wrote: 'I look forward to sending you a paper on Aphasia [*On Aphasia*] for which I have a good deal of feeling. I have been very cheeky in it, and have crossed swords with [the German neurologists] and have even scratched the high and mighty idol Meynert' (1891).[57] The book included the dedication 'to Dr. Josef Breuer in friendship and respect' (1891)[58] – an honour not lightly given by anyone. It would appear, however, that it was not well received by Breuer. To his sister-in-law, Minna Bernays, Freud revealed Breuer's reaction:

The 'Aphasia' . . . has already caused me deep disappointment. Breuer's reception of it was such a strange one; he hardly thanked me for it, was very embarrassed, made only derogatory comments on it, couldn't recollect any of its good points, and in the end tried to soften the blow by saying that it was well written. I believed his thoughts were miles away. The breach between us is widening all the time, and my efforts to patch things up with the dedication have probably had the opposite effect'. (1891)[59]

The book was not widely received (142 copies were sold in the first year and 115 in the following 9 years)[60] although among neurologists of the field, it has become something of a 'classic'.[61]

It was not just theoretical differences which were beginning to divide these two researchers, it was something deeper. In order to understand just what the key was to their estrangement it is necessary to backtrack slightly and uncover some more details of the additional material which Freud was to draw upon, prior to the publication of the *Studies*. In the *Studies* Breuer was to assert 'concerning "Anna O"' that 'the element of sexuality was astonishingly underdeveloped in her'.[62] Freud, on the other hand, in a paper published in 1894' wrote 'in all the cases I have analyzed it was the subject's *sexual life* that had given rise to the distressing affect . . . Moreover, it is easy to see that it is precisely sexual life which brings with it the most copious occasions for the emergence of incompatible ideas' (1894).[63] In other words Freud had discovered that those 'memories which . . . correspond to the precipitating causes [and are] at the root of *chronic* hysterical symptoms'[64] were specifically *sexual* memories. What had led to that discovery?

Whilst Freud was at Nancy with Bernheim he had been struck by one particular occasion when Bernheim demonstrated that 'despite a patient's profuse denials' she could be made to remember any supposedly forgotten event – Bernheim had put his hand on the patient's forehead and insisted she revealed some ostensibly forgotten situation. This demonstration had impressed Freud, and so when he began to find difficulty in eliciting patient's memories – so disturbing were they to the patient that they would not come out (even under hypnosis) – Freud decided to follow Bernheim and supplement hypnosis with 'the pressure technique' of therapy. Freud described this method thus:

I decided to start from the assumption that my patients knew everything that was of any pathogenic significance and that it was only a question of obliging them to communicate it. Thus when I reached a point at which after asking a patient some question such as: 'How long have you had this symptom?' or: 'What was its origin?' I was met with the answer: 'I really don't know.' I proceeded as follows. I placed my hand on the patients forehead or took her head between my hands and said: 'You will think of it under the pressure of my hand. At the moment at which I relax my pressure you will see something in front of you or something will come into your head. Catch hold of it. It will be what we are looking for. – Well, what have you seen or what has occurred to you?' (1895)[65]

Freud later explained that his task as a therapist was to overcome by his efforts the psychic resistance of his patients to the painful memories. In the very last chapter of the *Studies* – that devoted to the psychotherapy of hysteria and written by Freud alone – Freud elaborated on this theme. Therapeutic success with patients was most assured when their personal relationship with the physician was one of complete trust – those 'who have decided to put themselves into his hands and place their confidence in him' (1895).[66] When this is the case, explained Freud, 'it is almost inevitable that their personal relation to him will force itself, for the time at least, unduly into the foreground. It seems, indeed, as though an influence of this kind on the part of the doctor is a *sine qua non* to a solution of the problem' (ibid.). A little later in the same chapter Freud expounded this idea further and coined the technical term 'transference' to describe the phenomenon. During the course of analysis Freud discovered as 'a frequent, and indeed in some analyses a regular, occurrence' that a patient 'is transferring onto the figure of the physician the distressing ideas which arise from the content of the analysis' (1895).[67] This phenomenon Freud interpreted as the appearance of a 'new symptom' but significantly one 'that has been produced on the old model [and can] be treated in the same way as the old symptoms' (ibid.). At first Freud was annoyed at this phenomemon, regarding it as an obstacle to the real task of therapy, an increase in the work he had to do to clean out the system. Gradually, however, he began to realize that this very phenomenon provided both the physician and the patient with a means of insight into the condition (Freud was to develop his thoughts about 'transference' still further, see chapter 4).

The 'pressure technique' was one of the means whereby Freud sought to overcome his patient's resistance. He used the technique on two of the patients whose cases are reported in the *Studies on Hysteria*, Fraulein Elizabeth von R. and Miss Lucy R. He subsequently came to abandon this technique in favour of an alternative means of eliciting that hidden and repressed material – 'free association'. 'Free-association' is the name that is given to the technique which gradually replaced both hypnosis and the pressure technique. As a method of delving into the unconscious it was to prove more enduring for it relied less on the doctor and more on the patient to uncover the hidden problems. It was a very simple technique – for that reason often ridiculed and caricatured – it simply allowed a patient to carry on talking and divulging anything and everything that came into her head. Freud subsequently described his instructions to his patients in the following terms 'say whatever goes through your mind. Act as though, for instance, you were a traveller sitting next to the window of a railway train and describing to someone inside the carriage the changing views which you see outside . . . never forget that you have promised to be absolutely honest, and never leave anything out because, for some reason or other it is unpleasant to tell it' (1913).[68] The patient, as it were, gave the game away.

Freud chanced upon this technique when one day one of his patients reproved him for interrupting her train of thought with a question. Freud, acting on what he called an obscure intuition, allowed her to continue and 'free association' was born. There have been many accounts of the origins of this classic technique of psychoanalysis, some of them even hinted at by Freud himself – he speculated that his intuition may have been based upon his half-remembering a particular essay he had read at school. Others have pointed out the similarities between this technique, and the ideas of certain neurologists writing at the time, one of whom had recently produced a 'word association test'. Whatever the specific precursors of the technique, it was a powerful tool in the hands of a man committed to a view of psychic determinism – every association and idea was related to others in a causal way. Specifically neurotic symptoms could then be traced back to particular psychic causes. The term '*free* association' can, perhaps, conjure up a misleading image of the process for Freud readily admitted that time and time again he was forced into 'leading back the attention of patients . . . to the repressed sexual ideas *in spite of all their protestations*' (1894).[69] Likewise he spoke of rejecting patients' own accounts of things in favour of one 'which would harmonize better with my own views on the aetiology of the neuroses' (1895).[70]

Using hypnosis, the cathartic method, the pressure technique and 'free association' can, perhaps, conjure up a misleading image of the process for Freud readily admitted that time and time again he was forced into however, a picture profoundly coloured by his 'own ideas on aetiology'. These, he maintained, had their origins in three casual remarks made by physicians of Freud's acquaintance – Charcot, Breuer and Chrobak (this latter a Viennese gynaecologist whom Freud had consulted in 1886 concerning one of his patients). Freud suggested in his *On the History of the Psycho-Analytic Movement* that it was the chance remarks of these men who first put him on the track of sexuality as *the* cause of neurosis. He had once heard Charcot discussing a case with a colleague in which he had said 'je vous assure . . . dans des cas pareils c'est toujours la chose genitale, toujours-toujours-toujours'. Similarly Breuer had once remarked to Freud concerning a hysterical patient's problems: 'these things are always *secrets d'alcove!*' (secrets of the bedchamber). The third remark, made by Chrobak, concerning a patient was that the only hope for her was a regular dose of normal penis as a cure.[71] Armed with this hunch that it was the sexual secrets of his patients which he was to elicit Freud attempted to discover confirmation of his views from his patients apparently with their cooperation – to his friend Fliess he wrote 'the sexual business attracts people. They all go away impressed and convinced, after exclaiming: "No one had ever asked me that before!"' (1893).[72] Although Freud was subsequently to suggest that his identification of the link between hysteria and sexuality was *totally* revolutionary, there were many psychiatrists pursuing similar researches at the time, including Moritz Benedikt in Vienna, and Pierre Janet in France. Sexuality, both in its own right, and as a cause of other phenomena, was very much part of the currency of intellectual discourse.

Freud's case material though, was hardly lavish; he was still building a theory on a very small data base. To his friend Fliess he confided: 'the sexual business is becoming more and more firmly consolidated, and the contradictions are fading away, but new material is very meagre because of the unusual shortage of patients' (1893).[73] *Studies on Hysteria* itself was only to report 'in depth' five cases ('Anna O'; Frau Emmy von N; Miss Lucy R.; Katharina; and Fraulein Elizabeth von R.). Even one of those (Katharina) was an account of a single, chance meeting, in August 1893. Freud had met a girl who had served him a meal at a mountain refuge and had begun talking with her. Concerning Katharina's case Freud stated that 'if someone were to assert that the present case history is not so much an analysed case of hysteria as a case solved by guessing, I should have nothing to say against him' (1895).[74] In addition to the five case studies presented *Studies on Hysteria* made reference to three other named, and eleven unnamed, case histories. Of these, one case, the only one to be studied jointly with Breuer, Frau Cäcile M., deserves some mention here. Freud described the case 'as my most severe and instructive one' (1895).[75] Indeed, in a footnote to one of the published case studies he remarked:

> In the case of another patient, Frau Cäcile M., whom I got to know far more thoroughly than any of the other patients mentioned in these studies . . . I collected from her very numerous and convincing proofs of the existence of a physical mechanism of hysterical phenomena such as I have put forward above. Personal considerations unfortunately make it impossible for me to give a detailed case history of this patient, though I shall have occasion to refer to it from time to time. (1895)[76]

The case material presented by Freud, for all the wealth of detail he provides, actually remains thin. Freud was indefatigable in his search for the sexual basis of the hysterical symptoms and so as a persistent researcher he pressed his patients for confirmation of his theories. To his friend Fliess he confided, regarding one particular case 'you are right – the connection between [the] neurosis and sexuality does not always lie so near the surface. I can assure you that in my Case II [the case of a woman with problems breast feeding] it was not so easy to find. *If it had been sought by anyone less obstinately wedded to the idea, it would have been overlooked*' (1894).[77]

If enthusiasm to uncover the 'secrets of the bedchamber' was to mark his therapeutic approach to his patients in private, in the public sphere, enthusiasm for his theories was again to be a hallmark. To his friend in Berlin, Fliess, he wrote 'I am pretty well alone here in tackling the neuroses. They [meaning the public at large, but particularly the Viennese academic community] regard me rather as a monomaniac, while I have the distinct feeling that I have touched on one of the great secrets of nature' (1894).[78] Freud was at this time enjoying all the popularity of 'a freshly painted wall', as he once put it.[79] Freud was subsequently to interpret the reactions of those around him as indications of their hostility to his ideas on sexuality. In his *On the History of the Psychoanalytical Movement* for example, he wrote 'I unhesitatingly sacrificed my growing popularity as a doctor, and the increase in attendance during my consulting hours, by making a systematic enquiry into the sexual factors involved in the causation of my patients' neuroses' (1914).[80] But Freud's perception of hostility as being evoked principally by the content of his theories, does not tally with the fact that sexuality itself was becoming an important and fashionable field of study in its own right in Vienna of the *fin de siècle* under the tutelage of Meynert's successor as Professor of Psychiatry, Richard von Krafft-Ebing. He was the man recognized by his contemporaries as 'the true founder of modern sexual pathology'. Krafft-Ebing had created a considerable scientific interest in the field following the publication of his study of sexual perversion, *Psychopathia Sexualis* (in 1886). The book went through twelve editions and was translated into seven languages even within his own lifetime. Sexuality *per se* was not a taboo subject in Vienna, or in the rest of Europe.

Perhaps people's reactions to Freud were not so much reactions to the *content* of his ideas but to the *style* in which he delivered them – Breuer later wrote of Freud that 'Freud is a man given to absolute and exclusive formulations: this is a physical need which, in my opinion, leads to excessive generalization. There may in addition be a desire *d'épater le bourgeois* [to shock the old fogies]'.[81] Freud loved to be the 'bold oppositionist' but in doing so he frequently ignored the opinions of others and went beyond the limits of his evidence. It was to his friend Fliess that he confessed: 'we cannot do without men with the courage to think new things before they can prove them' (1895),[82] and, Freud might have added, men with the courage to *proclaim* new things. That said, Freud himself was the first to lament the number and type of case and the evidence he was to present in his *Studies:*

> We have [produced] a series of case histories, the selection of which could not unfortunately be determined on purely scientific grounds. Our experience is derived from private practice in an educated and literate social class, and the subject matter with which we deal often touches upon our patients' most intimate lives and histories. It would be a grave breach of confidence to publish material of this kind, with the risk of patients being recognized and their acquaintances becoming informed of facts which were confided only to the physician. It has therefore been impossible for us to make use of some of the most instructive and convincing of our observations. This of course applies especially to all those cases in which sexual and marital relations play an important aetiological part. Thus it comes about that we are only able to produce very incomplete evidence in favour of our view that sexuality seems to play a principal part in the pathogenesis of hysteria as a source of physical traumas and as a motive for 'defence' – that is, for repressing ideas from consciousness. It is precisely observations of a markedly sexual nature that we have been obliged to leave unpublished.[83]

The *Studies on Hysteria* was then an ambiguous book – advocating sexuality as the cause of hysteria but with only a few examples, and even those highly selected and, as Freud has just said, censored, to back up the claim – not surprisingly it had a muted reception. One neurologist who reviewed the book questioned the legitimacy of 'fathoming . . . the most intimate private affairs' of patients, whilst another reviewer said that it contained 'nothing but the kind of psychology used by poets', and yet another that Anna O's treatment had 'long been recognized in the Roman Church, by the institution of confession'.[84] Under 600 copies of the book were to be sold in the next decade, but for Freud it was the beginning of a new era for it marked a transition from his earlier neurological specialism to his new field of psychoanalysis – a term which, incidentally, Freud first used in 1896.

Publication of the book marked the formal end of his relationship to Breuer, who Freud admitted later was 'hurt and discouraged'[85] by its reception, although Breuer publicly defended Freud and the *Studies* on a number of occasions. Concerning this break with Breuer, Freud was to write to Fliess:

> Our personal relations, externally restored, throw a deep shadow on my existence here. I can't do anything right for him, and have given up trying. According to him I should ask myself everyday whether I am suffering from moral insanity or scientific paranoia. Yet I think of myself as the psychically more normal of the two of us. I believe he cannot forgive me

for having dragged him along and involved him in the *Studies on Hysteria*, since he invariably knows three candidates for the position of the one truth, and abhors all generalizations, regarding them as presumptions. It is decidedly sad that one must pay so dearly for all that one has enjoyed in life. Will the same thing also happen to the two of us one day? (1896)[86]

In fact Freud's rhetorical question was to be answered in the affirmative within 5 years. The break with Breuer was not just over style, in many respects it was a matter of mutual personal antagonism arguably not over sexuality in theory, but over it in practice. Before we can understand this fully we need to explore a little more fully Freud's own sexuality.

SEXUALITY: IN PRACTICE AND IN THEORY

The more I set about looking for such disturbances – bearing in mind the fact that everyone hides the truth in matters of sex – and the more skilful I became at pursuing my enquiries in the face of a preliminary denial, the more regularly was I able to discover pathogenic factors in sexual life. (1906)[87]

Given all that we have seen about the circumstances of Freud's work at the time, and given the problems Freud was having with his collaborator, Josef Breuer and his former colleagues, we are faced with the question of why Freud persisted in searching for sexual clues in the neuroses of his patients. Why did Freud pursue so wholeheartedly the sexual origins of the neuroses? Particularly as he suggested in the *Studies* that in the first instance he 'regarded the linking of hysteria with the topic of sexuality as a sort of insult – just as the women patients themselves do' (1895).[88] Of course, it may have been true that in Vienna there was a high proportion of women with sexual problems, and that these invariably became revealed by Freud's perceptive probings. It was, however, in the *linkage* between sexuality and contemporary problems which Freud saw his most significant contribution at this time. Indeed, he regarded his uncovery of the sexual roots of the neuroses as restoring a whole new dimension to the understanding of human behaviour. One of his favourite pictures of his task in uncovering these vestiges of the past was of his task being like that of the archaeologist – digging to reveal the traces of past peoples. This was a powerful metaphor to his contemporaries whose imaginations had so recently been captured by the discovery of Troy by Heinrich Schliemann. Just as for Schliemann traces and fragments pointed to hitherto undiscovered glories so for Freud the symptoms and pathology of the neuroses pointed to hitherto undiscovered patterns: in particular to the sexual side of life. In sexuality Freud believed that he had discovered

Plate 5. Freud c.1898 with, reading from left to right and front to back: Sophie, Anna and Ernst Freud; Oliver and Martha Freud and Minna Bernays; Martin and Sigmund Freud

the key to the neuroses: '[I have] demonstrated to them the solution to a more than thousand-year-old problem – a "source of the Nile"!' he wrote to his friend Fliess.[89]

But his theories received 'an icy reception from the asses', to use his own phrase to describe the reception of his views by the Viennese academic establishment, and were described by Professor Krafft-Ebing as sounding 'like a scientific fairy tale'. Despite this Freud continued to advance his theories about the sexual origins of the neuroses ('they can all go to hell' was his private and previously unpublished reaction to the asses),[90] and thus we must pose the question: why did he remain uncompromising? Clearly one significant factor in his espousal of sexuality was his belief in the 'organic foundation' that it provided for his psychological theories – and yet the investigation of those foundations he did not pursue: he was far more interested in the superstructure. Were there other factors in his interest? Was there perhaps some personal element in his views which meant that he could not give them up? This is certainly the conclusion of one of his former pupils, Carl Jung, who believed that Freud was gripped with an obsession over the question of sex. Many years later Jung, having long since broken with Freud over this very issue, recollected his first encounters with Freud. He wrote:

> Freud was the first man of real importance I had encountered: in my experience up to that time [1907], no one else could compare with him. There was nothing the least trivial in his attitude. I found him extremely intelligent, shrewd, and altogether remarkable. And yet my first impressions of him remained tangled: I could not make him out . . . I could not decide to what extent [his] strong emphasis upon sexuality was connected with subjective prejudices of his, and to what extent it rested upon verifiable experiences.[91]

As time went on Jung was able to resolve his confusion to his own satisfaction and concluded that:

> There was no mistaking the fact that Freud was emotionally involved in his sexual theory to an extraordinary degree. When he spoke of it, his tone became urgent, almost anxious, and all signs of his normally critical and sceptical manner vanished. A strange, deeply moved expression came over his face, and the cause of which I was at a loss to understand. I had a strong intuition that for him sexuality was a sort of *numinosum* . . . it was something to be religiously observed . . . One thing was clear: Freud, who had always made much of his irreligiosity, had now constructed a dogma; or rather, in the place of a jealous God whom he had lost, he had substituted another compelling image, that of sexuality . . . He remained the victim of the one aspect he could recognise, and for that reason I see him as a tragic figure; for he was a great man, and what is more, a man in the grip of his daimon. (ibid.)[92]

Jung also observed of Freud's substitution that it had the advantage for Freud that 'he was able to regard the new numinosity as scientifically irreproachable and free from all religious taint' (ibid.).[93] For all that he longed to be 'scientific' and 'rational' in his emphasis on the sexual roots of all behaviour Freud may be said to have created and served an idol. The sociologist Jacques Ellul has observed, with some percipience, that modern man is no less religious than his medieval counterpart; but whereas medieval man's demons were defined by the Church our contemporary demons are science, or the state, or, as with Freud, sexuality.[94]

Before going on to talk about some of the personal elements which might have been involved in Freud's idolization of sex I want, briefly, to outline the specific theory which Freud was propounding at this time. *Studies on Hysteria* which was published in 1895 is in many ways a cautious and ambiguous book. Nowhere does the book explicitly state a coherent theory relating sex to the neurosis – there are hints, but those hints are self-contradictory. Following the publication of the book Freud began to develop his theories further, at first only privately, but later, in 1896, publicly. In October 1895 he wrote to Fliess, 'note that among other things I suspect the following: that hysteria is conditioned by a primary sexual experience (before puberty) accompanied by revulsion and fright; and that obsessional neurosis is conditioned by the same accompanied by pleasure' (1895).[95] Never one to prevaricate for long, his next letter to Fliess showed that his suspicions had become more concrete; 'have I revealed the great clinical secret to you, either by writing or by word of mouth?' he asked Fliess. 'Hysteria is the consequence of a presexual *sexual shock*. Obsessional neurosis is the consequence of presexual *sexual pleasure* later transformed into guilt' (1895).[96] By 'presexual' Freud explained that he meant before puberty – in other words in childhood. Children, Freud maintained, had been subjected to sexual advances by adults, the effects of which were so traumatic as to generate neurotic illnesses in them once they had grown up – 'infantile seduction' were the source of the neuroses.

This is the so-called 'seduction-theory of the neuroses' which in 1896 Freud began to publicly propound. Freud was well aware of its provocative overtones and noted 'I am quite sure that this theory will call up a storm of contradictions from contemporary physicians' (1896).[97] The details of the theory were quite specific: 'the subject's sexual life, whether they lie in a disorder of his contemporary sexual life or in important events in his past life' is the aetiological cause of the disorder. This idea, Freud admitted was not new but, he insisted:

What gives its distinctive character to my line of approach is that I elevate these sexual influences to the rank of specific causes, that I recognize their action in every case of neurosis, and finally that I trace a regular parallelism, a proof of a specific aetiological relation between the nature of the sexual influence and the pathological species of the neurosis. (1896)[98]

In particular, Freud distinguished between the *actual neuroses* which were caused by a current sexual problem (excessive masturbation or frustrated sexual stimulation), and the *psychoneuroses* which were caused by sexual events in the past (sexual abuses and seductions of children by adults). The problems of hysterics and obsessional patients were then the direct result of other people: 'foremost among those guilty of abuses like these, with their momentous consequences, are nursemaids, governesses and domestic servants' (1896).[99] It was this theory which Krafft-Ebing called a 'scientific fairy tale'.

At first sight it might be easy for us to concur with Krafft-Ebing's derisory description for this theory seems so simple and straightforward that it almost defies credibility. However, Freud's position was more complex than it might seem. He was, simultaneously, working on a 'theoretical' model of the mind which would provide the necessary 'psychic' apparatus to support his theory. In April 1895 he announced to Fliess that he was writing a 'Psychology for Neurologists.' This 'Psychology' was begun at about the time when he was finishing his final contribution to the *Studies* and can be seen in some senses as Freud's alternative rendering of the theoretical part of that book (the theoretical part proper having been written by Breuer). To Fliess he confessed 'on the scientific side I am in a bad way; I am so deep in the "Psychology for Neurologists" that it quite consumes me, until I have to break off out of sheer exhaustion. I have never been so intensely preoccupied by anything. And will anything come of it? I hope so, but the going is hard and slow' (1895).[100] Freud continued to work in spurts upon the text throughout the summer. Breuer observed to Fliess that 'Freud's intellect is soaring at its highest. I gaze after him as a hen at a hawk'.[101] In September 1895 Freud visited Fliess in Berlin. As a result of his conversations there he immediately started rewriting the whole 'psychology' (he began this revision on the train back to Vienna). By October 1895 two notebooks were duly sent to Fliess for his comments, with the promise of a third to follow.

These manuscripts have become known as the *Project for a Scientific Psychology*. They represent Freud's most systematic attempt to integrate his earlier neurological understanding of the mind with his more recent psychological investigations. Freud's English translator has described the work as an 'extraordinarily ingenious working model of the mind as a piece of neurological machinery.[102] It is a complex and enigmatic work for Freud later abandoned it unfinished, and never referred to it in his subsequent writings; it is, as that same translator wrote, 'a torso disavowed by its creator'.[103] We only know of its existence because of the discovery of the two notebooks among the letters to Fliess. First published (in German) in 1950, it has become a subject of much controversy: many argue for its irrelevance to psychoanalysis given that Freud himself abandoned it, while others stress the significance of its strategic timing and themes. Despite the varied interpretations of its importance most would acknowledge its similarities with his earlier work *and* with his latter work. In the words of his translator again 'the *Project*, or rather its invisible ghost, haunts the whole series of Freud's theoretical writings to the very end'.[104] More recently the work has been described as

> . . . neither a purely neurological document nor a projection of wholly psychological insights into imagined neuroanatomical structures; rather it combines clinical insight and data. Freud's most fundamental psychophysicalist assumptions, certain undeniably mechanical and neuroanatomical constructs, and a number of organismic, evolutionary, and biological ideas – all into one remarkably well-integrated psychobiological system.[105]

Freud himself saw the *Project* at the time as the theoretical grounding for his sexual theories on the neuroses: in short he saw his task as providing a *neurophysiological* account of his clinical data and of how that clinical data related to normal psychology. He described his interests to Fliess in May 1895:

> A man like me cannot live without a hobby-horse, a consuming passion – in Schiller's words a tyrant. I have found my tyrant, and in his service I know no limits. My tyrant is psychology; it has always been my distant, beckoning goal and now, since I have hit on the neuroses, it has come so much the nearer. I am plagued with two ambitions: to see how the theory of mental functioning takes shape if quantitative considerations, a sort of economics of nerve-force, are introduced into it; and secondly, to extract from psychopathology what may be of benefit to normal psychology. Actually a satisfactory general theory of neuropsychotic disturbances is impossible if it cannot be brought into association with clear assumptions about normal mental processes. (1895)[106]

Specifically the *Project* was written with 'the intention . . . to furnish a psychology that shall be a natural science: that is, to represent psychical processes as quantitatively determinate states of specifiable material particles, thus making those processes perspicuous and free from contradiction' (1895).[107] Freud may well have been inspired in this goal by one of his former teachers, Sigmund Exner, who in 1894 had published a work entitled *Sketch of a Physiological Explanation of Psychical Phenomena* which dealt with the same subjects as Freud's *Project*.

To facilitate his aims Freud postulated that the mind was an energy system within which psychic energy or quantity (which he labelled Q) was processed in ways very similar to the ways in which ordinary energy behaves. This energy flows along specific pathways provided by the nerve cells of the brain, the neurones. In order to account for the three primary processes of perception, memory, and consciousness Freud found it was necessary to introduce a three-fold distinction into his neuronal system: there were the (phi), the (psi) and the (omega) systems. These systems behaved in different ways: being permeable or impermeable to the flow of psychic energy as Freud thought fit to explain the various psychological properties of the mind. In fact, Freud found himself having to explain more than he wished, in order to explain the little that he had set out to explain: to Fliess he confided 'this psychology is really an incubus . . . all I was trying to do was to explain defence, but I found myself explaining something from the very heart of nature. I found myself wrestling with the problems of quality, sleep, memory – in short, the whole of psychology' (1895).[108] The repression of the painful memories of sexual abuse, defence – a crucial part of Freud's sexual theory – was the 'core of the riddle'[109] which Freud was attempting to solve at this time.

In October 1895 shortly after announcing to Fliess that he had solved 'the great clinical secret' of the causes of the neuroses, Freud wrote to Fliess about the *Project*:

> Now listen to this. One strenuous night last week, when I was in the stage of painful discomfort in which my brain works best, the barriers suddenly lifted, the veils dropped, and it was possible to see from the details of neurosis all the way to the very conditioning of consciousness. Everything fell into place, the cogs meshed, the thing really seemed to be a machine which in a moment would run of itself. The three systems of neurones, the 'free' and 'bound' states of quantity, the primary and secondary processes, the main trend and the compromise trend of the nervous system, the two biological rules of attention and defence, the indications of quality, reality, and thought, the state of the psycho-sexual group, the sexual determination of repression, and finally the factors determining consciousness as a perceptual function – the whole thing held together, and still does. I can naturally hardly contain myself with delight. (1895)[110]

Despite that, perhaps in response to the fatigue such intense work created, or perhaps in response to the failure of his patients to confirm the newly 'held-together' theory, Freud was soon, once again doubting his own theory – a month later he wrote to Fliess:

I no longer understand the state of mind in which I concocted the psychology; I cannot conceive how I came to inflict it on you . . . it seems to me to have been a kind of aberration. The clinical explanation of the two neuroses will probably stand after some modifications. (1895)[111]

Once again it was the theory of repression which proved to be a problem: Freud did not seem able to provide an adequate account of this phenomenon. The theory seemed to be too weak to account for the clinical data so that Freud suggested that 'in the end I may have to learn to content myself with the clinical explanation of the neuroses'[112] and not with the more fundamental, neurophysiological account he had so desired. Nine months after having completed the *Project* he despaired still further of achieving his declared aim of theoretically grounding his clinical work; to Fliess he wrote:

I am in a rather gloomy state, and all I can say is that I am looking forward to our congress as to a slaking of hunger and thirst. I shall bring with me nothing but a pair of open ears, and shall be agape. Also I expect great things – so self-centred am I – for my own purposes. I have run into some doubts about my repression theory which a suggestion from you . . . may resolve. Anxiety, clinical factors, etc. – perhaps you may supply me with solid ground on which I shall be able to give up explaining things psychologically and start finding a firm basis in physiology! (1896)[113]

Perhaps, Freud would have continued to run round in circles over this vexed problem had it not been for the fact that at this very crucial time in his work he was thrown into a personal turmoil over the death of his father. On 23 October 1896 Jacob Freud died. His death plunged Freud into a period of depression and intense introspection – writing to Fliess he wrote 'it all happened in my critical period, and I am really down over it' (1896).[114] Personal tragedy intervened to throw the theoretical question into sharper focus: Freud began to examine his own feelings, memories and responses:

By one of the obscure routes behind the official consciousness the old man's death affected me deeply. I valued him highly and understood him very well indeed, and with this peculiar mixture of deep wisdom and imaginative light-heartedness he meant a great deal to my life. By the time he died his life had been long over, but at a death the whole past stirs within one. I feel now as if I had been torn up by the roots. (1896)[115]

In the very same letter where he describes that stirring Freud reports to Fliess an account of one of his dreams with the theme of duty to the dead.

He concludes by suggesting to Fliess that: 'the dream was thus an outlet for the feeling of self-reproach which a death generally leaves among the survivors' (1896).[116] He continued to work on his ideas on the connection between sexuality and the neuroses still hoping to ground his 'psychology' in biology. To Fliess, who was developing his own biology of sexuality based on periodicity, Freud wrote towards the end of the year: 'I am busy thinking out something which would cement our work together and put my column on your base, but I have a feeling that I ought not to write about it' (1896).[117] The theoretical work Freud was doing was, however, complicated by the personal effects of Jacob's death.

Jacob's death provoked such feeling within Freud that his inner life, and his most significant personal relationships were thrown into turmoil. In June 1897 the effects of this were so great as to prompt him to reveal to Fliess: 'I have been through some kind of neurotic experience, with odd states of mind not intelligible to consciousness – cloudy thoughts and veiled doubts, with barely here and there a ray of light . . . I believe I am in a cocoon, and heaven knows what sort of creature will emerge from it' (1897).[118] In July, Freud was still confused about what was occurring within him, to Fliess he wrote:

> I still do not know what has been happening to me. Something from the deepest depths of my own neurosis has ranged itself against my taking a further step in understanding of the neuroses, and you have somehow been involved. My inability to write seems to be aimed at hindering our intercourse. I have no proofs of this, but merely feeling of a very obscure nature. (1897)[119]

By August, Freud was able to write to Fliess with the news that 'things are fermenting inside me, but I have nothing ready . . . and have done nothing here to get the better of the turbulence of my thoughts and feelings' (1897).[120] Indeed, this letter contains the admission that 'the chief patient I am busy with is myself. My little hysteria . . . has yielded one stage further . . . This analysis is harder than any other . . . But I believe it has got to be done and is a necessary stage in my work' (ibid.). Freud was embarking on his famous 'self-analysis' – which Jones called his 'unique instrument' for 'the achievement of self-mastery'.[121] His 'self-analysis' is intimately connected to the development of his theories on sexuality.

The beginnings of this self-analysis coincided with another significant development in his thoughts, possibly a crucial one in the evolution of his ideas.[112] He began to study the prehistory of psychiatry. Specifically he started to study the work of the influential sixteenth-century physician,

Johann Weier. Johann Weier was the first person to suggest (in a treatise published in 1563) that the confessions of women charged with being witches and being in league with the devil were in reality not true descriptions of their state but rather fantasies and delusions. In doing so he suggested that such poor women should be treated with compassion rather than persecuted. Freud began reading about Weier's ideas, probably as a result of the suggestions contained in Krafft-Ebing's *Psychopathia Sexualis* which he was also reading at the time. He was also treating a patient, Emma Eckstein, whose symptoms and lurid descriptions of sexual abuse taxed even Freud's imagination. In January 1897 he announced to Fliess:

> What have you got to say, by the way, to the remark that my brand-new primal history of hysteria is already well known and published a hundred times over, albeit a few centuries ago? Do you remember my always saying that the theory of possession of the Middle Ages and the ecclesiastical courts is identical with our theory . . .? But why did the Devil who possessed the poor creatures invariably commit acts of indecency with them, and in a disgusting manner? Why do the confessions under torture so resemble the reports of my patients in psychical treatment? I shall soon absorb myself in the relevant literature. (1897)[123]

Indeed, within a week having received yet more lurid tales from Emma, and from another patient (Herr E) Freud was even more convinced of the power of the parallelism; to Fliess he wrote: 'the parallel with witchcraft is taking shape, and I believe it is conclusive' (1897).[124] Exploring the theme further Freud considered that all perverse sexual actions – whether the confession of witches or those of his patients – 'are always alike, always have a meaning, and are based on a pattern which can be understood'(ibid.). He then indicated to Fliess the dominance this idea was gaining in his mind: 'I am beginning to dream of an extremely primitive devil religion the rites of which continue to be performed secretly, and now I understand the stern therapy of the witches' judges. The links are abundant' (ibid.).[125] Freud's mind was thus engrossed in the whole phenomenon of how to understand witchcraft, so much so that he arranged for his next meeting with Fliess, in April, to be at Nuremberg, a city replete with museums containing various torture implements and relics of the witch persecutions. At first Freud believed that, like his patients, these 'witches' were the victims of sexual molestation in infancy, which under the pressure of the torturers insistence they transfer onto the Devil. However, despite receiving patients who 'brought confirmation of my theory of paternal aetiology' (1897),[126] it slowly began to dawn upon him that many of these reports were actually fictions or inventions of the witches' minds. In Freud's mind now his patients and the witches of old were reporting not memories of actual seductions – as his old 'seduction theory' suggested – but fantasies of seductions shaped unconsciously by the memories of earlier seductions.

It was with these stories in mind, and with his own thoughts and feelings in 'turbulence' that Freud set out in September to tour Tuscany and Umbria in Central Italy with his brother Alexander and a young physician, Felix Gattl, whom Freud had earlier reported to Fliess was 'becoming much attached to me and my theories'.[127] It was a trip on which Freud had specifically promised Fliess that he would reconsider his earlier antagonism to the Christian aspects of Italian art, and attempt to reassess their value. The trip was a most significant one – indeed Freud even suggested to Fliess that it was only *after* his holiday that his self-analysis began: 'before the holidays I mentioned that my most important patient was myself, and after my holiday trip my self-analysis, of which there had previously been no trace, began' (1897).[128] Certainly, it is only after his trip to Italy that Freud was able to report to Fliess the childhood material that he deemed so crucial in understanding his feelings. Certainly too, the trip was influential in that on his return to Vienna he immediately wrote to Fliess with an important repudiation. On 21 September 1897 he announced to Fliess: 'let me tell you straight away the great secret which has been slowly dawning on me in recent months. I no longer believe in my *neurotica*' (1897).[129] Freud had abandoned his 'seduction theory'.

The seduction theory which he had previously considered to be the 'source of the Nile' had turned out to be none other than an obscure tributary. His hopes of achieving lasting fame through his discovery vanished: 'the hope of eternal fame was so beautiful', he confessed to Fliess 'and so was that of certain wealth, complete independence, travel, and removing the children from the sphere of the worries which spoiled my own youth' (ibid.). Again to Fliess he confessed his reasons for abandoning his *neurotica* as first being his lack of success with patients – he never seemed able to achieve therapeutic success even though he had discovered the cause of their disease. Secondly, he found it astonishing that in every case – even his own – 'blame was laid on perverse acts by the father' but he conceded 'it was hardly credible that perverted acts against children were so general' (ibid.).[130] In other words as he later explained the 'aetiology broke down under the weight of its own improbability and contradiction' (1914).[131] For the unconscious mind Freud admitted there is no distinction between 'truth and emotionally-charged fiction', these seduction stories were the product of the patient and not (except in some circumstances) of a perverse adult. In the words of his autobiography: 'I was at last obliged to recognize that these scenes of seduction had never taken place, and that they were only fantasies which my patients had made up or which I myself had perhaps forced on them . . .' (1925).[132] Even then though he continued to flirt with the 'seduction theory' announcing to Fliess in December 'my confidence in the father-aetiology has risen greatly', and of another case it 'speaks for the intrinsic authenticity of infantile trauma' (1897).[133]

In the light of the fact that it was immediately after his tour of Italy that he repudiated his original *neurotica*, and in the light of the fact that it was only after the same trip that he considered his self-analysis to have begun in earnest, we are prompted to ask questions about what happened to Freud during this holiday. Clearly, prior to the trip much had been brewing within him – the turbulence of his thoughts and feelings following his father's death; the reference to his 'little hysteria'; his inability to effect cures in his patients; his immersion into the interpretation of witchcraft all attest to this – but we may legitimately ask whether there was something specific on that trip which really was a key to understanding Freud more fully at this period. Ernest Jones, intriguingly, in the second volume of his biography (presumably on the basis of some unpublished material) has hinted that there was one very significant encounter on the trip – however, he only hinted and indicated that he would include an account of it in the revision of his first volume (one which he never, in fact, managed to make). Jones stated that on this particular trip Freud went to Orvieto 'where he especially enjoyed the Signorelli pictures', and that they were 'connected with a significant episode that must have played an important part in the inception of [his] self-analysis'.[134] It was these very same pictures, and the name of the artist who painted them, which were later to become the focus of one of his famous Freudian slips (see chapter 3).

At Orvieto, in the chapel of San Brizio in the cathedral there are a set of frescos depicting 'the last things', the final *eschaton* of creation. The designs for this were originally conceived in 1447 by Fra Angelico, and partially fulfilled by him, but left incomplete. In 1499 Luca Signorelli, an Umbrian painter was invited to complete the designs – in part on the basis of the preliminary work done by Fra Angelico, but largely under his own inspiration. Signorelli produced a depiction of the four last things – the preaching and fall of the Anti-Christ; the Fall of the Damned; the Resurrection and the Crowning of the Elect – with tremendous visual and emotional impact. One art historian has said of the frescos: 'few figure compositions of the fifteenth century have the same awesome psychic impact'.[135] To Sigmund Freud, arriving at the chapel half-way through his tour of Central Italy, we can only speculate on their impact, but in the light of all that had been on his mind prior to the trip we may suggest that he was immediately drawn to their themes. We can imagine his studying intensely the scenes of the damnation filled as they are with nude figures tortured by demons, these would surely resonate with the themes of his own recent reading on demonology and witchcraft. We can also note the resonance that may well have been struck on discovery of the self-portrait of Signorelli in the preaching of the Anti-Christ fresco – after all Freud was at that time conceiving of a book of dreams in which he would be depicted within the work itself. Not only that but Signorelli painted himself with Fra Angelico just behind him, representing the biblical figures of 'the two witnesses' of the end times, Freud may well have thought of himself and Fliess as being analogous to those two witnesses – indeed he saw himself and Fliess as lonely prophets proclaiming a new gospel of sexuality. The fresco of the Preaching of the Anti-Christ is also infused with a sense of the *fin de siècle* (the period in which Signorelli was working was a time of turbulence and trouble) that would probably have evoked a similar awareness in Freud. The Austro-Hungarian Empire had, within the last few months, been thrown into turmoil by the granting of linguistic autonomy to the Czechs. In Vienna Karl Lueger had made anti-Semitism the focus of his political platform. The Empire was so ripe for change – cataclysmic change – that within a few years Karl Kraus could pen his mammoth epic *Last Days of Mankind* as the scenario of the period. Above all, however, we may reflect upon the effect of these 'Christian' images upon Freud, a Jew of humble origins whose career was hampered by anti-Semitism and who had only very recently indicated to his friend Fliess that he would try to appreciate the art of Italy despite its manifest Christian content. By medieval tradition the Anti-Christ was to have been a Jewish avenger – a last desperate attempt by Satan to win the souls of the elect and overthrow the Christian Church. How did he react to this image? How did he respond to the idea of the last days and the coming of the Anti-Christ?

Some glimmering of the emotions Freud encountered when gazing at the frescos may be gleaned from reflecting upon the reactions of a friend and former mentor of Freud's, Professor Theodor Gomperz, who visited Orvieto in 1889. Gomperz described his reactions in a series of letters to his wife. Gomperz, who, unlike Freud, was one of the rich Austrian aristocracy and of high social standing with the coveted professorship already, reflected thus:

> The Cathedral . . . [in Orvieto] is stupendous; the [frescoes] . . . of Fra Angelico and Signorelli really interesting beyond words.
> There is so much to see here it makes one quite dizzy. With the [Roman] Catholic Middle Ages, it is a strange thing; there is more behind it than we, the Enlightened, like to admit. Fra Angelico and Signorelli . . . really get to me. What bowls me right over is the imposing realism . . . the simple but at the same time magnificent rendering of reality . . . I begin to understand the inquisitors and religious wars. If one possesses so glorious

and harmonious a civilization, then one can be forgiven if one defends its
central standpoint, the foundation and cornerstone, the mental and spiritual
status quo – in a word, the religion – with [hell] fire and flames . . . Anyone
who today defends the social structure against the socialist acts no
differently [than did the defenders of the Christian faith]. Only that the
world which he [today] believes he must defend is a much less beautiful
and euphonious one than the heyday of the so-called dark ages. 'Dark
Ages' – what an epithet for an epoch that produced Dante and Fra Angelico,
an epoch so infused with jubilation and so saturated with beauty that it
gushed out of all its pores and transfigured everything down to the [very]
floor on which it stood.[136]

If Gomperz, a man who had to a certain extent not been hampered by
his Jewish background, could feel these emotions in the face of such an
overtly 'Christian' set of images, we may imagine what the disadvantaged,
discriminated-against Freud must have felt. He probably would have noted
the beauty, yes, but also experienced profound repugnance. Christian
civilization was an otiose creation, profoundly in need of the emergence
of a Semitic avenger.

We do not have any direct evidence to suggest that he even took much
notice of these aspects of the frescos at all. It may be that he simply
took in the whole scene and carried on oblivious of any particular personal
elements in his encounter. I suggest that such a possibility was unlikely
for one of the dominant themes in his psychology was his willingness
to identify with heroes – within a few days he was to follow in Hannibal's
footsteps and recover his own sense of identification with Hannibal
principally in Hannibal the 'Semitic avenger'. Within a few months his
'Rome neurosis' was to develop – a neurosis intimately connected with
his feeling on religion and on Christianity in particular. Indeed, soon after
his return to Vienna, in the throws of his 'self-analysis', he was to speak
of his own pilgrimage, his own 'via dolorosa' on his route to Rome.
Similarly in October, just after his return from Italy, Freud was to write
to Fliess of his interest in the theme of the 'founders of religion'.[137] In
December he was writing to Fliess of his own ability to construct religious
illusions.[138] Given this plethora of themes which emerge immediately
after his Italian trip, and given Jones' hint that the Signorelli pictures
were 'connected with a significant episode' we are led to conclude that
the central motif of the frescos – the coming of the Anti-Christ – may
well have had an important influence upon Freud. Indeed we may even
speculate on whether Freud did not see himself in this role – as Christ had
been the founder of a new religion he too could, through his 'self-analysis',
be the founder of a new secular alternative world view. Freud's 'self-
analysis' far from being the forging of a new scientific technique for the
founding of a new science, may in its inception have been Freud's response

to a religious crisis and his attempt to construct a secular solution to his own problems.[139]

Having returned from Italy and having renounced his *neurotica* the coming months of his life were to become dominated by his 'self-analysis' – early in October he wrote to Fliess with the news that 'outwardly very little is happening to me, but inside me something very interesting is happening . . . my self-analysis, which I regard as indispensable for clearing up the whole problem, has been making progress in dreams and yielding the most valuable conclusions and evidence. At certain points I have the impression of having come to the end, and so far I have always known where the next night of dreams would continue' (1897).[140] In his dreams Freud unearthed memories of his feelings for his mother and father and nurse – all of which he took to be determinants of his 'hysteria'. Less than 2 weeks later he wrote again to Fliess describing his 'self-analysis' [as] the most important thing . . . in hand and [as promising] to be of the greatest value to me when it is finished' (1897).[141] Progress with it was not inexorable though, for in the same letter he described how 'in the very midst of it it suddenly broke down for three days, and I had the feeling of inner binding about which my patients complain so much . . . I was inconsolable' (ibid.). He was also able to report the discovery of ' a number of real points of reference' by asking his mother about persons and events in his childhood.[142] By the end of the month Freud had seized upon a metaphor to describe his impressions in his analysis, and had begun to talk of a resolution to all the disparate strands of his recent experiences:

I am living only for 'inner work'. It gets hold of me and hauls me through the past in a rapid association of ideas; and my mood changes like the landscape seen by a traveller from a train . . . Some sad secrets of life are being traced back to their first roots, the humble origins of much pride and precedence are being laid bare. I am now experiencing myself all the things that as a third party I have witnessed going on in my patients – days when I slink about depressed because I have understood nothing of the day's dreams, phantasies or mood, and other days when a flash of lightning brings coherence into the picture, and what has gone before is revealed as preparation for the present. I am beginning to perceive big general framework factors (I should like to call them) which determine development, and other minor factors which fill in the picture and vary according to individual experiences. Simultaneously a number of my doubts about the interpretation of the neuroses, if not all of them, are being resolved. (1897)[143]

Despite that sense of resolution within a few days he was to report to Fliess: 'everything is still dark, including even the nature of the problems, but at the same time I have a reassuring feeling that one only has to put one's hand in one's store-cupboard to be able to extract – in its own good time – what one needs' (1897).[144] This sense of licence which the richness of the psychic produced even prompted Freud to question the value of the whole enterprise: 'I can only analyse myself with objectively acquired knowledge (as if I were a stranger); self-analysis is really impossible' (1897).[145] Freud pressed on though, at times having 'to wait until things move inside me and I experience them', at times dreaming 'whole days away' (1897).[146] Freud had become fascinated by his inner world of phantasies and dreams – to Fliess he confessed 'since I have started studying the unconscious I have become so interesting to myself' (1897).[147] With the wealth of dream material emerging his self-analysis slowly became transformed into the ground work for his dream book – dreams and their interpretation were to dominate the next 2 years of his life (see chapter 3).

Whatever the validity of speculations into the Italian origins of Freud's 'self-analysis' (the 'Orvieto encounter'), and whatever the strengths of particular predisposing factors in the repudiation of the seduction aetiology the fact remains that he did change his views significantly at this time. The abandonment of this theory of traumatic seduction and his 'self-analysis' created the possibility of an alternative understanding of sexuality in the neuroses. In particular it pointed towards the possibility that 'from behind the fantasies, the whole range of a child's sexual life came to life' (1914).[148] Freud had stumbled upon infantile sexuality – infants and children experience sexual feelings towards their parents. The arrest of the normal development of these now became the source of the neuroses. Having stumbled upon this, and having confided the news to Fliess, Freud was in no mood to admit his error to the Viennese establishment; Krafft-Ebing had, it seems, been right to ascribe to Freud's theories the description of 'scientific fairy-tales' but Freud was not prepared to concede his error. To Fliess he confided: 'it is curious that I feel not in the least disgraced, though the occasion seems to require it. Certainly I shall not tell it in Gath, or publish it in the streets of Askalon, in the land of the Philistines' (1897).[149] It was not until 1905 in his book *Three Essays on the Theory of Sexuality* that he publicly admitted what he privately called 'that first great error' (1907). Jeff Masson has, however, recently noted that in 1904 the Munich psychiatrist Leopold Löwenfeld published a book containing extracts of letters written by Freud in the early 1900s specifically on the subject of the seduction theory. Reporting that Freud's views had changed since they were first published in 1896 Löwenfeld reported that Freud now held that 'As a rule it is the experiences of puberty which have a harmful effect. In the process of repression these events are fantasied back into early childhood, following the pathways of sexual impressions accidentally experienced during the illness or arising from the [sexual] constitution' (c.1902).[150]

The new theory of sexuality, which the repudiation of his first 'great error' precipitated, was forged out of the material unearthed during those vital months at the end of 1897 when his self-analysis was at its height. Using the dreams, memories and phantasies thrown up during this time, and relying very heavily upon Fliess' theories of sexual development (Sulloway has described the emergence of the psycho-analytic understanding of sexuality as 'Freud's transformation of the Fliessian [conception]')[151] Freud was forced to attack a whole host of conventional assumptions about sexuality. When opening his discussion of sexuality in the *Essays* of 1905 he was quite plain about the conception he was opposed to.

> Popular opinion has quite definite ideas about the nature and characteristics of [the] sexual instinct. It is generally understood to be absent in childhood, to set in at the time of puberty in connection with the process of coming to maturity and to be revealed in the manifestations of an irresistable attraction exercised by one sex upon the other; while its aim is presumed to be sexual union, or at all events actions leading in that direction. We have reason to believe, however, that these views give a false picture of the true situation. If we look into them more closely we shall find that they contain a number of errors, inaccuracies and hasty conclusions. (1905)[152]

Sexuality, Freud argued, was a phenomenon which, in contrast to these popular views, was more widespread (notably in childhood) and more diverse (notably in having facets and aspects to it that were not solely concerned with sexual intercourse). Despite the popularity of the narrower view of sexuality, Freud was quick to point out that the work of the sexologists – Krafft-Ebing, Havelock Ellis and others – had already refuted such a narrow conception. Using a distinction between the terms 'sexual object' ('the person from whom sexual attraction proceeds') and 'sexual aim' ('the act to which the instinct tends') Freud went on to develop a theory of human sexual development. First, Freud maintained infantile sexuality emerged 'spontaneously from internal causes' (1905).[153] In the first instance that sexuality is indifferentiated in terms of both its object and aim – Freud called this condition the 'polymorphously perverse' (ibid.) state. From his unstructured state the child's libido develops through specific phases of 'pregenital organization' in which the sexual instinct is attached to, and finds release through, the various 'erotogenic zones'. These zones – the mouth, the nose, the anus, the genitals – had been identified by Fliess as providing pleasure and as thus having sexual significance, Freud took up this idea and developed it suggesting that human sexual development follows a course (one which in the perversions is incomplete or arrested) through quite specific phases – the oral stage, the anal stage, the phallic stage, and the latency period. Freud was later to regard the discovery of the 'polymorphosely perverse' nature of infantile sexuality and the 'erotogenic zone' conception of development as two of the most fundamental ideas of psychoanalysis. The development of the libido during these childhood years is intimately connected with sexual feelings towards the parents and maturity can only be achieved through the mastery of these feelings. The fact that most people do not remember much about these early crucial years of their development, let alone remember anything about their own sexuality during this time was, Freud argued, part of the reason why the subject of infantile sexuality had been ignored. That, in itself gave Freud a clue to the significance of this material; using the analogy of hysterical amnesia Freud suggested that the infantile material had been repressed:

> We must assume, or we can convince ourselves by a psychological examination of other people, that the very same impressions that we have forgotten have none the less left the deepest impression on our minds and have had a determining effect upon the whole of our later development. There can, therefore, be no question of any real abolition of the impressions of childhood, but rather of an amnesia similar to that which neurotics exhibit for later events, and of which the essence consists in a simple with-holding of these impressions from consciousness, viz, in their repression. (1905)[154]

In the depths of the experiences of childhood future behaviour was thus being forged – Freud's theory was strongly deterministic.

Before elaborating Freud's views on sexuality any further, in order for us to understand their important place in his thinking (and indeed his idolization of sex) we must place them within the context of his own sexual life. Freud himself noted 'it is impossible to understand anyone without knowing his sexual constitution' (1934).[155] Delving into the sexuality of the founder of psychoanalysis is no mere academic exercise not least because of the centrality of sexuality within psychoanalysis. Such archeological pursuits can give us the necessary personal context in which to understand some of his otherwise obscure interpretations. Throughout his psychoanalytic work interpretations often hinge around his own understanding of, for instance, marriage, or homosexuality, or sexual phantasy – it is thus imperative to discover the sources of his vision of these states. Freud's own sexuality, not surprisingly, has been the subject of a continuous stream of speculations and interpretations – it is a notorious battle-field for his supporters and his detractors. On the face of it, perhaps more than any other figure in the history of science, we have considerable material available to us from Freud's own pen which should furnish us with the basic evidence for our picture of his sexuality – indeed Freud claimed towards the end of his life that he would not supply any more information on this side of things for a biography because he had revealed so much about himself already. But Freud was a person who for all the surface candour was like the rest of us, prone to be deceitful in this most private of areas – as he hinted 'everyone hides the truth in matters of sex' (1906).[156]

In 1913 Freud wrote to a friend 'for each of us fate assumes the form of one (or several) women'.[157] Biographers and critics have waxed eloquent on which particular woman (or women) Freud regarded as being the most important to him. It is clear, as chapter 1 shows, that Freud's mother Amalie, is the prime candidate for this role. She dominated his early years, while he was the apple of her eye; *'mein goldener Sigi'* had a very deep and intimate relationship with his mother. Of the mother/son relationship in general Freud once wrote: 'a mother is only brought unlimited satisfaction by her relation to a son: that is altogether the most perfect, the most free from ambivalence of all human relationships' (1933).[158] Clearly Freud had his own relationship with his mother in mind when he praised the mother/son relationship so highly. Indeed, having identified infantile sexuality as existing in 1897 Freud went on to develop his ideas further and identify as a *universal* human experience the Oedipus complex. Children – all children – experience sexual desires for their parents; for sons that desire is for their mother – a desire which puts them in conflict with their father – this was called by Freud the Oedipus complex after the hero in Sophocles play *Oedipus Rex*. To Fliess he expained the significance:

> Only one idea of general value has occurred to me. I have found love of the mother and jealousy of the father in my own case too, and now believe it to be a general phenomenon of early childhood . . . if that is the case, the gripping power of *Oedipus Rex*, in spite of all the rational objections to the inexorable fate that the story presupposes, becomes intelligible . . . the Greek myth seizes on a compulsion which everyone recognises because he has felt traces of it in himself. Every member of the audience was once a budding Oedipus in phantasy. . . . (1897)[159]

In his dream book published at the end of this intense period Freud spelled out the theory more explicitly: 'it is the fate of all of us, perhaps, to direct our first sexual impulses towards our mother and our first hatred and our first murderous wish against our father' (1900).[160] Having become aware of these feelings the child then develops a castration anxiety – he fears punishment from his powerful father. From out of the half-serious threats of parents about the dangers of 'playing with oneself' castration fears are generated (Freud later suggested that what he called 'phylogenetic' factors reinforced these fears – see chapter 5). The Oedipus complex, which Freud later asserted could 'justly be regarded as the nucleus of the neuroses' (1916/1917),[161] was an idea which he regarded as fundamental to his thought. In his very last publication, published posthumously, he reiterated its importance: 'if psycho-analysis could boast of no other achievement than the discovery of the repressed Oedipus complex, that alone would give a claim to be included among the precious new acquisitions of mankind' (1940).[162] Freud's interpretation of the story of Oedipus which places the emphasis on the *son's* feelings for his mother and father rather than on the parent's feelings for the child gives a clear indication of the direction of Freud's interest. It is interesting to note that the abandonment of the seduction theory marks a transition too from his earlier preoccupations with understanding how *females* develop neuroses, to an emphasis on the generation of neuroses in *males* – a transition which reflects the underlying shift from the analysis of mainly women patients (as in the *Studies*) to the analysis of himself. The analagous complex for women – dubbed by some 'the Electra complex' (a term which Freud explicitly repudiated) maintained that girls too, initially love their mothers, but turn against them in favour of their fathers when they discover their own lack of a penis.

Maturity and growth were conceived by Freud in terms of the successful resolution of these complexes. When an individual developed normally he was able to transcend these early, infantile sexual feelings and eventually after puberty to transfer them to other more appropriate women. Clearly Freud's first calf-love for Gisela Fluss and his other 'strong passion' for her mother, Frau Fluss, were stages in that development in Freud. Freud's sexual longings were becoming detached from his mother (though, arguably, they never quite became fully detached given the very deep feelings he expressed for her even quite late in life); Gisela and Frau Flüss represent a transition phase for Freud in the development of his sexuality.

The four years of his engagement to Martha Bernays represent a further stage. It was a long and difficult engagement in part because for the majority of this time Freud was in Vienna and Martha in Wandsbeck, Hamburg. During that time Freud wrote Martha over a thousand letters, usually writing daily, some were a mere four pages long whilst the longest was twenty-two. Very few of these letters have yet been published, but those that have been show Freud to be passionately 'in love' with 'my dearest Princess', 'my dearest treasure', 'my sweet Marty', 'my little woman' – to use but a few of his titles for her. The range of sentiments expressed in these letters show Freud to be a man of intense passion full of sensitivity, curiosity, warmth but also full of jealousy, possessiveness, rage, selfishness and dependency – in short they portray a real human being full of all the ambiguities of human nature. Ernest Jones remarks of this period that his relationship to Martha was a 'veritable *grande passion*' through which Freud 'was to experience in his own person the full force of the terrible power of love with all its raptures, fears and torments'. Four years of engagement, mostly separated by many miles must have been a long, trying experience for Freud: Jones called this experience 'a fiery apprenticeship' which 'qualified [Freud] to discourse authoritatively on love'.[163]

Given then that this period was marked specifically by the arousal of 'all the passions of which his intense nature was capable' (Jones) what may be said specifically about Freud's sexuality at the time? For a long time people have assumed that his sexuality was carefully kept under control and that like many *petit-bourgeois* middle-class men he did not engage in any specifically sexual experience. Some have even suggested that this abstinence was a formative influence in nurturing the genius that was to emerge in the 1890s – the sexual energy accumulating and being sublimated to creative work.[164] Others, basing themselves upon this premise, that he did not explore his sexuality at the time, have taken this lack of exploration to be a sign of his psychological (psychosexual) ill health.[165] There is, however, a good deal of evidence – gleaned from Freud's reported dreams and his 'case studies' – that the primary premise of these estimates must be rejected. It is known for certain, from his own lips, that Freud was not a virgin when he married,[166] although Freud himself, and every biographer since, has tried to create the impression that Martha was his first and only sexual partner. Similarly it is also clear that Freud was engaged in sexual activity during this time but of an auto-erotic kind, that is to say, during his engagement Freud found sexual release through masturbation. Masturbation, a solution that he had sought for the frustrations of his calf-love in his teens, was the only solution for Freud at this time. Martha was miles away and probably would not have consented to any premarital sexual activity anyway. Recourse to prostitutes was ruled out given that syphilis and gonorrhoea were rife in such people. Masturbation coupled with sexual fantasy was the answer to Freud's frustration.[167] Years later, in 1908, Freud was to say this about masturbation, which he regarded as the 'primal addiction', 'in the phantasies that accompany satisfaction, the sexual object is elevated to a degree of excellence which is not easily found again in reality' (1908).[168]

This interpretation of Freud's sexual life runs counter to the whole thrust of Freud biography as it has so far been written. It is, however, a matter of crucial significance for it is tied up with the interpretation of the most important source of material about Freud's sexuality, namely a paper published in 1899 entitled 'Screen Memories'. This paper purports to present a case study of a young man some 5 years Freud's junior. In reality the paper is an autobiographical account of Freud's own case. The paper recounts how the patient indulges in phantasies of 'gross sexual aggression' onto a virgin – 'defloration phantasies' – which, on account of their 'coarsely sensual element' the patient transposes into an 'innocent' childhood memory. The 'screen memory' consists of the man remembering himself in a sloping meadow, full of yellow flowers, with his two cousins. The man recalls that he and his male cousin pounce upon the female cousin and steal her bunch of flowers. The girl runs off to be comforted by a peasant woman who gives her black bread. The boys then throw away her ill-gotten flowers in order to gain some of the bread. The twin themes of 'love' and 'hunger' are those that Freud stressed in his 'interpretation' of his patients' memory. Ernest Jones, and Siegfried Bernfield, the man who originally uncovered the autobiographical nature of this paper, both agreed that the material in the paper was closely connected with Freud's involvement with masturbation, but Jones did 'not think it right' to mention this in his biography of Freud.[169] The alleged patient's phantasies are specifically related to the patient's longing to get married and experience for himself the pleasures of the promised land of sexuality. The patient says 'the most seductive part of the whole subject [of marriage] for a young good-for-nothing is the picture of the wedding night – little does he know what comes afterwards' (1899). Understanding the 'Screen Memories' paper is vital to understanding not only his sexual experiences in engagement but also his whole concept of phantasy, indeed the central dogma of psychoanalysis – the relationship between the past and the present in an individual's psychic life. 'Screen memories' shows Freud's own personal phantasy life to have been far more complicated, and suspect, than many biographers have yet allowed.[171]

Freud's remark (put into the lips of the supposed patient) – the caustic aside about what comes afterwards – gives us an indication of the transformation which was to happen in his relationship with Martha. Having literally dominated his every thought, his dreams, his fantasies, on marriage Martha suddenly disappeared from his consciousness. She became transformed into a 'non-sexual' background figure – all passion, so evident before, disappeared. Jones generously asserted that Frau Freud was 'an excellent wife and mother . . . and admirable manager . . . never the kind of *Hausfrau* who puts things before people' but that appears to be *all* she was. She was a woman whose task was 'ruling her household with great kindness and with an equally great firmness' (to use her son, Martin's description of her role). Jones, again with a fair amount of generosity maintained 'his wife was assuredly the only woman in Freud's love life and she always came first before all mortals'.[171] In reality Martha ordered the household around Freud (as even a cursory examination of his daily routine reveals) and Freud took up his all-consuming passion, psychoanalysis. There is evidence to suggest that Freud resumed his fantasy sex life which was *not* directed at Martha, who had now become merely the bearer of his children and a *Hausfrau*.[173]

Some indication of this transformation of Martha from the longed for sexual object into the mother and 'admirable manager' is provided by Freud himself in a letter he wrote to his son-in-law. He wrote, concerning his relationship with his wife that: 'I have really got along very well with my wife. I am thankful to her above all for her many noble qualities, for the children who have turned out so well, and for the fact that she has neither been abnormal nor very often ill' (1912).[174] This summary of his wife's 'noble qualities' is so bland as to be positively insulting: as one woman psychoanalyst has commented on this passage, if that was all her husband could summon up to describe her 'noble qualities' after so many years of marriage she would 'most certainly divorce him'.[175] Similarly, in 1936 on his golden wedding anniversary, Freud wrote to the woman who had become his close confidant, Marie Bonaparte, herself a woman of intense sexuality, that Martha 'was really not a bad solution of the marriage problem, and she is still today tender, healthy and active' (1936).[176] A description again, which belies little real intimacy or affection.

Obviously, given that they did have six children (the first, Mathilde being born in 1887 and the last, and most famous, Anna born in 1895 – see plate 5) their sexual relations did not cease immediately after marriage – disappointing as the desired object of his fantasies was he still expressed himself sexually with her. In fact the number of children they had, in the short space of 8 years, gives one indication of a possible reason for a decline in the passion of their relationship, i.e. Martha was frequently either pregnant or recovering from pregnancy during these early years of their marriage. These years, it would seem reasonable to suppose, would then have been characterized either by a periodic cessation of sexual activity (out of deference for the pregnant partner or out of sexual taboo), or by sexual activity marred by the fear of pregnancy. Given Freud's continuing precarious financial position during these years, it is by no means far-fetched to assume that the fear of pregnancy dominated their early years.

Freud's feelings about sexuality can be clearly seen in his writings at this time, most notably in his correspondence with Wilhelm Fliess. Fliess, a nose and throat specialist from Berlin, had developed a theory about the connection between the nasal membranes and the genitals especially in women. The changes he observed in the nasal mucous membranes of women during menstruation were extrapolated by Fliess into a general theory of nasal reflexes and a general theory of periodicity in all animals. Given their mutual marginality in their respective cities the two men were thrown together in an intense and intimate way – they both depended on each other for support and encouragement sharing every new idea together. It is difficult to exaggerate the importance of these two men to each other. Freud called Fliess 'the Kepler of biology',[177] and his letters to him are full of references to his indebtedness to Fliess for his ideas (see plate 6).

During these early years of marriage he was developing his ideas about sexuality, and sharing his innermost thoughts about it with Fliess. Freud, as did others in the field, was convinced at this time (the early 1890s) that coitus interruptus (the practice of 'avoiding' contraception by the male withdrawing his penis from the vagina before ejaculation – one of the few forms of 'contraception' available at the time), and prolonged sexual abstinence were *the* causes of anxiety: Freud's own personal experiences here may well have had a marked influence upon his thought. Freud compared the transformation of what was normally so good, healthy and desirable into something as destructive and nasty as a neurosis as being akin to wine turning into vinegar. Indeed, he pictured the action of this 'souring' very much in physical terms of the build up of 'sexual toxins' which if they were not released properly would 'poison' the individual – much as 'cocaine' in large doses built up in the body and produced harmful effects. When he heard that Fliess had developed a 'safe' method of contraception based upon his ideas of periodicity (an early version of the 'rhythm method' of contraception) Freud wrote exultantly to Fliess: 'You could be the strongest of men holding in your hands the reins of sexuality which governs all mankind, you could do everything and prevent everything' (1895);[178] and in another letter he wrote: 'I could have shouted with joy at your news. If you have really solved the problem of contraception I will ask you what sort of marble would best please you' (1895).[179]

There can be no questioning the fact that sexual relations between Freud and Martha ceased fairly soon after the birth of their last child, Anna. In fact both had hoped that the early symptoms of Martha's pregnancy with Anna were the first signs of the onset of the menopause for Martha – a condition which would solve the problem of contraception for them both.[180] Freud adopting a somewhat conventional definition, was later to write of sexual activity that it was: 'perverse if it had given up the aim of reproduction and pursues the attainment of pleasure as an aim independent of it' (1916/1917),[181] a situation which followed quickly on the birth of Anna. Jones records that 'the more passionate side of married life subsided with him earlier than it does with many men'.[182] Freud did indeed remark to Fliess that 'sexual excitation is of no more use to a person like me' in October 1897.[183] He also subsequently confided in the wife of his pupil, C. G. Jung, that his 'marriage had long been "amortized" [and that] there was nothing more to do except die'.[184] The decline of his sexuality occurred shortly after the death of his father (in October 1896), a loss which he felt very keenly and which initiated the psychological processes which were to necessitate his 'self-analysis'. Years later he wrote that the loss had 'revolutionalized my soul' (1920).[185] There may well have been a connection between the revolution in his soul and the 'amortization' of his marriage for Freud later wrote about a particular case he was studying the following revealing analysis:

> He was the most pronounced rebel imaginable . . . on the other hand at a deeper level he was still the most submissive of sons, who after his father's death denied himself all enjoyment of women out of a tender sense of guilt. (1922)[186]

It is further worth noting that Freud made his observation in the context of a discussion on homosexuality. The question of homosexuality in relation to Freud needs some consideration, for he was involved in a relationship at this time with Wilhelm Fliess which years later, after it had broken up, Freud described to a fellow psychoanalyst as being an aspect of his homosexuality. Freud's relationship with Wilhelm Fliess is perhaps the most misunderstood aspect of his early career. It was begun at a crucial stage in his development, in 1887, it continued through the years of what he called his 'splendid isolation' (the 1890s) and finished with traumatic effect early in the 1900s. Freud himself was concerned to eliminate all reference to this period, and when he learnt of the preservation of his letters to Fliess he wrote 'I don't want any of them to become known to so called posterity'. Concerning those letters he wrote:

> Considering the very intimate nature of our relationship, these letters naturally deal with anything and everything, factual as well as personal matters. The factual matter concerns all the hunches and false paths connected to the birth of analysis and in this case is also quite personal. (1937)[187]

The letters were eventually published in 1950 but only in what one biographer has called 'bowdlerized form'[188] for the editors of the letters (which included Freud's daughter Anna) saw fit, presumably out of some sense of being fair to the spirit of Freud's wishes, to cut portions from them. Not only did they cut significant portions but they also failed to mention, on numerous occasions, when they were doing this. When later, some of Freud's followers broke ranks and published a little more of the material censored, it became clear that the meaning of certain sentences and letters was significantly different from the 'sanitized' version. The behaviour of Freud's 'protectors' is a matter of profound disgrace, for in marketing an image of Freud, they have done his cause a disservice – Freud's greatness, or otherwise, should be able to stand up to the truth. In the words of one of his closest followers: 'The demolisher of mankind's sweetest illusion who drew the curtain from the holiest of self-deception, is no fit object for fine words and the services of a beautician'.[189]

In 1980, it was announced that Anna Freud had given permission for a new, complete edition of the Freud/Fliess correspondence to be published. This new edition will certainly help dispel the impression left after their original, incomplete, publication that 'the personal Freudian cupboard is as full of skeletons as a graveyard'.[190] Even on the evidence of the published material we can conclude that Freud had a homosexual love for Fliess which dominated his life in the 1890s and, even though they had broken off their relationship, in the early 1900s. All of the passion that we have seen before in his childhood friendships, his adolescent ones, and his engagement days are present in this relationship. Hitherto Freud's biographers have sought to suppress this passionate aspect of the relationship and attempted to suggest that Fliess was just a 'father figure', or a sounding board for his ideas; such a playing down of this relationship cannot be continued – it was an expression of Freud's 'dominant sexual disposition' (1899).[191] The editor of the new edition of the letters, on the basis of his having studied all of them in full, writes 'nobody would disagree that Freud was enraptured with Fliess'. He then goes on to quote the opinions which Jones and Strachey held privately on the relationship. Strachey had written to Jones suggesting that the 'suppressed passages' revealed 'a complex instance of *folie à deux*, with Freud in the unexpected role of hysterical partner to a paranoiac'. Jones wrote to Strachey in return that Freud 'never really emancipated himself from Fliess'.[192] It is interesting that Freud himself made an observation that for many people of maturer years 'a blocking of the main stream of their libido has caused a widening in the side-channel of homosexuality' (1908).[193]

So great was the emotional attachment between these two men that 10 years after his last meeting with him (in 1900) Freud wrote to a friend that his dreams were *entirely* concerned with 'the Fliess affair' (1910).[194] This was written at a time when Freud was having the first radical dissension among his pupils, Alfred Adler and Wilhelm Stekel. Adler and Stekel were both promising students who were in the process of severing their connections with Freud at this time. Freud wrote to a fellow, loyal, psychoanalyst: 'I have now overcome Fliess, about whom you were so curious. Adler is a little Fliess, come back to life, and equally paranoid. Stekel, as his appendix, is at least called Wilhelm' (1910). It was to that fellow analyst that Freud specifically outlined the exact nature of how and what he 'overcame' with Fliess:

> You not only noticed, but also understood that I no longer have any need to uncover my personality completely and you correctly traced this back to the traumatic reason for it. Why would you then insist upon it? Since Fliess' case, with the overcoming of which you recently saw me occupied, that need has been extinguished. A part of homosexual cathexis has been withdrawn and made use of to enlarge my own ego. I have succeeded where the paranoiac fails. (1910)[195]

Freud went on to suggest that it would be impossible for anyone to fully understand the depth of the relationship with Fliess, and the consequent pain of the break. When pressed for more information by his fellow analyst on the grounds that he was 'an unmitigated therapist'[196] and therefore wanted to help Freud, Freud responded by stating that on the contrary he did not need a therapist since, he argued 'I feel capable of handling everything and am pleased with the resultant greater independence that comes from having overcome my homosexuality' (1910).[197] A fuller understanding of the complicated theoretical processes Freud is alluding to here becomes clearer when it is seen that Freud was concerned at that very same time to understand the case of a paranoic, Schreber (see chapter 4). In that study Freud spoke of 'the liberated libido' returning to the ego such that 'a person's only sexual object is his own ego' (1911).[198] In 1912 Freud had a fainting fit in the presence of yet another of his dissenting pupils, Jung. Explaining later to Ernest Jones that the fit had occurred in a room where he had once met Fliess, Freud explained the fit with the words: 'there is some piece of unruly homosexual feeling at the root of the matter' (1912).[199] Clearly even after 1910 his 'dominant sexual disposition' was not as successfully overcome as he would have liked everyone to believe.

The formal break with Fliess occurred in 1906 when Fliess denounced Freud for plagiarism. Well before that break with Fliess, that is, before

1900, Freud's relationship with Fliess satisfied not only his scientific researches – the two shared every new fact and theory with each other – but also, significantly, in some measure his sexual feelings. That is not to suggest that these found physical expression, but emotionally Freud found satisfaction in his homosexual love for Fliess. When in 1935 he wrote to a mother over her concern about her son's homosexuality, he wrote from an informed perspective.

> Homosexuality is assuredly no advantage, but it is nothing to be ashamed of, no vice, no degradation; it cannot be classified as an illness: we consider it to be a variation of the sexual function, produced by a certain arrest of sexual development. Many highly respectable individuals of ancient and modern times have been homosexuals, several of the greatest men among them (Plato, Michelangelo, Leonardo da Vinci, etc.). It is a great injustice to persecute homosexuality as a crime – and a cruelty, too . . . By asking me if I can help, you mean, I suppose, if I can abolish homosexuality and make normal heterosexuality take its place. The answer is, in a general way we cannot promise to achieve it. In a certain number of cases we succeed in developing the blighted germs of heterosexual tendencies, which are present in every homosexual; in the majority of cases it is no more possible . . . what analysis can do for your son runs in a different line. If he is unhappy, neurotic, torn by conflicts, inhibited in his social life, analysis may being him harmony, peace of mind, full efficiency, whether he remains homosexual or gets changed. (1935)[200]

The presence of these two elements in his sexual constitution – heterosexuality (in his marriage) and homosexuality (in his relation to Fliess) would have been no great theoretical problem to Freud, for in their theories of sexuality developed during these years both men affirmed the diverse, and frequently contradictory nature of the libido. In particular both Fliess and Freud upheld the idea that human nature ·was fundamentally bisexual and that the development of a unisexual disposition is always only partially successful. Freud always considered the idea of 'the bisexuality of all human behaviour' to have been one of Fliess' major contributions to science. Fliess had reached his conclusions partly on the basis of the knowledge that sexual differentiation occurs in embryonic development only after a stage when the sexual organs of both sexes are present in all vertebrates (including man), and partly on the basis of his theories of periodicity. Having determined the presence of a 28-day period in female physiology and behaviour, and the presence of an analogous one of 23-days in male physiology and behaviour, Fliess concluded that since he could detect the presence of both periods in the behaviour of any individual then everybody has a 'bisexual disposition'.

Freud and Fliess first discussed the question of the permanent bisexuality of human behaviour at Nuremberg on one of their congresses in 1897, although they had touched upon the theme in their letters following Fliess' publication of the theory. What was significant about the Nuremberg discussion was that there was a suggestion that the theory of bisexuality might help explain the riddle of repression. As Freud was later to describe the theory: 'the dominant sex of the person, that which is the more strongly developed, has repressed the mental representation of the subordinated sex into the unconscious. Therefore the nucleus of the unconscious (that is to say, the repressed) is in each human being that side of him which belongs to the opposite sex' (1919).[201] Freud described the impact of this idea to him in a letter to Fliess: 'I literally jumped at the emphasis on bisexuality and consider this your idea the most significant in my themes since that of "Defence"' (1898).[202] Accordingly Freud began to view all behaviour in this light – in 1899 he wrote to Fliess telling him of how he was 'accustoming [himself] to the idea of regarding every sexual act as a process in which four persons are involved' (1899).[203] Bisexuality was, in the words of his *Essays* of 1905 – 'the decisive factor' and that: 'without taking bisexuality into account I think it would scarcely be possible to arrive at an understanding of the sexual manifestations that are actually to be observed in men and women' (1905).[204]

Freud's sexual make-up was clearly very complicated, within him torrents of passion ebbed and flowed in ways scarcely discernible now. However, since Freud himself used autobiographical material, notably relating to his own sexuality as *evidence* to support his theory of the neuroses, and ultimately his whole theory of human functioning, it is important to try to establish, as much as it is possible at so great a distance, the precise nature of that autobiographical material. The central Freudian doctrine, that infantile sexuality is *the* determinant of subsequent behaviour – that the Oedipus complex is at the heart of adult action – was forged out of the depths of Freud's own self-analysis. The very material of that self-analysis – the dreams, the memories, the phantasies – constitute the empirical base of psychoanalytic theory. True, Freud drew upon material gleaned from other patients and true, psychoanalysis now boasts a whole range of clinical data as its support, but at the outset it was Freud and his inner life which provided the necessary insight into the human soul. It is, therefore, of profound significance that we understand Freud the man as part of our assessment of psychoanalysis the science. Freud's own sexuality and his views on sex, largely gained in this early period of his psychological work, percolate through and infuse the whole of the rest of his writings – we cannot understand those without our prior understanding of these foundations.

3

Decoding the Mind
Dreams, Slips and Jokes

I see light: To Dream is to think, and to think is to Dream.
(Descartes)

Since time immemorial people have been both fascinated and often
perplexed by their dreams. In the traces of humanity's earliest thoughts
that have survived to our day we find an intrigue and respect (if not awe)
for dreams – they surely tell us something, it's been argued. Achilles, when
the Greek army encamped around Troy was being destroyed by a
pestilence, thought recourse to dreams the most natural way to obtain
a solution 'because dreams descend from Zeus'. The Bible, throughout
the Old and the New Testament is full of people receiving guidance and
revelation in their dreams, from Jacob with his stairway to heaven to
St John with his visions in the night, or else is peopled with men requiring
the interpretation of their dreams. Indeed, one of the promised signs of
the coming of the Holy Spirit at Pentecost, the dawning of the new age,
was that 'your old men shall dream dreams' (Joel 2:28; Acts 2:17).
Dreams, have then, in most traditions been accorded a special place in
our understanding of ourselves and our context.

Given this rich, Biblical heritage and given Freud's Jewish upbringing it
comes as no surprise to find an emphasis upon dreams in Freud's thought.
Freud strongly identified himself with the Old Testament character of
Joseph, the dream-interpreter, and wrote, in what is one of his most
famous statements: 'the interpretation of dreams is the royal road to a
knowledge of the unconscious activities of the mind' (1909).[1] This
assessment of the importance of dreams Freud added to the second edition
of his monumental study entitled *The Interpretation of Dreams*. The first
edition was published in November 1899, though the publisher dated the
title page: 1900 (see plate 7). Of all Freud's books this was the one he considered to be his most enduring contribution to psychology. The book only
sold 351 copies during the first 6 years following its publication, yet Freud
constantly sought to revise it and improve it throughout his lifetime.[2]

Freud himself is reported to have recorded his own dreams even as a
young man, but since we do not have any of his early manuscripts and

notebooks (since he burnt them all in 1885) we can only record his early *interest*, not the form and content of that interest. Some time later he was to suggest that his interest in dreams was rekindled spontaneously as a result of his experiences with his patients:

> It was discovered one day that the pathological symptoms of certain neurotic patients have a sense. On this discovery the psycho-analytic method of treatment was founded. It happened in the course of this treatment that patients, instead of bringing forward their symptoms, brought forward dreams. A suspicion, thus arose that the dreams too had a sense. (1916/17)[3]

The genesis of the idea that dreams made sense may well have been prompted by the presentation of dreams by patients, but the context in which Freud was writing his book makes it clear that in many respects he began systematically to study dreams in order to understand himself, his chief patient. Later, in 1909, when lecturing in America, he was to suggest that if he was ever asked how one might become a psychoanalyst he replied 'By studying one's own dreams' and further that 'if . . . you can accept the solutions of the problems of dream life, the novelties with which psychoanalysis confronts your minds will offer you no further difficulties' (1910).[4] It may well have been Freud's desire to understand the complexities of his own sexual constitution which prompted him to begin to explore dreams systematically as a means of coming to grips with the unconscious – the chronology of his self-analysis points towards this. Whatever the particular route of his discovery that 'royal road to knowledge of . . . the mind', was one which he regarded as of cardinal importance to him. Indeed, he said of dream interpretation that it was 'the securest foundation of psychoanalysis and the field in which every worker must acquire his convictions and seek his training' (1910).[5] Not surprisingly, given the weight he attached to this work, Freud could recall a specific occasion when the *sense* of dreams began to be clear to him. He mentioned it to Fliess in a letter he sent him just after the publication of *The Interpretation of Dreams:*

> Life at Bellevue[6] is turning out very pleasantly for everyone. The evenings and mornings are enchanting; the scent of acacia and jasmine has succeeded that of lilac and laburnum, the wild roses are in bloom and everything, as even I notice, seems suddenly to have burst out.
>
> Do you suppose that someday this house will have a marble plaque with the inscription:

Here, on July 24th, 1895
the mystery of dreams
revealed itself to Dr. Sigm. Freud

(1900)[7]

The reference here is to a dream about one of his patients which served as one of the main illustrative cases in *The Interpretation of Dreams*. He also provided a preliminary account of the dream and its interpretation in the section on dreams which he wrote for the *Project* in the Autumn of 1895. The dream has since become known as 'the dream of Irma's injection'. This dream, Freud wrote in a footnote appended to the account in *The Interpretation of Dreams*, was the first dream which he has subjected to a 'thorough interpretation' – although in conclusion he also stated: 'I will not pretend that I have completely uncovered the meaning of this dream or that its interpretation is without a gap' (1900).[8] What Freud was alluding to here will become clear during the course of this chapter, but for now suffice it to note that the events of 23 and 24 July 1895 were so important that they became fixed in his mind and, over the next few years, the interpretation of dreams became of paramount importance. In the *History* he looked back on those days and noted:

The interpretation of dreams became a solace and a support to me in those arduous first years of analysis, when I had to master the technique, clinical phenomena, and therapy of the neuroses all at the same time. At that period, I was completely isolated, and in the network of problems and accumulation of difficulties I often dreaded losing my bearings, and also my confidence. There were often patients with whom an unaccountably long time elapsed before my hypothesis – that a neurosis was bound to become intelligible through analysis – proved true; but these patients' dreams, which might be regarded as analogues of their symptoms, almost always confirmed the hypothesis. It was only my success in this direction that enabled me to persevere. (1914)[9]

Many years later, he described dream analysis as the 'sheet-anchor during those difficult times . . . Whenever I began to have doubts of the correctness of my wavering conclusions, the successful transformation of a senseless and muddled dream into a logical and intelligible mental process in the dreamer would renew my confidence of being on the right track' (1933).[10] Specifically, dream analysis proved to be a key to Freud's own self-analysis, and thus it was the 'royal road' to his own solace. In trying to understand his own conflicts dreams were the one sure route to the hidden sources. In the midst of his grief over the death of his father, they literally provided a route out of the turmoil. In the *History* he wrote: 'I soon saw the necessity of carrying out a self-analysis, and this I did with the help of a series of my own dreams which led me back through all the events of my childhood' (1914). Indeed, in Freud's opinion this route out of turmoil was so successful that he added a coda to his own history: 'I am still of the opinion today that this kind of analysis may suffice for anyone who is a good dreamer and not too abnormal' (ibid.).[11]

One consequence of the fact that the writing of the *Interpretation of Dreams* coincided with his own self-analysis is that the book itself contains considerable autobiographical material. In the preface to the second edition of the book he wrote that the book was a 'portion of my own self-analysis, my reaction to my father's death – that is to say, the most important event, the most poignant loss, of a man's life' (1909).[12] To his friend Fliess he confided 'none of my works has been so completely my own as this; it is my own dung-heap, my own seedling and a *nova species mihi (sic!)*' (1899).[13] Freud felt that the material was so important that, despite its personal nature he had to publish it. To Fliess he wrote 'I have decided that all the efforts at disguise will not do, and that giving it all up will not do either, because I cannot afford to keep to myself the finest – and probably the only lasting – discovery that I have made' (ibid.). Later, when writing a preface for yet another revised edition he added 'insight such as this falls to one's lot but once in a lifetime'.[14] Dream interpretation became for Freud the successor to his earlier attempts to make his mark on the world – the new histological technique of the 1870s, cocaine, hypnosis and hysteria, the seduction theory.

Freud's work on the interpretation of dreams had a twofold significance for him beyond the personal solace it gave him. First, he felt that he had discovered something no-one else had: *the* key to the meaning of dreams. To Fliess he confided: 'when I read the latest psychological books . . . all of which have the same kind of aims as my work, and see what they have to say about dreams, I am as delighted as the dwarf in the fairy tale because "the princess doesn't know"' (1900).[15] To Freud's mind, nobody but himself and Fliess were on the right track, that is 'on the track of sexuality' (1894).[16] Freud's *way* of interpreting dreams, however, was not the only novel feature for him. The interpretation of dreams had a second significance for Freud in that it enabled him to make a strategic leap. Prior to his work on dreams Freud's work had been concerned only with the *abnormal* and the *pathological*, with his dream work he could enter the world of the *normal*. The book marks, then, the beginning of a general psychology not just a branch of psychopathology. This was an important step for Freud, as he recalled in his autobiography:

What constitutes the enormous importance of dream-interpretation . . . is not the assistance they give to the work of analysis but another of their attributes. Previously psycho-analysis had only been concerned with solving pathological phenomena . . . But when it came to dreams, it was no longer dealing with a pathological symptom, but with a phenomenon of normal mental life which might occur in any healthy person. If dreams turned out to be constructed like symptoms, if their explanations required the same assumptions . . . then psychoanalysis was no longer an auxiliary science in the field of psychopathology, it was rather the starting point of a new, a deeper science of the mind which would be equally indispensable for the understanding of the normal. Its postulates and findings could be carried over to other regions of mental happenings; a path lay open to it that led far afield, into spheres of universal interest. (1925)[17]

Given what we already know of Freud's interests and of his desire to really make his mark on the world, we can see the appeal of his dream work and the importance he attached to it. In the course of a few years he was to extend that 'new, a deeper science' to encompass 'slips of the tongue' and other seeming, ordinary 'accidents' with the publication in 1901 of *The Psychopathology of Everyday Life*, and to encompass the world of wit and jokes in 1905 with *Jokes and their Relation to the Unconscious*. Freud's letters to Fliess show that over the period from 1895 to 1905 dreams, slips, jokes and symptoms all provided material for this model of the mind – they were the basis of his 'new, a deeper science of the mind'. It was on this seemingly trivial foundation –.that the unconscious could be studied through the messages it sent out – that Freud went on to colonize other ostensibly unrelated fields – religion, anthropology, art criticism, literary studies. The place that the interpretation of dreams assumed for Freud – as a stepping stone out of the pathological into the normal – is pivotal.

The book, as I have already indicated, received a muted reception (though not, note, as muted as Freud subsequently maintained),[18] but Freud was still able to write to Fliess: 'it has been a consolation to me in many a gloomy hour to know that I have this book to leave behind me' (1900).[19] Some time later, writing to Jung, Freud was even more explicit about the central place of the work for him personally. He recalled that in 1900 he had experienced an eruption of superstition – a superstition that he was going to die between the ages of 61 and 62. He further noted that this eruption coincided 'with the conviction that with *The Interpretation of Dreams* I had completed my life work, that there was nothing more for me to do and that I might just as well lie down and die' (1909).[20]

'TO SLEEP, PERCHANCE TO DREAM'

> I have finished; that is to say, the last of the manuscript has gone off . . .
> the matter about dreams I believe to be unassailable; what I dislike about
> it is the style. (1899)[21]

Despite Freud's early interest in dreams, and their interpretation, he himself regarded his analysis of the dream of the night of 23/24 July 1895 as the most significant first step towards a new understanding of dreams. Since Freud himself put so much weight on this 'specimen dream', which he describes as having been given a 'thorough interpretation', we shall devote some time to understanding it. The dream is called 'the dream of Irma's injection', since it refers to an imagined treatment of a patient 'Irma' by injection. In my account of the dream, and Freud's interpretation of it, I am going to distinguish three levels of explanation: first I shall consider the dream and what Freud says about it in *The Interpretation of Dreams* – this might be called the 'face-value' level. Secondly, I shall consider material which is clearly pertinent to a full understanding of the dream which Freud fails to mention – this might be called the 'background' level. Lastly, I shall attempt to relate the first two levels of explanation to a third, integrative level of explanation as provided by comments that Freud made elsewhere about dreams in general, and about this dream in particular.

To begin at the beginning, Freud prefaced his book with a few observations about the subject of his work; he remarked:

> The only dreams open to my choice were my own and those of my patients
> undergoing psycho-analytic treatment. But I was precluded from using the
> latter material by the fact that in its case the dream-processes were subject
> to an undesirable complication owing to the added presence of neurotic
> features. But if I was to report my own dreams, it inevitably followed that
> I should have to reveal to the public gaze more of the intimacies of my
> mental life than I liked, or than is normally necessary for any writer who
> is a man of science and not a poet. Such was the painful but unavoidable
> necessity; and I have submitted to it rather than totally abandon the
> possibility of giving the evidence for my psychological findings. Naturally,
> however I have been unable to resist the temptation of taking the edge off
> some of my indiscretions by omissions and substitutions. But whenever
> this has happened, the value of my instances has been very definitely
> diminished. (1900)[22]

Freud was then, faced with a dilemma with respect to interpreting his dreams for the public: interpretation led to self-disclosure but self-disclosure could lead to possible social censure, but without self-disclosure the interpretations were worthless. In the process of offering an interpretation in line with his theories about the functioning of the unconscious, he would inevitably open himself up to the charge of being an evil man or one harbouring dark and perverse desires. However, with the caveat lodged by Freud that he did take the edges off some of his interpretations he gives us the clear impression that in the interests of science he is, in general, being candid about the most important aspects of the dream and its interpretation. Indeed, as he introduced the specimen dream, he quoted from a French psychologist (in French) the statement: 'every psychologist is under an obligation to confess even his own weaknesses if he thinks that it may throw light upon some obscure problem' but out of a concern to guard 'against misinterpretation by strangers' Freud added a footnote to say:

> I am obliged to add, however, by way of qualification of what I have said above, that in scarcely any instance have I brought forward the *complete* interpretation of one of my own dreams, as it is known to me. I have probably been wise in not putting too much faith in my readers' discretion. (1900)[23]

Freud thus presents us with interpretations which he regarded as 'thorough' but *incomplete*.

The specimen dream of 23/24 July 1895; 'the dream of Irma's injection', is introduced with a preamble explaining Freud's own personal circumstances at the time. In the summer of 1895 Freud was treating a young widow, 'Irma'. 'Irma' had problems which he described as 'hysterical anxiety'; she was also a close friend of both himself and his family. Just before going on summer holiday Freud had presented 'Irma' with a (psycho-analytic) solution to her problems which she had refused to accept. In this unsatisfactory state, Freud had been forced to leave her in order to go on holiday. On 23 July a mutual friend of both Freud and Irma had come to visit him, having just been staying at the home of 'Irma' and her family. When asked by Freud how she was, his friend 'Otto' (in reality Oskar Rie, a friend and collaborator of Freud) had replied that she was 'better but not quite well'. Freud reported that he detected reproach in the voice of his friend and suggested to himself that this was caused by 'Otto' siding with 'Irma's' family. That evening Freud decided to write out 'Irma's' case history with a view to justifying himself and exculpating himself from blame for her condition. He thought he would send this case report to his former mentor (and by this time estranged), Dr M. (in reality Josef Breuer). These are the circumstances Freud brought forward as being pertinent to 'the dream of Irma's injection' which he dreamt that very same night.

At risk of tedium to the reader it is best to report Freud's dream verbatim, as he himself does in the book:

Dream of July 23rd–24th, 1895

A large hall – numerous guests, whom we were receiving. – Among them was Irma. I at once took her on one side, as though to answer her letter and to reproach her for not having accepted my 'solution' yet. I said to her: 'If you still get pains, it's really only your fault'. She replied: 'If you only knew what pains I've got now in my throat and stomach and abdomen – it's choking me.' – I was alarmed and looked at her. She looked pale and puffy. I thought to myself that after all I must be missing some organic trouble. I took her to the window and looked down her throat, and she showed signs of recalcitrance, like women with artificial dentures. I thought to myself that there was really no need for her to do that. – She then opened her mouth properly and on the right I found a big white patch; at another place I saw extensive whitish grey scabs upon some remarkable curly structures which were evidently modelled on the rubinal bones of the nose. – I at once called in Dr M., and he repeated the examination and confirmed it . . . Dr M. looked quite different from usual; he was very pale, he walked with a limp and his chin was clear-shaven . . . My friend Otto was now standing beside her as well, and my friend Leopold was percussing her through her bodice and saying: 'She has a dull area low down on the left'. He also indicated that a portion of the skin on the left shoulder was infiltrated. (I noticed this, just as he did, in spite of her dress.) . . . M. said: 'There's no doubt it's an infection, but no matter; dysentery will supervene and the toxin will be eliminated' . . . We were directly aware, too, of the origin of the infection. Not long before, when she was feeling unwell, my friend Otto had given her an injection of a preparation of propyl, propyls . . . propionic acid . . . trimethylamin (and I saw before me the formula for this printed in heavy type) . . . Injections of that sort ought not to be made so thoughtlessly . . . And probably the syringe had not been clean.[24]

The first point worth noting about this dream is what I might call the blandness of its substance (what Freud goes on to call its 'manifest content'). The dream, as described seems innocuous, even ordinary, with points of obvious correspondence with the immediate context that Freud has described. This may come as a shock to some people who have a picture in their minds of what Freudian dreams are all about. True Freud also sought to stress the central role of 'symbolism in dreams', and from that stress there has emerged a popular conception of classic dreams of boats and sticks and caves and cabinets (a theory which Freud admits he 'resurrected and [gave] proper recognition' to from an older source).[25] Freud's dream, as here reported, seems dull in comparison.

In his interpretation Freud attempted to correlate items in the dream (in the 'manifest content' that is) with events and people of his immediate circumstances. The method he adopted for this purpose was the technique which had proved so successful with his hysterical patients – free association. Freud allowed his mind to wander over the events and associations each specific part of the dream conjours up until he feels he has a coherent picture of the origins of each element and their relations We can reconstruct Freud's thinking behind this procedure and illustrate it with a simple diagram:

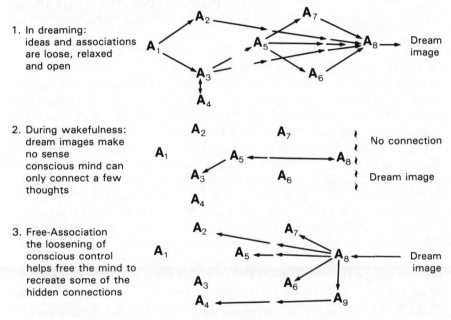

1. In dreaming: ideas and associations are loose, relaxed and open

2. During wakefulness: dream images make no sense conscious mind can only connect a few thoughts

3. Free-Association the loosening of conscious control helps free the mind to recreate some of the hidden connections

Figure 1. Adapted from Foulkes, 1978.[26]

By the use of free association each element was given a specific context such that the sum of those contexts constructed and illustrated an underlying theme (this Freud called the 'latent content' of the dream).

Most of the significant people of Freud's life are represented in the dream, and in the dream their portrayal gives an indication of Freud's true feelings towards those persons – Dr M. (Joseph Breuer) with whom Freud was having considerable disagreements about hysteria is shown up in a bad light with his inappropriate diagnosis. Otto (Oskar Rie) who had originally provoked the dream with his reproach is shown to be the cause of the patient's problems. Leopold (Ludwig Rosenstein, a Viennese colleague) is portrayed in the dream as a friend. In the interpretation Freud offers Fliess was also mentioned as the man who had put Freud on the track of sexuality (he had recently suggested to Freud that the substance trimethylamin was the chemical responsible for sexuality). Irma (whose real identity is not made explicit by Freud but about whom there are various clues) is clearly shown to be 'guilty' for her condition. Above all, in fact in many mutual contradictory ways, blame for Irma's condition is shifted in the dream – it was this that Freud saw as the underlying theme: 'the dream acquitted me of the responsibility for Irma's condition by showing that it was due to other factors – it produced a whole series of reasons. The dream represented a particular state of affairs as I should have wished it to be' (1900).[27] Freud then generalizes this understanding with the statement that 'its content was the fulfilment of a wish and its motive was a wish' (ibid.).

Here we see the genesis of the 'wish-fulfilment' theory of dreams – or at least of many dreams – as the *Project* stated clearly: 'the aim and sense of dreams (of normal ones, at all events) can be established with certainty. They are *wish-fulfilments* – that is, primary processes following upon experiences of satisfaction' (1895).[28] Freud's initial insight into the interpretation of dreams was that dreams were a means whereby we experience gratification of our deepest, unarticulated wishes. In *The Interpretation of Dreams*, which was written some years after both the *Project* and the 'specimen dream' was first recorded, and which relied heavily upon material churned up from Freud's self-analysis, Freud went further than this and stated that *every* dream (even unpleasant ones) represent wish-fulfilments. Once the latent content had been uncovered, this, Freud believed, could be shown in *every* case to be a wish-fulfilment. Even unpleasant dreams often represented '(disguised) fulfilment of a (suppressed or repressed) wish' (1900).[29] The extension of the hypothesis to *all* dreams was a novel departure from the views of his contemporaries, many of whom had already noted that *some* dreams were wish-fulfilment ones.

The Irma dream Freud maintained had a 'connection with the previous day . . . so obvious as to require no further comment' (1900).[30] The connection between the immediate circumstances and the 'manifest content' Freud called 'day residues'. However, such 'day residues' were insufficient alone to create the dream. Dreams were only formed when there was a further element present: an unconscious wish. A deep unconscious wish was required to provide the motive force for the dream. Freud used an analogy drawn from economics to explain this aspect of his theory:

A daytime thought may very well play the part of *entrepreneur* for a dream, but the *entrepreneur*, who, as people say, had the idea and the initiative to carry it out, can do nothing without capital; he needs a *capitalist* who can afford the outlay and the capitalist who provides the psychical outlay for the dream is invariably and indisputably, whatever may be the thought of the previous day, a *wish from the unconscious*. (1900)[31]

Such wishes 'from the unconscious' were not just any old wishes. Freud believed that all such wishes were infantile and sexual. He was quite specific in the book about this: 'the deeper one carries the analysis of a dream, the more often one comes upon the track of experiences in childhood which have played a part among the sources of that dream's latent content' (1900).[32] In a letter he wrote to Fliess in 1898 he explains this infantile component fully:

It seems to me as if the wish-fulfillment theory gives only the psychological and not the biological, or rather metapsychological explanation. (Incidentally I am going to ask you seriously whether I should use the term 'metapsychology' for my psychology which leads behind consciousness.) Biologically dream-life seems to me to proceed directly from the residue of the prehistoric stage of life (one or three years), which is the source of the unconscious and alone contains the aetiology of all the psychoneuroses; the stage which is normally obscured by an amnesia similar to hysteria . . . a recent wish leads to a dream only if it can be associated with material from that period, if that recent wish is derivative of a prehistoric wish or can get itself adopted by such a wish. I do not know yet to what extent I shall be able to stick to this extreme theory, or let it loose in the dream book (Freud 1898).[33]

Freud did indeed let loose his theory of the infantile origins of dreams in his dream book, and it became *the* most important element in his ideas about dreams, and in his 'new and deeper science of the mind'. The proper interpretation of dreams (as propounded by Freud) used the techniques of free association; was aware of all the psychological tricks that the unconscious plays (condensations, displacement, censorship, etc.), and, as he subsequently was to stress further (following the work of one of his pupils, Wilhelm Stekel), made use of the interpretation of symbols. When this was carried out dreams *always* revealed infantile sexual wishes seething in the unconscious.

This infantile material is usually hidden from consciousness and can only be revealed when, in sleep, the mind's defence mechanisms are lowered. Dreams thus became the most useful tool available to study the psychosexual development of individuals. They provided access to material that would otherwise have been unavailable to the normal 'conscious' memory: 'The fact that dreams have at their command memories which are inaccessible in waking life is so remarkable and of such theoretical importance that I should like to draw . . . more attention to it' (1900),[34] he called it the 'hypermnesic' function of dreams. Towards the end of the dream book he outlined that theoretical importance and, in consequence, their precise practical importance: 'the fact that dreams are hypermnesic and have access to material from childhood has become one of the corner-stones of our teaching. Our theory of dreams regards these wishes originating in infancy as the indispensable motive force for the formation of dreams' (1900).[35]

However, for all of that stress in the dream book Freud's interpretation of the 'Irma' dream seems to lack that level of interpretation. Indeed it is almost as if the wealth of contemporary meaning and significance (the host of 'day-residue' material) so overwhelms us in its plausibility that in consequence we do not ask the question, which Freud was prepared to ask everybody else, namely what are the sexual origins and the sexual wishes expressed by Freud in his 'Irma' dream? Freud does not tell us; he only gives us an 'incomplete' analysis of his dream. This omission can be found in the interpretations of other dreams that Freud reports. For instance, soon after the publication of *The Interpretation of Dreams*, a massive work by any standards, Freud decided to publish a short, popular introduction to his ideas. *On Dreams* was published in 1901; it contained a different specimen dream, and Freud's analysis of it concluded with this admission:

> In analyzing my specimen dream I was obliged to break off my report of the dream thoughts . . . because, as I confessed, there were some among them which I should prefer to conceal from strangers and which I could not communicate to other people without doing serious mischief in important directions. (1901)[36]

This lack of openness over his own dreams was noticed by a number of his contemporaries, some of which were able to confront him over the matter. The surrealist painter André Breton was given the following answer:

> I believe that if I have not analyzed my own dreams as extensively as those of others the cause is only rarely timidity with regard to the sexual. The fact is, much more frequently, that it would have required me regularly to discover the secret source of the whole series of dreams in my relations to my father, recently deceased. I maintain that I was in the right to set limits to the inevitable exhibition (as well as of an infantile tendency since surmounted). (c. 1931)[37]

It is an interesting confession, though it is not clear to which infantile tendency he was referring at the end. In locating the origin of his inability/unwillingness to reveal more of the 'secret sources' of his dreams in his relationship to his father Freud was once again being less than candid, for the dream book was written in part to explore and analyse these very relationships and their influence – father and son, mother and son etc. At other times, in other contexts, Freud was to suggest alternative reasons for his desire to 'conceal from strangers' elements in his interpretations.

Carl Jung, for instance, at the time when he was still a trusted pupil of Freud, was asked by him if he had any suggestions to make, and revisions to suggest, for a third edition of *The Interpretation of Dreams*. Jung responded with a number of specific points, most notably over Freud's reports of children's dreams, which, Jung noted, 'seem to me insufficiently interpreted; the interpretation uncovers only a superficial layer of the dream, but not the whole, which . . . is clearly a sexual problem whose instinctual energy alone explains the dynamism of the dreams'.[38] He then widens the scope of his comments to make the same observation about Freud's own dreams:

> But you may have reasons (didactic?) for not revealing the deeper layer of interpretation, just as in the preceding dreams (your own). I also miss a specific reference to the fact that the essential (personal) meaning of the dream (e.g. Irma . . .) has *not* been given. I insist on my students learning to understand dreams in terms of the dynamics of libido [unconscious sexual energy]; consequently we sorely miss the personally painful element in your own dreams. Perhaps this could be remedied by your supporting the Irma dream with a typical analysis of a patient's dream, where the ultimate real motives are *ruthlessly* disclosed, so that the reader will realize (right from the start) that the dream does not disintegrate into a series of individual determinants, but is a structure built around a central motif of an exceedingly painful nature . . . Naturally one cannot strip oneself naked, but perhaps a model would serve the purpose.[39]

This was indeed, as Jung confessed, a 'bold criticism' for it touched upon material that was most sensitive.

Freud's reply to this bold criticism was not as Jung had feared 'anger' but seeming gratitude and thanks – 'Many thanks for your remarks about *The Interpretation of Dreams*' Freud replied 'in principle I shall take account of them *all*, but everything you say cannot be reflected in changes in the third edition' (1911).[40] Freud conceded Jung's points about the children's dreams but then defended his original text on the grounds that his intention in some of his interpretations was 'expository or pedagogic'. He then referred to the specific question of his own dreams:

> You have very acutely noticed that my incomplete elucidation of my own dreams leaves a gap in the overall explanation of dreams, but here again you have put your finger on the motivation – which was unavoidable. I

simply cannot expose any more of my nakedness to the reader. Of each dream, consequently, I explain only as much as is needed to bring out a specific point; one throws light on dissembling, the second on the infantile material, the third on wishfulfilment. In none do I bring out all the elements that can be expected of a dream, because they are my personal dreams. As for the *corpora vilia* ['vile bodies' – an obscure biblical allusion] in whose dreams we may *ruthlessly* disclose everything, these can only be neurotics, that is patients; and it was not possible to communicate their dreams, because I could not presuppose the secrets of neurosis, which were precisely what the interpretation of dreams was intended to disclose. (1911)[41]

There are two things worth noting in particular about this reply: first Freud admitted that he did *not* reveal the secrets of his dreams, even though he may have purported to; he revealed just what material was necessary to make his (didactic) point. Secondly he admitted another motivation for writing about the interpretation of dreams: that was to reveal the secret of neurosis. The book which purported to be about the interpretation of dreams, was thus by his own admission coloured by less obvious motivations.

Whatever his motivations – to reveal the secret of neurosis, to create a new science of the mind – since these personal dreams are offered as evidence in support of his theories we can only be disappointed that Freud did not expose more of 'his nakedness' in his interpretations, for only then would it be possible to make a fair evaluation of the doctrine. In providing just such material as he deemed would make his point the evidential value of these dreams was diminished. Freud, strangely, regarded the absence of these personal details as a virtue: 'the book proves the principles of dream interpretation by its own nature, so to speak, through its own deficiencies' (1911),[42] i.e. on that most Freudian principle of repression that which Freud omits is as important as that which he includes – the real key to the book lies elsewhere. Having made that point Freud confided to Jung that he intended to 'remedy this mischief in another way'. Just what Freud's remedy was is shown in the same paragraph. He wrote that *The Interpretation of Dreams* 'will not be re-issued, but will be replaced by a new and *impersonal* one',[43] i.e. Freud intended (although he never carried it out – *The Interpretation of Dreams* ran to eight editions in German in Freud's lifetime) to remove *all* of 'his nakedness' from the text. His reasons became clearer in a subsequent letter where he reports to Jung that he has received back from the publishers the draft of his new preface to *The Interpretation of Dreams:* 'It will have to be changed' Freud noted 'it might make an unfavourable impression. And I must admit that the rabble who read these things don't deserve a shred of honesty' (1911).[44]

Acting on the principle that Freud himself recommended, i.e. that we try to discover what he left out/repressed from his interpretations, we must seek other sources of information about the background to his dreams and their meaning. The most obvious source of such information must be the letters to Fliess, for during the course of his self-analysis, and during the whole time he was writing *The Interpretation of Dreams* Freud was in constant communication with him. Not only did they discuss their ideas fully at their regular 'congresses', but they also wrote to each other extensively about their new ideas, and new twists and turns in their thinking. Indeed, having decided to formalize his ideas on dreams in a book early in 1898, Freud used Fliess as his audience, critic and even censor. Everything he wrote he sent off to Fliess for examination. He hung on Fliess' responses to his text. He called him his 'first reader and supreme arbiter'.[45] We can get some ideas of Fliess' function at this time from one of Freud's letters – the full depth of their mutual appreciation can also be seen here as the ground upon which Freud felt able to send Fliess material, and to accept his criticism:

I am completely absorbed in the dreams, I am writing eight to ten pages a day, and have just got over the worst in the psychological chapter – under great torment. I dare not think how it has turned out. You must tell me whether it will do, but in the galley-proof stage, because reading manuscript is too great an imposition, and in the galley-proof stage everything can still be altered. I ended by putting more into it than I intended – one always goes deeper and deeper as one goes on – but I am afraid it is rubbish. And the things I shall be told about it! When the storm breaks I shall fly to your room. You will find something to praise in it anyway, because you are as prejudiced in my favour as others are against me.

I have received sixty more galleys, which I am sending you by the same post. I am almost ashamed of exploiting you in this way, because in biology you can discriminate for yourself and do not need any *quid pro quo* from me, you deal in light, not darkness, with the sun and not the unconscious. But please do not tackle the whole thing at once, but send me the galleys on which you find something to censor when you have a number ready; then I shall get your corrections before sending off my own; they can all go in together. There are a lot of new things in it which I can mark for you. I have avoided sex, but 'dirt' is unavoidable, and craves your indulgence. (1899)[46]

It is interesting that Freud wrote this letter, which is obviously so appreciative of Fliess, after Fliess had insisted Freud make a radical revision to his text. The reasons Fliess thought that Freud needed to change his work may well be most revealing to us, in the light of our aim to recover the hidden aspects of Freud's own dreams.

Way back in February 1898, Freud had written to Fliess with the news that: '[I] have found my interest in life. I am deep in the dream book, writing it fluently and smiling at all the matter for "head-shaking" it contains in the way of indiscretions and audacities' (1898).[47] As the book stands now, chapter 1 is not the chapter which was written first. Freud added an introductory chapter, on 'the scientific literature dealing with the problems of dreams', much later – indeed he was worried lest this initial 'heavy' material deter potential readers from pressing on to the crucial part of the text – to Fliess he confessed 'most readers will stick in this thicket and never get through to see the Sleeping Beauty within' (1899).[48] As far as we can tell Freud sent his interpretation of the 'Irma dream' to Fliess ('the thorough analysis') together with an interpretation of another dream which Freud later called 'the completely analysed example dream'.[49] This second dream evidently contained too many 'indiscretions and audacities', such that Fliess felt obliged to urge Freud to leave it out of the text. Freud's response to this suggestion was not published in the original edition of his letters to Fliess; the editors did not think it was of sufficient importance in understanding Freud's work. Fortunately, however, his response has become available through the courage of his physician, Max Schur, who, in 1966, published some of the unpublished material in the letters. Freud replied to Fliess on 9 June 1898:

> I also thank you cordially for your criticism. I am aware of the fact that you have undertaken a very thankless task. I am reasonable enough to recognize that I need your critical help, because in this instance I myself have lost the feeling of shame required of an author. So this dream is condemned. However, now that the sentence has been passed, I would like to shed a tear for it and confess that I regret it and that I cannot hope to find a better one as a substitute. You must know that a beautiful dream and no indiscretion do not go together. At least write me to which topic you took exception, and where you feared an attack by a malicious critic. Was it my anxiety, or Martha, or the *Dalles* [A Jewish word for poverty, frequently used colloquially by Viennese Jews], or my being without a fatherland? [Please let me know] so I can omit the topic you designate in a substitute dream, because I can have dreams like that to order . . . (1898)[50]

Freud did eventually leave out the dream, and its complete interpretation from his dream book, so we cannot say with certainty what it was about. Freud's last sentence, presumably indicates that the topic of the dream was fairly fundamental for Freud at that time. If it were not it would make a mockery of his whole thesis – *The Interpretation of Dreams* is all about how our dream life is not determined by our conscious will but rather a reflection of our unconscious life. This dream may well have been about some fundamental aspect of Freud's sexuality. On 20 June 1898, Schur shows us that Freud once again returned to the topic of the forbidden dream in his letters:

> My mourning for the lost dream is not yet over. As if in spite I recently had a substitute dream in which a house constructed of building blocks collapsed (we had built a *staatliches* house); this dream, therefore, because of that reference, cannot be used either. (1898)[51]

Freud's reference to a *staatliches* house, which is probably one of his associations, is a pun on a word which means both stately or grand and appertaining to politics. Schur feels sure that this reference, and the one earlier to Freud 'being without a Fatherland' indicate that the subject of the dream must have been something manifestly 'political'. He does also countenance the possibility that the 'collapsed house' is a reference to Freud's relationship to Fliess which even by this time was showing signs of strain, for Freud was beginning to desire a greater degree of independence from Fliess. On the other hand, a more plausible explanation of the source of the 'indiscretion' in the dream may have something specifically to do with his wife, and with his own sexuality. Since the dream must have been concerned with really basic desires (Freud could dream 'like that to order'), and since it also may have contained an offence against Martha, it is reasonable to suggest that the forbidden 'completely analysed' dream touched upon matters to do with this area. It is worth noting that Freud explicitly implicates Fliess in this area: '*we* had built a . . . house'. Whatever it was about Freud removed it from the text and only made mention of it once more to Fliess in August 1899 when he wrote: 'the gap made by the big dream which you took out is to be filled by a small collection of dreams (innocent and absurd dreams, calculations and speeches in dreams, affects in dreams). Real revision will only be required for the last, psychological chapter . . .' (1899).[52]

Our conclusions about the content of the big dream and its interpretation can only be tentative at present for we do not have all the relevant background information. We can gain more evidence to help us if we turn to the 'Irma dream' once more and consider some of the background to that. *The Interpretation of Dreams* was published in 1900. Since then many people have tried to understand the specimen dream more fully for there are aspects of it that do not hang together. When Freud's correspondence with Fliess was first published in 1950 it was hoped that there would be some hint or clue to the dream which had hitherto been hidden. Strangely, no reference to the dream, which Freud clearly saw as vital to his work was found other than the brief note made by Freud in 1900 about the possibility of having a plaque erected at Bellevue. This was confusing to those who were trying to unravel the mystery of the man and his work, for it was as if *the* most important insight Freud had during this period left him so unmoved that he did not report any of it to his closest friend. Once again though, the situation was clarified when Max Schur published more portions of the unpublished letters; it became clear that Freud had talked more fully with Fliess about material apertaining to the 'Irma dream' but that his protectors had sought to suppress this material. Schur has published a series of Freud's letters which deal with an incident which has marked similarities to the 'Irma dream'. Indeed it might be said that the Irma dream uses the dramatic context of this real incident to express Freud's hidden feelings.

Early in 1895 Freud had begun to treat a woman patient called Emma Eckstein, for hysteria. At the time Freud fully accepted the views of his friend Fliess that some of the symptoms could be related to a problem in the nasal passages. Fliess believed in the 'nasal origin' of many disorders, particularly sexual disorders, and attempted remedies using cocaine (administered to the nasal mucous membranes) and surgery (of the nose). Accordingly, Freud referred Emma to Fliess who travelled to Vienna and performed an operation on her nose. Emma did not get better, in fact she became worse such that on 4 March 1895 Freud felt obliged to write to Fliess (by now returned to Berlin) for his 'authoritative advice' on the fact that she was in severe pain, had a 'purulent secretion' coming from her nose, had a dreadful sickeningly foetid smell coming from her wound, and had haemorrhaged badly.[53] Four days later Freud wrote again with 'a report which will probably upset you as much as me'. He then unravelled the tale of how he had been called out early in the morning to attend Emma who was bleeding profusely and in great pain. Freud called another physician to attend Emma with him. When they got to Emma Freud reported the following incident:

There was moderate bleeding from the nose and mouth; the foetid odour was very bad. R. [the helping physician] cleaned the area surrounding the opening, removed some blood clots which were sticking to the surface, and suddenly pulled at something, like a thread. He kept right on pulling, and before either of us had time to think, at least half a meter of gauze had been removed from the cavity. The next moment came a flood of blood. The patient turned white, her eyes bulged, and her pulse was no longer palpable. However, immediately after this he packed the cavity with fresh iodoform gauze, and the haemorrhage stopped. It had lasted about half a minute, but this was enough to make the poor creature, who by then we had lying quite flat, unrecognizable. (1895)[54]

Fliess had, it seems, bungled the operation and had left half a metre of gauze in the wound which had turned putrid and was severely affecting the patient. This surgical bodge by Fliess was a dramatic and traumatic challenge to Freud who had hitherto regarded Fliess as little short of a genius. Freud's whole perception of his friend and mentor faced a serious crisis. However, just like in the Irma dream, where his unconscious attempted to deflect blame for the condition of his patient away from himself, Freud managed to parry the blow to his image of Fliess and deflect blame away from him. Even in the letter reporting the discovery of the gauze Freud subtly shifts the blame from Fliess to the gauze by suggesting that 'it' tearing away was the cause of the problem.

Freud, was, however, very shocked by the whole incident and lamented over the fact that there was something seriously wrong with her, and that she was not just (hysterically) putting-on the symptoms – to Fliess he wrote: 'so we had done her an injustice. She had not been abnormal at all'.[55] The whole incident, potentially, could have undermined all his theories – which were based on the premise that psychological problems were causing the physical symptoms. It could also have undermined his professional standing – to have a patient die in your care as a result of a procedure that you had 'inflicted' on her would have had dire consequences (Freud actually described his horror at having 'inflicted violence' on the poor girl). Freud concluded his letter to Fliess with this assurance:

> Of course no-one blames you in any way, nor do I know why they should. And I only hope that you will come quickly as I did to feel only pity. Rest assured that I felt no need to restore my trust in you. I only want to add that I hesitated for a day to tell you about it, and that then I began to be ashamed, and here is the letter. (1895)[56]

Throughout March and April 1895 Freud continued to send reports of Emma's progress to Fliess. In each successive letter Freud managed to exculpate Fliess further from any blame for the incident. On 28 March, after reporting that Emma was doing 'tolerably well' Freud concluded his letter with the report that 'she is a nice, decent girl who does not blame either of us in this affair, and who speaks of you with high esteem' (1895).[57] Unfortunately, by 11 April, Emma had suffered a relapse with further massive haemorrhaging – so much so that one of the other attending physicians suggested that they had to perform further major surgery on one of Emma's main arteries. In his letter to Fliess, Freud confessed 'I'm really quite shaken that such a misfortune can have arisen from this operation, which was depicted [by you!] as harmless' (1895).[58]

Fliess must have been offended by some of the remarks Freud reported as having been made by the attending doctors for he evidently asked Freud for some sort of 'testimonial' from the most senior surgeon present (G). On 20 April Freud replied:

> Of course I immediately informed R. of your suggestions concerning Emma. Naturally things look different from close up . . . The writer of this is still very miserable, but is also quite offended that you should deem it necessary to have a testimonial from G for your rehabilitation. Even if G should have the same opinion of your skill as [the other physician who had cast aspersions on it], for me you remain the healer, the prototype of a man into whose hands one confidently entrusts one's life and that of one's family. I wanted to tell you of my misery, perhaps ask you for some advice about Emma, but not reproach you for anything. This would have been stupid, unjustified, in clear contradiction to my feelings . . . (1895)[59]

So deep were the feelings of trust that Freud had for Fliess that even in the face of a dreadful accident that could have caused the death of one of his patients, Freud could still view Fliess as a wonderful healer into whose hands he could trust anyone and anything. Freud's love for Fliess was of paramount importance to him at this time and it coloured his perceptions of everything else. As time went on this became even clearer such that by April 1896, approximately a year after this last letter, Freud wrote to Fliess explaining that he had 'surmised' a 'surprising explanation of Emma's haemorrhages, which will give you great satisfaction' (1896).[60] In his next letter to Fliess he revealed that 'with regard to Emma, I shall be able to prove to you that you were right; her haemorrhages were hysterical, brought on by *longing* probably at the "sexual period" [the menstrual time]' (1896).[61] Emma had now become totally to blame for her bleeding, Fliess could in no way be held responsible for her own hysterical haemorrhaging. Emma, not Fliess, was the guilty one as Freud categorically stated in yet another letter about the subject: 'as far as the blood is concerned, you are altogether innocent' he reported to Fliess.[62] Indeed, so confident was Freud in 'the healer' that within a year of the Emma incident he himself had allowed Fliess to perform a similar piece of nasal surgery on his own nose! Emma herself must have made a good recovery, and must have somehow managed to retain some semblance of confidence in Freud and Fliess, because in December 1897 Freud reported to Fliess that she had her own psycho-analytic patients. Emma Eckstein had become the very first practising psychoanalyst (after Freud himself). Even this reference to Emma was omitted from the published version of the letters.[63]

The Emma Eckstein incident happened in February, March and April of 1895; it preoccupied and depressed him throughout this period. Her condition had become stabilized for about a month by the time that Freud left for his summer holiday at Bellevue. Two months after it had become stable Freud had the 'dream of Irma's injection' the ostensible, central theme of which was concern about a patient's welfare (Irma's), and the question of whose responsibility it was. It stretches our credulity to believe that this incident did *not* spring to mind when Freud was presenting his associations. It is true that all of the material for the dream book was sent to Fliess for his perusal and censorship and thus Freud might well have felt it inappropriate to recount any of these associations. However, given that Freud knew that Fliess would probably be able to make the connection himself, we are forced once again to be wary of even the most thoroughly analysed material in the book for yet again it is used as evidence for his theories. If, in order to understand the 'Irma dream' we need to be aware of the 'Emma incident' (if only as, in Schur's words, 'additional day-residues') then since Freud could not make reference to it out of deference to Fliess, the specimen dream loses much of its value as an example to be analysed. Indeed the omission of *any* of this material from those associations leads us to ask serious questions about Freud's self-professed honesty. Ronald Clark, in his recent biography of Freud talks of having 'deliberately created a gap [in his interpretation] of Grand Canyon proportions'.[64] The publication, by Max Schur, of the previously censored portions of Freud's correspondence with Fliess has helped us to see the magnitude of Freud's public omissions, it also points to one area of motivation in Freud's life that he was less than candid about: namely his deep affection for, and utter reliance upon, Fliess. It does not, however, provide the complete picture necessary to understand Freud and his dreams, for there is still more material to be unearthed.

Despite the obvious similarities between the two, it is not possible simply to equate the two people Emma and Irma – and thus relate the dream to the real-life trauma. The two 'events' do share many similarities but a number of the associations Freud does present do not tally with Emma. Irma, while taking part in a dream-drama just like the real drama Freud had witnessed with Emma, does not stand for Emma but rather stands for someone else. Actually, in the dream-world Freud maintained that figures could represent several people – Freud called this process condensation – the dreamer takes elements and features of a number of people and allows them to be expressed in just one figure (see Fig. 1 where many associations converge on *one* figure that produces the image). In fact, later in his book Freud used the Irma dream to illustrate what he meant by condensation – he showed that 'Irma' stood for a number of women about whom he had some particular feeling:

None of these figures whom I lighted upon by following up 'Irma' appeared in the dream in bodily shape. They were concealed behind the dream figure of 'Irma', which was thus turned into a collective image with, it must be admitted, a number of contradictory characteristics. Irma became the representative of all these other figures which had been sacrificed to the work of condensation, since I passed over to *her*, point by point, everything that reminded me of *them*. (1900)[65]

That said, it is possible to identify one of Freud's patients as the figure in the dream, although she represents a number of other women about whom Freud was concerned. Anna Hammerschlag Lichtheim (who was born in 1861 and who died in 1938) was a widow in 1895 (Emma Eckstein never married). She was also the daughter of one of Freud's oldest 'fatherly' friends, Samuel Hammerschlag, and was a 'close friend of Freud's wife (Emma Eckstein was not a friend of the family at that time). Anna Lichtheim was also related by marriage to Josef Breuer with whom Freud was having considerable problems at the time. Further evidence about the identity of 'Irma' being 'Anna' is given by the fact that Freud named his youngest child, Anna, after her – it was this child that Martha was carrying at the time – the gestation of Anna Freud was occurring at the time when Freud had his specimen dream. Indeed, the fact that Martha was pregnant (again!) was one of the major precipitating causes of the dream – it was the backdrop to the dream drama.

We learn more of this aspect of the dream from the pen of Freud himself, admittedly only as revealed to his closest most trusted pupil, the German psychoanalyst, Karl Abraham. Abraham, like Breton and Jung, had perceived the shallowness of Freud's interpretation of this dream and had attempted to quiz Freud on it in one of his letters. He wrote:

I should like to know whether the incomplete interpretation of the first dream in *The Interpretation of Dreams* is intentional (Irma's Injection). I find that trimethylamine leads to the most important part, to sexual allusions which became more distinct in the last lines. After all everything points to the suspicion of syphilitic infection in the patient; the spot in her mouth is the plaque representing the infection, the injection of trimethylamine which had been carelessly given, the dirty syringe (??) Is not this the organic illness for whose continued existence you cannot be made responsible, because syphilis or a nervous disease originating from it cannot be influenced by psychological treatment?[66]

In the absence of any knowledge of the Emma incident this is reasonable supposition on Abraham's part – not least because Freud himself beguilingly uses an unusual word for syringe. The word he actually uses in the dream report is *Spritze* which means a 'squirter': Irma's problems are caused by a 'dirty squirter'. Freud replied to Abraham's suggestions by denying that the problem concerned syphilis – the drama, after all, Freud knew was a recapitulation of the Emma incident. He did not reveal just what the organic problem was though (you will recall from chapter 2, that in 1908 he had not yet 'overcome' his homosexual feelings for Fliess, even though they were estranged). He then went on to reveal the true motivation for the dream:

> Sexual megalomania is hidden behind it, the three women, Mathilde [Breuer], Sophie [Paneth] and Anna [Lichtheim], are my daughter's three godmothers, and I have them all! There would be one simple therapy for widowhood, of course. All sorts of intimate things, naturally. (1908)[67]

This quite extraordinary confession of Freud gives us a clue to the real meaning of the 'Irma dream' but it needs a little further explanation. First, Freud had his Irma dream when his wife, Martha, was 4½ months pregnant; it is not unreasonable to assume that in the light of this he was both sexually frustrated and feeling guilty over inflicting her with one of his solutions (another pregnancy and child). Throughout his associations to the dream Martha is portrayed as a rather pathetic, unwilling victim of his potency. At the same time his former friend and reluctant collaborator, Joseph Breuer, was objecting to Freud's preoccupation with sex in his theoretical work. The 'Irma dream' is a sort of revenge on Breuer, for all the women mentioned by Freud in connection with his sexual megalomania are Breuer's women – Freud has, or wants to, inflict his own sexual solution on them. Thirdly, Freud's current theory of anxiety neurosis was that sexual toxins (notably trimethylamine) built up in the body (like cocaine) to poison the individual – sexual satisfaction released that toxin and regulated its influence as, he believed, his new psychoanalytic therapy did. The very structure of trimethylamine (the formula of which was printed in heavy type in the dream) may indeed have been the real clue to Freud as to the meaning of the dream – the people mentioned in the dream group in threes in such a way as to be strikingly reminiscent of the formula of trimethylamine (so much so that two French psychoanalysts discerned the underlying themes of the dream without reference to the confession to Abraham).[68] Recalcitrant patients were then refusing to allow Freud to regulate their sexual energy and therefore they needed to have a 'solution' forced upon them.[69] Psychoanalysis was for Freud a means whereby he could vicariously enjoy sexual gratification with women.

The dream of Irma's Injection was not then, as Freud would have us believe the simple, chance, discovery of the fundamental truth that all dreams are wish-fulfilments. Rather, the specimen dream is a complex drama in which Freud's deep sexual feelings – both his homosexual feelings and his desires for sexual megalomania – seethe below the surface and get deliberately hidden by Freud in order to prove his theories. Indeed, in 1897, he wrote to Fliess identifying Fliess and himself as equivalent to the medieval torturers who, for sexual pleasure, forced innocent victims to reveal their sexual secrets and imposed their own solutions onto them. The vision of Freud as the man of science primed and ready to stumble over some hitherto unobserved facts about dreams which would enable him to erect a noble theory of dreams and their interpretation, could not be further from the truth. He was a man obsessed with the dark aspects of his own sexual being who sought to justify and rationalize them by careful manipulation of evidence and by the deliberate presentation of half-truths. He was racked by the complexity of his own sexuality – psychoanalysis helped him achieve a measure of satisfaction without receiving the opprobrium which would be attached to him had he indulged himself in reality.

In presenting his dream theory Freud claimed that the evidence he presented proved the theory true and thus that his interpretations were definitive. Secondly, he claimed that having provided an account of dreams two other things were established: the validity of his earlier theories on the neuroses, and the mandate for establishing a new psychoanalytic theory of normal psychology. Doubt cast on the dream theory must cast doubt on these two conclusions. At the beginning of this section I suggest that we can distinguish between three levels of explanation in Freud's theory of dreams: 'the face level', the background level, and the integrative level. On the face level Freud suggests three things: that all dreams are *wish-fulfilments*; that they are specifically fulfilments of *sexual* wishes; that they are fulfilments of *infantile* sexual wishes. The corollaries of this analysis of dreams are that infantile sexuality exists and that it has a determining effect on people's behaviour (in this case dreams but as time goes on, slips, jokes, art, literature, etc.). When the background level is considered it becomes clear, if the analysis of the dream of Irma's injection is typical, that Freud only presents evidence to support the first contention. When all of the background material is collected it does provide some sort of evidence for the second contention but in a slightly obscure way. The background information on the 'dream of Irma's injection' merely demonstrates that Freud's contemporary sexual problems could become manifest in his dream life; it provides no information about the infantile component. Freud asserts 'every dream [is] linked in its manifest content with recent experience and in its latent content with the most ancient experiences' (1900); in other words the infantile material is an 'essential precondition of dreaming' (ibid.).[70] Analysis of the dream of Irma's injection provides no support for this thesis, indeed all of the background evidence points to the location of the conflicts of the latent content in the contemporary circumstances. Such a conclusion has radical implications for the whole of the psychoanalytic edifice Freud constructed after *The Interpretation of Dreams*.

Freud opened his dream book with the observation that 'in spite of many thousands of years of effort, the scientific understanding of dreams has made very little advance' (1900).[71] Ironically, for all of his stress on the *scientific* aspects of his theories Freud did not entitle his great thesis the *explanation* of dreams, or the *cause* of dreams. He gave his book the title *Die Traumdeutung*, which in English translates as *The Interpretation of Dreams* (see plate 7). The German word, however, has far more pejorative connotations than its simple English equivalent; it has associations with fair-ground-type divinations of dreams. In one sense Freud's remark still stands: the *scientific* understanding of dreams still has a very long way to go.

Most of the recent work in this field (apart from that conducted by analytically committed researchers who manage to find Freudian or Jungian or neo-Freudian motives and themes in any dreams) concentrates on observations about sleep first established 30 years ago. It was discovered then that sleep can be divided up into two qualitatively different states – in all mammals, mankind included, there are alternating periods of D sleep (also called paradoxical sleep) and S sleep (also called orthodox sleep). These two states of sleep have a number of different physiological correlates; D sleep, the most interesting from our point of view, is usually known by its most prominent feature – the eyes move very quickly behind the eyelids (Rapid Eye Movement) it is thus known as REM sleep – this is the period when dreaming occurs. In all, each night, we have about 1 to 2 hours of REM sleep during which time we dream; we rarely recall any of these dreams unless we are specifically woken in or just after a period of REM sleep. Newborn babies have as much as 8 hours REM sleep per day, and even babies in the womb have substantial periods of REM sleep. All of these biological findings point towards the fact that REM sleep (and its associated dreaming) have a far more important biological function rather than a strictly psychological function. The few dreams that are remembered are perhaps less important than the many which are not – dreaming appears to be part of a mechanism whereby the brain is cleared of unwanted traces that would clutter the neuronal system if allowed to accumulate.[72] Psychoanalytic dream theory – the royal road to knowledge of the unconscious mind – needs revision to take account of the fact that remembered dreams are but a tiny fraction of the whole biological phenomenon of REM sleep – they may only be a faint footpath to knowledge.

'WHOOPS – YOUR SLIP IS SHOWING!'

I cannot avoid confessing a certain disappointment. In [your] book you honour me highly, mention my name together with the greatest names of our people [the Jews] (which far transcends my ambition), and so on; in the chapter of the doctrine of Lapses you express disbelief concerning just that part of psycho-analysis that has most readily found general recognition. How then are you likely to judge our other less attractive discoveries? My impression is that if your objections to the conception of lapses are justified I have very little claim to be named besides Bergson and Einstein among the intellectual sovereigns . . . (Freud, 1930, in a letter to an author who had sent him a book on The Jewish Influence on Culture).[73]

Next to his ideas on dreams the second most commonly held idea which is associated with the name of Freud is that of the Freudian slip. The phrase 'a Freudian slip', has become a widely accepted, if not frequently abused, idiom. When people have some hidden worry on their minds they often allow that to show through some apparently meaningless, apparently random mistake. Freud himself has furnished us with two of his own classic examples of this sort of slip (Freud's English translator's have found great difficulty in translating the German word Freud used for these occurrences, Freud used a word that meant literally a 'faulty function' or 'faulty act'. Freud's translator, James Strachey, introduced a new word 'parapraxis' to cover Freud's generic term).[74] The first example is a slip of the tongue produced by the President of the Lower House of the Austrian Parliament during the opening ceremony. The President was apparently concerned that the forthcoming session of the assembly would be difficult for him, he feared that it was to be a sitting 'from which little good was to be expected'. He opened the session with the words: 'Gentlemen: I take notice that a full quorum of members is present and herewith declare the sitting *closed!*' His slip showed that 'the President secretly *wished* he was already in a position to close the sitting' (1901).[75] The second example, again a slip of the tongue which Freud cites, concerns an eminent, Viennese, Professor of Anatomy who was lecturing on the subject of female anatomy. He announced to his students: 'In the case of the female genitals, in spite of many *Versuchungen* [temptations] – I beg your pardon, *Versuche* [experiments] . . .'.[76] Parapraxes were not limited to slips of the tongue, however. Freud included in this term, bungled actions, the forgetting and substituting of words and names, slips of the pen and misreadings.

So important did Freud deem these apparently casual accidents, that in 1901 he wrote a whole book on the subject *The Psychopathology of Everyday Life*. Indeed, throughout his life, when he was called upon to

Plate 6. Freud with Wilhelm Fliess, August 1890

expound and defend his views, or to outline the main principles of
psychoanalysis he frequently gave his theory of parapraxes a didactic
prominence even over the subject of dreams – he did this, in 1915 for
instance, in his *Introductory Lectures on Psychoanalysis* and, in 1923,
in an encyclopaedia article. The quotation, taken from one of his letters,
at the beginning of this section, shows that even towards the end of his
life he regarded parapraxes as the most easily understood aspect of, and
entry to, psychoanalysis. *The Psychopathology of Everyday Life* was one
of his most successful and popular books going through many editions,
and being translated into many languages, within Freud's lifetime. One
of Freud's pupils, A. A. Brill, the man responsible for introducing the

main body of Freud's works in translation, in English, to the USA has described the impact of these particular Freudian views on himself and his contemporaries:

> Those were the pioneer days of Freud [and his theories] among psychiatrists, and we observed and studied and noted whatever was done or said about us with unfailing patience and untiring interest and zeal. We made no scruples, for instance, of asking a man at table why he did not use his spoon in the proper way, or why he did such and such a thing in such and such a manner. It was impossible for one to show any degree of hesitation or make some abrupt pause in speaking without being at once called to account. We had to keep ourselves well in hand, ever ready and alert, for there was no telling when and where there would be a new attack. We had to explain why we whistled or hummed some particular tune or why we made some slip in talking or some mistake in writing. But we were glad to do this if, for no other reason, than to learn to face the truth.[77]

Freud's interest in parapraxes has arisen as a result of a number of influences converging on him in the middle of 1898. First, as he confided in *The Psychopathology of Everyday Life*, once again his patients had provided some of the initial instances which had first drawn his attention to the subject. He explained:

> I am very often faced with the task of discovering from the patient's apparently casual utterances and associations, a thought-content which is at pains to remain concealed but which cannot nevertheless avoid unintentionally betraying its existence in a whole variety of ways. Slips of the tongue often perform a most valuable service here . . .(1901)[78]

Secondly, he derived a considerable insight into the phenomena of parapraxes, as he had done with his studies of dreams, as a result of exploring his own mind – he was, after all, his own chief patient. In August 1898 he wrote to Fliess about a discovery he had made:

> I have at last understood a little thing that I have long suspected. You know how you can forget a name and substitute part of another for it, to which you could swear, though it invariably turns out to be wrong. That happened to me not long ago over the name of [a] poet . . . I felt it must be something ending in *an* – Lindan, Feldan, or the like. Actually of course, the poet's name was Julius Mosen; the 'Julius' had not slipped my memory. I was able to prove (i) that I had repressed the name Mosen because of certain associations; (ii) that material from my infancy played a part in the repression; and (iii) that the substitute names that occurred to me arose, just like a symptom, from both groups of material. The analysis resolved

the thing completely; unfortunately, I cannot make it public any more than my big dream . . . (1898)[79]

This piece of self-observation, which, like the 'big dream', we do not know much more about (except, perhaps the supposition that it may have been an allusion to his patient Fanny Moser), is the first example of such a parapraxis that Freud described anywhere in his work. It may have remained the only one had he not simultaneously been reading a particular work on psychology by a German psychologist, Theodor Lipps. Lipps was the first psychologist Freud had attempted to read in preparation for writing the historical introduction to his dream book. To Fliess, in the same letter which contains the Julius Mosen parapraxis, Freud wrote: 'I have set myself the task of making a bridge between my germinating metapsychology and what is in the books, and have therefore plunged into the study of Lipps, whom I suspect of being the best mind among present-day philosophical writers. So far he lends himself very well to comprehension and translation into my terms' (1898).[80]

Five days later Freud again wrote to Fliess, this time eulogizing over Lipps' work even more he wrote:

In Lipps I have rediscovered my own principles quite clearly stated – perhaps rather more so than suited me. 'The seeker often finds more than he seeks' . . . In details the correspondence is close too; perhaps the divergence on which I shall be able to base my own contribution will come later. (1898)[81]

In Freud's copy of one of Lipps' works (which has been preserved at the Freud Library) we find the following passage marked by Freud:

[We believe] not only in the existence of unconscious mental processes side-by-side with the conscious ones. We further believe that unconscious processes lie at the bottom of all conscious ones and accompany them. As we have already said, the conscious, when fortune favours, arises from the unconscious and then sinks back into it again.[82]

Freud himself cited Lipps as the person to whom he owed his 'courage and ability' to tackle the problems of humour and jokes in his book of 1905 *Jokes and Their Relation to the Unconscious* (see the next section). Clearly, Lipps' firm statements of the unconscious origins of all conscious thought, resonated in Freud: 'he says in his jargon just what I worked out about consciousness, quality, etc.' Freud reported a little later to Fliess.[83]

Parapraxes continued to fascinate him, so much so that in the very next month Freud was reporting yet another example to Fliess about his forgetting a name. The incident happened to Freud himself whilst he was on holiday in Bosnia (an area of Yugoslavia now called Dalmatia). Freud was travelling alone in a railway carriage when he began making conversation with a lawyer from Berlin. They were discussing some of the customs of the Turks who lived in the region. Two facets of Turkish psychology were foremost in Freud's mind: their resignation in the face of death and their horror at the thought of the cessation of sexual activity. Having engaged himself in conversation 'about death and sexuality' Freud's mind moved on to 'the magnificent frescos of the 'Four Last Things' in Orvieto cathedral', those which he described to Fliess as 'the finest I have seen' (indeed the very frescos that had had such an important influence upon Freud the summer before). Freud could not remember the name of the artist who had painted the frescos, Signorelli, but could only think of Botticelli or Boltraffio whom he knew 'with . . . certainty that they were wrong'. Freud interpreted his parapraxis as being caused by repression – specifically related to the theme of 'death and sexuality'. He ended his report with a plaintive cry 'how can I make this seem credible to anyone?' (1898).[84] Within a week, however, he had felt so confident in this latest example that he had written it up and sent it off for publication in a German journal *Monatsschrift für Psychiatrie und Neurologie*. Indeed, so pleased was he with it as an example that it was chosen as the basis for his first chapter in the *Psychopathology of Everyday Life*. Freud examined the parapraxis quite extensively, explaining why he had substituted *Bo* and *traffio* in place of the real name; what is most interesting, however, is the fact that he did *not* posit any connection between the first part of the real name and his own, Sig – as with his dreams we are left to wonder whether that which he has left out of his analysis was as important as that which he included.[85]

Freud was not able to develop his ideas of parapraxes until after his dream book had been completed. In fact, he left the drafting of his book on parapraxes until he had completed a further short book on dreams – disappointed at the public response to his huge tome on dreams he set about writing a simple introduction to the topic. In October 1900 he wrote to Fliess 'I am writing the dream pamphlet [*On Dreams*] without real enjoyment and am becoming an absent-minded professor while collecting material for the psychology of everyday life. It has been a lively time, and I have a new patient, a girl of eighteen (1900).[86] Between September 1900 and February 1901, with consummate productivity Freud wrote: the booklet, *On Dreams*; a case-history of the new patient (subsequently, on publication in 1905, immortalized as 'Dora' – see chapter 4); and *The Psychopathology of Everyday Life*. Like *The Interpretation of Dreams* all three of these works contain subtle allusions to Freud's life at the time. Hidden within the case histories presented, there may be found the bare-bones of a story which has been the subject of a host of speculations and rumours; namely the suppressed details of a possible love-affair between Freud and his sister-in-law Minna Bernays.

The role of Minna Bernays in Freud's life is one of the most controversial questions posed to those who are seeking to understand Freud as a man. It is a subject upon which tempers wax hot. It is, however, a matter which demands our attention for it touches upon all the central themes of Freud's life. Minna Bernays was Martha's younger sister, who despite being 6 years younger than Martha was very close to her. From early in his courtship of Martha he had grown to share her appreciation of Minna, and had frequently assumed a brotherly role with her, writing letters to her as 'your brother Sigmund' and addressing her as 'sister' not 'sister-in-law'. When Minna became engaged to one of his close friends (one of the *Bund* of his youth), Ignaz Schönberg, he looked forward to the development of a friendly foursome of himself and Martha, and Ignaz and Minna. Ernest Jones recounts in his biography of Freud how Freud wrote to Martha about this quartet. Jones confusingly only summarizes the contents of the letter by saying that Freud wrote 'that two of them were thoroughly good people, Martha and Schönberg, and two were wild passionate people, not so good, Minna and himself: two who were adaptable and two who wanted their own way'. Jones then added Freud's interpretation of this observation: 'That is why we get on better in a criss-cross arrangement; why two similar people like Minna and myself don't suit each other specially; why the two good-natured ones don't attract each other'.[87] As Paul Roazen has noted 'an entirely different (and prophetic) construction might be put on this characterization'.[88]

Unfortunately, things did not go well for Ignaz and Minna. Ignaz had contracted pulmonary tuberculosis, which in 1883 worsened such that Freud had to take him to a spa in Hungary where he could attempt to recuperate. The following year Freud successfully treated Ignaz's mother, but could do little to help Ignaz himself. Concerned lest the possibility of an imminent death afflict Minna too greatly, Ignaz broke off his engagement, and subsequently died in February 1886. Freud wrote a long letter of consolation to Minna when he heard of the death of his friend expressing the following sentiments:

> Your sad romance has come to an end, and when I think it over carefully I can only consider it fortunate that the news of Schönberg's death should reach you after such a long time of estrangement and cooling off. Let us give him his due by admitting that he himself tried and succeeded in sparing

you the pain of losing your lover, even though it was less high-minded
intention than the moral weakness of his last years that prompted him to
do so . . . You haven't been made so unhappy as you so easily could have
been; fate has grazed you only lightly; but you have suffered a lot, you
have little joy and a lot of worry, and in the end a great deal of pain from
this relationship. You were hardly out of your teens when you took upon
you tasks normally faced in life only by adults. Now all this is over and
I would like to ask you one thing; try to regain something of the lost youth
during which one is meant to do nothing but grow and develop, give your
emotions a long rest and live for a while quietly with the two of us who
are closest to you now. (1886)[89]

In fact, it was to take just under 10 years for Minna to take up that
offer, having tried her hand at being a governess and lady's companion
in the provinces. In 1895, during Martha's last pregnancy she moved into
the Freud household – she became a permanent part of it until she died
in 1941. She became a mother to the children, a companion to Martha,
and a friend and confidant of Freud. It was Minna who was present when
Freud learnt of the death of his father in October 1896 (Martha was away
with her mother in Hamburg – her first time away from her family since
she had become married). She took an active interest in psychoanalysis,
in contrast to her sister Martha who once remarked to a visitor 'if I did
not realise how seriously my husband takes his treatments, I should think
that psychoanalysis is a form of pornography'.[90] Jones made the
following observations about Minna:

[Minna] deserved a book to herself so interesting and decided was her
personality. She certainly knew more about Freud's work than did her sister,
and he remarked once that in the lonely nineties Fliess and she were the
only people in the world who sympathised with it. She had more leisure
for reading than her sister . . . Her caustic tongue gave rise to many
epigrams that were cherished in the family. Freud no doubt appreciated
her conversation, but to say that she in any way replaced her sister in his
affections is sheer nonsense.[91]

Jones took great care to repudiate the suggestion which had long
surrounded the Freud/Minna relationship that it was anything other than
a meeting of minds, or a touching of kindred spirits. He believed it was
utterly alien to Freud's constitution to have allowed the relationship to
have developed any further. He staunchly maintained that Minna, and
a whole series of devoted women disciples and patients 'had no erotic
attraction for him . . . [for] Freud was quite peculiarly monogamous.
Of few men can it be said that they go through the whole of life without
being erotically moved in any serious fashion by a woman beyond the

one and only. Yet this really seems to have been true of Freud'.[92] Freud
himself was party to this conception of his own sexuality and its expression,
for he once wrote to an American follower, James Putnam: 'sexual
morality as society – and at its most extreme American society – defines
it, seems very despicable to me. I stand for a much freer sexual life.
However, I have made little use of such freedom, except in so far as I
was convinced of what was permissible for me in this area' (1915).[93] This
last somewhat cryptic allusion to 'what was permissible . . . in this area'
may have referred to his interest in his sister-in-law; the evidence for this,
though tendentious, can be gleaned from his writings of the very early
1900s, notably from *The Psychopathology of Everyday Life*.

   The Psychopathology of Everyday Life opens with the expanded
account, previously published in December 1898 in the *Monatsschrift fur
Psychiatrie*, of an example, which had happened to Freud, of how one
can forget a name through 'unconscious' motivation. This autobiographical example, which Freud describes in detail, concerned his
failure to recall the name of Signorelli, and his substitution of the names
of two other painters, Botticelli and Boltraffio. In his analysis of this
case Freud alludes to the 'unconscious' source of his forgetting what he
calls a 'delicate topic', namely the thought which had preoccupied him
since the cessation of sexual activity with Martha that 'once a man's sexual
life comes to an end then life is of no value', i.e. a man is as good as
dead once he can no longer function sexually. Later, to Jung, Freud
referred to this parapraxis and mentioned his '"Old-age complex" whose
erotic base is known to you' (1911).[94] The repression of this thought led
to the seemingly innocent substitution of false names for the true name.
To Freud's mind, the slip showed the power of the repressed thoughts,
just as dreams and symptoms had previously done so. The 'Signorelli
parapraxis' is an example of a slip motivated by a current sexual problem;
Freud did not relate this in any way to the infantile material that he alleged
was so necessary for repression.

   Shortly after the 'Signorelli parapraxis' had first been published, as
a journal article, Freud also published in the same journal a paper entitled
'Screen memories'. This paper purports to be an analysis of a patient
who is undergoing psychoanalysis with Freud. It has since been shown
to be an autobiographical account of Freud's own life – the very first
published product of his self-analysis. The biographical detail, except in
a few instances where Freud changed material in order to disguise his
identity, correlates exactly with all that is known of Freud. It is this paper
which contains the descriptions of the patients with masturbatory fantasies
about violently deflowering a virgin. This paper again purports to be an
account of the childhood memories of the patient, but Freud is using
'screen' memories in a special sense, they are *masks* which are constructed

by the mind to represent current or recent conflicts and desires. The infantile scenes of the patients 'screen memories' were not, then, recollections of actual events, but reconstructions of those memories through the grid of contemporary feelings (in his later writings on this idea he was to use the idea of a 'screen memory' in a more sophisticated way – being a construction from a variety of sources from early sexual experiences). Freud expressed this idea to Fliess at the time he was writing the paper: 'First of all I have accomplished a piece of self-analysis which has confirmed that fantasies are products of later periods which project themselves back from the present into earliest childhood' (1899).[95] There are two points worth noting from this 'screen memory' idea (an idea which incidentally Freud expanded upon in *The Psychopathology of Everyday Life* where he pointed out the similarities between the production of slips and the production of memories). In the first place once again it is a *current* or recent sexual desire or anxiety which is the motive force behind the seemingly distant memory. In the second place Freud resorted to subterfuge in presenting his case; in particular, he adopted the clever device of having fictitious people (in this case the patient) present material that confirmed his ideas.

This is the necessary background to understand Freud's second example of a parapraxis presented in *The Psychopathology of Everyday Life*. The second example we may call the '*aliquis*' example. The case concerned 'a certain young man of academic background' whom Freud met on holiday and engaged in conversaion with. The two of them talked together of the social status of the Jews in Austria–Hungary, in particular of the difficulty with which Jews of his generation could get on in society and advance themselves. In concluding what Freud called 'a speech of impassioned fervour' the young man tried to quote from a line of Virgil's *Aeneid* in which Dido, having been abandoned by Aeneas and, about to commit suicide exclaims, '*Exoriar(e) aliquis nostris ex ossibuis ultor*' ('Let someone [*aliquis*] arise from my bones an avenger'). The young man failed to remember the lines correctly and 'forgot' the word '*aliquis*' and inverted the words '*nostris ex*' (So he actually said '*Exoriar(e) ex nostris ossibus ultor*'). He realized that this was incorrect, but could not remember the correct line, finally he asked Freud to help him out with the full quotation. This Freud supplied, and then, on being asked by the young man to explain why he had misquoted as he had, supplied an elaborate chain of reasoning by the use of free association, ultimately linking the young man's parapraxis to his concern about the possibility that he had made a young 'Italian' girl pregnant.[96]

There are a number of points which have to be made about this example which throw doubt on whether it is a report of an actual meeting rather than another example of Freud resorting to deception to present his views.

First, the young man is described by Freud as being 'familiar with some of my psychological publications', in particular, he is aware that Freud claims 'that one never forgets a thing without some reason'. This is strange for most of Freud's publications up to that time had been available only to a specialist audience of neurologists and psychiatrists, indeed the very paper in which Freud developed that argument had been in a journal published in Berlin and was by no means a widely circulated journal. Secondly, the young man is reported by Freud to quote the 'well-known line of Virgil', not only that, but he quoted from the edition that Freud himself always quoted from. However, it just is not the case that the *Aeneid* was that well known and used in Vienna at the time; Freud is quite exceptional in his use of quotations from Virgil (he quoted Virgil in both his 'Screen Memories' paper and in the dream book). Thirdly, all of the associations the young man produces in 'free association' have a distinctly 'Freudian air' about them – they reflect perfectly Freud's own interests and concerns, not least Freud's recent unsuccessful application for a professorship. Fourthly, the young man capitulates with such ease under the inexorable logic of Freud's reasoning, that as Swales has remarked it 'eclipses even the fictional feats of Sherlock Holmes'.[97]

All of the evidence points to the fact that Freud was not here reporting an actual case, but in reality, as he had done with the 'Screen Memories' paper, he was presenting an analysis drawn from his own experience. In coming to this conclusion, we go against the testimony of Freud himself who made great play in the book, on the importance of the fact that this case derived from someone other than himself. In the presentation of the argument in *The Psychopathology of Everyday Life* the *'aliquis'* example comes at a crucial point. Having revamped the Signorelli example in chapter 1 the credibility of the thesis would have been diminished considerably by the production of yet another example from himself. Freud himself noted the point:

I have several reasons for valuing this brief analysis; and my thanks are due to my former travelling-companion who presented me with it. In the first place, this is because I was in this instance allowed to draw on a source that is ordinarily denied to me. For the examples collected here of disturbances of a physical function in daily life I have to fall back mainly on self-observation. I am anxious to steer clear of the much richer material provided by my neurotic patients, since it might otherwise be objected that the phenomena in question are merely consequences and manifestations of neurosis. My purpose is therefore particularly well served when a person other than myself, not suffering from nervous illness, offers himself as the object of such an investigation. (1901)[98]

This statement by Freud can be regarded as being very similar in intent to his statement at the beginning of the 'Irma dream' that a psychologist is morally bound, in the interests of his science, to disclose even his own weaknesses. It also has similarities to a statement made at the beginning of the 'Screen Memories' paper about the value of the material there being 'certainly increased by the fact that it related to someone who is not at all or only very slightly neurotic' (1899).[99] Freud disarms his potential critics by supplying an example which purports to come from someone else. The internal evidence of the example, and the fact that he had previously, recently published a successful pseudo-case history must cast doubt on the reality of the former travelling companion.

If one accepts that this example is a disguised version of something that actually happened to Freud, then one is immediately faced with a problem, for the content of the *aliquis* case concerns a man's worries over the possibility that he had made a mistress pregnant, but Freud, as we have already discovered, had earlier confessed to Fliess that 'sexual excitation' was of no use to him. He had also been preoccupied with the thought that once a man's sexual activity finishes then his life is not worth living. Finally, as Jones and so many others have attested Freud was quite 'peculiarly monogamous.' The resolution of this problem may be sought through supposing that Freud had a temporary revival in his sexual potency as a result of turning his attention away from his wife Martha, to his sister-in-law, Minna.

What sort of evidence is there to support this contention? The first lot of evidence comes from the reports of some of Freud's friends and colleagues at the time, for instance, Oskar Rie, one of Freud's oldest, and closest, Viennese friends is reported to have said to one of his relatives that 'for children Freud went to Martha; but for pleasure he took Minna'.[100] Similarly, Carl Jung, recounting, many years later, his first visit to the Freud household in 1907 noticed the discrepancy in the interest that Martha and Minna took in Freud's life and work. Jung noted that Martha knew 'absolutely nothing about what Freud was doing', and further recalled that 'it was obvious that there was a very superficial relationship between Freud and his wife'. In contrast, Jung was able to say of Minna that she was 'very good looking and she not only knew enough about psychoanalysis but also about everything Freud was doing'. Jung then added that one day Minna took him aside to have a few words in private: 'She was very much bothered by her relationship with Freud and felt guilty about it. From her I learned that Freud was in love with her and that their relationship was indeed very intimate. It was a shocking discovery to me, and even now I can recall the agony I felt at the time'.[101]

Two years after Jung learned of this intimate relationship, i.e. in 1909, Freud and Jung went to America together to lecture on psychoanalysis.

This was Freud's first major international breakthrough and it marks the initiation of that continent to the movement which was to dominate cultural activity and psychiatry for over half a century. During the course of that trip Freud and Jung began to analyse each other's dreams. Jung suggested that because Freud developed certain neuroses he had to 'do a limited analysis with him'. Jung later recounted how Freud soon put a stop to that activity when Freud's dreams focused upon an intimate triangle and revealed material about his relationship with Minna. Jung suggested that Freud should undergo free association with him, but Freud refused. Jung recalled Freud's attitude exactly: 'He looked at me with bitterness and said "I could tell you more, but I cannot risk my authority"' (Jung, 1961). Jung then recounted that, for Freud to allow the examination of these secret aspects of his personal life would have meant that his sexual theories would have become open to challenge – something which he could not countenance.[102]

Such evidence, from Freud's colleagues, is, however, only circumstantial, and it would remain far from persuasive were it not for the fact that in Freud's own writing we have evidence, albeit skilfully hidden, for a passion for his sister-in-law. If Freud did have an affair with Minna, it was hardly something to be blazened across the headlines of the world's newspapers, it had to be hidden, for by the standards of the Old Testament, and by the standards of Roman Catholicism, it constituted incest. Freud had to be very careful, when reporting his dreams and his slips that he did not give the game away about this affair – in short he had to distort and dissimulate in order to both publish his own material (upon which his theories were based) and yet not reveal the secret, incestuous relationship. Freud himself confessed, in *The Psychopathology of Everyday Life*, that when lying he found he was incapable of 'carrying through the distortion or concealment of thoughts . . . without leaving some trace of them behind' (1901).[103] The traces that survive in Freud's writings, together with the circumstantial evidence cited earlier, give us just enough evidence to tip the balance in favour of maintaining that Freud not only had an affair with Minna in 1900 but also, as a result of the liaison, that he may have got Minna pregnant, and may even have provided money for her to have an abortion in the same year.

Such a bold assertion needs some substantiation for it is in direct contradiction to most Freud scholars – Clark, for instance, in reviewing Jung's allegations about Freud and Minna, concludes by saying 'maybe [Freud] was an unsublimated randy young man who grew into an unsublimated randy old man, but there is not a tatter of evidence for this, and the known context of his life makes it distinctly improbable'.[104] That dismissive treatment of the subject, however, hardly does justice to the *precise* context of his life at this time nor to the content of the

'Screen Memories' paper, and to Freud's own 'real' interpretations of his dreams. It certainly does not account for the discrepancies in the autobiographical fragments that pepper Freud's writing at the time. When Freud's writings are put into the context in which they were written, and when you make certain, reasonable assumptions that cases, purportedly about patients or colleagues, actually refer to Freud himself then that very context makes it distinctly probable that an affair, and subsequent abortion, took place. It is important to establish that the question of whether Freud did indeed have an affair with his sister-in-law is of central concern to the whole Freudian enterprise. It is not just of mildly academic interest – a controversy to add spice to a biography – it is not just of passing biographical significance – an interesting fact to slot into Freud's life – it casts the shadow of its significance over Freud's theories of dreams, of parapraxes, of the neuroses, of the human mind. If Freud seriously entertained sexual longings and desires for Minna, and if those desires and phantasies span the period from his self-analysis through to (at least) 1909 – Freud's most fertile and productive period for his ideas – then many of those theories, dreams and parapraxes, need to be reinterpreted. Traditionally, the material Freud presents about himself has been regarded as confirming his theories about the infantile origins of human behaviour; if Freud did indulge in sexual phantasies and feelings about Minna then that traditional view would require some radical revision.[105] What other evidence is there for making this suggestion?

First, there is evidence, in Freud's letters to Fliess, and in the dreams he reports in *The Interpretation of Dreams*, that in 1898 Freud began to entertain sexual phantasies about Minna (who had by that time joined the Freud household). One of Freud's dreams in June 1898, shortly after having visited his mother-in-law with Minna, has an interpretation which Freud admitted was incomplete; he then noted 'it will rightly be suspected that what compels me to make this assumption is sexual material'.[106] The dream hinged around a lack of gratitude towards an old lady for hospitality, and in his interpretation Freud mentioned a particular play. The plot of this play concerns a man whose love for a vestal virgin can never be consummated because she is permanently watched-over. Less than a week later Freud sent Fliess the very first analysis of a piece of literature. The book in question has the theme of incest with a sister. Freud noted that 'all neurotics create a so-called family romance . . . on the one hand it serves the need for self-aggrandizement and on the other as a defence against incest. If your sister is not your mother's child, you are relieved of the guilt' (1898).[107] Minna, whom Freud had long considered as a sister, was not his mother's child, but, as Freud knew only too well, in strictly biblical terms sexual relations with her were still forbidden; perhaps he contemplated it, but did not go any further. Once again, Freud's dreams provide some evidence for this, for shortly after this piece of literary analysis, Freud had another dream, the contents of which he again admitted are heavily censored on account of their compromising sexual material. This dream had a central theme about whether a person should sieze the opportunity to have sexual pleasure even though it is known to be wrong. Some time later Freud referred again to the theme and noted that it 'appeals to the uncertainty of life and the unfruitfulness of virtuous renunciation' (1905).[108]

In 1900 shortly after having had his last traumatic meeting with Wilhelm Fliess, Freud spent a long summer holiday touring Northern Italy with Minna (the holiday had begun with Martha too, but she had returned to Vienna as she did not enjoy travelling). Freud and Minna were alone in countryside that Freud described to Fliess as 'dreamlike' and 'beautiful as paradise'.[109] At the end of this tour Freud suddenly took Minna to an Austrian health-spa called Merano. Jones tells us that the purpose of this trip was for Minna 'to pass some time in the hope of recovering from her tuberculosis'.[110] Jones' statement may be taken at face value as a true statement about the reason for the visit to Merano – except that Merano, at that time, was a spa that was definitely not recommended for people with tuberculosis, and Minna herself is never ever mentioned at any other time as having TB. Pictures of her which are available indicate that she was the very opposite image of a typical consumptive – she was an unusually robust woman (one clearly up to the onerous task of accompanying Freud on his travels, something Martha felt unable to face). Minna was not at Merano for long but while she was there Freud experienced (i.e. himself committed) the '*aliquis*' parapraxis.[111]

Such an account still does not provide sufficient evidence to suggest that Freud and Minna partook of incestuous sexual relations during this time. However, there is evidence to support this contention – again from Freud's dreams. Having returned from his holiday with Minna, Freud set about writing his introductory work concerning dreams, *On Dreams*. In this work he reported a new specimen dream and presented an interpretation of it. The exact details of the dream are complicated but it concerned two women – his wife and a Frau E. L. Freud contrasted their behaviour in the dream, his wife was inattentive to him and unduly interested in other people while Frau E. L. 'was turning her whole attention to me and laid her hand on my knee in an intimate manner'.[112] As the drama of the dream unfolded Freud was reminded of cab-drives and their expense.

When Freud set out to interpret this specimen dream one particular theme emerged from his associations – at first in a general sense and then subsequently in a more specific sense (the interpretation spans several pages). Initially, Freud reached the thought: 'I have always paid dearly for whatever advantage I have had from other people'. Then Freud noted: '[The] bitter thought . . . that I had never had anything free of cost'; emerged as an association. Then a little later he added. 'I should like to get some enjoyment without cost'. Finally he discovered that 'in the dream thoughts the chief emphasis is laid on a wish for once to enjoy unselfish love, love which "costs nothing"' (1901). The theme of the dream was then, his desire to have 'enjoyment in love' which 'costs nothing'. Freud continued to provide an account of the context of this wish, in which he recounted how he had recently had a number of cab drives with a relative (in an obscure footnote to another story, it is plain that the relative in question was a 'sister'). One ride in particular had been an expensive one, for on behalf of that 'member of my family of whom I am fond' Freud had had to pay out 'a considerable sum of money'.[113] In *The Psychopathology of Everyday Life* (written at the same time as *On Dreams*) there is a clue to the size and purpose of this sum of money. There Freud recounted a story of a parapraxis involving the writing out of a cheque for 300 Kronen (worth, in those days, about £30). The purpose of that cheque, Freud wrote, was to 'send to a relative absent for purposes of cure'. In connection with this payment Freud also mentioned both his regrets at having to pay, and his obligation to pay too. Concern and guilt are intermingled in all the material pertaining to this incident.[114]

Having unravelled his dreams thus, Freud then broke the train of revelation and closed the door on the dream's real secrets. He closed his interpretation with the following admission:

> While I was producing the thoughts behind the dream, I was aware of intense and well founded affective impulses; the thoughts themselves fell at once into logical chains, in which certain central ideas make their appearance more than once. Thus, the contrast between 'selfish' and 'unselfish', and the elements 'being in debt' and 'without paying for it' were central ideas of this kind, not represented in the dream itself. I could draw closer together the threads in the material revealed by the analysis, and I could then show that they converge upon a single nodal point, but considerations of a personal and not of a scientific nature prevent my doing so in public. I should be obliged to betray many things which had better remain my secret, for on my way to discovering the solution of the dream all kinds of things were revealed which I was unwilling to admit even to myself . . . there were some among them which I should prefer to conceal from strangers and which I could not communicate to other people without doing serious mischief in important directions. (1901)[115]

So, just like the main dream book with its partially analysed dreams, and with the 'big dream' left out, Freud once again gave a glimpse into his mind and its deepest thoughts, but avoided revealing the crucial elements and facts which made the whole thing hang together. In the present context, his illicit relationship with Minna, phantasized about for so long and consummated in the summer of 1900 – with dire, expensive consequences – was the single nodal point which provides the explanation for so many of the veiled references in his writing at this period. Minna provided a solution, albeit an expensive one, for his mood of despair following the cessation of sexual activity with his wife, she may also have provided a solution to a neurosis which Freud was afflicted with throughout the 1890s – his 'Rome neurosis'.

Throughout his correspondence with Fliess Freud had made reference to this desire to go to Rome. During his self-analysis Freud reported to Fliess dreams and phantasies which centred around the idea of going 'to Rome'; at times this idea was expressed through analogous images – of journeying to Karlsbad (a spa outside Vienna renowned for its cures); of visiting Sienna; of being in Prague. Rome had come to symbolize for Freud so many important ideas in his mind; but like his great phantasy mentor, Hannibal, he had not succeeded in reaching Rome. In *The Interpretation of Dreams* Freud explained that going 'to Rome' had a number of connotations for him:

> The wish to reach Rome has become in my dream-life a mask and a symbol for several other passionately held wishes, the realization of which one would like to pursue with all the perseverance and single-mindedness of the Carthaginian, and whose fulfilment seems at times just as little favoured by destiny as Hannibal's life-long wish to march into Rome. (1900)[116]

Of those passionately held wishes, we may already surmise a few on the basis of the information I have presented – a desire to avenge his father; a desire to strike at the heart of anti-Semitism; a desire to overturn Christianity may all have been just such wishes. It is also clear that one very definite wish he entertained was to achieve professional advancement, in particular a coveted professorship. In 1897 Krafft-Ebing and Nothnagel had proposed Freud for a professorship, but this application was turned down, in part, on the grounds that Freud was a Jew. Freud, no doubt seething inside, let the matter rest until after the publication of *The Interpretation of Dreams*, and until after he had finally visited Rome. The conquest of Rome, however, required a preliminary conquest, for Freud, steeped in classical history and mythology, knew that the conquest of Rome could only be affected by someone who had fulfilled an obscure condition. In his 1911 revision of *The Interpretation of Dreams* Freud referred to the 'well-known' prophecy of the Tarquins that Rome would fall to the man who should first 'kiss' the mother. In other words, in

Freud's mind, once he had conquered his 'mother' sexually, then Rome would lie at his feet. In Freud's complicated inner-fantasy world his 'mother' in this context did not mean Amalie but rather actually meant Minna – the two were interchangeable.[117]

In 1912, long after he had conquered Minna, and had subsequently 'taken Rome', Freud wrote:

> It sounds not only disagreeable but also paradoxical, yet it must nevertheless be said that anyone who is to be really free and happy in love must have surmounted his respect for women and have come to terms with the idea of incest with his mother or sister. (1912)[118]

Freud once referred to Martha and Minna as 'the two mothers' of his children (see plate 5),[119] but equally significantly Freud also refers in some of his 'screen memories' to his two mothers – Amalie and the Catholic nurse. Given the fact that such 'screen memories' are the results (albeit with some childhood components) of contemporary phantasies projected backwards, Martha and Minna can be seen in some senses as being represented in his phantasies by his two earlier mothers. It is worth noting too that Oedipus, the central figure in Freud's solution of his own self-analysis, had two mothers. Oedipus violated the incest taboo with his (real) mother and was condemned, Freud violated the incest taboo with his (phantasy) mother and conquered Rome. Through his incest with Minna Freud felt able to go on to realize his other passionately held wishes – to go to Rome; to begin to expose the 'lie of salvation' (as he called religion); to seek the long-desired professorship; and to create a new secular movement to replace the displaced Christian religion.[120]

'A THEORY OF JESTING: YOU MUST BE JOKING!'

> So far reaching an agreement between the methods of the joke-work and those of the dream world can scarcely be a matter of chance. (1905)[121]

In 1905 Freud published a work on the subject of jokes or of wit. Although appearing some time after *The Interpretation of Dreams* and *The Psychopathology of Everyday Life*, the book can be seen as being directly related to them, and as being a product of the same period and concerns. Freud himself in his autobiography remarked on the confluence of his interests in dreams, slips and jokes and summarized his conclusions thus:

> My book on *Jokes and their Relation to the Unconscious* was a side-issue directly derived from *The Interpretation of Dreams*. The only friend of mine who was at the time interested in my work remarked to me that my

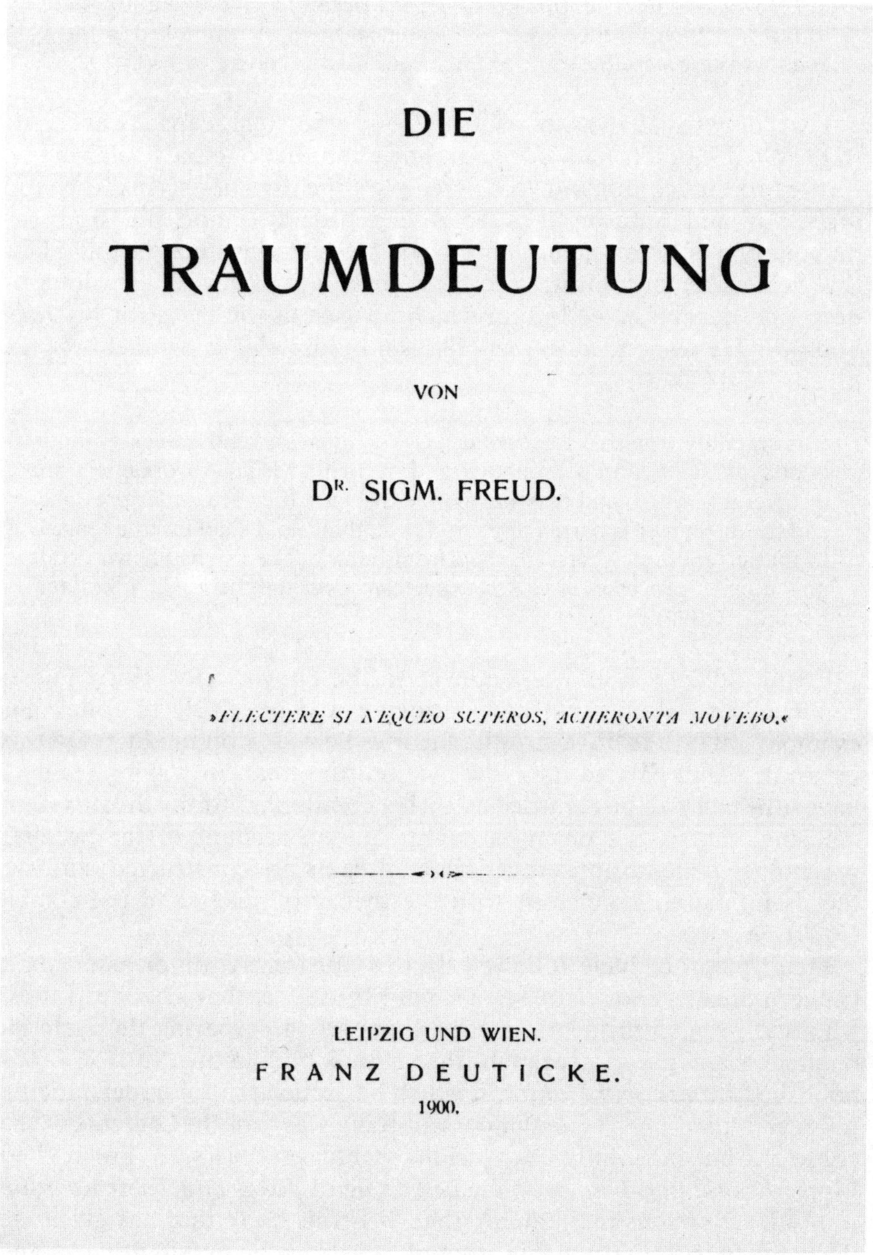

DIE

TRAUMDEUTUNG

VON

DR. SIGM. FREUD.

»FLECTERE SI NEQUEO SUPEROS, ACHERONTA MOVEBO.«

LEIPZIG UND WIEN.

FRANZ DEUTICKE.

1900.

Plate 7. Title page of the first edition of *The Interpretation of Dreams*, 1900

interpretations of dreams often impressed him as being like jokes. In order to throw some light on this impression, I began to investigate jokes and found that their essence lay in the technical methods employed in them, and that these were the same as the means used in 'dream-work'. (1925)[122]

That 'only friend' was, of course, Fliess, who, in his capacity as censor to the *Dream* book, had lodged an objection that one particular dream showed too much humour to be credible: 'the dreamer seems to be too ingenious and amusing'.[123] Freud had already made the study of humour one of his on-going concerns (in 1897, for instance, he told Fliess that he had begun 'putting together a collection of Jewish anecdotes of deep significance', a collection which he used as the basis for his *Joke* book).[124] He responded to this criticism by drawing a parallel between dreams and jokes:

> It is certainly true that the dreamer is too ingenious and amusing, but it is not my fault, and I cannot be reproached with it. All dreamers are insufferably witty, and they have to be, because they are under pressure, and the direct way is barred to them. If you think so, I shall insert a remark to that effect somewhere [in the dream book]. The ostensible wit of all unconscious processes is closely connected with the theory of jokes and humour. (1899)[125]

Freud did indeed add a comment to the *Dream* book citing Fliess' comment and noting that other critics would be 'likely to follow his example', and thus disregard the theories he was propounding. On this occasion Freud parried the blow by admitting that 'in waking reality I have little claim to be regarded as a wit', continuing, 'if my dreams seem amusing, that is not on my account, but on account of the peculiar psychological conditions under which dreams are constructed; and the fact is intimately connected with the theory of jokes and the comic' (1900).[126]

Freud may not have followed up this apparently minor association between dreams and jokes, were it not for the fact that Theodor Lipps, who had been so influential on his thoughts in preparing the material on dreams and parapraxes, published a book on humour. In 1898 Lipps published *Komik und Humor* in which he argued that in understanding jokes and humour the most important thing was 'not the contents of the conscious but inherently unconscious mental processes'.[127] Freud cited Lipps' *Komik und Humor* at the beginning of *Jokes and Their Relation to the Unconscious* maintaining that 'it is this book that has given me the courage to undertake this attempt as well as the possibility of doing so' (1905).[128] Throughout the book Freud made reference to Lipps and his ideas asserting that 'they seem to me of the highest importance'

(1905),[129] although naturally, he differed from Lipps in his interpretation of just which unconscious processes were paramount in 'joke-work'. For Freud, as ever, the sexual motives of the joker, and of his audience, were the key elements in understanding jokes.

As with his earlier works on dreams and slips Freud spent some time classifying jokes and then explaining how each type – word plays, puns, jests, innocent jokes, tendentious ones involving obscenity or hostility – could be rendered intelligible in terms of the release in psychic energy they produced. Just as the mechanism of dreams served as a means whereby dammed-up psychic energy could be released harmlessly, so jokes fulfilled a similar function: 'the pleasure in the case of a . . . joke arises from a purpose being satisfied whose satisfaction would not otherwise have taken place' (1905).[130] The mechanism of repression can be outwitted in the process of joking, and the suppressed desire can find partial fulfillment thereby producing a measure of satisfaction: 'the direct and easiest pathway to the expression of . . . [unconscious] thoughts is barred [i.e. by repression]';[131] however, indirect, ingenious routes are found in dreams, slips and jokes. The mechanisms and techniques used in the psyche to form dreams and jokes are essentially the same. Freud maintained this was the key:

> This led to an economic enquiry into the origin of the high degree of pleasure obtained from hearing a joke. And to this the answer was that it was due to the momentary suspension of the expenditure of energy upon maintaining repression, owing to the attraction exercised by the offer of a bonus of pleasure (*fore-pleasure*). (1925)[132]

Interestingly, in the light of Freud's admission that he was incapable of 'carrying through the . . . concealment of thoughts . . . without leaving some trace of them behind' (1901),[133] one of the jokes which Freud analyses is the anecdote 'a wife is like an umbrella – sooner or later one takes a cab'. Freud saw this simple vignette as part of protest against the institution of marriage – 'there is no more personal claim than that for sexual freedom and at no point has civilization tried to exercise severe suppression than in the sphere of sexuality' (1905).[134] Freud's interpretation of this interesting anecdote is revealing in the light of his experiences during the summer of 1900:

> The simile [of the anecdote] may be worked out as follows. One marries in order to protect oneself against the temptations of sensuality, but it turns out nevertheless that marriage does not allow of the satisfaction of needs that are somewhat stronger than usual. In just the same way, one takes an umbrella with one to protect oneself from the rain and nevertheless gets wet in the rain. In both cases one must look around for a stronger

protection: in the latter case one must take a public vehicle, and in the former a woman who is accessible in return for money. The joke has now been almost entirely replaced by a piece of cynicism. One does not venture to declare aloud and openly that marriage is not an arrangement calculated to satisfy a man's sexuality unless one is driven to do so perhaps by a love of truth . . . The strength of this joke lies in the fact that nevertheless – in all kinds of roundabout ways – it *has* declared it. (1905)[135]

This 'personal claim' about marriage, with its jaundiced assessment of the institution is a clear statement about Freud's feelings about his own marriage – the joke is (if our reconstruction of events is correct), that Freud may have found his 'stronger protection' against the repressive nature of his own marriage precisely in a carriage – with Minna.

Jokes and Their Relation to the Unconscious is a difficult book to read now; much of it is hard to translate, particularly Freud's own jokes, the meanings of which hinge upon the sense and sound of the original German. Indeed, when the book was first translated into English by A. A. Brill, he found it was necessary to replace a number of Freud's own original examples with ones that would be more intelligible to an English-speaking audience. Though relatively well received at the time it was published it is frequently passed by nowadays as 'merely' a clever, but obscure, piece of work by Freud – by no means one of his classic texts. Its significance lies in the way in which Freud was able to extend his theories away from the abnormal and the pathological into the realm of normal psychology. It was, as he remarked about his dream-work, part of the creation of 'a new a deeper science of the mind', an extension of psychoanalysis into 'spheres of universal interest'. Freud himself conceived this extension to be part of an inexorable logic – from pathology to normality and from normality on to what he termed the super-normal. In 1919, for instance, he wrote:

Psycho-analysis was born of medical necessity . . . its further progress led away from the study of the physical conditions of nervous illnesses in a degree surprising to the physician, and gradually the whole mental content of human life came within its sphere, including the healthy – the normal as well as the super-normal. (1919)[136]

The extension, through dreams, slips and jokes, was only just beginning. Art, religion, anthropology, morality were all soon to come under the critical attention of this man whose avowed aim was to put humanity firmly in its place in the world.

4

The Psychoanalytic Movement
Cases, Theories and Followers

*Everything will change at the same time, literature, art, education,
everything after the general upheaval which I am expecting this year,
next year, in five years, but which will come, I am certain.* (Octave
Mirbeau writing in the 1890s)

As the last days of the 1890s drew on the *fin de siècle* spirit of the age
expressed itself in seeing the coming new century as a turning point – the
year 1900 began to take on an almost cosmic significance. Of course,
the full impact of the historical processes was not to be realized until the
carnage of the First World War, and until the Bolshevik Revolution in
Russia initiated a new age – an age in which Communism became a force
to be reckoned with. Nevertheless the turn of the century did see the
presage of a new age in many areas of culture, as had been predicted.
In 1895 Wilhelm Röntgen initiated a new atomic age with his discovery
of X-rays. Radioactivity and the new atomic theories of Rutherford and
Bohr were just around the corner. In 1900 Max Planck took the crucial
step of dividing energy into discrete units and the new 'quantum' physics
was born (both these developments were soon to find their synthesis in
the work of Albert Einstein who introduced us to the world of relativity).
Also in 1900 the work on genetics by an obscure monk, Gregor Mendel,
was rediscovered – a discovery that effectively revived the flagging
Darwinian paradigm and paved the way for what Julian Huxley was later
to call 'the new synthesis' biology. Ludwig Wittgenstein, a young man
in Vienna, was preparing to effect his revolution in philosophy, the
Tractatus. Change was afoot throughout Europe and Freud both partook
of its influences and precipitated it.

   For Freud the year 1900 may be seen as a turning point; he
had completed and published, what he hoped would be his masterpiece,
The Interpretation of Dreams. He had established the general
principles of his idea, and had begun the crucial transition – from
pathological to normal phenomena. His official biographer, Ernest Jones,
wrote, in near eulogistic tones about his achievements at this time:

In 1901 Freud, at the age of forty-five, had attained complete maturity,
a consummation of development that few people really achieve . . . In 1897
he embarked, all alone, on what was undoubtedly the greatest feat of his
life. His determination, courage and honesty made him the first human
being not merely to get glimpses of his own unconscious mind – earlier
pioneers had often got as far as that – but actually to penetrate into and
explore its deepest depths. This imperishable feat was to give him a unique
position in history. But three or four years of herculean struggles with those
powerful forces in the mind that so strenuously resist such an endeavour
brought their reward. He obtained the insight and knowledge that made
possible the life's work for which his name has become famous.[1]

Such idealizations only serve to perpetuate myths. True, they are myths
initiated and sustained by Freud himself. Interestingly, Freud himself
believed that the tendency to develop a 'romanticization of origins' was
one exhibited by 'paranoics – heroes, founders of religion' (1897).[2] A
more balanced picture about origins does better service to the truth,
however. Freud himself was actually pessimistic about his position in the
early 1900s; to Fliess he confided:

The new century – the most interesting thing about which for us is, I dare
say, that it contains the dates of our death – has brought me nothing but
a stupid review . . . I do not count on recognition, at any rate in my
lifetime . . . I have to deal in dark matters with people I am ten to fifteen
years in advance of, who will never catch me up. (1900)[3]

In many respects Freud's pessimism was justified although his
interpretations of the causes of his rejection are probably suspect. He
believed anti-Semitism and fear of sexuality were the causes, but he had,
as Breuer was to say of him 'a desire *d'épater le bourgeois*' so that it
would be true to say that *some* of the hostility and incomprehension he
met was more due to his style of arguing. There are, of course, instances
reported of outright vilification of him, such as the man who confronted
him in the street one day with the condemnation: 'Let me tell you what
a dirty-minded filthy old man you are'.[4] Freud's response to such
attacks was knowing silence, as he explained to Fliess: 'I know that my
work is odious to most people. So long as I behave perfectly correctly,
my opponents are at a loss. If once I start doing the same as they do,
they will regain their confidence that my work is no better than theirs'
(1900).[5]

Freud's perception of that period recounted in his autobiography is
decidedly coloured: 'For more than ten years after my separation from
Breuer, I had no followers. I was completely isolated. In Vienna I was
shunned; abroad no notice was taken of me. My *Interpretation of Dreams*,

published in 1900, was scarcely reviewed in the technical journals'
(1925).[6] Ernest Jones, himself the object of considerable critical
attention when he began propounding psychoanalysis in England in 1908,
has perpetuated this image of the hostile reception of psychoanalysis. It
became part of the standard stock-in-trade of all psychoanalysts that
Freud's views were unacceptable and had never been accepted, even when
they were first put forward.[7] Freud himself, writing his polemical *On the
History of the Psycho-Analytic Movement* was the chief instigator of these
origin myths. Recalling the early years of the Movement he wrote:

> I pictured my future as follows:- I should probably succeed in maintaining
> myself by means of the therapeutic success of the new procedure, but science
> would ignore me entirely during my life time; some decades later, someone
> else would infallibly come upon the same things – for which the time was
> not now ripe – would achieve recognition for them and bring me honour
> as a forerunner whose failure had been inevitable. Meanwhile, like
> Robinson Crusoe, I settled down as comfortably as possible on my desert
> island. When I look back to those lonely years, away from all the pressures
> and confusions of to-day, it seems like a glorious heroic age. My 'splendid
> isolation' was not without its advantages and charms . . . My publications,
> which I was able to place with a little trouble, could always lag far behind
> my knowledge, and could be postponed as long as I pleased, since there
> was no doubtful 'priority' to be defended. (1914)[8]

The truth is that this picture of the beginnings of psycho-analysis has
no validity whatsoever. As countless modern historians of science have
shown Freud's work was reviewed, and his ideas were aired.

His reception, throughout society, was on the whole, mixed – some
disliked his work intensely, some thought his ideas strange, some were
prepared to learn more, and some, gradually, became his disciples. The
range of reactions to his work was far more diverse than he would have
us believe. One early American reviewer described his work as 'perhaps
not quite convincing [but] interesting and timely'.[9] That same
American, a distinguished New England psycho-pathologist, was *later*
to withdraw even his modest praise. Writing in 1914, after a Psycho-
Analytic Movement had been started and had begun to break up, and
after the issue of sexuality had been made the shibboleth of orthodoxy,
he wrote: 'Psychoanalysis is a conscious and more often a subconscious
or unconscious debauching of the patient. Nothing is so diabolically
calculated to suggest sexual perversion as psychoanalysis. Psycho-
analysis . . . is a menace to the community . . . Better Christian Science
than psychoanalysis'.[10] Meanwhile in Vienna, in certain circles, Freud
was receiving less calumny than mockery. A Viennese musicologist, Max
Graf, has recalled the mood in his circle:

In those days when one mentioned Freud's name in a Viennese gathering, everyone would begin to laugh, as if someone had told a joke. Freud was the queer fellow who wrote a book about dreams and who imagined himself as interpreter of dreams. More than that, he was the man who saw sex in everything. It was considered bad taste to bring up Freud's name in the presence of ladies. They would blush when his name was mentioned. Those who were less sensitive spoke of Freud with a laugh, as if they were telling a dirty story . . .[11]

Jones recounted that Freud would counter such rejection privately to his friends with one of his characteristic personal remarks: 'they may abuse my doctrines by day, but I am sure they dream of them by night'.[12]

Recognition began to come, however, not least because he actively pursued it. Having conquered Minna, and having conquered Rome, Freud resolved to make a concerted effort to achieve promotion. He announced his determination to do that to Fliess: 'When I got back from Rome . . . I made up my mind to break with my strict scruples and take appropriate steps, as others do after all. One must look somewhere for one's salvation, and the salvation I chose was the title of professor' (1902).[13] The title of professor could only be granted on application to the Ministry of Education, this had been done once before in 1897 but nothing had come of it. On consulting his former teacher, Exner, he learnt that there were 'obscure . . . personal influences' blocking his application. Freud thus marshalled a 'counter-influence' (a practice perfectly common in Vienna at the time) to aid his reviewed application. Thanks to the intervention of that 'counter-influence' – a patient had offered the Minister a picture for a new gallery he was opening – Freud received his professorship. He was ecstatic and wrote to Fliess:

It was done . . . the news spread quickly from the Ministry. The public enthusiasm is immense. Congratulations and bouquets keep pouring in, as if the role of sexuality had been suddenly recognised by His Majesty, the interpretation of dreams confirmed by the Council of Ministers, and the necessity of the psycho-analytic therapy of hysteria carried by a two-thirds majority in Parliament. (1902)[14]

However, even the title of professor does not guarantee the growth of a practice – in the very same letter as he wrote of his recognition by the authorities he confessed 'I myself would still gladly exchange five congratulations for one good case coming for extensive treatment'.[15] Cases not only provided a reliable source of income, but they could also, with careful writing up, be used to illustrate his therapy and theories. Freud did, in fact receive considerable kudos from treating Bruno Walter and Gustav Mahler in the early years of the century, but when we think now of his case-studies, we think not of these famous figures of the Viennese musical scene, but of a series of studies where he presented in-depth analyses of some of his more obscure patients. The Case Studies have become immortalized through convenient, if somewhat bizarre, names: 'the Dora Case' (first published in 1905); 'Little Hans' (which appeared in 1909); 'the Rat Man' (another case published in 1909); 'the Schreber case' (published in 1911); 'the Wolf Man' (of 1918); and the last in-depth study Freud published 'the case of homosexuality in a woman' (published in 1920). These are to be the subjects of the next section.

THE CASE STUDIES: DORA AND COMPANY

> No doubt it was awkward that I was obliged to publish the results of my enquiries without there being any possibility of other workers in the field testing and checking them, particularly as those results were of a surprising and by no means gratifying character. But it will be scarcely less awkward now that I am beginning to bring forward some of the material upon which my conclusions were based and make it accessible to the judgement of the world. I shall not escape blame by this means. Only, whereas before I was accused of giving *no* information about my patients, now I shall be accused of giving information about my patients which ought not to be given. I can only hope that in both cases the critics will be the same, and that they will merely have shifted the pretext for their reproaches; if so, I can resign in advance any possibility of ever removing their objections. (1905)[16]

On 14 October 1900 Freud announced to Fliess that he had taken on a new patient 'a girl of eighteen'. It seems that she presented no peculiar problems to Freud for he remarked calmly 'the case has opened smoothly to my collection of picklocks' (1900).[17] For all that, the young girl herself seemed dissatisfied with Freud's approach for by 31 December she had broken off the analysis. Undaunted by the abruptness of the analysis, within 4 weeks Freud had written up the material as a paper, thus late in January 1901 he announced to Fliess: 'I finished "Dreams and Hysteria" yesterday, . . . It is a fragment of an analysis of a hysteria, in which the interpretations are grouped round two dreams, so it is really a continuation of the dream book' (1901).[18]

Evidently, Freud was pleased with his paper for he described it to Fliess as 'the subtlest thing I have so far written, and will put people off more than usual'. He also told Fliess that it had been accepted for publication, however, he withdrew his permission for it to 'meet the gaze of an astonished public'.[19] His reasons for withdrawing permission for it to be published were complex. They may have had something to do with his growing estrangement from Fliess. Equally they may have been due to his isolation and depression at this time – he showed the paper to his friend Oskar Rie who was unimpressed ('it gave him little pleasure' he recounted to Fliess). He responded by holding the paper back until 1905 (to Fliess he wrote 'I will make no further attempts to break through my isolation . . . The time is otherwise bleak, outstandingly bleak'[20]).

The Dora case is a strange one for Freud to devote so much time to, for by any standards it was a failure. It was fragmentary – Freud constantly admitted that – and it was terminated abruptly, and, to judge from what is known of the life of the woman in question, it had no appreciable impact on her life. An analyst who subsequently followed up her case reported that 'her death . . . seemed to be a blessing to those who were close to her [for] she had been . . . one of the most repulsive hysterics he had ever met'.[21] Freud had didactic reasons for wanting to use the case though:

> In publishing this paper, incomplete though it is, I had two objects in view. In the first place, I wished to supplement my book on the interpretation of dreams by showing how an art, which would otherwise be useless, can be turned to account for the discovery of the hidden and repressed parts of mental life . . . In the second place, I wished to stimulate interest in a whole group of phenomena of which science is still in complete ignorance today because they can only be brought to light by the use of this particular method . . . I was further anxious to show that sexuality does not simply intervene, like a *deus ex machina*, on one single occasion, at some point in the working of the processes which characterize hysteria, but that it provides the motive power for every single symptom and for every single manifestation of a symptom. The symptoms of the disease are nothing else than the patient's sexual activity . . . sexuality is the key to the problem of the psychoneuroses and of the neuroses in general. No one disclaims the key will ever be able to unlock the door. (1905)[22]

Indeed, so important did he view the sexual aspect of the case (the case is after all his very first full-length case after the *Studies* and by this time Freud was fully convinced of his infantile *neurotica*) that he resolved to present the case history with a candor that he knew would provoke his critics: 'sexual questions will be discussed with all possible frankness, the organs and functions of sexual life will be called by their proper names' (1905).[23] For all that Freud was still forced to concede that the actual case material was incomplete. He assured the reader though that there was no problem here for 'I have restored what is missing, taking the best models known to me from other analyses . . . like a conscientious archaeologist, I have not omitted to mention in each case where the authentic parts end and my constructions begin' (1905).[24]

Dora was the daughter of a wealthy businessman who had earlier received some treatment from Freud. He brought his daughter to Freud, when, after a series of minor problems, such as shortness of breath, fits of coughing and fainting, she had written a suicide note. Dora, it seems, had been part of an elaborate nexus of relationships. Her father was unhappily married to a woman Freud described as having a 'housewife's psychosis' (she was always cleaning and washing things such that it was 'almost impossible [for her] to use or enjoy them'). He had though, formed a friendship with another couple, called by Freud, Frau and Herr K. He had also started an affair with Frau K. In order to enhance his chances of sustaining his affair the father had also effectively given Herr K. a free hand in seducing his daughter (you scratch my back and I'll scratch yours). Accordingly Herr K. had one day, connived to get Dora alone. Then he had 'suddenly clasped the girl to him and pressed a kiss upon her lips'. Freud recounted her reaction and gave us his interpretation of that reaction:

> This was surely just the situation to call up a distinct feeling of sexual excitement in a girl of fourteen who had never before been approached. But Dora had at that moment a violent feeling of disgust, tore herself free from the man, and hurried past him . . . In this sense . . . the behaviour of this child of fourteen was already entirely and completely hysterical. I should without question consider a person hysterical in whom an occasion for sexual excitement elicited feelings that were preponderantly or exclusively unpleasurable. (1905)[25]

Freud's perception of 'Dora' and her circumstances was certainly coloured by his own feelings – which young girl would normally want to resist the advances of an older married man? It was coloured too by his own theories – he found evidence for sexuality in everything. Thus Dora's gastric complaints were symptoms whose cure Freud knew how to effect: 'it is well known that gastric pains occur especially often in those who masturbate. According to a personal communication made to me by Wilhelm Fliess, it is precisely gastalgias of this character which can be interrupted by an application of cocaine to the 'gastric spot' discovered by him in the nose, and which can be cured by the cauterization of the same spot' (1905).[26] Dora, had she continued analysis, might have become another Emma Eckstein (see chapter 3 on the Dream of Irma's Injection).

Time and time again as the case unfolds Freud interpreted the actions reported, and the material presented in ways that reflected his own understanding of the situation. Indeed he even expressed his aims in the following terms:

When I set myself the task of bringing to light what human beings keep hidden within them, not by the compelling power of hypnosis, but by observing what they say and what they show, I thought the task was a harder one than it really is. He that has eyes to see and ears to hear may convince himself that no mortal can keep a secret. If his lips are silent, he chatters with his finger-tips; betrayal oozes out of him at every pore. And turns the task of making conscious the most hidden recesses of the mind one which is quite possible to accomplish. (1905)[27]

Armed with this ability Freud felt himself able to pick up any of Dora's actions and interpret them to his own satisfaction. The repetition of complaints against her father which she produced 'with wearisome monotony' became linked in Freud's mind with her continuing cough. Eventually Freud was able to suggest that there was a connection between this symptom and the knowledge she professed to know about her father's impotence and his indulgence of 'sexual gratification *per os*' with Frau K. Dora herself seems to have objected to the linkage: 'she would not hear of going so far as this in recognizing her own thoughts; and indeed, if the occurrence of the symptom was to be made possible at all, it was essential that she should not be completely clear on the subject' (1905).[28] Nevertheless, Freud reported 'a very short time after she had tacitly accepted this explanation her cough vanished' (ibid.). Other symptoms indeed all of her behaviour became amenable to Freud's interpretations – her playing with her purse became a confession that she had masturbated in childhood as did her supposition that her cousin had masturbated ('it is a very common thing for patients to recognize in other people a connection which, on account of their emotional resistance, they cannot perceive in themselves'[29]). In particular Freud felt able to insist on his own perception of Dora's feelings in contradistinction to her own. When, for instance, he suggested that Dora was really in love with Herr K. she denied it; Freud was unperturbed and, in a passage which opens up the possibility of unlimited abuse, remarked:

My expectations were by no means disappointed when this explanation of mine was met by Dora with a most emphatic negative. The 'No' uttered by a patient after a repressed thought has been presented to his conscious perception for the first time does no more than register the existence of a repression and its severity; it acts, as it were, as a gauge of the repression's strength. If this 'No', instead of being regarded as the expression of an impartial judgement (of which, indeed, the patient is incapable), is ignored, and if work is continued, the first evidence soon begins to appear that in such a case 'No' signifies the desired 'Yes'. (1905)[30]

The similarities of this line of argument with those of men accused of rape who protest that they thought that when the girl said 'no' she really meant 'yes', are striking, as many feminist writers have pointed out. Indeed, as D. M. Thomas has observed in connection with one of Freud's earlier cases, Elizabeth von R., Freud's approach to his women patients is infused with a kind of verbal eroticism. Elizabeth, for instance, was the object of the following sequence: '[The truth] . . . now forced itself irresistibly upon her once more, like a flash of lightning in the dark . . . the analyst's labours were richly rewarded . . . fending off . . . excitations . . . resistance . . . a shattering effect on the poor girl . . . the most frightful pains . . . one last desperate effort to reject . . . we probed . . . I was able to relieve her once more . . .' (1895).[31] Thomas remarks 'apart from the analytical terminology, it is the style of mildly sadistic pornography'.[32]

The problem is that just as the patient may be incapable of being impartial so, too, Freud, rooted and grounded thoroughly in nineteenth-century patriarchy and sexism, is incapable of making such an impartial assessment. Indeed, in a note obviously added to the text as he reflected upon the case just prior to its publication in 1905, Freud himself admitted that he had misinterpreted the central concerns in her life. He wrote: 'it seems to me that the fault in my technique [in his particular case] lay in this omission: I failed to discover in time and to inform the patient that her homosexual . . . love for Frau K. was the strongest unconscious current in her mental life' (1905).[33] Dora was in many respects a victim and pawn in a complex marital and extra-marital power play. Throughout the case though, Freud merely betrays his prejudices by colluding with her father and with Herr K. in interpreting 'Dora' as the abnormal, neurotic woman. It would be naïve of anyone to deny that people do sometimes say one thing when they mean another; or that they are prone to discern in others just those traits and desires which they themselves have or wish to have; or that seemingly random movements or actions can betray unacknowledged tensions. Human behaviour is far too complex not to countenance all those aspects. The problem with Freud's use of such insights was that he consistently ignored other interpretations in such a way as to deny crucial elements in the situation. When we examine the interpretations Freud adopted in Dora's case we are led to conclude that he perceived her case through a pre-set grid of expectations – Dora became a victim not only of her father and Herr K. but also of Freud himself.

The fact that Dora terminated her analysis prompted Freud to suggest that the case history he presented was merely a 'fragment of an analysis'. Quite apart from any incompleteness Dora introduced into the study by terminating the therapy Freud himself admitted that he introduced 'another kind of incompleteness' namely to do with the technique of analytic therapy. Towards the end of his 'prefatory remarks' on the study Freud indicated 'apart from the dreams . . . the techniques of the analytic work has been revealed in only a very few places' (1905).[34] In particular, Freud continued since it was such a short analysis 'precisely that portion of the technical work which is the most difficult never came into question with the patient; for the factor of 'transference' . . . did not come up for discussion during the short treatment' (ibid.).[35] Nevertheless, Freud did engage himself in some preliminary discussions of this phenomenon as part of his concluding remarks. Just as in the *Studies* Freud was prompted to reflect on this phenomenon, so too with the Dora case 'transference' emerged as a matter that demanded his attention. Freud explained the origins of this phenomenon in this way:

> It may be safely said that during psychoanalytic treatment the formation of new symptoms is invariably stopped. But the productive powers of the neurosis are by no means extinguished; they are occupied in the creation of a special class of mental structures, for the most part unconscious, to which the name of '*transference*' may be given. (1905)[36]

He further explained that the novel feature of these new products of the 'productive power of the neurosis' was that 'they replace some earlier person by the person of the physician'. Indeed that they emerge as 'a whole series of psychological experiences are revived, not as belonging to the past, but as applying to the person of the physician at the present moment' (ibid.). He saw these as 'an inevitable necessity' and as unavoidable and yet as holding the very key to therapeutic success for having been aroused 'they are then turned to account for the purposes of the analysis by being made conscious, and in this way the transference is constantly being destroyed' (ibid.). Accordingly Freud concluded: 'transference, which seems ordained to be the greatest obstacle to psychoanalysis, becomes its most powerful ally, if its presence can be detected each time and explained to the patient' (ibid.).[37] The therapeutic power of transference was a theme which Freud was to develop further, indeed during a discussion of the role of transference in one of the early psychoanalytic meetings Freud was unequivocal about its vital place in the therapeutic *armamentarum* of the analyst:

> There is only one power which can remove the resistance, the transference. The patient is compelled to give up his resistance to *please us*. Our cures are cures of love. There would thus remain for us only the task of removing the *personal* resistances (those against the transference). To the extent that transference exists – to that extent can we bring about cures: the analogy with hypnotic cures is striking. It is only that in psychoanalysis, the power of the transference is used to produce a *permanent* change in the patient, whereas hypnosis is nothing but a clever trick. The vicissitudes of the transference decide the success of treatment. The only thing the method

still lacks is authority; the element of suggestion must be added from without. But even so, the need of the unconscious for liberation meets us half way. The neurotic does not fall ill again because we have made conscious the infantile content (1907).[38]

During the second decade of the new century Freud elaborated his ideas on transference still further in a series of papers on psychoanalytic technique. In these Freud concluded that every conflict 'had to be fought out in the sphere of transference' (1912)[39] thus a phenomenon which had appeared initially as an unwanted distraction came over the years in the refinement of his techniques to represent the most crucial aspect of psychoanalytic therapy for Freud. The phenomenon whereby the analyst transferred his feelings onto his patient was also considered and dubbed 'countertransference' by Freud.

As may be expected, the Dora case, and Freud's subsequent case of the 'homosexual woman' (of 1920) have been subjected to considerable scrutiny from women, notably feminist, writers. Their researches have confirmed that Freud, in common with so many men of his own time and subsequently, consistently failed to provide an adequate account of female sexuality, and further that he perpetuated many positively detrimental myths about the subject. Freud's psychology of women, entirely derivative from his explorations into his own psyche during his self-analysis, and supplemented by material gained from such case studies as Elizabeth and Dora, rarely transcends the male perspective.

We may note the dominance of this perspective in most of his writings. Thus, in his essay on feminity in his *New Introductory Lectures on Psycho-Analysis* in which he dwelt at some length on the nature of the female psyche, he made the following observations:

We do not lay claim to more than average validity for these assertions; nor is it always easy to distinguish what should be ascribed to the influence of the sexual function and what to social breeding. Thus we attribute a larger amount of narcissism to feminity, which also affects women's choice of object, so that to be loved is a stronger need for them than to love. The effect of penis-envy has a share, further in the physical vanity of women, since they are bound to value their charms more highly as a late compensation for their original sexual inferiority. Shame, which is considered to be a feminine characteristic *par excellence* but is far more a matter of convention than might be supposed, has as its purpose, we believe, concealment of genital deficiency. We are not forgetting that at later time shame takes on other functions. It seems that women have made few contributions to the discoveries and inventions in the history of civilization; there is, however, one technique which they may have invented – that of plaiting and weaving. If that is so, we should be tempted to guess the unconscious motive for the achievement. Nature herself would seem to have given the model which this achievement imitates by causing the growth at maturity of the pubic hair that conceals the genitals. The step that remained to be taken lay in making the threads adhere to one another, while on the body they stick into the skin and are only matted together. If you reject this idea as fantastic and regard my belief in the influence of the lack of a penis on the configuration of feminity as an *idée fixe*, I am of course defenceless. (1933)[40]

There are indeed grounds for suggesting that he feared women and their differences: in 1927, for instance he wrote: 'probably no male human being is spared the fright of castration at the sight of a female genital' (1927).[41] That fear pervades his work – in the words of one (male) analyst 'his theories about them were naïve rationalizations of male prejudices, especially of the male who needs to dominate in order to hide his fear of women'.[42]

It is a weakness which runs through his whole work, from his earliest formulations to his late mature work. To his friend Silberstein, as early as 1875 he had revealed his conception of women in an extended song of praise to the virtues of manhood. Men could, in Freud's opinion indulge in passions without danger, explore and create new boundaries of morality and act as their own arbiters. In contrast Freud went on 'but a woman . . . has no inherent ethnical yardstick; she can only act correctly if she keeps within the bounds of convention, observing what society deems proper . . . all her dignity and worth rest in general in one point' (1875).[43]

During the crucial years of his self-analysis and the early years of the new century this view of women as indisciplined, inferior beings became encapsulated within his theory of sexuality. It was to women that he likened 'polymorphously perverse' infants – at least what he called the 'average uncultivated women'. Having outlined the nature of this unstructured sexuality in the infant Freud wrote:

In this respect children behave in the same kind of way as an average uncultivated woman in whom the same polymorphously perverse disposition persists. Under ordinary conditions she may remain normal sexually, but if she is led on by a clever seducer she will find every sort of perversion to her taste, and will retain them as part of her own sexual activities. Prostitutes exploit the same polymorphous, that is infantile, disposition for the purposes of their profession; and considering the immense number of women who are prostitutes or who must be supposed to have an aptitude for prostitution without becoming engaged in it, it becomes impossible not to recognize that this same disposition to perversions of every kind is a general and fundamental human characteristic. (1905)[44]

Little wonder then that he concluded his lecture on feminity in 1933 with the words: 'what I've had to say about feminity doesn't always sound friendly . . . It is incomplete. If you want to know more, look at your own experience of life . . .' (1933).[45] Indeed, when he was near the end of his life he told one of his close women collaborators: 'The great question that has never been answered and which I have not yet been able to answer, despite my thirty years of research into the feminine soul, is "what does a woman want?"'.[46]

The fact that Freud's perceptions of women were irremediably coloured by his sexist, patriarchal, conception of them, may lead us to suppose that in his case studies of men, he was more fair. Such a supposition would be unwarranted, however, for in the case studies of men – the 'Rat Man', the 'Wolf Man' and Schreber – we may discern a similar disregard for context, and the same preoccupation with his own theories. If Freud's understanding of women and of sexuality was a function of his acceptance of common stereotypes and of his own marital experiences, so too, with his case studies of men, do we find themes which bear more than a passing resemblance to his own experiences of men, notably his own bisexuality and suppressed homosexuality.

In order to understand in what way his own experiences controlled his interpretation of the case material it is necessary here to recapitulate some of the events surrounding the break-up with Fliess, and its subsequent ramifications. There is a direct link between Freud's own experiences with Fliess and one of his case studies, the 'Schreber case'. The link becomes clear from a letter that Freud wrote to Karl Abraham. In 1911 Freud admonished Abraham not to forget 'that it was through him [Fliess] that both of us came to understand the secret of paranoia' (1911).[47] In December of 1910 Freud completed 'Psycho-Analytic notes on an Autobiographical Account of a Case of Paranoia' which was an analysis of the memoirs of a judge who had gone mad, Daniel Paul Schreber. On its completion he wrote to Abraham describing the paper as dealing with Schreber's book and using 'him as a point of departure to try to solve the riddle of paranoia' (1910).[48] Freud then went on to describe how he 'followed the path shown by your paper' and of how he 'had to plagiarise you very extensively in this paper' (ibid.). Since Abraham had not yet met Fliess it is difficult to understand how Freud could claim that they both received their insight into paranoia through Fliess. What is clear, however, is that Freud himself believed that he had unravelled paranoia through his encounter with Fliess and that he used that understanding to interpret the Schreber case. He published his analysis in 1911.

Daniel Schreber had published his *Memoirs of my Nervous Illness* in 1903 following his release from detention in an asylum. They contain material which he wrote down during a period when he was insane (actually the second period in his life). He was described in an official judgement in the following terms:

> The court is in no doubt that the appellant is insane. One would not wish to argue with him whether in fact he suffers from a mental illness known as paranoia. He lacks insight into the pathological nature of the inspirations and ideas which move him. What to objective observation is hallucination and delusion is for him irrefutable certainty. Even now he holds fast to the conviction that God manifests Himself to him directly and continuously performs his miracles on him. This conviction, as he says himself, towers high above all human insight and science. (Court judgement on Schreber, 1902)[49]

Part of the delusional world that Schreber lived in included the belief that he had a divine mission to redeem the world. However, in order to do that, God was in the process of transforming him into a woman. Freud's interpretation of the case – based only on study of the *Memoires* (he never met Schreber) – was that Schreber's paranoia was directly related to his unconscious homosexuality. In Freud's own words: 'what lies at the core of the conflict in cases of paranoia among males is a homosexual wishful fantasy of *loving a man*, we shall certainly not forget that the confirmation of such an important hypothesis can only follow upon the investigation of a large number of instances of every variety of paranoic disorder' (1911).[50] For Freud this case was not an isolated case; it was the confirmation of his theories already worked out as a result of reflecting upon the Fliess affair. In consequence, Freud did not bother to investigate Schreber's life more fully (his intention in the case study was not to present a new theory that might be further confirmed, but to confirm his existing theory). Had he done so he would have discovered, as William Niederland and Morton Schatzman have done, that there is a considerable basis in reality for Schreber's strange delusions – Schreber's father, a prominent German educationalist had concocted, and inflicted, a variety of wierd inventions on his son to 'improve his posture', to stop him from masturbating etc.[51] Freud's case study was merely a reconstruction, using selected evidence from another man's life, of Freud's own experience with Fliess.

What had happened with Fliess was that in 1900 the two men had had their last meeting, their last 'congress'. This had ended acrimoniously. Fliess later was to describe Freud's attitude to him as one of 'violence' and 'personal animosity' deriving from 'envy'.[52] It is indeed the case that just prior to the meeting Freud had written to Fliess saying, if they were to meet and talk 'your beautiful and secure biological discoveries would arouse my innermost (impersonal) envy' (1900).[53] Fliess had only recently finished acting as editor to the *Dream* book. There he learnt of Freud's death wishes towards him and of Freud's delight, in one particular dream, of surviving him and leaving Freud 'in [sole] possession of the field [of the neuroses]'.[54] He had also learnt there of Freud's identification with a patient with a 'Cain fantasy' who was 'capable of wanting to push his own father over a precipice from the top of a mountain'.[55] In the fateful last meeting the two men had gone for a walk into the mountains. Fliess maintained that on this walk Freud had tried, or had intended to try, to push him over a precipice, but being wary of Freud's intentions he had declined to take the proposed path that was 'too steep and dangerous'. The two men returned from their walk estranged and soon parted company – Fliess back to Berlin and Freud off eventually to travel round Northern Italy with Minna Bernays (it was on this holiday that, if we are to believe that he did, he consummated his passion for her).

Though they continued to exchange letters (until 1902) they never again met, and in 1903 and 1904 fell out further when two young Viennese philosophers published works on the two theories, bisexuality and periodicity, which Fliess had been working on for so long. It turned out that the two Viennese men had been put on the track of their ideas by their contact with Freud. Freud had made a suggestion to one of them who was his patient at the time, but had not acknowledged that the idea came from Fliess. Fliess was incensed, and though he came to Vienna to discuss it with Freud, could not because Freud had left Vienna just in time to avoid him. In 1906, Fliess took the unprecedented step of authorizing publication of part of their correspondence in order to substantiate his claim that he had been plagiarized – and that Freud had been the perpetrator of the dastardly deed. Freud took this act to be not only an act of betrayal but also a sign that Fliess had developed 'a dreadful case of paranoia'.[56] As Russian psychiatrists have found, there is no better defence (provided you can get enough people to agree with you) against legitimate claims than undermining them by attributing them to the ravings of a paranoic. The whole incident had a dramatic effect on Freud. In 1907, just as he had done after the debacle of his cocaine studies in 1885, he destroyed all his letters and papers.

For the next three years he grappled with his own feelings of homosexuality and paranoia. In 1911 he was very concerned when Abraham announced that he was going to see Fliess thinking Fliess might corrupt and influence him. He wrote to Abraham 'taking the liberty of giving you my advice unasked' and suggested:

I cannot see why you should not call on him. In the first place you will meet a remarkable, indeed fascinating man, and on the other hand you will perhaps have an opportunity of getting scientifically closer to the grain of truth that is surely contained in his theory of periodicity, a possibility that is denied to me for personal reasons. He will certainly try to side-track you from psycho-analysis (and, as he thinks, from me) and to guide you into his own channel. But I am sure you will not betray both of us to him. You know his complex, and are aware that I am the centre of it, and so you will be able to evade it. You know in advance that he is a hard man, which I took many years to discover. (1911)[57]

When Abraham eventually met Fliess, and reported to Freud 'I had a friendly reception [and] he refrained from any attacks on Vienna'[58] Freud, in turn responded: 'you must not think Fliess so crude as to betray any intention in the first hour. Unfortunately he is the opposite, subtle or even cunning. You will certainly come across his complex' (1911).[59] Although in 1910 he claimed to Ferenczi that he had conquered his homosexuality (see chapter 2) between 1906 and 1910 he had numerous fainting fits in which he claimed that there was 'some piece of unruly homosexual feeling at the root of the matter' – it was always related to the former friendship. The 'Schreber Case', written at the same time as all this inner turmoil was going on over Fliess, is almost a parody of a case study unless it is considered in the light of this background material, and in the light of the considerable basis in reality of Schreber's delusions.

Of the other case studies, the 'Rat Man' and the 'Wolf Man' received their titles from various aspects of each particular case. The 'Rat Man' was a lawyer who in 1907 came to Freud complaining of obsessions. These obsessions had got worse as a result of hearing of a certain Eastern military punishment in which a pot containing live rats was strapped to a man's buttocks. The horror this induced in the man exacerbated his concern for his father and another lady whom he admired. The details of this case cannot be expounded here due to the limitation of the scope of the book – there seems to be little to add other than to point out that Freud added a note to the text in 1923 saying 'The patient's mental health was restored to him by the analysis which I have reported upon in these pages. Like so many other young men of value and promise, he perished in the Great War' (1923).[60]

The 'Wolf Man' is in some respects more interesting for he completed his analysis with Freud, and continued to remain in Vienna, there to re-emerge throughout the century having had further analytic work done on him – Anna Freud even refers to him as 'our Wolf Man'.[61] The 'Wolf Man' case was written quite specifically to refute the views of the renegade disciples Adler and Jung. It is interesting to note that time and time again his case study was used by Freud to counter the objections to his theories, thus when Rank and Ferenczi later broke with him it was the 'Wolf Man' case that Freud used to refute their arguments. Clearly he became in Freud's words 'a piece of psychoanalysis' (1937).[62] He was a Russian emigré who had lost his family fortune in the Russian Revolution and had come to Freud for help with his obsessions – he was obsessed with many digestive problems, his tailor and the buttocks of servant women. Ernest Jones described their first encounter in the following way:

> When he first came to Freud, at the beginning of February 1910, he was a helpless young man of twenty-three accompanied by a private doctor and valet and unable to dress himself or face any aspect of life . . . he initiated the first hour of treatment with an offer to have rectal intercourse with Freud and then to defaecate on his head.[63]

Jones' perception of this first meeting is, as has subsequently become clear following the publication of his source of the story, somewhat less than fair to the Wolf Man. Freud wrote about their first encounter in a letter to Ferenczi – this is the very first mention he made of the case, and predates the final written case-history by 4 years:

> A rich young Russian whom I have taken on because of compulsive falling in love, confessed to me, after the first session, the following transference [phantasies]: Jewish swindler, he would like to use me from behind and shit on my head. When he was six years old his first symptom was blasphemous complaints against God: Pig, dog etc. If he saw three piles of dung on the street, because of the holy trinity, it was unpleasant for him, and he would anxiously search for a fourth to destroy the suggestion [of the association]. (1910)[64]

Freud probably reported this to Ferenczi out of a sense of pleasure at having generated childhood phantasies so quickly – that which was soon to provide the battleground for his break with Jung. Freud, undaunted at the ascription that he was a 'Jewish swindler' took on the case for analysis. Once again, as with Dora, Freud felt the breakthrough in understanding came with a dream – he dreamt of a scene in which his bedroom window opened to reveal white wolves perched on a walnut tree, frightened they were going to eat him he woke up in terror. Freud interpreted this dream as representing 'a primal scene' in which he had witnessed his parents copulating – the whiteness represented their underwear, his obsession with buttocks derived from this event, a castration fear on seeing his naked mother. As a result of this experience, Freud argued that the Wolf Man adopted, psychologically, her passive position and thus became a suppressed homosexual.

Freud was particularly gratified with this revelation because for the first time [sic] he felt he had uncovered the infantile material that he alleged was so crucial to all of his work: 'the description of such early phases and of such deep strata of mental life has been a task which has never before been attained' (1918).[65] A remark which has prompted one psychoanalyst to remark that 'the Wolf man . . . led to the El Dorado, the long promised arrival at childhood memories which could only be heralded in "Dora" and the "Rat Man"'.[66] Once again, though, the question of whether the scene was a reality or a phantasy was 'the most delicate question in the whole domain of psychoanalysis' (1918).[67] The question was still unresolved despite Freud's constant assumption that it was. What is interesting about this case is that, because the Wolf Man lived on, it is possible to explore his life subsequently after analysis and see how he fared. The Wolf Man himself together with a number of analysts who had concerned themselves with his case has written an account of his encounter with Freud and of his subsequent life.[68] More recently an Austrian journalist, Karin Obholzer, has recorded a series of conversations with him just prior to his death, in which he refutes many of Freud's interpretations – the book makes a fascinating addition to the Freud case studies correcting and putting into context many of the more stark facts of the original.[69]

The last case study to be described in this section is the case of 'Little Hans', the 5-year-old son of Max Graf (whose comments on the atmosphere with respect to Freud in Vienna we reported earlier). The background to the 'Little Hans' case was Freud's growing awareness that in his 1905 essays on sexuality, for all his talk about children's sexuality, there is no evidence *from children* about it. By 1905 Freud had affirmed his theory of infantile sexuality which had replaced the 'seduction theory', a considerable part of the evidence Freud had for his views on infantile sexuality was derived from adults – his patients and himself. Direct evidence from work with children on the nature of pre-pubertal sexuality was scarce. True, Fliess had assiduously observed the sexual development of his son Robert and had passed on these observations to Freud. Freud himself has been barred from using his own children by his none-too-sympathetic wife who has been reported to have said: 'psychoanalysis stops at the door of the children's room'.[70] Indeed Freud himself on one occasion when he was asking Fliess for some clarification on the matter of children eating excrement confirmed the likely validity of this prohibition on his work. He asked: 'why do I not go to the nursery and – experiment?' to which his answer was plain: 'because with twelve-and-a-half hours work I have no time, and because the womenfolk do not back me in my investigations' (1897).[71] In the absence of such direct observations for himself Freud longed to be able to provide a more solid foundation to his views:

When a physician treats an adult neurotic by psychoanalysis, the process he goes through of uncovering the physical formations, layer by layer, eventually enables him to frame certain hypotheses as to the patient's infantile sexuality; and it is in the components of the latter that he believes he has discovered the motive forces of all the neurotic symptoms of later life. I have set out these hypotheses . . . [but] I am aware that they seem as strange to an outside reader as they seem incontrovertible to a psycho-analyst. But even a psycho-analyst may confess to the wish for a more direct and less roundabout proof of these fundamental theorems. Surely there must be a possibility of observing in children at first hand and in all the freshness of life the sexual impulses and wishes which we dig out so laboriously in adults from among their own debris – especially as it is also our belief that they are the common property of all men, a part of the human constitution, and merely exaggerated or distorted in the case of neurotics. (1909)[72]

When Max Graf, by this time a passionate devotee of psychoanalysis, reported that his son was showing a quite peculiarly lively interest in that portion of his body he used to describe as his "widdler" ' (1906),[73] the opportunity seemed present for Freud, working through the boy's father, to explore this matter more fully. Hans continued to be interested in all sorts of sexual matters until one day Max announced to Freud that Hans had developed a 'nervous disorder' – he became afraid to go out into the street for fear that a horse might bite him. Freud conducted an analysis of Hans through his father (in terms of the principles of psychoanalysis later enumerated a very unorthodox procedure). To Freud the material seemed to confirm his theories and to vindicate his approach. Thus in 1910 having just published the case of 'Little Hans' Freud was able to add a footnote to his *Essays* claiming that 'direct observation has fully confirmed the conclusions arrived at by psychoanalysis [giving] good evidence of the trustworthiness of that method of research' (1910).[74] He did, however, confess that:

. . . during his analysis Hans had to be told many things that he could not say himself, that he had to be presented with thoughts which he had so far shown no signs of possessing, and that his attention had to be turned in the direction from which his father was expecting something to come. This detracts from the evidential value of the analysis; but the procedure is the same in every case. For a psycho-analysis is not an impartial scientific investigation, but a therapeutic measure. In a psycho-analysis the physician always gives his patient (sometimes to a greater sometimes to a less extent) the conscious anticipatory ideas by the help of which he is put in a position to recognize and to grasp unconscious material. (1909)[75]

Plate 8. The Third International Congress in Weimar, 1911

Freud was partially gratified to add a postscript to the study in 1922 prompted by the arrival in his office of 'a strapping youth of nineteen' who announced that he was the 'Little Hans' of the case study. Publication of the case had apparently evoked a great storm of protest from people suggesting he had corrupted an innocent child. 'Strapping Hans' assured Freud that he was 'perfectly well', and suffered from no troubles or inhibitions' and had not only weathered puberty but also the divorce and remarriage of both his parents – to Freud this was vindication indeed.[76]

The significance of this analysis is not in whether it confirms Freud's theories or not but rather in the field of work with children that it opened up. Jung was to call the study 'indeed the first time insight into the psychology of the child'[77] and to follow it with his own study of a child, Agathli. Freud's study became the starting point for a movement of child-analysis.

Child-analysis was taken up in Berlin where Karl Abraham analysed his own daughter – he called the case 'Little Hilda' – and where he supported the work of Melanie Klein. Melanie Klein, recognizing the problems of relying on verbal communication with young children (psychoanalysis was after all 'the talking cure' and young children do not necessarily have a sufficient level of articulation to express their feelings adequately), developed a means of interpreting the play of children. Others, such as Margaret Lowenfelt and D. W. Winnicott in England, also developed approaches to children along these lines. Melanie Klein moved to England and began to develop a Kleinian school of child-analysis, which with the support of Ernest Jones became the dominant English tradition in psycho-analysis. Anna Freud, Sigmund Freud's youngest daughter, after teaching in a nursery school, also began to apply

Plate 8. Key

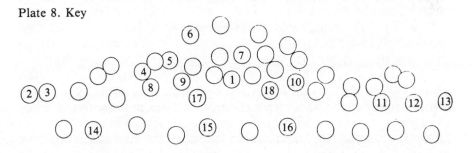

1 Sigmund Freud; 2 Otto Rank; 3 Ludwig Binswanger; 4 Ludwig Jekels; 5 Abraham A. Brill; 6 Eduard Hitschmann; 7 Paul Federn; 8 Oskar Pfister; 9 Max Eitingon; 10 Karl Abraham; 11 James J. Putnam; 12 Ernest Jones; 13 Wilhelm Stekel; 14 Eugen Bleuler; 15 Lou Andreas-Salomé; 16 Emma Jung; 17 Sándor Ferenczi; 18 C. G. Jung.

psychoanalysis to children. She remained truer to her father's original formulations, whereas Melanie Klein nurtured ideas which were contrary to the orthodox Freudian understanding. The Freud/Klein controversy threatened to split English psychoanalysis in the 1940s, and even now there is veiled antagonism between the various schools of thought.[78]

THE THEORIES: FOUNDATIONS OR SUPERSTRUCTURE

You may then ask why, since I have such a laudable appreciation of the limitations of my own infallibility, I do not at once give in to these new suggestions but prefer to re-enact the familiar comedy of an old man obstinately clinging to his opinions. My reply is that I do not yet see any evidence to induce me to give in. In early days I made a number of alterations in my views and did not conceal them from the public. I was reproached on account of these changes, just as today I am reproached for my conservativeness. Not that I should be intimidated by the one reproach or the other. But I know that I have a destiny to fulfil. I cannot escape it and I need not move towards it. I shall await it, and in the meantime I shall behave towards our science as earlier experience has taught me. (1912)[79]

The previous section of this chapter was concerned with the 'case studies', that is, with material which is *clinical* in orientation. In this section I shall consider in more detail some of the ideas which are *theoretical* in orientation. Of course, all of Freud's works are a complex blend of the two aspects – clinical material and theoretical interpretation – however, it is possible to characterize the evolution of Freud's theoretical ideas and to examine the relationship between the two.

If we look at Freud's work over the course of his life we find that although there are discernible trends (which I shall be outlining later in this section) there are also underlying constancies – basic assumptions, or fundamental beliefs that do not seem to change. His model of the mind evolved as his early formulations failed to account adequately for some phenomena, but the basic premises did not. One premise that did not change was that within individuals there is some sort of mental apparatus (a mind) which though, in some sense, related to the brain and its anatomy and physiology, can be described in psychological terms, and can be considered to be relatively constant and permanent. Similarly another unchanging premise was that a large part of that mind is hidden from direct scrutiny (the unconscious). Likewise Freud's belief that within that apparatus a form of psychological determinism acts such that observable events can reliably be attributed to some psychological cause remained constant. The belief that the abnormal and the normal lay on some sort of continuum remained as a bedrock belief in psychoanalysis.

Freud retained a faith in science and its methods throughout his life. Freud took an early interest in science – in particular in science as the source of answers to life's problems (he once wrote to Silberstein, his student friend, 'you are searching for truth in life with the same urgency as I try to seek it in science'[80]). He also thought the discipline he had obtained as a result of studying philosophy at the University had given him an acute awareness of questions of the relationship between theory and observation, and of the danger of abstract theorizing. He once gave Silberstein a warning about getting involved in the politics of the social democrats, in terms which are remarkably similar to many criticisms which were subsequently directed at his own system. Freud, argued to Silberstein that the social democrats had 'turned their views into a dogma' permitting 'no discussion of it' – a fact which should certainly not endear them to any thinking professional. He concluded that 'their ideological system, which you praise, is the worst possible proof of the validity of their convictions, for all their claims and hopes are based on these 'speculative theories' (1875).[81]

As his own theories grew Freud was particularly keen to maintain that psychoanalysis was a neutral scientific technique with the usual relationship between observations and theories. It did, he argued, arise out of observations ('the psychoanalytic view . . . is . . . empirical – either a direct expression of observations or the outcome of a process of working them over' (1916/1917),[82] but it had a developed theory ('[it is] an impartial instrument like the infinitesimal calculus, as it were' (1927).[83] Thus, when he was outlining the development of his theories in his autobiography it was almost with despair that he exclaimed 'psycho-analysis is a natural science – what else could it be?' (1925), and with venom that he retorted that he 'always felt it was a gross injustice that people have refused to treat psycho-analysis like any other science' (1925).[84] Drawing on an analogy with physics (where the new theories of relativity, 'quantum' energy had but recently overturned the long-established 'certainties' of Newtonian physics) Freud felt it 'a legitimate course to supplement the theories that were a direct expression of experience with hypotheses that were designed to facilitate the handling of the material and related to matters which could not be a subject of immediate observation' (1925).[85] But since such introductions could produce 'uneasiness' Freud suggested that 'these ideas are not the foundation of science, upon which everything rests: that foundation is observation alone. They are not the bottom but the top of the whole structure, and they can be replaced and discarded without damaging it' (1914).[86]

Freud's idea of science forms a basic assumption that underlies his theoretical ideas; indeed he constantly makes appeal to the idea of science to justify and legitimate his theoretical conclusions and findings. Such an appeal is by no means devoid of significance, as Jung observed (of Freud):

> Today, the voice of one calling in the wilderness must perforce ring out with scientific tones if the ear of the contemporary world is to be reached. At all costs we must say that it is science which has brought such facts to the light of day, regardless of whether science has done it or not. That alone is really convincing.[87]

Jung's use of a religious metaphor – that of John the Baptist – may be even more apt than he intended. There is a link between men's thought systems (their ideologies) and their religious commitments (their idolatries). The linkage has been cogently explored by a number of Christian sociologists, notably Jacques Ellul. He has argued that 'the forms and meanings of the sacred today can no longer be those of an enduring sacred. Man is forced to create something to serve as sacred'.[88] In particular he notes that 'modern man (by which he means post-Enlightenment man) is just as religious as medieval man . . . and the sacred is proliferating all around us'. The investment of meaning and significance into these new masters – science, the state, the individual – creates what Ellul calls the 'new demons'. Having thus been created, those 'new demons' control and dominate us in just the same way as medieval man was enslaved by his demons. Freud, in addition to being under the sway of the 'new demon' sex (see chapter 2) was also dominated by an idolatrous conception of science. Freud's talk of having to fulfil his destiny, and of sticking to his scientific principles to await that destiny, point to the serious way in which he took his science.

Turning now to the evolution of his theoretical ideas, I should like to suggest that the development of psychoanalysis can be seen as having four phases.[89] Freud himself, in 1925, suggested that 'the history of psycho-analysis falls from my point of view into two phases'[90] but the additional two phases of my scheme represent post-1925 developments and so can be integrated into his scheme.

The first phase of his work represents his views from the time he returned from working with Charcot in Paris in 1886 until 1897 when he abandoned – at least privately – his seduction theory, what he later called his 'first great error' (see chapters 1 and 2). In this phase of his work he believed that his patients were the victims of 'forgotten' childhood seductions (actually not consciously forgotten but repressed, and, as it were, half 'remembered' in the symptoms of the illnesses). In this phase of his work there was an emphasis on discovering the effects of the real world on people – his patients had been affected by reality. Although 1897 marked a turning point for his ideas, he did not let on publicly that they had changed until 1905 when, in his famous essays on sexuality, he casually dropped the news that he had previously overrated the importance of seduction. He wrote there

> I cannot admit that [earlier in my work] I exaggerated the frequency or importance of that influence, though I did not then know that persons who remain normal may have had the same experiences in their childhood, and though I consequently overrated the importance of seduction in comparison with the factors of sexual constitution and development. Obviously seduction is not required in order to arouse a child's sexual life; that can also come about spontaneously from internal causes. (1905)[91]

The abandonment of the seduction theory marked the beginning of the second phase in psychoanalysis. The second phase ran from 1897 until 1923. The key theoretical idea of this phase was the Oedipus complex – that theory which suggested that young children entertain wishful phantasies of sexual desire for their parents. Freud saw this concept as the most important discovery he had made, and much of the second-phase work is related to exploring its ramifications and dimensions. In his autobiography Freud recalled the discovery:

> When, however, I was at last obliged to recognize that these scenes of seduction had never taken place, and that they were only phantasies which my patients had made up or which I myself had perhaps forced on them, I was for a time completely at a loss. My confidence alike in my technique and in its results suffered a severe blow; it could not be disputed that I had arrived at these scenes by a technical method which I considered correct, and their subject-matter was unquestionably related to the symptoms from which my investigation had started. When I had pulled myself together, I was able to draw the right conclusions from my discovery: namely that the neurotic symptoms were not related directly to actual events but to wishful phantasies, and that as far as the neurosis was concerned psychical reality was of more importance than material reality. I do not believe even now that I forced the seduction-phantasies on my patients, that I 'suggested' them. I had in fact stumbled for the first time upon the *Oedipus Complex*, which was later to assume such an overwhelming importance, but which I did not recognize in its disguise of phantasy. (1925)[92]

The shift in emphasis – from material reality to psychical reality – where the causes of neurosis are sought for *within* the individual has become one of the dominant orthodoxies of all subsequent psychoanalytic thought.

It is only more recently when psychologists have turned once more to the context of distressed individuals that a more balanced, realistic account of the genesis of neurosis has become possible; in the words of Jeff Masson (the translator of the complete edition of the Freud/Fliess letters):

> [In] shifting the emphasis from a real world of sadness, misery and cruelty, to an internal stage on which actors performed invented dramas for an invisible audience of their own creation Freud began a trend away from the real world that, it seems to me, has come to a dead halt in the present-day sterility of psychoanalysis throughout the world'.[93]

The second phase is often called the topographical phase of Freud's work after the theory he propounded of mental functioning (the so-called topographical approach). Freud was using a topographical model of the mind. Freud first introduced this model in his dream book, but he developed and elaborated it further throughout his writings until 1923. He proposed that the mind could be considered to consist of three systems – the Conscious, the Preconscious and the Unconscious – these systems were related to each other spatially. Freud described his intentions in these terms:

> The subdivision [of the mind] is part of an attempt to picture the apparatus of the mind as being built up on a number of *agencies* or *systems* whose relations to one another are expressed in spatial terms, without, however, implying any connection with the actual anatomy of the brain. (I have described this as the *topographical* method of approach). Such ideas as these are part of a speculative superstructure of psycho-analysis, any portion of which can be abandoned or changed without loss or regret the moment its inadequacy has been proved. (1925)[94]

It is never an easy task to simplify a complex phenomenon such that it becomes readily understandable and yet retains those essential features that are in need of explanation. When Freud tried to outline his topographical model he had to resort to analogies that he admitted were 'crude' and 'incorrect' but nevertheless instructive. Freud outlined the model thus:

> The crudest idea of these systems is the most convenient for us – a spatial one. Let us therefore compare the system of the unconscious to a large entrance hall, in which the mental impulses jostle one another like separate individuals. Adjoining this entrance hall there is a second, narrower, room – a kind of drawing room – in which consciousness, too, resides. But on the threshold between these two rooms a watchman performs his function: he examines the different mental impulses, acts as a censor, and

will not admit them into the drawing-room if they displease him . . . The impulses in the entrance hall of the unconscious are out of sight of the conscious, which is in the other room; to begin with they must remain unconscious. If they have already pushed their way forward to the threshold and have been turned back by the watchman, then they are inadmissible to consciousness; we speak of them as *repressed*. But even the impulses which the watchman has allowed to cross the threshold are not on that account necessarily conscious as well; they can only become so if they succeed in catching the eye of consciousness. We are therefore justified in calling this second room the system of the *preconscious*. (1916/1917)[95]

We may picture this model on a diagram.

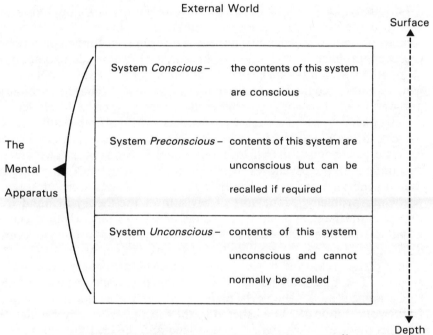

Figure 2. Adapted from Sandler, Holder and Dare, 1973.[96]

The unconscious was for Freud something that could never fully be understood: '[it] is as unknowable as electricity'[97] he declared at the end of his life. Despite that its existence could be inferred. Thus, in 1925 he suggested: 'Analysts refuse to say what the Unconscious is, but they can indicate the domain of phenomena whose observations has obliged them to assume its existence' (1925).[98]

From observations Freud posited that the Unconscious system contained basic instincts and drives which Freud thought were primarily sexual –

he called the energy behind these drives the 'libido'. These drives, Freud posited, were constantly seeking discharge (in much the same way as the build up of electrostatic charge seeks discharge through earthing). Since, these drives included infantile bisexual impulses, sexual longings and jealousies directed at and against parents (the Oedipal desires), these instincts were seen as threatening, or dangerous, or as giving rise to unpleasant contradictions. They were thus prevented from reaching consciousness by repression or censorship. The only means of effecting their release (other than by 'talking them out' in psychoanalysis) was through the diversion of their energies into substitute activities – symptoms, dreams and parapraxes. Freud also believed that the energy of these instinctual drives could be diverted to creative and scientific activity; indeed that civilization was built on the sublimated energy of the sexual drives.

Gradually, however, he found as the new century wore on and, as he extended the range of phenomena subjected to his scrutiny, that the topographical model begun to appear too simplistic. Rather than revise the topographical model initially he simply introduced incompatible elements to it in ways that solved his initial precipitating problem but which contradicted the basic assumptions of the model. Thus he introduced a second form of censorship between the preconscious and the conscious; he introduced a second category of instincts – the self preservative drives (or 'ego drives') to account for the problem of aggression; he introduced the concept of narcissism (self-love) to account for some of the phenomena encountered in the psychoses. By the beginning of the 1920s it was clear that no matter how helpful individual new concepts were at solving particular problems, some sort of revision of the theory of mind was necessary for the sake of clarity and consistency. Accordingly he declared when introducing that revision 'we land in endless obscurities and difficulties if we keep to our habitual forms of expression' (1923).[99]

In 1923 he published a new model, the structural model, in a paper entitled 'The Ego and the Id'. He continued to talk in terms of the topographical model, he never abandoned completely its concepts and framework, but in 1923 he ushered in the third phase of psychoanalysis with his theories on the ego, the super-ego and the id. In the preface to *The Ego and the Id* Freud suggested that 'it is more in the nature of a synthesis than of a speculation and seems to have had an ambitious aim in view. I am conscious, however, that it does not go beyond the roughest outline and with that limitation I am perfectly content' (1923).[100] His 'ambitious aim' was quite clearly the reformation of his theory of the mind. Despite this initial contrast between the synthetic and the speculative aspects of the ideas, Freud continued to suggest that they were indeed speculative ideas. Thus in 1925 he saw these new ideas as being very tentative when he wrote in his autobiography: 'in the works of my later years . . . I have given free rein to the inclination, which I kept down for so long, to speculation' (1925).[101] He described the new view in this way:

> In my latest speculative works I have set about the task of dissecting our mental apparatus on the basis of the analytic view of pathological facts and have divided it into an *ego*, and *id* and a *super-ego*. The super-ego is the heir of the Oedipus complex and represents the ethical standards of mankind. (1925)

For all of his suggestions that these new ideas, and this new model were the products of unfettered speculation, there was a more immediate source of them. That source was a psychoanalyst called Georg Groddeck. In 1921 he sent Freud five chapters of a book he was writing. In those chapters Groddeck used the German word '*Es*' to describe the unconscious. It means simply 'it'. Freud himself used the same word which is now translated 'id'. Freud was enthusiastic about the ideas in the manuscript: 'your style is enchanting, your speech like music' he declared.[102] Groddeck, encouraged, sent Freud the rest of the book and asked Freud to decide a title. In July 1922 Freud announced to one of his other pupils that he was 'occupied with something speculative . . . it will result in either a small book or else nothing at all. I will not reveal to you the title, only that it has to do with Groddeck' (1922).[103] Both Groddeck's book called *The Book of It*, and Freud's called *The Ego and the Id*, appeared in the early part of 1923.

Freud congratulated Groddeck on the book's publication:

> I like the little book very much. I believe it is very important to keep bringing home to people the fundamentals of psycho-analysis to which they are so inclined to close their eyes. The work, moreover, expounds the theoretically important point of view which I have covered in my forthcoming *The Ego and the Id* (1923).[104]

Groddeck in turn congratulated Freud on the publication of his book, although to his wife he complained 'in reality it was written to appropriate secretly loans made by . . . me'.[105] While it is true that Freud did adopt and adapt Groddeck's term (he did acknowledge he had taken up 'a suggestion by Groddeck') he did so within the context of his own evolving thought so that we might say that Groddeck's ideas were the immediate stimulations for Freud to make his long-needed revision to his theory of the mind, not the sole factor in the revision.

We may find clarification of 'the new model' diagrammatically, first in relating the two frames of reference (as in fig. 3), and secondly in drawing a representation of the structural model (as in fig. 4).[106]

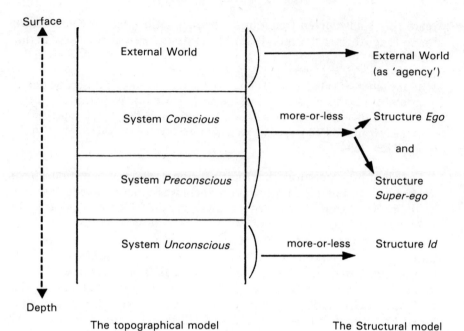

The topographical model   The Structural model

Figure 3. Adapted from Sandler, Dove and Holder, 1982.

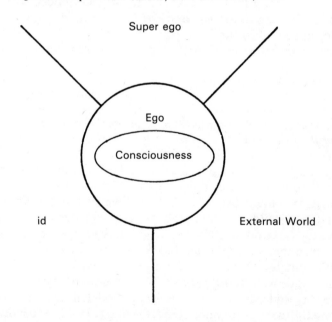

Figure 4. Adapted from Sandler, Dove and Holder, 1982.

A number of points may be made about this new model. First what is implied by structural is some sort of more-or-less permanent organization – again, as before in the psychological sphere, not directly related to brain anatomy or physiology. Secondly, the new structures are heirs to the old ideas. The 'id' is seen, as the *Unconscious* system had been before, as the reservoir of the instinctual drives – the sexual, and, by this time, the aggressive drives – these continue to remain permanently unconscious. Freud thought it particularly appropriate to call this aspect of the mind by the impersonal pronoun 'id' as it expressed 'the main characteristic of this province of the mind – the fact of its being alien to the ego'.[103] Freud's conception of the 'id' was of a decidedly murky place:

> It is the dark, inaccessible part of our personality . . . a chaos, a cauldron full of seething excitations . . . It is filled with energy reaching it from the instincts, but it has no organization, produces no collective will, but only a striving to bring about the satisfaction of the instinctual needs subject to the observance of the pleasure principle (ibid.).

The ego which had been an idea that had long hovered around uneasily within his topographical model, came to be seen as that part of the mind (that part of the id) which under pressure from the outside world began to differentiate to control the tempestuous id. Gone are the static pictures of entrance halls and drawing rooms, the chaos of the id requires some more dynamic control:

> The ego's relation to the id might be compared with that of a rider to his horse. The horse supplies the locomotive energy, while the rider has the privilege of deciding on the goal and of guiding the powerful animal's movement. But only too often there arises between the ego and the id the not precisely ideal situation of the rider being obliged to guide the horse along the path by which it itself wants to go. (1933)[108]

The ego has an even rougher time for another portion of the id became differentiated to form the 'super-ego'. This is the heir to the Oedipus complex in the topographical system – using energy derived from the id it acts as a conscience constantly castigating the ego for failing to control the id. The ego is seen to be the vital arbiter between the conflicting demands of the instincts, the external world (which in the structural model, potentially, receives as much attention as in the first phase of Freud's work) and the *super-ego* (the demands of which generate guilt); in Freud's own words:

We are warned by a proverb against serving two masters at the same time. The poor ego has things even worse: it serves three masters and does what it can to bring their claims and demands into harmony with one another . . . Its three tyrannical masters are the external world, the super-ego and the id. (1933)[109]

Freud himself was the first to admit that these formulations were but preliminary explorations into the complexities of human nature. He concluded one of his *New Introductory Lectures* on the new structural model with the following *caveat:*

Here is . . . [a] warning . . . In thinking of this division of the personality into an ego, a super-ego and an id, you will not of course, have pictured sharp frontiers like the artificial ones drawn in political geography. We cannot do justice to the characteristics of the mind by linear outlines like those in a drawing or in primitive painting, but rather by areas of colour melting into one another as they are presented by modern artists. After making the separation we must allow what we have separated to merge together once more. You must not judge too harshly a first attempt at giving a pictorial representation of something so intangible as psychical processes. (1933)[110]

With this model of the mind Freud saw psychoanalysis as having a quite specific task. In *The Ego and the Id* he expressed that task in these terms: 'Psycho-analysis is an instrument to enable the ego to achieve a progressive conquest of the id' (1923).[111] In his *New Introductory Lectures* he was more expansive on this theme:

Its intention is . . . to strengthen the ego, to make it more independent of the super-ego, to widen its field of perception and enlarge its organization, so that it can appropriate fresh portions of the id. Where id was, there ego shall be. It is the work of culture – not unlike draining the Zuider Zee. (1933)[112]

To a certain extent Freud knew that this task belonged to the future – that psychoanalysis as a movement must, like the ego conquering the id, conquer the minds of the world to foster that individual conquest. This was to be the task of his followers. The fourth phase of psychoanalysis is the phase of his followers not of himself. He is reported once to have said to a pupil: 'What will they do with my theory after my death? Will it still resemble my basic thought?'[113] As Freud grew older, and as he drew followers around him, psychoanalysis grew and developed on many fronts through the ideas and personalities of others – this growth is to be the subject of the next section.

Plate 9. The 'Committee' in 1922 including, clockwise from the far left: Rank, Abraham, Eitingon, Jones, Sachs, Ferenczi, Freud.

THE FOLLOWERS: STARTERS AND STAYERS

> I find myself in the midst of a great movement in the interpretation and treatment of nervous diseases, one that is probably not unknown in Roumania either, since it has gained many adherents in Russia, Switzerland and America. (1910)[114]

These words are taken from a letter Freud wrote to his student friend Silberstein some 20 years after they had last written to each other. Silberstein had obviously written to Freud and asked how he was. Freud's reply shows us something of his perception of his position and achievements at this time. The letter explained how he considered himself relatively well off having established a full, lucrative, private practice (this is in marked contrast to the 1890s where a constant theme of his letters to Fliess was his lack of money and his concern over it); he had acquired a number of pupils who were prepared to do as he suggested (again in marked contrast to the period that he called his 'splendid isolation', the late 1890s); he had acquired a measure of international repute (whereas in the 1890s he only had the acceptance of Fliess and Minna Bernays); and finally he had continued to meet opposition to his views (he wrote of the 1890s that he began to experience 'the reaction of distaste and repudiation which was later to become so familiar to me').[115] Freud also reveals that he had by this time become part of a 'great movement', he had become caught up, as it were, in something bigger than just a scientific research tradition. In the very same year he wrote to one of his 'many pupils', Karl Abraham, with a more personal assessment of his involvement with that 'great movement'.

> On the whole, I think, our cause is going very well, and is no longer restricted to my four eyes only [an allusion to a contemporary German aphorism which suggested that secrets should be restricted to four eyes only]. Advances will now be more difficult, the surface has been creamed, the final results are perhaps not yet plainly visible, and defence is required not only against enemies but also against rash fellow-workers. But perhaps it is merely I who feel the necessity to slacken my pace while the younger generation is vigorously pressing forward. (1910)[116]

In order to understand in what senses Freud was caught up in, and in what senses he created, a movement, and in order to understand the nature of that movement, it is necessary to draw back slightly and outline and assess the events and their significance during this period. Despite what Freud says about his period of isolation (he says 'a vacuum rapidly formed itself about my person')[117] Freud did have a group of people to whom he could relate, the Jewish B'Nai B'Rith Society. Years later he was to write to the group that:

> It happened that in the years from 1895 onwards I was subjected to two powerful impressions which combined to produce the same effect on me. On the one hand I had gained my first insight into the depths of the life of the human instincts; I had seen some things that were sobering and even, at first, frightening. On the other hand, the announcement of my unpleasing discoveries had as its result the severance of the greater part of my human contacts; I felt as though I were despised and universally shunned. In my loneliness I was seized with a longing to find a circle of picked men of high character who would receive me in a friendly spirit in spite of my temerity. Your society was pointed out to me as the place where such men were to be found. (1926)[118]

The fact that Freud sought such a group of 'picked men of high character' to support and encourage him, and the fact that the found his solace in the company of other Jews are two significant facts if we are to consider the developments of the twentieth century for they remain features of the 'psychoanalytic movement'.

In 1900, on holiday at Achensee in the Alps, Freud has his final 'congress' with Fliess – they never met again, although they continued to correspond. As a result of that 'congress' Freud felt himself to be yet more isolated. Following the congress, assuming that he did, Freud finally managed to consummate his passion for Minna. The conquest of Minna represented, in Freud's complicated phantasy world, the route whereby he felt able to conquer Rome (he who would first kiss the mother . . .). The conquest of Rome, the task that his childhood hero, Hannibal, had failed to do, had origins that were 'deeply neurotic'. In 1901 he accomplished this; he described it as 'an overwhelming experience for me, and, as you know, the fulfilment of a long cherished wish' (1901).[119] Part of the experience that had been overwhelming was directly related to the fact that Rome was the principal city (the mother city) of the Roman Catholic Church – the source, as he saw it, of racial hatred, bigotry, and error. He confided to Fliess:

> I could not freely enjoy [Christian] Rome; I was disturbed by its meaning, and, being incapable of putting out of my mind my own misery and all the other misery which I know to exist [i.e. as a result of it], I found almost intolerable the lie of the salvation of mankind which rears its head so proudly to heaven. (1901)[120]

The sterility of the Catholic rituals he had witnessed as a child; the years of being the victim of anti-Semitism largely perpetrated by the Catholic

Church; and an intense dislike of Christianity all crystallized in Rome for Freud to produce an inner conviction, the pursuit of which became the dominant, but covert, aim of his life – to expose the 'lie of salvation' and show it to be just that, a lie.

Such a concern goes way beyond any scientific pretensions that Freud purports to have. In Eric Fromm's words 'under the disguise of a scientific school [Freud] realized his old dream, to be the Moses who showed the human race the promised land, the conquest of the Id by the Ego, and the way to this conquest'.[121] Many may cavil at such a proposition about a man who professed only to be a scientist who discovered new facts and constructed theories to explain them but the overwhelming evidence is that Freud and his followers conceived their task, at least in private, in religious and ethical terms. Ferenczi, writing to Freud at the end of the First World War described his involvement in the movement in precisely those terms:

> The only thing that has kept up my spirits in these days, and will continue to do so, is the optimism I owe to the circumstances of being a collaborator in psychoanalysis, a spiritual movement which undoubtedly has a future. Regarded *subspecie* psychoanalysis, the recent frightful events fall into place as merely episodes in a still very primitive social organization. And even if our hopes deceive us and mankind remain the victim of their unconscious to the very end, still we have been vouchsafed a glimpse behind the senses, and knowledge of the truth can compensate us for much we are deprived of and also for much suffering.[122]

For Freud involvement in such a movement drew upon his earlier political aspirations. These are seen in his aspirations of entering politics with his *Bund* companion Heinrich Braun; his aspirations to emulate certain Austrian political leaders, Victor Adler and the German socialist leader Lassalle (whose translation of Virgil Freud makes use of in his introductory quotation to the dream book, and whose translation is used by the 'young man' in the 'aliquis' parapraxis). It also draws upon his earlier emotional identifications: with Hannibal ('to my youthful mind Hannibal and Rome symbolized the conflict between the tenacity of Jewry and the organization of the Catholic Church'[123]) and with Moses ('Another time someone led me to the top of a hill and showed me Rome half-shrouded in mist; it was so far away that I was surprised at my view of it being so clear. There was more in the content of this dream than I feel prepared to detail; but the theme of 'the promised land seen from afar' was obvious in it'[124]).

That his dominant, covert aim was directed at exposing the pretensions of the hated Catholic Church, and *a fortiori* against the 'lie of salvation' is clear from the opening quotation in the *Dream* book. At the time that he was writing this he was convinced that he had been denied his rightful professorship because of Catholic anti-Semitism. Unlike his compliant father, he had longed to rear up and fight that anti-Semitism – to attack Rome as the source of all hatred for the Jews. The *Dream* book was the beginning of his revenge. Freud prefaced the book with a quotation from his beloved Lassalle's translation of Virgil: '*Flectere si nequeo superos, Acheronta movebo*'. It means 'If I cannot bend the higher powers, I shall stir up Hell' (see plate 7). This is clearly an allusion to his theories of dreams – where the unconscious is seen as the source of dreams, and where base motives can be ascribed to even the most noble sentiments and ideas – but it also contains other allusions. Lassalle first used this quotation in the context of a (Jewish) stand against the state, and the words themselves were uttered by Juno who calls from Hell a fury to prevent the founding of Rome and to defend the 'Semitic' Dido against Aeneas. They are also clearly a reference to Freud's intended disturbance of the higher powers of the church – he was out to attack Christianity. Freud himself later flatly denied that the question had any other significance than 'merely to emphasise the most important part in the dynamics of the dream' (1927).[125] – that there was nothing 'Promethean' about it, but then he was always careful to conceal his true motives.

Freud hated Christianity, he hated all that it stood for – anti-Semitism; the hypocrisy of 'Christian' civilization; the stern demands of its morality; and the suggestion that man's destiny was ultimately linked with an eternal purpose. From 1900, his opposition to Christianity, hitherto mostly expressed as caustic comments in his letters, found an increasing outlet in his theories and in the movement they spawned. As the psycho-analytic movement was in its infancy it is tempting to relate the religious nature of this movement, its cultic significance, to that profound encounter which I have called the 'Orvieto encounter'. There is no doubt that at Orvieto Freud experienced something which had a dramatic effect upon his life – not least because out of it the famous 'self-analysis' grew. We may further wonder whether in the figure of the 'Anti-Christ' Freud found a symbol whereby he was able to focus his antagonism to Christianity. Freud certainly did not disavow the association when in 1930 the novelist Arnold Zweig wrote to him proclaiming him as the *true* Nietzsche. Zweig wrote: 'psycho-analysis has reversed all values, it has conquered Christianity, disclosed the true Antichrist, and liberated the spirit of resurgent life from the ascetic ideal'.[126] Freud's overt aims may well have been scientific – furthering the new science of depth psychology – but his covert aims were far more subtle and complex – to conquer the source (as he saw it) of Christianity, Rome, to accomplish that which Hannibal failed to do. I have looked at the achievements of his scientific work in the first two sections of this chapter: the covert aspects of his mission become clearer as the history of the psychoanalytic movement unfolds.

Interestingly, it was Freud's dream book, *The Interpretation of Dreams*, which was largely responsible for initiating the movement and the cause. It was through reading this book that many of his early followers first became interested in his work. Throughout the 1890s, but particularly since the publication of his joint work with Breuer, Freud's reputation in Vienna was largely based upon his advocacy of two dubious theories – the theories on cocaine, and the seduction theory of the neuroses. There was justifiable distrust of both of these theories among his contemporaries, indeed Freud himself had probably stopped using cocaine by about 1896, and had certainly abandoned the seduction theory by 1897, so that in a sense, he no longer accepted his own (public) position. In 1899 he complained to Fliess that in Vienna 'I have a few readers here . . . the time is not yet ripe for followers. There is too much that is new and incredible, and too little strict proof' (1899).[127] With the publication of *The Interpretation of Dreams* and with the subsequent publication of the short introductory book, *On Dreams* (in 1901) the time for followers was ripe.

The early years of the new century are as shrouded in myths as the 1890s. Both in his letters, and in his subsequent autobiographical essays, Freud staunchly maintained that 'not a leaf has stirred to show that the interpretation of dreams meant anything to anyone' (1900).[128] However, this feeling is much more a reflection of Freud's covert expectations than an accurate description of the actual reception of the work. True there were critical reviews, but equally there were those whose appreciation for Freud's work shone through. Of the forty or so reviews that Freud's dream books received between them many were very complimentary, as shown by one example produced by a German reviewer who wrote that '[*The Interpretation of Dreams*] is psychologically the most profound that dream psychology has produced thus far . . . in its entirety the work is forged as a unified whole and thought through with genius'.[129] Even such high praise and recognition was not enough for Freud who longed for public recognition for his hard-won ideas. Recognition was coming but at a pace out of step with Freud's aspirations.

Gradually, following the publication of his two dream books, Freud began to attract followers who liked what they had read and wanted to know more. Two of the first, Wilhelm Stekel and Alfred Adler, were young doctors in Vienna. Stekel a general practitioner, who had first learnt of Freud's work through reading a critical review of *The Interpretation of Dreams*, had immediately sought Freud out. Years later he recalled that Freud 'lent me his new book. I was enraptured, I wrote a long paper in two parts [for an Austrian newspaper] and emphasized the importance of this book which was inaugurating a new science of dream interpretation'.[130] He became an ardent follower of Freud proselytizing for him in the Viennese press. Freud in turn was influenced by his stress on the importance of symbols in dreams, and dedicated one of his books to him. Alfred Adler, an ophthalmologist who had become interested in the field of emotional illness, read the *Interpretation of Dreams* when it first appeared and felt as a result 'This man has something to say to us!'[131] When, in the autumn of 1902, Stekel suggested to Freud that a small discussion group be started, Freud leapt at the idea and promptly invited Adler to attend.

The group became a regular weekly discussion forum. It was the first opportunity Freud had had to try out, and nurture his ideas in a supportive atmosphere in Vienna. These Wednesday evening meetings were the Viennese heirs of the 'congresses' Freud had had with Fliess in the 1890s – they became the testing pan of his ideas. Stekel recalled, of the early meetings that 'there was complete harmony among [us] no dissonances; we were like pioneers in a newly discovered land, and Freud was the leader. A spark seemed to jump from one mind to the other, and every evening was like a revelation'.[132] Stekel's testimony is not alone in the vividry of its imagery about those early meetings. Fritz Wittels, one of Freud's earliest biographers, who joined the group a few years after it had started (after it had become, in 1906, the Vienna Psychoanalytical Society) noted that the group fulfilled Freud's needs for 'collaborators who would line the walls of the tunnel with glazed bricks'.[133] Those collaborators though had to maintain a very special role of receptivity to Freud for as Wittels had put it 'what he wanted was to look into a Kaleidoscope lined with mirrors that would multiply the images he introduced into it'.[134] This sense of the importance of *Freud's* ideas was further reinforced by the mystery that shrouded the origins of those ideas themselves. Freud as the elder statesman had somehow managed to produce a system as it were *ex nihilo*; as one analyst was later to write 'psychoanalysis itself had, to all appearances, sprung from his head like Athena from the head of Zeus'.[135] Intellectual ferment was constrained by Freud's autocratic control over the group; he could not tolerate deviance from his view point. Hans Sachs, one of the early members of the group recalled that he developed a useful rule of thumb to 'spare frictions and a lot of superfluous arguing'. The rule was to state his opposition to an idea and give his reasons, then to acquiesce 'unreservedly with his decision and [act] in the way he wished, stopping all further remonstrances'.[136] As Thomas Szasz had shrewdly observed, in the group 'Freud abandoned the kind of leadership we associate with the progress of science and adopted in its stead the kind of leadership typical of big business or of imperialistic nationalism [or, we might add, a new cult]'.[137]

The Psychological Wednesday Society grew steadily to some twenty members, not all of which were medically qualified. Freud, in keeping with his desire to move from the pathological to the normal, welcomed to his ranks a music critic, an artist, a journalist, a former glass-blower – anyone prepared to accept his views. Most came from marginal social positions and most were Jews. Prominent in the group was a young Jew, Otto Rank, who from 1905 to 1925 acted as 'research worker . . . proof reader . . . adopted son'. Rank was entrusted with revising *The Interpretation of Dreams*, and Freud even used him to present to the Society ideas that he wished to be considered. Freud once noted that he had a 'deferential air' about him. One modern commentator has suggested '"deference" seems too mild a term [to describe Rank's attitude] and yet "slavery" would miss the eagerness of Rank's collaboration'.[138] Rank's role in fostering the sense of mission and the importance of the Jewish aspect of Freud and his movement was if anything even greater than Freud's himself. Rank was one of the first analysts to apply psychoanalysis to religion – the paper 'The Essence of Judaism' being the first psychoanalytic study of Judaism, presaging even Freud's studies on the subject.

Many of this early group eventually committed suicide (including Stekel),[139] and many eventually seceded from the movement usually in the most bitter and acrimonious of circumstances (Stekel and Adler were forced out in 1911, Jung in 1914, Rank in 1926, Ferenczi in 1932). Freud, reflecting on the early disagreements, admitted that 'personal differences – jealousy or revenge or some other kind of animosity always came first, scientific discoveries came later. If people were really friendly, differences of scientific opinion would not make enemies of them'.[140] In particular it was Freud's desire to dominate the group, and to maintain the purity of the doctrines, which was the source of most of the tensions. When Adler was in the process of developing an alternative interpretation of the roots of human behaviour, just prior to his final estrangement from Freud, Freud wrote to another pupil with these thoughts on the affair:

> Adler's theories digress too far from the right road, it was high time to take a stand. He forgets those words of the Apostle Paul – you will know the exact text better than I – 'And if I have not charity'. He has created a world system for himself without love, and I am about to avenge the goddess Libido he has offended. I was always determined to be tolerant and not to exercise authority; in reality this is not possible. (1911)[141]

There is an interesting photograph of Freud with his followers, taken in 1911, which gives an indication of Freud's desire to have pre-eminence in the group – he stands in the centre dominating the group – in order to increase his stature Freud had stood on a box, and Jung, a tall man, had stooped forward next to him (see plate 8).

Paradoxically, Freud's pre-eminence in the group did not put people off joining it; rather the reverse, initially it helped to establish a strong sense of group identity. The followers became the enlightened ones, and the hostile world became the enemy. The group became self-consciously Freudian; those who opposed them were seen as being victims of their own repressions. Wittels recalled how they used to attend Freud's public lectures and accompany him 'in triumph' as he left the auditorium making themselves 'as conspicuous as possible'. In this atmosphere, Freud's works and words, even obscure footnotes, became the very foundation of wisdom. Wittels again recalled they 'were as proud . . . as the pupils of Aristotle in the days before the philosopher's works had become widely known'.[142] Theodor Reik, who joined the Society after 1910, has defended his pupils 'unconscious identification' with Freud on the grounds of the 'things we shared in common'. He continued: 'together, we endured the world's reaction against our efforts to convey to it the new knowledge that had been vouchsafed us . . . Together, we endured scorn and destructive criticism . . . Together, we arrived . . .'.[143]

Ironically, given Freud's avowed opposition to religion, this 'togetherness' transcended mere solidarity and took on religious overtones. Many of the early followers expressed their support for Freud in distinctly religious terms. Hans Sachs spoke of his 'first opening of the *Traumdetung* [as] the moment of destiny for [him] – like meeting the *"femme fatale"* . . .'; he continued in like vein suggesting that on finishing the book 'I had found the one thing worthwhile for me to live for; many years later I discovered that it was also the only thing I could live by'.[144] Stekel goes so far as to admit that he was 'the apostle of Freud who was my Christ!'.[145] Jung, recalling his first meeting with Freud in 1907, recounted how Freud himself encouraged this atmosphere:

I can still recall vividly how Freud said to me, 'My dear Jung, promise me never to abandon the sexual theory. That is the most essential thing of all. You see we must make a dogma of it, an unshakeable bulwark'. He said that to me with a great emotion, in the tone of a father saying 'And promise me this one thing, my dear son: that you will go to church every Sunday'. In some astonishment I asked him, 'A bulwark – against what?' To which he replied, 'Against the black tide of mud' – and here he hesitated for a moment, then added – 'of occultism'. First of all, it was the words 'bulwark' and 'dogma' that alarmed me, for a dogma, that is to say, an indisputable confession of faith, is set up only when the aim is to suppress doubts once and for all. But that no longer has anything to do with scientific judgement; only with a personal power drive.[146]

Max Graf, the musicologist and father of Little Hans was as explicit as Jung in observing the religious nature of Freud's new movement. Concerning the weekly Wednesday meetings he wrote: 'there was an atmosphere of the foundation of a religion in that room. Freud himself was its new prophet who made the theretofore prevailing methods of psychological investigation appear superficial. Freud's pupils – all inspired and convinced – were his apostles' (Graf, 1942).[147] The movement slowly became a 'church' with excommunication as the ultimate threat: 'Freud – as the head of the church – banished Adler; he ejected him from the official church. Within the space of a few years I lived through the whole development of a church history' (ibid.).

The Psychoanalytic Movement grew, and with it the cause of psychoanalysis. By 1905, not only had Freud's infamy spread to England, the USA and Switzerland, but also in these three places in particular Freud was beginning to get adherents to his ideas. In England Ernest Jones had been so stimulated by what he had learnt of Freud's views in reviews that he decided to learn German in order to read Freud in the original. In the USA James Putnam, in the very first issue of a new journal, the *Journal of Abnormal Psychology*, had published a favourable review of Freud's work. In Switzerland in the prestigious Bürgholzli Sanitorium under the direction of Eugen Bleuler, a small group was gathering and, drawing upon Freud's ideas, began to apply them to the new and hitherto untouched field of the psychoses. Eugen Bleuler is best known for his work in determining the existence of a psychiatric syndrome, schizophrenia, but he was also, in these early days, a supporter of psychoanalysis. It was through him that Jung first came to read *The Interpretation of Dreams*. Some of the ideas in that seemed to tie up very neatly with Jung's work on patients with dementia praecox (the disease which Bleuler was soon to designate schizophrenia), and with his diagnostic studies using word-association studies. By 1907, Bleuler had encouraged Max Eitingon, Carl Jung and Ludwig Binswanger to go to Vienna to see Freud. The interest from abroad, and the calibre of the three men, was a great fillip to Freud. Jung was soon to become adopted by Freud as the 'crown prince' of the movement, Eitingon was to become one of the stalwarts of the movement after Jung had seceded, and Binswanger, though remaining a close personal friend of Freud, was to found the immensely influential school of 'existential analysis' (a line of psychoanalytic theory which has found contemporary expression in the work of R. D. Laing and the anti-psychiatrists).

Just as in the 1890s Freud has formed a very deep friendship and dependency on Fliess, now after 1907 until he broke with him in 1914 Jung became the most important figure in Freud's life. Admittedly the relationship was different than it had been with Fliess for Jung became

Freud's 'son and heir'.[148] Fliess was rather more like a father or brother to Freud whereas with Jung, Freud could assume the fatherly role. He wrote 'when the Empire I founded is orphaned, no one but Jung must inherit the whole thing'. Similarly in 1909 he wrote to Jung of the progress of the movement 'if I am Moses, then you are Joshua and will take possession of the promised land of psychiatry, which I shall only be able to glimpse from afar' (1909).[149] Accordingly Jung was groomed for his role as 'crown prince' – becoming the chairman of the 1st International Congress in 1908, and the editor of the psychoanalytic yearbook.

This rise to power offended some of Freud's earlier followers particularly as it became known that Jung's opinion of the Viennese analysts was that Freud had no followers of any weight in Vienna, and that he was surrounded there by a 'degenerate and Bohemian crowd who did him little credit'.[150] Freud was prepared to overlook this aspect of Jung's personality because he had an important use for Jung – to be his ambassador. Freud was hoping here to draw upon two facts about Jung – that he was a Gentile and that he had a persuasive manner. To Abraham, who had himself worked at the Bürgholzli under Bleuler, Freud confessed: 'Our Aryan comrades are really completely indispensable to us, otherwise psychoanalysis would succumb to anti-Semitism' (1908).[151] As a 'Christian' and a pastor's son Jung could serve the cause of psychoanalysis by helping it to escape 'the danger of becoming a Jewish national affair' (ibid.). Jung also had an ease of manner wholly conducive to Freud's cause; 'to you all hearts are open' Freud wrote.[152] In 1909 Freud, Jung and Ferenczi were invited to Clark University, in the USA, to expound psychoanalysis. The trip was to consolidate the work done there of Jones, Brill and Putman. It was a great success, with their ideas receiving a thorough write up by Putnam in the *Journal of Abnormal Psychology*. Putnam had proved to be 'altogether a wonderful acquisition' to the psychoanalytic movement.[153] The lectures were of vital importance in the establishment of psychoanalysis in the USA. Indeed it is only now with the rise of a new confidence in the biology of mental disorder that psychoanalysis is losing its grip on American psychiatry.

As the cause grew, and numbers increased both in Vienna and abroad so too did the danger to Freud's supremacy. When eventually the differences of opinion between Freud and Jung and his colleagues in Switzerland became so great as to make a rift inevitable, Freud took the initiative in writing a none-too-impartial account of the development of psychoanalysis, his *On the History of the Psycho-Analytic Movement*. To Putnam Freud confided: 'I hope that the Swiss and their following will desert the association after reading my polemic . . . so that we can conduct our Congress in unity and with friendly feelings towards one another'. (1914)[154] In *On the History of the Psycho-Analytic Movement*, Freud described his reasons for tightening the organizational side of the movement:

> I considered it necessary to form an official association because I feared
> the abuse to which psychoanalysis would be subjected as soon as it became
> popular. There should be some headquarters whose business it would be
> to declare: 'All this nonsense is nothing to do with analysis; this is not
> psychoanalysis'. (1914)[155]

To Bleuler, in 1910 during the time when the International Psycho-
Analytical Association was being created, Freud was rather more candid
in his aims. Objecting to the fact that he was being 'represented as the
founder of a religion, as one who is worshipped and whose word is
infallible' he hoped to distance the *movement* from his *person:* 'it appeared
to me necessary to create an organization with a central office which would
conduct its external policies and give authentic information about what
should be permitted to be called psychoanalysis' (1910).[156] The new
'central office' would, it seemed, take the place of Freud himself. Stand
in the brink, as it were, between him and his critics. The International
Association was then formed out of

> . . . the need to present to the public genuine psychoanalysis and protect it
> from imitations (conterfeits) which soon would arise, and . . . [it] must be
> ready now to answer our opponents . . . it is not proper to leave these
> answers up to the whim of individuals. It is in the interest of our cause to
> bring a personal sacrifice and relegate polemics to a central office. (1910)[157]

Freud was adamant that people were confusing his 'steadfastness with
intolerance' (1910);[158] but as Bleuler was to add in a letter to Freud in
1911 after he had left the Association: 'the principle "all or nothing"
is necessary for religious sects and for political parties . . . for science
I consider it harmful'.[159] Similarly, during his break with Jung Freud
was insistent that, for the sake of the movement, he had to make a stand
against dissention. At the height of the tension he wrote to Putnam

> I must protect myself against people who have called themselves my pupils
> for many years and who owe everything to my stimulus. Now I must accuse
> them and reject them. I am not a quarrelsome person, nor do I share the
> widespread opinion that a scientific quarrel brings about clarity and
> progress. However I am not in favour of sloppy compromises nor would
> I sacrifice anything for the sake of an unproductive reconciliation.
> (1914)[160]

It is clear in the light of the comments I have quoted earlier that Jung
and Freud began to fall out over their respective emphases on the role
of sex in determining neuroses. Jung felt that Freud's emphasis on the
dogma of the sexual theory detracted from the growth of science. Freud,

in his turn distrusted Jung's mysticism despite the fact that he had exhorted Jung to 'conquer the whole field of mythology'.[161] The break between the two of them was fraught and unedifying with both of them jockeying and manoeuvring for power. To Putnam Freud revealed some of the dimension of the split: 'Jung . . . I found sympathetic so long as he lived blindly, as I did. Then came his religious-ethical crisis with higher morality, "rebirth", Bergson, and at the very same time, lies, brutality and anti-Semitic condescension towards me. It has not been the first or the last experience to reinforce my disgust with saintly converts' (1915).[162] To Freud such Christian hypocrisy was just too much to bear, he'd had enough of it before, and he was not going to let it take over *his* movement. He was once asked why it was that many of his followers left him after a time in the movement. He replied: 'precisely because they too wanted to be Popes' (1913).[163] When they finally broke Freud wrote to Abraham that he could not suppress a cheer at the prospect of the freedom it restored to his cause. Again, to Abraham, he confided:

So we are at last rid of them, the brutal sanctimonious Jung and his disciples. I must now thank you for the vast amount of trouble, the exceptional clear-sightedness, with which you supported me and our common cause. All my life I have been looking for friends who would not exploit and then betray me, and now, not far from its natural end, I hope I have found them. (1914)[164]

The net result of this, the second and the most painful, split in the psychoanalytic movement was to make Freud and his disciples close ranks still further. The church needed some sort of bishopric to act as the guardians and the protectors of orthodoxy. Even before Jung had finally been ousted the idea was mooted (most probably by Freud himself) that a small, select group be gathered together. It was as if the *Academia Castellana* of Freud's youth, and the B'Nai B'Rith of his middle years, now became resurrected to serve as the models for the new Committee; Freud admitted that 'there is a boyish and perhaps romantic element too in this conception'. To Jones, himself enamoured with the prospect of becoming a 'Paladin of Charlemagne', Freud confessed:

What took hold of my imagination immediately is [the] idea of a secret council composed of the best and most trustworthy among our men to take care of the future development of psychoanalysis and defend the cause against personalities and accidents when I am no more. (1912)[165]

The idea stuck and soon Jones had gathered Ferenczi, Rank, Sachs, and Abraham together to form 'the Committee'. Each member of the committee received a gift from Freud, a gold ring with an antique Greek intaglio mounted on it. In 1918 Max Eitingon was also introduced into the Ring making the Committee up to seven (see plate 9). Jones, whose enthusiasm for the idea never wavered has suggested that they 'acted as a sort of Privy Council to Freud, who mostly presided at our meetings, and we either made or influenced all the decisions concerning the doings of the Association, the periodicals, and many other affairs'.[166] The undisputed Pope could now speak '*ex cathedra*' and uphold the principle of infallibility still more strictly.

Even a religious movement cannot survive without converts. For Freud such 'converts' were of two sorts – patients and followers. The case studies discussed earlier in this chapter were but a tiny fraction of the patients Freud gradually built up. These patients were very important to Freud not only for the clinical material they provided but also for the financial support their fees provided. As the fame of psychoanalysis spread across the world so did Freud begin to receive patients from all over the world, particularly from America. In the dire economic circumstances of post-First World War Vienna any such foreigners, with their more secure currencies quite literally kept Freud solvent. True, they helped support a very large extended family in the Freud household, even, at times, extended to former patients (the impoverished Wolf Man received help from Freud). Freud, writing to his English nephew Samuel wrote: 'I am dependent on foreign patients and scholars, as it would be impossible to get from Austrians fees sufficient to live thereon' (1921).[167]

The reference here to scholars probably is one to that other group of 'converts' that Freud had begun to attract, would-be psychoanalysts. At that time it was by no means clear how one should become an analyst. Earlier, in 1912, Freud had spoken of the need for people practising analysis to have 'purification' by which he probably meant some sort of personal analysis but it was in no sense formalized. Most of his early followers became analysts through reading his works, or coming to his lectures, or becoming associated with an analytic group. The old guard were all like this – Rank, Federn, Abraham, Ferenczi, Tausk, Sachs, Reik, Wilhelm Reich, Brill, Putnam, Jones – they had no formal training. The only formal requirement, in the early years of the movement, was to present a paper to the analytic society. In 1918 Freud initiated a change in direction that would alter that rather casual arrangement. At the International Congress of Psychoanalysis in Budapest Freud instigated two important changes in the movement. First he declared that the movement should become, as it were, the 'church militant' and take psychoanalysis out to the world. In the first place the publishing side of psychoanalysis was set on a firm footing thanks to the generosity of a wealthy, Budapest brewer, Anton von Freund. Then in an unprecedented move he *read* out his proposals for the future of psychoanalysis:

> Institutions or out-patient clinics will be started, to which analytically-trained physicians will be appointed, so that men who would otherwise give way to drink, women who have nearly succumbed under the burden of privations, children for whom there is no choice but between running wild or neurosis, may be made capable, by analysis, of resistance and of efficient work. Such treatments will be free. It may be a long time before the state comes to see these duties as urgent. Present conditions may delay its arrival even longer. Probably these institutions will first be started by private charity. Some time or other, however, it must come to this. (1919)[168]

Though we might be tempted to note Freud's propensity for wishful thinking exhibited here, we should also note the introduction of the second novel feature – the key notion of 'analytically trained physicians'. The very same congress also had a paper given by a young psychoanalyst on the need for every analyst to have a 'didactic analysis'. The idea was that in order to practise analysis it should become a necessary requirement that the prospective analyst be analysed himself first. The idea was actually voted down at that meeting, largely on account of the efforts of two of the senior psychoanalysts of the movement, Rank and Tausk. The idea, however, lodged; principally with Freud himself. In 1920 he spoke to one such prospective analyst of his duties in 'the instruction of disciples' (1920).[169] The notion to make a 'didactic' analysis mandatory for the practice of psychoanalysis was finally accepted by the International Psycho-Analytic Association in 1925.

Hans Sachs, himself a keen exponent of the idea of a 'didactic analysis', and the instigator of the scheme to conduct such analyses in Berlin, in his reflections on the idea made the following interesting observations:

> Religions have always demanded a trial period, a novitiate, of those among their devotees who desired to give their entire life into the service of [the church] those in other words, who were to become monks or priests . . . It can be seen that analysis needs something corresponding to the novitiate of the church.[170]

Freud was totally in favour of such 'training analyses' to instruct 'his disciples' – it became the cornerstone of the new profession of psychoanalysis. The new generation of analysts, many of whom have been responsible for exporting analysis and sustaining it throughout this century, were all reared on this doctrine – Alexander, Bernfield, Fromm, Horney, Nunberg, Wortis, Erikson, Hartmann and most significantly

Anna Freud. When psychoanalysis became attacked in Germany, and analysts were forced to flee Europe it was this 'novitiate' that spread the message – the psychoanalytic diaspora was peopled by those who had been through analysis themselves. Personal analysis, by this time, a long and expensive process became the only route into psychoanalysis. To Freud this became essential to maintain purity:

> You can believe me when I tell you that we do not enjoy giving an impression of being members of a secret society and of practising a mystical science. Yet we have been obliged to recognize and express as our conviction that no one has a right to join in a discussion of psychoanalysis who has not had particular experiences which can only be obtained by being analysed oneself. (1933)[171]

Ignoring the temptation to adopt Freud's principles of interpretation, as enumerated in the Dora case – a denial really means an affirmation – that apparently simple dictum is contrary to the normal practices of science.

Freud was aware that the great public disputes and the overt schisms in the movement did damage his image considerably, and seemed to point to intolerance. He used to counter such accusations by citing the evidence of those pupils who had remained loyal to him. Such loyalty, he argued, gave the lie to his critics for 'an intolerant man, dominated by an arrogant belief in his own infallibility, would never have been able to maintain his hold upon so large a number of intellectually eminent people, especially if he had at his command as few practical attractions as I had' (1925).[172] At least that was what he used to say in public; in private he once admitted to a patient 'the goody-goodys are no good, and the naughty ones go away' (1920).[173] Those who remained loyal, the 'goody-goodys' were those who found security in orthodoxy – as Abraham was to write to Freud 'one feels so secure in the clear and unassailable structuring of your thoughts'.[173] The behaviour of the 'naughty ones' though distressing provided Freud with yet more grist for the mill, as each defection was interpreted by the theories of psychoanalysis. For Freud every break had a neurotic element at the heart of it – Breuer could not face the truth of the sexual basis of neurosis; Fliess could not accept Freud out of paranoia; Jung could not overcome his anti-Semitism; Rank was said to have 'depression [with] manic phases'.[175] Many indeed became cited as case studies in his later works either by name or as anonymous examples. The effects of these defections went deeper still with Freud.

Throughout his life, until his later years, one can find examples of Freud's strong identification with, and his closeness to, key figures in his contemporary setting. These figures were always men. As a student it had been von Fleischl and Brücke. In his early days in practice Breuer and Fliess had assumed the mantle. With the break in relations with these men, and the beginnings of the psycho-analytic movement, Rank and Jung were suitably honoured. With Jung's 'defection', Abraham and Ferenczi assumed a more prominent position in Freud's life. In the 1920s he began to lose these last close companions: Abraham died in 1925, Rank eventually broke with Freud in 1926, and Ferenczi began the slow distancing, which only his premature death in 1933, stopped making a final break. If we examine Freud's relationships during the 1920s we find a shift in emphasis. As the decade progressed Freud began to draw close to himself a group of highly able women. Pride of place in this entourage must be given to his daughter Anna, but there were others who made these later years totally unlike the earlier ones. Marie Bonaparte, Ruth Mack Brunswick, Helene Deutsch were but a few of his companions and protectors in these last years, as were the women that Anna herself introduced to the circle, Dorothy Burlingham and others. Significantly, Freud gave at least eleven women rings such as 'the Committee' had received, including his daughter Anna. The rings which had meant so much to those who received them during the years of the 'secret Committee' were now dispersed to his new vanguard for the future – his faithful women pupils.

The Psychoanalytic Movement, instigated by Freud after the turn of the century, from its humble beginnings as the Wednesday Society with its handful of interested practitioners grew to an International movement with supporters in virtually every continent and every sphere of influence. Politicians, poets, scientists, doctors, all were represented in the portals of psychoanalysis by the time that Freud died. In that sense his insistence on maintaining the purity of his doctrines paid off in the end – he established both a thriving profession, and a group of sympathetic, interested supporters. Others who seceded were less successful and their names and therapies are now merely historical phenomena. Still others who broke with Freud, with valid cause have developed their own particular schools of thought with their particular stresses. The loss of these heterodox interpretations to the development of an adequate new science of the mind is an unfortunate consequence of Freud's original desire to protect the cause.

Concerning the Last Things
From Eros to Thanatos

It is dangerous to show man too often that he is equal to beasts, without showing him his greatness. It is also dangerous to show him. too frequently his greatness without his baseness. It is yet more dangerous to leave him ignorant of both. But it is very desirable to show him the two together. (Blaise Pascal)

In 1897 Freud, writing to his friend Fliess, had noted: 'So one still remains a child of one's age, even with something one had thought was one's very own'.[1] He made this statement on discovery that other psychologists were working on the very same subjects as he was concerned with. It is a remark, however, that may be taken as applicable to his whole life and work. Taken in isolation, the views Freud developed, and the twists and turns he took, seem strangely unpredictable, even when they can be shown to follow some sort of biological logic. When they are put into their context, though, they become much more understandable. Freud himself was concerned to systematically hide and distort that personal and intellectual context in order to further the vision of himself as the psychoanalytic hero bringing the tablets of the new science to an ignorant, recalcitrant public.

In the last section of the previous chapter I have pointed out how the Psychoanalytic Movement was not just a scientific society but how it was also a vehicle for the expression of Freud's wider philosophical views. The history of the Psychoanalytic Movement expresses both the development of a research tradition – the growth of the new depth psychology – it also expresses the development of a deeply pessimistic conception of being human. If we are to redress the balance, as Pascal indicates we must, and present a picture of humanity which is less one-sided we have to understand the origins of Freud's pessimism. Just as Freud was a child of his time in *fin de siècle* Vienna in the 1890s so too was he a child of his time in this century, and his theories and ideas reflect those times. In this chapter I want to suggest that Freud's theories, and the developing research tradition, are a function of three facets of his times: they are a function of his personal history; a function of his involvement

Plate 10. Freud and his daughter Anna in 1913

with 'the Movement' and its renegades; and a function of the historical
context of early twentieth-century Europe. Freud's later theories are then,
reactions – they are reactions to his personal circumstances, his immediate
(intellectual) environment, and to his historical context. Throughout this
chapter it will become plain that the content, form and timing of all of
Freud's later works reflect these three levels of reaction. His works this
century fall conveniently into three specific categories. His work can be
divided into those which deal with a meeting with man and his creations;
those which deal with a meeting with God, with humanity's religious
sentiments; and those which deal with his meeting with death. The three
encounters with these most fundamental issues should evoke a profound
dialogue; in Freud's case, all too often, they produced a monologue as
he harangued them to conform to his theories:

MEETING MAN: FREUD ON ART AND CIVILIZATION

> But creative writers are valuable allies and their evidence is to be prized
> highly, for they are apt to know of a whole host of things between heaven
> and earth of which our philosophy has not yet let us dream. In their
> knowledge of the mind they are far in advance of us everyday people, for
> they draw upon sources which we have not yet opened up for science.
> (1907)[2]

Freud had always been a widely read scholar who had both enjoyed works
of literature, and saw their potential usefulness in providing additional
support for his ideas. As a youth, not only had he been held spellbound
by many of the great literary works (most notably, of course, Cervantes,
who was the inspiration behind the '*Academia Castellana*'). Throughout
his life there were figures, usually drawn from some literary work that
dominated his inner perceptions of himself – Joseph, Don Quixote, Faust,
Leonardo, Mephistopheles, Moses. Such figures acted as the foci of his
phantasy world. He himself also engaged in literary pursuits exercising
his hand at poetry. When his first calf-love, Gisela, got married Freud
wrote a 'poetic effusion' in praise of 'Ichthyosaura communa'.[3] It is the
only poem he wrote that survives (there may well have been others but
they probably went up in smoke in his special burning ceremonies). In
itself, apart from showing the magnitude of the impression that Gisela
made on him, it also shows Freud's early literary interest. It was an interest
that flared again under the influence of Martha in their betrothal. In 1884
Freud wrote to Martha: 'You will be astonished to hear that I am becoming
aware of literary stirrings when previously I could not have imagined
anything further from my mind' (1884).[4] However, such stirrings may
well have been prompted not from some resurgence of his earlier artistic

skills but from a practical desire to out thwart two rivals for Martha's hand. Two other young men were actively pursuing Martha, both were 'artistic' in contrast to Freud who was but a natural scientist. Freud wrote to Martha:

> I think there is a general emnity between artists and those engaged in the details of scientific work. We know that they possess in their art a master key to open with ease all female hearts, whereas we stand helpless at the strange design of the lock and have first to torment ourselves to discover a suitable key to it. (1884)[5]

With such a linkage between creativity and potency it is strange that Freud did not pursue the line of investigation further. Freud did address himself to the question of the meaning and origin of art and literature in a rather haphazard way during his 'self-analysis' with Fliess and his dream interpretations are replete with literary allusions. The crucial period, during which time he abandoned his seduction theory, was a period in which he was studying the work of Johann Weier (whose book on witches Freud was later to suggest was one of the ten most important books in world literature). The constant theme of this period was the similarities between the accounts of seduction of his patients and those of the witches in Weier's work – Freud was here confronted by the similarity of reality and fiction or rather he was confronted by the 'stranger than fiction' natures of them both – 'Where do all patients derive the horrible perverse details which are often as alien to their experience as to their knowledge?' he declared at the key point of his self-analysis in 1897.[6] It was Sophocles' play, *Oedipus Rex*, which had helped crystallize his own resolution of his feelings, and formulate the 'Oedipus complex'. Albeit, it is worth noting the frankly one-sided, and heterodox, interpretation he gave the play – Freud's concentration upon the fundamental sin of the son (incestuous relations with his mother) overshadowed, with fateful consequences, the problematic role of the father in the play thus producing a distortion into the meaning of the myth.[7] The Oedipal origins of all neurosis, in turn found confirmation for Freud in *Hamlet*. Freud felt that the 'Oedipus complex' lay 'at the root of *Hamlet*'. The example gives us a clear clue to Freud's theory of art and literature, he writes: '*I am not thinking of* Shakespeare's *conscious intentions*, but supposing rather that *he was impelled* to write it by a real event because his own unconscious understood that of his hero' (1897).[8] He incorporated this idea into his dream book and it ultimately spawned a whole tradition of psychoanalytic studies of Hamlet. Freud's thesis, and that of his followers, was that artistic or literary creations have the same psychic origins as the symptoms of the neuroses – the unconscious literally finds its expression in the work of art.

However important these literary works were in actually helping Freud to formulate his ideas, and resolve to his own satisfaction the dilemmas he was facing with respect to the contributions of reality and phantasy to the neuroses, in terms of a theory of art and literature they were merely throw-away conjectures from Freud to his confidant at this time. They had not yet become the pieces of confirmatory evidence they were soon to become in the early part of the new century. Prior to 1900 Freud did use another piece of literature to confirm his ideas, again only in private to Fliess. In 1898 he sent Fliess an analysis of a novel. Freud's interpretation of the novel is only 500 or so words, but it's a good example of the way in which his literary studies were to progress. The central thesis of the analysis was once again that the author's creation (the book) is a product of his unconscious mind – specifically that it was 'a defence against the writer's memory of an affair with his sister' (in fact, Freud may well have known that C. F. Meyer did indeed have an intense relationship to his sister).[9] In other words psychic turmoil in the unconscious erupts in a creative person to produce a work of art – in a less-creative person it would produce a neurotic symptom, or a dream, or a parapraxis. Interestingly, on those very principles, the content of the book and its interpretation – the story of the family romance in which incest is deemed acceptable if the sister is not your mother's daughter – provides one of the pieces of evidence we have advanced that points to Freud's early desires for Minna (see chapter 3).

It was not until 1906, when on a summer holiday, that Freud was able to devote himself to a literary study. He had recently completed his book on jokes, further extending the application of psychoanalysis into the realm of the normal. It was natural for him at this juncture to turn to his earlier thesis about art and literature with a view to using that as a further example. From psychoanalysis being a therapy for neurotics in the 1890s, Freud had slowly extended his ideas to turn it into the 'new science of the mind'. Dreams had succumbed in 1900, parapraxes in 1901, jokes in 1905, now in 1907 literature was to yield to the logic of psychoanalysis.

Freud chose a short novel by Wilhelm Jensen entitled *Gradiva* to apply his ideas to. The story is of a German archaeologist who had become obsessed with a plaster cast of a young girl which is to be found in the Vatican. The archaeologist had a dream about her in which he saw her at the time of the destruction of Pompeii where she perished. He feels compelled to travel to Pompeii where he finds a young girl that he believes to be his beloved. She in turn recognizes that he is deluded, but undertakes to cure him. Through her care he comes to realize that she is none other than his forgotten childhood playmate from his home town. Freud interpreted the story to show that it had been generated from Jensen's sadness at losing a childhood companion – possibly a sister lost through death. In the story of the *Gradiva* much is made of the beautiful gait of the girl. Freud postulated that Jensen's childhood companion had had a physical deformity in one of her limbs – possibly a club-foot – which had been converted into the beautiful gait. Freud himself may well have enjoyed the book in part because of his own feelings for lost childhood companions regained in early youth.

Freud sent a copy of his interpretation to Jensen, who replied that Freud's analysis followed his own aims. He considered that this was due to his own intuition, perhaps reinforced by some early medical studies, but that he had not read any of Freud's work. Freud, delighted at this reply wrote for more information, but Jensen did not feel able to supply any more, other than the fact that he had written the book in an uninterrupted flow. Freud read Jensen's replies out to the Vienna society. Jung was particularly thrilled with the work, writing to Freud that it was 'magnificent . . . one would have to be struck by the gods with seven fold blindness not to see things now as they really are'.[10] Freud, in turn, was most gratified by this response, and in a typical passage replied:

> Many thanks for your praise of *Gradiva*. You wouldn't believe how few people have managed to say anything of the kind; yours is just about the first friendly word I have heard on the subject . . . This time I knew that my work deserved praise; this little book was written on sunny days and I myself derived great pleasure from it. True, it says nothing that is new to us, but I believe it enables us to enjoy our riches . . . To tell the truth, a statement such as yours means more to me than the approval of a whole medical congress . . . (1907).[11]

In fact Jensen admitted that he did not have a sister but that he had had a childhood friend who had died of consumption when she was eighteen; and that later he had met another girl who had reminded him of her but that she had, likewise, died. However, the important thing for Freud was that he had publicly propounded his theory of the genesis of art and literature. *Gradiva*, and by implication all creative products of the mind, was 'another egocentric fantasy' analysis of which 'would lead through . . . childhood to [the] most intimate erotic experience' (1907).[12] Just as the dream book had made dreams legitimate objects of (psychoanalytic) study, and *The Psychopathology of Everyday Life* had generated an effusion of studies of mistakes and slips, *Gradiva* opened the door to a whole tradition of analytic studies of literature and art. Freud himself was to extend the tradition but many of his pupils also followed his example.

Freud's most famous (infamous) studies of art and creativity appeared in 1910 and 1914. In 1910 he produced his study of the great, Renaissance polymath, Leonardo; and in 1914 he brought out a paper, anonymously, entitled 'The Moses of Michelangelo'. It is fitting that Freud should have devoted himself to the study of these two artists for he felt himself to have a fair measure of similarity with both. Both studies probably tell us very little of the people they purport to be about but do reveal a considerable amount of information about Freud himself.

The Leonardo study, was an analysis of a personality who had long interested him (in 1898 he had discussed him with Fliess). In 1909, under the stimulus from Jung, Freud announced to Jung that he had discovered the secret of Leonardo's personality and work:

> I am glad that you share my belief that . . . we need men for more far reaching campaigns . . . We must take hold of biography. I have had an inspiration since my return. The riddle of Leonardo da Vinci's character had suddenly become clear to me. That would be a first step in the realm of biography. But the material concerning L. is so sparse that I despair of demonstrating my conviction intelligibly to others. I have ordered an Italian work on his youth and am now waiting eagerly for it. In the meantime I will reveal a secret to you. Do you remember my remarks in the 'Sexual Theories of Children' . . . to the effect that children's first primitive researches in this sphere were bound to fail and that this first failure could have a paralysing effect on them? Read the passage over: at the time I did not take it as seriously as I do now. Well, the great Leonardo was such a man; at an early age he converted his sexuality into an urge for knowledge and from then on the inability to finish anything he undertook became a pattern to which he had to conform in all his ventures: he was sexually inactive or homosexual. (1909)[13]

Freud's study of Leonardo is less a study of the actual person – as might be revealed in his diaries and records about him – but more a study of a literary creation of the Russian novelist, Merezhkovsky's. Freud's English translator dryly noted 'the most important influence was the German translation of Merezhkovsky's Leonardo book, which, as may be seen from the marked copy in Freud's library, was the source of a very great deal of his information about Leonardo'.[14] In consequence of using this 'fictitious' account of Leonardo, Freud's venture into the realm of biography only managed to produce a mythology. In particular the crucial passage upon which Freud based a considerable weight turned out to contain a mistranslation of the vital central idea. Leonardo had recalled his earliest childhood memory: 'it seems that I was always destined to be so deeply concerned with vultures; for I recall as one of my very earliest memories that while I was in my cradle, a vulture came down to me, and opened my mouth with its tail, and struck me many times with its tail against my lips' (Leonardo cited by Freud, 1910).[15] Freud's German translation of this text contained two errors – the most important being the mistranslation of 'Kite' as 'vulture'. Freud's interpretation drew upon the significance of the bird being a vulture. He further drew upon his theory of symbols in dreams to make the following deductions:

> We may venture to translate the phantasy from its own special language into words that are generally understood. The translation is then seen to point to an erotic content. A tail, *coda*, is one of the most familiar symbols and substitutive expressions for the male organ, in Italian no less than in other languages; the situation in the phantasy of a vulture opening the child's mouth and beating about inside it vigorously with its tail, corresponds to the idea of an act of fellatio, a sexual act in which the penis is put into the mouth of the person involved. It is strange that this phantasy is so completely passive in character; moreover it resembles certain dreams and phantasies found in women or passive homosexuals. (1910)[16]

Drawing upon the fact that Leonardo reported it to have been a vulture (so Freud believed) Freud then made a connection 'from such a remote quarter that it would be tempting to set it aside' (ibid.) namely in Egypt (as Leonardo would have known) the mother goddess is always represented by a vulture. Freud was thus able to decode the childhood memory to produce an account of the infantile relationships of Leonardo with his mother. The interpretation, however, hinges upon a number of either obvious errors, or dubious assumptions. In addition Freud's knowledge of the Renaissance context of Leonardo's work, particularly the Catholic context, was also so inadequate as to render his interpretations readily refutable. Freud himself regarded the essay as 'the only truly beautiful thing I have ever written' (1919).[17] He also saw objections to it as being predictable from his enemies: the essay, he wrote to a friend will 'cause plenty of offence, but I write really only for a small circle of friends and followers' (1910).[18] His disciples took the study to be *the* definitive word on Leonardo, and even, when once the errors had been exposed, attempted to rationalize away such potentially damning evidence as irrelevant.

The theory he propounded, as with the family romance analysis, and with *Gradiva* was that 'artistic activity derives from the primal instincts of the mind'. Indeed, Freud emphasized the fact – 'which it is hardly any longer possible to doubt – that what an artist creates provides at the same time an outlet for his sexual desire' (1910).[19] In other words, artists are able to convert their sexual energy (their libido) into artistic creations – Freud called this their 'capacity for sublimation'.[20] Freud, and here we may note the element of self-identification, wrote of Leonardo that he was 'a man whose sexual need and activity were exceptionally reduced, as if a higher aspiration had raised him above the common animal needs of mankind' (1910).[21] However, as with his dream theory, this theory went further than that to suggest that artistic creations not only represented sublimated sexual desires but actually gave expression to, and manifested, sublimated *infantile* sexual desires. Thus, Leonardo's work provided evidence of his infantile sexuality, and was in reality a product of it: 'the key to all his achievements and misfortunes lay hidden in the childhood phantasy of the vulture, accordingly 'only a man who had had Leonardo's childhood experiences could have painted the Mona Lisa and the St. Anne, have secured so melancholy a fate for his works and have embarked on such an astonishing career as a natural scientist' (1910).[22] The fact that the interpretation not only represents a distortion of Leonardo's known life and context, and that the interpretation is systematically distorted to conform to known features of Freud's own life (Leonardo was seen by Freud as being doted upon by his mother, as having a mysterious step-mother so that he had two mothers etc.) render this example of the psychoanalysis of art rather more useful as an interpretation of what Freud was like, than as an example of what Leonardo was like.

Exactly the same conclusion must be drawn from Freud's interpretation of the statue of Moses which had been commissioned for the tomb of Pope Julius II. Michelangelo's Moses is an unfinished statue which Freud had discovered on a trip to Rome, although it is likely that he had already studied a copy of it which is to be found in the Vienna Academy of Art. In contrast to his earlier speculations on art and literature which stressed the unconscious, infantile, origins of human art forms, Freud uncharacteristically announced to Martha: 'I have come to understand the meaning of the statue by contemplating Michelangelo's intention' (1901).[23] The statue exerted a strange influence on him such that in 1912 on another visit to Rome he wrote again to Martha how he paid a visit to 'Moses' everyday. Similarly his grasp of the importance of the *intentions* of the artist must have remained with him for in 1913 he began to dwell further on the meaning of the statue. To a friend he later wrote:

> My relationship to this work is something like that to a love child. Everyday for three lovely weeks in September of 1913 I stood in the church in front of the statue, measuring and drawing it until there dawned on me that understanding which in the essay I only dared to express anonymously. Not until much later did I legitimize this non-analytic child. (1933)[24]

Freud's interpretation of the statue was a radical deviation from the traditional interpretation, based on the biblical account of Moses. The traditional view of the statue saw it as capturing Moses' initial anger at seeing the children of Israel dancing round the Golden Calf on his return from Mount Sinai with the Tablets of the Law. Freud disagreed with the traditional view that Michelangelo had intended to capture just that moment before he broke the Tablets. Freud's view was that the Moses of the statue was rather at the end of a sequence in which he had stopped himself from breaking the stone tablets in anger – Moses had sublimated his emotion. Thus, in contrast to the recorded story of the events (as described in the Bible) Freud suggested:

> . . . the Moses we have reconstructed will neither leap up nor cast the Tables from him. What we see before us is not the inception of a violent action but the remains of a movement that has already taken place. In his first transport of fury Moses desired to act, to spring up and take vengeance and forget the Tables; but he had overcome the temptation, and he will now remain seated and still, in his frozen wrath and in his pain mingled with contempt. Nor will he throw away the Tables so that they will break on the stones, for it is on their especial account that he has controlled his anger. (1914)[25]

If we ask the question, what has led Freud to 'reconstruct' the historical allusion in the statue? We are led to the inescapable conclusion that it was Freud's identification with Moses that has coloured his perception of the statue. Freud, who had so often compared himself with Moses, was, at the time he was writing this essay, in the throes of the final disintegration of his relationship with Jung, his 'crown prince'. At the height of the bitter struggle he wrote to his faithful colleague, Ferenczi: 'At the moment the situation in Vienna makes me feel more like the historical Moses than the Michelangelo one' (1912).[26] As the break continued, Freud, as he had done when he had been vilified before, attempted to remain calm and collected – Freud saw in Michelangelo's Moses the perfect model for this response. Accordingly, on Freud's theory, Michelangelo:

> . . . modified the theme of the broken Tables; he does not let Moses break them in his wrath, but makes him be influenced by the danger that they will be broken and makes him calm that wrath, or at any rate prevent it from becoming an act. In this way he had added something new and more than human to the figure of Moses; so that the giant frame with its tremendous physical power becomes only a concrete expression of the highest mental achievement that is possible in a man, that of struggling successfully against an inward passion for the sake of a cause to which he has devoted himself. (1914)[27]

There can be no doubt that Freud had himself in mind when he penned these words. When he sent a copy of the essay to his American follower, James Putnam, Freud included a note explaining that 'its author does not publicly acknowledge having written it because in this exceptional instance, it does not deal with sexuality' (1914).[28] The personal significance of the article was not missed by Putnam, who wrote back to Freud on receipt of the text 'as for the fine essay on Moses, its style seems familiar to me: I note its significance in more than one respect most willingly and need only affirm that reading it is a real pleasure'.[29]

Many of his works after the 'defections' of Stekel, Adler and Jung are replete with conscious and unconscious references to his former disciples who 'took their own paths, or turned themselves into an opposition which seemed to threaten the continuity of the development of psychoanalysis' (1924).[30] Thus, his English translator, James Strachey, could say of the Wolf Man case that it was 'largely designed as an empirical refutation of Adler and Jung, and contains many attacks on their theories'[31] (see chapter 4), and, similarly, many of his other works were thus designed. Freud's personal circumstances did not just influence the overt form of his writings, but impinged upon his examples and his interpretations. For example, in 1920, he introduced a new concept into his theories, 'the repetition compulsion' (that phenomenon exhibited by 'people all of whose human relationships have the same outcome'). As an illustration of the condition he described the case of 'the benefactor who is abandoned in anger after a time by each of his *protégés*, however much they may otherwise differ from one another, and who thus seems doomed to taste the bitterness of ingratitude' (1920).[32]

If the vicissitudes of his own disciples, the starters and the stayers, coloured his theories indelibly throughout the century so too did events in the real world beyond the Psychoanalytic Movement. *Fin de siècle* Europe finally erupted into the Great War with its moral cant, its gross carnage, and its destruction of the old order. Freud, in keeping with most of his fellow citizens, was initially enthusiastic about the war, and optimistic about its outcome. To the loyal Abraham in Berlin he wrote in 1914 'for the first time for thirty years I feel myself to be an Austrian and feel like giving this not very hopeful Empire another chance' (1914).[33] Later in the summer, again to Abraham, he confessed himself to be living 'from one German victory to the next' and to be keen to hear of the fall of Paris.[34] However, such uncharacteristic patriotism began to dissipate as the war drew out and pessimism began to loom on, and eventually to dominate, his horizon of thought. In July 1914 the events that had led to the war had begun with the assassination of the heir to the Austro-Hungarian Empire. Soon across Europe the world super-powers were locked in battle. Freud saw the conflict as a confirmation of his psychoanalytic theories. He wrote, explaining this to one of his disciples:

> I do not doubt that mankind will survive even this war, but I know for certain that for me and my contemporaries the world will never again be a happy place. It is too hideous. And the saddest thing about it is that it

is exactly the way we should have expected people to behave from our knowledge of psycho-analysis. Because of this attitude to mankind I have never been able to agree with your blithe optimism. My secret conclusion has always been: since we can only regard the highest present civilization as burdened with an enormous hypocrisy, it follows that we are organically unfitted for it. We have to abdicate, and the Great Unknown, He or It, lurking behind Fate will someday repeat this experiment with another race. I know that science is only apparently dead, but humanity seems to be really dead. (1914)[35]

The gradual emergence of pessimism at the 'unleashed brutality'[36] of war soon prompted Freud to write a lecture entitled 'Thoughts for the Time on War and Death'. To Abraham he described it as 'some twaddle . . . to appease the publisher. But I do all this against my will' (1915).[37] He concluded that the old saying *Si vis pacem, para bellum*, if you want to preserve peace, arm for war, should be adapted to read *Si vis vitam, para mortem*, if you want to endure life, prepare yourself for death.[38] It was a theme that was to remain with him for the rest of his life, in particular in his postulation, in 1920, of the death instinct (see the coming two sections).

If pessimism was the mood of his feelings, and death was to become the primary focus for his thought he was able to draw some consolation out of the fact that his new science had now found the ultimate justification. Neurotics, dreamers, jokers, artists Freud felt had given some support to his ideas but now the very drama of history appeared to yield evidence for his theories. He wrote to a correspondent

What is happening in this war . . . the cruelties and injustices for which the most civilized nations are responsible, the different way in which they judge their own lies and wrong-doings and those of their enemies, and the general lack of insight which prevails [has proved] that the primitive, savage and evil impulses of mankind have not vanished . . . [but] lie in wait for opportunities of becoming active once more. (1914)[37]

I have not lived through the deprivations and ravages of a war, but I have seen their effects as it were from a distance – it is a problem that demands attention. Clearly, war is evidence of some pathological condition in humanity. Freud was quite specific in his understanding of its origins – the unconscious, uncontrollable, infantile impulses of the human mind. In seeing the origins of war in the depths of the unconscious Freud extended the psychic determinism that had governed his earlier studies of individuals into a psychic determinism of society. In doing this he yielded to a biological fatalism, which largely ignored other important moral, economic, political, or religious questions which have some input into the vexed questions of why wars happen. For Freud there was only one alternative to war – that was the diversion of these infantile impulses into other acceptable channels of dissipation, namely into cultural activity. Thus, when he was asked to contribute to a series of open letters on the subject 'Why War?' by Albert Einstein, Freud concluded his answer to the question by suggesting that the only options available for avoiding war were 'indirect' methods, in particular, the 'diversion' of the instinctual energy into cultural activity 'what ever fosters the growth of culture works at the same time against war' (1932).[40] I would suggest, however, that such an option is not a sufficient solution to the problem of war. It does not get to the heart of the problem.

From what has been said in this section already Freud's ideas about civilization are in part discernible. In keeping with his views on the production of dreams, symptoms, parapraxes, and art Freud saw human civilization as being derived from the unconscious. This idea has three principle consequences: first it reflects its origins; secondly it has an inevitable quality about it (it cannot really be changed); and thirdly it is a delicate creation of the interplay of impulses which at any moment can be tipped to produce its own destruction. Part of this theory derives from his analysis of the origins of society and the origins of religion, which I shall be covering in my next section. Freud believed that primitive man gave full vent to his instincts, and consequently had no 'psychic' energy 'left over' to produce cultural artefacts. As man learnt to sublimate his instincts, so civilization developed: 'The whole course of the history of civilization is no more than an account of the various methods adopted by mankind for "binding" their unsatisfied wishes' (1913).[41]

Freud drew all of his thoughts on civilization together in 1930 in a book entitled *Unhappiness in Civilization*, a book which Freud intended should consider 'man's discomfort in civilization'. By some quirk the book has become known as *Civilization and its Discontents*, expressing in its title a word that never even appears in the text, 'discontents'. To a friend Freud wrote that the book 'deals with civilization, guilt feelings, happiness and similar lofty matters, and it strikes me, no doubt rightly, as quite superfluous in contrast to earlier works, which after all always derived from some inner urge . . . I have discovered the most banal truths' (1929).[42] The book reflected all the themes I have outlined – his pessimism, his fascination with death, his dislike of humanity, his resignation to fate. In 1918 he had reached the conclusion that:

> I do not break my head very much about good and evil, but I have found little that is 'good' about human beings on the whole. In my experience most of them are trash, no matter whether they publicly subscribe to this or that ethical doctrine or to none at all. That is something that you cannot

say aloud, or perhaps even think, though your experiences of life can hardly have been different from mine. If we are to talk of ethics, I subscribe to a high ideal from which most of the human beings I have come across depart most lamentably. (1918)[43]

To his disciples he used to say 'Men are a wolf pack, simply a wolf pack'.[44] However, it was not until 1930 that he was to allow the full-force of this private 'trash theory' of man to become available for scrutiny. Thus, he wrote then:

I can at least listen without indignation to the critic who is of the opinion that when one surveys the aims of cultural development and the means it employs, one is bound to come to the conclusion that the whole effort is not worth the trouble and that the outcome of it can only be a state of affairs which the individual will be unable to tolerate. (1930)[45]

But here Freud was faced with a problem, for in opposing civilization, which was in some sense a biological necessity, the would-be dissident was having to fight his own biology. Man, driven by his libido to seek satisfaction ultimately had to realize that a balance had to be obtained between the unlimited expression of his own needs, and the needs of others around him. This mutual dependence, based on the satisfaction of needs, is essentially, though, a culture of selfishness, with no room for the creation of an alternative model. For Freud the creation of alternatives to society as it existed then was inevitably doomed to failure – a socialist state became a psychological impossibility, while the idea of establishing the Kingdom of God on earth was just manifest wishful thinking. Freud believed, 'human civilization rests upon two pillars, of which one is the control of natural forces and the other the restriction of our instincts. The ruler's throne rests upon fettered slaves' (1925).[46] Accordingly there could be no advancement for civilization except through the strengthening of the pillars. The natural sciences were created to strengthen the first and *only* the science of psycho-analysis can help strengthen the second by virtue of the way in which it provides the insight into how best to control those instincts. Alternatives that did not have at heart psycho-analysis were deemed utopian, and doomed to failure.

The two classic examples of such utopian thinking which Freud considered were Christianity and Marxism. Freud saw these two alternative perspectives as having remarkably similar psychological power and practical expression. In one particular passage in his *New Introductory Lectures* he drew out the parallels between the two systems in a way that could equally be applied to himself and his 'science':

Theoretical Marxism, as realized in Russian Bolshevism, has acquired the energy and the self-contained and exclusive character of a *Weltanschauung* [a world view], but at the same time an uncanny likeness to what it is fighting against. Though originally a portion of science and built up, in its implementation, upon science and technology, it has created a prohibition of thought which is just as ruthless as that of religion in the past. Any critical examination of Marxist theory is forbidden, doubts of its correctness are punished in the same way as heresy was once punished by the Catholic Church. The writings of Marx have taken the place of the Bible and the Koran as a source of revelation, though they would seem to be no more free from contradictions and obscurities than those older sacred books. (1933)[47]

Of course, he denied that such a description was applicable to his 'science' but the 'uncanny likeness' is clearly discernible.

While Marxism and Christianity were, in some senses, comparable ideological systems which posed an alternative to society as it existed then, Freud's treatment of the two systems was not equivalent. Throughout Freud's writings on civilization there is a sense in which he was prepared to countenance the options posed by Marxism, whereas with Christianity he *knew* it was a discredited, infantile option. Perhaps Freud found an intellectual kindred with Marxism with its avowed opposition to the illusions of religion – both he and Marx were early converted to Feuerbach's critique of religion. He found no such kindred with Christianity. Marxism was a bold, but misguided, try at solving the problems posed by humanity – a 'tremendous experiment' was what he called it. It was an experiment doomed to failure:

The tremendous experiment of producing a new order of this kind is now actually being carried out in Russia. At a time when the great nations announce that they expect salvation only from the maintenance of Christian piety, the revolution in Russia – in spite of all its disagreeable details – seems none the less like a message of a better future. Unluckily neither our scepticism nor the fanatical faith of the other side gives a hint as to how the experiment will turn out. The future will tell us; perhaps it will show that the experiment was undertaken prematurely, that a sweeping alteration of the social order has little prospect of success until new discoveries have increased our control over the forces of Nature and so made easier the satisfaction of our needs. Only then perhaps may it become possible for a new social order not only to put an end to the material need of the masses but also to give a hearing to the cultural demands of the individual. Even then, to be sure, we shall still have to struggle for an incalculable time with the difficulties which the untameable character of human nature presents to every kind of social community. (1933)[48]

Such magnanimity towards an alternative ideology was not extended
to the old enemy – religion. As the century progressed he set about
relentlessly attacking religion in general, and Christianity in particular.
Freud saw his task in this respect of educating humanity out of their
infantile beliefs – a task he conceived of as being one of replacing illusions
with reality. 'Men cannot remain children for ever' he wrote in one of
his most sustained critiques of religion, 'they must in the end go out into
"hostile life". We may call this *"education to reality"* . . . .' I confess
to you that the sole purpose of my book is to point out the necessity for
this forward step' (1927).[49] To that end he set about undermining the
central tenets of Christianity, specifically the words of the man he regarded
as possibly 'an ordinary deluded creature', Jesus Christ.[50] The ethical
standard he preached, if indeed any words could reliably be attributed
to him – Freud was sceptical – was dismissed as impractical and irrelevant.
Thus, the words which Christ used to summarize the requirements of the
law – 'love your neighbour as yourself' – were taken and analysed, with
no regard for their context which at the very least provides some
explanation for their rationale and logic. The analysis ignored the original
context of these words within a system of ethics which was premised upon
the idea that human relationships were to be reflective of, and grounded
in, a prior relationship to God – the Jews were, after all, the B'nai B'rith
(Sons of the Covenant). Similarly, he ignored the fact that Christ himself
assumed that framework in his adoption of that summary as an expression
of his requirements for his new Kingdom. Even a minimal understanding
of this context is surely required to understand the value and significance
of these words as a basis for social cohesion. Freud scarcely concealed
his dislike for both Christianity and humanity in discussing them:

We find ourselves unable to suppress a feeling of astonishment as at
something unnatural. Why should we do this? What good is it to us? Above
all, how can we do such a thing? How could it possibly be done? My love
seems to me a valuable thing that I have no right to throw away without
reflection. It imposes obligations on me which I must be prepared to make
sacrifices to fulfil. If I love someone, he must be worthy of it in someway
or other. (I am leaving out of account now the use he may be to me, as
well as his possible significance to me as a sexual object; neither of these
two kinds of relationship between us come into question where the
injunction to love my neighbour is concerned.) He will be worthy of it if
he is so like me in important respects that I can love myself in him; worthy
of it if he is so much more perfect that I that I can love my ideal of myself
in him; I must love him if he is the son of my friend, since the pain my
friend would feel if anything untoward happened to him would be my pain –
I should have to start it. But if he is a stranger to me and cannot attract
me by any value he has in himself or any significance he may have already

acquired in my emotional life, it will be hard for me to love him. I shall even be doing wrong if I do, for my love is valued as a privilege by all those belonging to me; it is an injustice to them if I put a stranger on a level with them. But if I am to love him (with that kind of universal love) simply because he, too, is a denizen of earth, like an insect or an earthworm or a grass-snake, then I fear that but a small modicum of love will fall to his lot and it would be impossible for me to give him as much as by all the laws of reason I am entitled to retain for myself. What is the point of an injunction promulgated with such solemnity, if reason does not recommend it to us? (1930)[51]

In order to understand how Freud could adopt his position which falls only just short of an endorsement of selfishness as the basis for culture and civilization, we must pass on to consider Freud's second significant meeting in this century, the encounter with God.

MEETING GOD: FREUD ON RELIGION

Let me add that I am in no way in awe of the Almighty. If we ever met one another, it is rather I who should reproach Him, than he me. (1915)[52]

I have already indicated in my earlier chapters that I regard Freud's religious position as crucial to his whole work. Freud's early experiences with his Catholic nanny, his disappointments over his father, his firm belief that it was anti-Semitism that had resulted in his not receiving academic recognition, his dislike for the Catholic hierarchy, all coloured his theories. It comes as little surprise then to learn that Freud made the attack on religion one of the principal foci of his work during his last years. To many this latter-day concern seems to be almost inexplicable. Gregory Zilboorg, for example, was one of the first psychoanalysts to chronicle the history of medical psychology, and he found this overriding emphasis of the latter years strange. In a lecture he gave on Freud's life and work he quoted a description of Tolstoy which said of him it was 'as if he was not satisfied with the positive values of that which he himself had created'. Zilboorg then continued about Freud: 'apparently not fully satisfied with what he had discovered and created, he seems to have had the need to undo religious faith . . .'.[53] When placed in context, however, Freud's 'need to undo religious faith' is far more understandable.

Like so many of Freud's ideas we may trace the rudiments of his theories, if not the whole of their essence, to that crucial period of self-reflection, his self-analysis, of the late 1890s. In particular we may suggest that it was in his 'Orvieto encounter' that Freud's feelings about religion were distinctly stirred and began to take shape. On his return from Italy

Plate 11. A page from Freud's correspondence register

he had repudiated the seduction theory and had become liberated to see the mind as capable of constructing many fantastic creations – phantasies, dreams, symptoms. In December 1897 Freud announced to Fliess that he had discovered that his own mind had produced some very curious ideas, ideas which gave him an insight into the origins of religious beliefs. He wrote:

> Can you imagine what 'endopsychic myths' are? They are the latest product of my mental labour. The dim inner perception of one's own psychical apparatus stimulates illusions, which are naturally projected outwards, and characteristically into the future and a world beyond. Immortality, retribution, the world after death, are all reflections of our inner psyche . . . psycho-mythology. (1897)[54]

We cannot be sure what precisely led Freud to make this connection particularly as he himself had written in his previous letter that 'one always keeps one's mouth shut about the most intimate things'.[55] Freud himself felt unable, at that time, to expand this insight. The discovery remained with him, and surfaced occasionally in his letters to Fliess, such as the time when he had just finished reading about the excavations by Sir Arthur Evans at Knossos (on Crete). Freud described the findings to Fliess: 'Zeus seems originally to have been a bull. It seems, too, that our old God [the God of our fathers] before the sublimation instigated by the Persians took place, was also worshipped as a bull. That provides food for all sorts of thoughts which it is not yet time to set down on paper . . .' (1901).[56]

In 1901 Freud did in fact set down his thoughts further on paper over the question of religion, in his *Psychopathology of Everyday Life*. There, in defence of his understanding of psychic determinism, he reproduced his earlier argument, this time, for the first time, in public:

> I believe that a large part of the mythological view of the world, which extends a long way into most modern religions, is *nothing but psychology projected into the external world*. The obscure recognition (the endopsychic perception, as it were) of psychical factors and relations in the unconscious is mirrored – it is difficult to express it in other terms . . . – in the construction of a *supernatural reality*, which is destined to be changed back once more by science into the *psychology of the unconscious*. One could venture to explain in this way the myths of paradise and the fall of man, of God, of good and evil, of immortality, and so on, and to transform *metaphysics* into *metapsychology*. (1901)[57]

In presenting his case thus, Freud had fallen into the logical fallacy called by one logician, 'nothing buttery'.[58] Jones, in his defence of

Freud minimized this element in Freud's attack by suggesting: 'all he asserted was that such beliefs could be fully accounted for by the psychological and historical factors he had investigated, so that he personally could see no reason for adding to them an external supernatural one'.[59] Jones was, however, always the persuasive apologist for Freud, and was prepared to play down his negative aspects. In reality, Freud was self-consciously asserting his fundamental opposition to *anything but* his own understanding of religion – he could countenance no alternative explanation. In contrast there is a good deal of cogency to the argument that sees the language of psychology as *one* way of talking about reality, and the language of religion as another, equally valid, way of talking about the same thing. Freud ruled out the language of religion by fiat – declaring it unnecessary and dispensable – his language, the reductionist language of metapsychology, became the only permissible mode of discourse. A full explanation of reality may, as in many other spheres, require us to recognize that there are different levels of explanation, each with their own appropriate concepts and theoretical terms. An exhaustive physico-chemical explanation of the mechanics of speech production does not provide a full account of why one person utters the words 'I love you' to another, nor do explanation in terms of hormones, or social conditions, or mother-fixations!

Freud's 'throw-away use' of this understanding of religion – as a bolster to his argument on psychic determinism – was soon to prove but one of the areas of its use. He began to develop his critique of religion in a two-fold way: first because it was another phenomenon that could yield to his psycho-analytic logic just as dreams, slips, symptoms and jokes had done; and secondly as its origins were traceable to the origins of civilization and society, and hence provided a clue to those. Freud's analysis of religion thus contains two aspects: an analysis of religious behaviour, and the psychological origins of individual's beliefs in general.

Concerning the first aspect, religion became for Freud a phenomenon just like a neurotic symptom. These, Freud maintained, were produced when hidden, unconscious, desires, normally repressed, were allowed to escape in distorted form. Religious behaviour, or particular religious beliefs were viewed similarly: psychological forces within individuals found expression in their religious activity and beliefs. Psycho-analysis, Freud asserted, led 'to a result that reduces religion to the status of a neurosis of mankind and explains its grandiose powers in the same way as we should a neurotic obsession in our individual patients' (1939).[60] Freud put forward this view particularly forcefully in his paper of 1907 'Obsessive Acts and Religious Practices'.

One corollary of this was that religion itself became a source of evidence to uphold the psychoanalytic view, in particular, it 'confirmed' Freud's central thesis that the Oedipus complex lay at the heart of all neurosis. If the cause of neurosis was the unresolved Oedipus complex then, since religion was a universal neurosis, it too would show Oedipal connections. Sure enough in 1910, in his essay on Leonardo, Freud made this explicit:

> Psycho-Analysis has made us familiar with the intimate connection between the father-complex and the belief in God; it has shown us that a personal God is, psychologically, nothing other than an exalted father, and it brings us evidence of how young people lose their religious beliefs as soon as their father's authority breaks down. Thus we recognize that the roots of the need for religion are in the parental complex; the almighty and just God . . . appear to us as grand subliminations of father and mother, or rather as revivals and restorations of the young child's ideas of them. (1910)[61]

To his pupil, Jung, he was equally blunt about the relationship between an individual's beliefs about God and his psychological needs: 'the ultimate basis of man's need for religion is *infantile helplessness*, which is so much greater in man than in animals. After infancy he cannot conceive of a world without parents and makes for himself a just God and a kindly nature, the two worst anthropomorphic falsifications he could have imagined . . .' (1910).[62] Belief in God is a childish, infantile, hang-over which should be abandoned if maturity is to be reached, if we are to adopt Freud's reasoning.

Freud was to develop this line of reasoning much later, in 1927, in his book *The Future of an Illusion*. Here Freud maintained that religion is an illusion. 'An illusion', he explained 'is not the same as an error, it is indeed not necessarily an error . . . we call a belief an illusion when wish-fulfilment is a prominent factor in its motivation' (1927).[63] A classic example of such an illusion, which Freud himself gave in explanation, is the case of a poor girl imagining that one day a prince will come and carry her off home. 'It is possible; some such cases have occurred' suggested Freud, but there are no rational grounds for it and thus it is a belief, the most important aspect of which, is to alleviate the girl's contemporary needs and desires. As might be anticipated he regarded such illusions with contempt as he explained later in his book *Civilization and Its Discontents:*

> In my *Future of an Illusion* I was concerned much less with the deepest sources of the religious feeling than with what the common man understands by his religion – with the system of doctrines and promises which on the one hand explains to him the riddles of this world with enviable completeness, and, on the other, assures him that a careful Providence will watch over his life and will compensate him in a future existence for any

frustrations he suffers here. The common man cannot imagine this Providence otherwise than in the figure of an enormously exalted father. Only such a being can understand the needs of the children of men and be softened by their prayers and placated by the signs of their remorse. The whole thing is so patently infantile, so foreign to reality, that to anyone with a friendly attitude to humanity it is painful to think that the great majority of mortals will never be able to rise above this view of life. It is still more humiliating to discover how large a number of people living to-day, who cannot but see that this religion is not tenable, nevertheless try to defend it piece by piece in a series of pitiful rearguard actions.[64]

To one of his pupils he explained that his 'wrath was not so much directed against [the Almighty] as against the gracious Providence and moral world-order for which he is, to be sure, responsible' and in an interesting defence of his excessive interest in unmasking that rather than any other illusion he suggested that it was worthy of attack since it made 'such mock of reason' (1927). Just how seriously Freud took these arguments is open to debate since he himself confessed to one pupil that there was little of value in the study but that it would help to raise cash for his publishing house. To another he described it as his worst book not even worthy of his name.[65] To yet another pupil he confided 'it already seems to me childish; fundamentally I think otherwise; I regard it as weak analytically and inadequate as a self-confession' (1927).[66] Indeed, he encouraged one of his faithful Zurich supporters, Pfister, in the production of his (psycho-analytic) rejoinder, *The Illusion of the Future*, which while accepting all of Freud's premises, argued that the particular illusion of Christianity would, and should, survive precisely because it did meet people's needs.[67] To another pupil, Binswanger, Freud explained the origins of religion in an individual, but also related it to the premise that underlies his theory: 'religions originate in the child's and young mankind's fears and need for help, it cannot be otherwise' (1927).[68]

Fundamental to his position in *The Future of an Illusion* was an overriding positivist stance. Positivism, the very philosophy which had been so evident in his early days of study, is a belief in the inexorable logic of progress in thought from religion to metaphysics to positive science. It found its *locus classicus* in the French sociologist August Comte writing in the mid-nineteenth century. Even by the turn of the century it was in many respects a discredited philosophy, but Freud was a firm believer in it. In January 1927 he wrote to a friend: 'In secret – one cannot say such things aloud – I believe that one day metaphysics will be condemned as a nuisance, as an abuse of thinking, as a survival from the period of the religious *Weltanschauung*' (1927).[69] In fact though Freud made little secret of his positivist faith as shown by a statement in

1913: '*Pari passu* with men's progressive control over the world goes a development in their *Weltanschauung*, their view of the universe as a whole. They turn away more and more from their original belief in their own omnipotence, rising from an animistic phase through a religious to a scientific one' (1913).[70]

Freud upheld some of the characteristic, Comtean, positivist, ideals notably the ultimate belief in the triumph of science – he wrote 'in the long run nothing can withstand reason and experience, and the contradiction religion offers to both is only too palpable' (1927).[71] He also, unlike Comte, held a pessimistic conception of the resultant 'progress'. As with so many of his contemporaries the *fin de siècle* spirit had produced a pessimism which 'the Great War', and the post-1918 settlement, and the demise of Austro-Hungary did nothing to remove. The end of the war was the time he affirmed his 'trash theory' of humanity, it will be recalled. However, such a reflection was by no means uncommon for the period; indeed many, like Freud in 1927 with *The Future of an Illusion*, combined the paradoxical beliefs of positivist progress with profound pessimism. Thus, a Scandinavian author could declare in the 1890s: 'After all, atheism is unspeakably tame. Its end and aim is nothing but a disillusioned humanity. The belief in a God who rules everything and judges everything is humanity's last great illusion, and when that is gone, what then? Then you are wiser; but richer, happier? I can't see it'.[72] It was the author, and the novel from which these words are taken, that Freud declared to Fliess, in 1895, have 'moved me more than anything I have read in the last nine years' (1895).[73] The perspective stayed with him.

Freud believed that it was his mission to unmask the illusions of religion. In 1913, he declared to Ferenczi, 'We possess the truth, I am as sure of it as fifteen years ago' (1913).[74] Freud's theoretical formulations were to change as the century drew on, but his belief in science, and in the necessity to oppose religion, were held with that same conviction. In 1933 he expressed his belief in his truth and its opposition to religion in the following terms:

It is simply a fact that the truth cannot be tolerant, that it admits of no compromises or limitations, that research regards every sphere of human activity as belonging to it and that it must be relentlessly critical if any other power tries to take over any part of it. Of the three powers [art, philosophy and religion] which may dispute the basic position of science, religion alone is to be taken seriously as an enemy. (1933)[75]

Accordingly, in keeping with his positivist conception of progress, he pronounced his considered opinion on the subject:

In summary, therefore, the judgement of science on the religious *Weltanschauung* is this. While the different religions wrangle with one another as to which of them is in possession of the truth, our view is that the question of the truth of religious beliefs may be left altogether on one side. Religion is an attempt to master the sensory world in which we are situated by means of the wishful world which we have developed within us as a result of biological and psychological necessities. But religion cannot achieve this. Its doctrines bear the imprint of the times in which they arose, the ignorant times of the childhood of humanity. Its consolations deserve no trust. Experience teaches us that the world is no nursery. The ethical demands on which religion seeks to lay stress need, rather, to be given another basis; for they are indispensable to human society and it is dangerous to link obedience to them with religious faith. If we attempt to assign the place of religion in the evolution of mankind, it appears not as a permanent acquisition but as a counterpart to the neurosis which individual civilized men have to go through in their passage from childhood to maturity. (1933)[76]

Freud's statement that religion bears the imprint of its primitive origins requires some further explanation. Indeed if we examine Freud's arguments he places considerable weight upon observations about the origins of religion. In fact Freud's analysis of the prehistory of religion constitutes the second aspect of his critique of religion – it requires some examination.

Throughout Freud's classic texts of the early 1900s one comes across suggestions, made *en passant* by Freud about the parallels he could find between individual's development and the nation's development, and about the value of psychoanalysis in studying *both*. Just as 'childhood memories' provided a means whereby Freud felt himself able to analyse the neuroses of adults, so too, did national legends and mythologies provide a clue, when suitably analysed, to the neuroses of mankind. In the second edition of his *Psychopathology of Everyday Life* he pointed out the analogy between the two: 'the "childhood memories" of individuals come in general to acquire the significance of "screen memories" and in doing so offer a remarkable analogy with the childhood memories that a nation preserves in its store of legends and myths' (1907).[77] Some 2 years later he wrote to a collaborator 'I have long been haunted by the idea that our studies on the content of the neuroses might be destined to solve the riddle of the formation of myths, and that the nucleus of mythology is nothing other than what we speak of as "the nuclear complex of the neurosis"' (1909).[78] Accordingly, since he felt the two to have the same core, he felt able to extend the logic of the one (the psychoanalysis of the neuroses) into the other (the interpretation of mythology and religion). However, although two of his followers,

Abraham and Rank, had already made forays into the field, Freud was at that time reticent to press on: 'We are amateurs, and have every reason to be afraid of mistakes. We are lacking in academic training and familiarity with the material' (1909).[79] Many years later, Freud, when reflecting upon the experience of the movement in the fields of the history of civilization and religion, admitted that these early attempts were, frankly, partial forays into alien territory which deserved some of the calumny they received. He believed that this situation was being remedied though, 'in every region', he wrote, 'there is a growing number of people who study psychoanalysis in order to make use of it in their special subject, and in order, as colonists, to replace the pioneers' (1933).[80] It was to require the specific stimulus of the impending divergence of his 'crown prince', Jung, from the movement to galvanize Freud into action and produce a detailed theory on the subject.

In one sense, studying religion was just a continuation of the logic that has led from symptoms, to dreams, to parapraxes, to jokes, to art and literature. Freud was convinced that the underlying mechanisms were the same – in a thoroughly naturalistic world where there was no other reality than man and nature the *only* source could be man himself. Freud believed that 'psychoanalysis has established an intimate connection between these physical achievements of individuals on the one hand and societies on the other by postulating one and the same dynamic source for both of them' (1913).[81] Individuals cope with the demands of their unfulfilled wishes by producing symptoms, dreams, parapraxes and jokes; nations, Freud argued, analogously did the same thing: 'Myths, religion, and morality . . . [are] attempts to seek a compensation for the lack of satisfaction of human wishes' (1913).[82] Freud needed more than logic to impel him into the analysis of the precise nature of the connection.

Freud's relationship to Jung was the specific impetus for Freud to work out his ideas further. Freud exhorted Jung to 'conquer the whole field of mythology' in 1908 soon after they had begun to collaborate and share insights. He felt compelled, however, by 1911, to join Jung in the field, perhaps out of worry over the direction Jung's thought was going. At first, the two of them joked about the implications of them both working in the same field with Freud being almost obsequious to Jung:

The reading for my psychology of religion is going slowly. One of the nicest works I have read (again), is that of a well known author [Jung] . . . In it many things are so well expressed that they seem to have taken on definitive form and in this form impress themselves on the memory . . . it is the best thing this promising author has written up to now, though he will do still better . . . Not least I am delighted by the many points of agreement with things I have already said or would *like* to say. Since you yourself are this author, I shall continue more directly and make an admission: it is a torment to me to think, when I conceive an idea now and then, that I may be taking something away from you or appropriating something that might just as well have been acquired by you. When this happens, I feel at a loss . . . Why in God's name did I allow myself to follow you into this field? You must give me some suggestions. But probably my tunnels will be far more subterranean than your shafts and we shall pass each other by . . . . (1911)[83]

Jung seems to have viewed the thought of prospecting with Freud in the same lode as alarming. He replied to Freud's letter with the words 'the outlook for me is very gloomy if you too get into the psychology of religion. You are a dangerous rival – if one has to talk of rivalry. Yet I think it has to be this way, for a natural development cannot be halted, nor should one try to halt it. Our personal differences will make our work different. You dig up the precious stones, but I have the degree of extension'.[34] With the deterioration of their relationship through 1912 and into 1913 Freud began to see the value of having his own tunnels in the lode in order to undermine the increasingly heterodox understanding of Jung. The importance of this work was underlined to Freud when in 1912, Jung began publicly to renounce the very doctrines that Freud held sacred, principally the theories of infantile sexuality and of the dominance of sexuality in all life. For Freud, who declared in 1919 that 'the theme of sexuality . . . is our shibboleth',[85] such a departure from orthodoxy was intolerable, particularly, when, as in Jung's case, it was also backed up with ideas taken from religion. Thus in 1914 he wrote: 'in the latest works of the Zurich school . . . we find analysis permeated with religious ideas rather than the opposite outcome that had been in view' (1914).[86] Freud's own studies in this field at this crucial time of tension and imminent rupture were to assume an importance to him little short of monumental.

Freud began his studies in the prehistory of mankind and in the origins of religion in the spring of 1911. To Jung he wrote that he hoped to have it finished by the summer and that he had 'unearthed strange and uncanny things and will almost feel obliged *not* to discuss them with you' (1911).[87] Jung responded to this veiled allusion by suggesting that 'if the auguries do not deceive us, it may very well be that thanks to your discoveries, we are on the threshold of something really sensational . . . the reincarnation of ancient wisdom in the shape of psychoanalysis' (1911).[88] In September, Freud dropped the allusions and informed Jung that his 'work in the last few weeks has dealt with . . . the origin of religion'. Freud, apparently believing that Jung was in agreement with him, continued that 'much to [his] relief [Jung] too [was] aware that the Oedipus complex is at the root of religious feeling' (1911). He then added that 'what evidence I have to contribute can be told in five minutes'.[89] It is strange that Freud should have concluded that Jung agreed with him about the Oedipal origins of religious feeling for within 2 months Jung was writing to Freud with an alternative hypothesis about the origins of such feeling: namely that it was rooted in the racial memories of mankind not in individuals' particular Oedipal struggles. So divergent were their views that Jung's wife Emma was even writing to Freud to enquire about the cause of the problem.[90]

Jung was working at the time on material drawn from Greek mythology and comparative religion. Freud, in contrast, chose to base his studies on the ideas of contemporary primitive people, in particular he drew upon the anthropological studies of Sir James Frazer. In 1910 Frazer, a British anthropologist of the English Evolutionary School, published a four-volume work entitled *Totemism and Exogamy*. It was to provide the majority of the examples Freud used. In November 1911 Freud was finding the going very heavy. To Jung he announced 'my psychology of religion is giving me a good deal of trouble; I have little pleasure in working and constant *douleurs d'enfantement* [labour pains]'.[91] To Ferenczi, at the end of the month, he wrote:

> The Totem work is a beastly business. I am reading thick books without being really interested in them since I already know the results; my instinct tells me that. But they have to slither their way through all the material on the subject. In the process one's insight gets clouded, there are many things that don't fit and yet mustn't be forced . . . with all that I feel as if I had intended only to start a little liaison and then discovered that at my time of life I have to marry a new wife. (1911)[92]

The study came out as a series of essays, the first, finished in January 1912, was entitled 'Horror of Incest among Primitive Peoples', and the fourth and last, entitled 'The Return of Totemism in Childhood' was completed in May 1913. All four essays were collated together later in 1913 to form the book *Totem and Taboo*. As he was completing the final essay he wrote to Ernest Jones that 'it is the most daring enterprise I have ever ventured. On Religion, Ethics and *quibusdem aliis* [literally: as each to others]. God help me!' (1913).[93] He even went so far as to assert to Ferenczi 'I am writing Totem at present with the feeling that it is my greatest, best, perhaps my last good work. Inner confidence tells me that I am right' (1913).[94] Indeed, as late in his life as 1935 Freud expressed his belief that this work represented the very zenith of his intellectual achievement for in it he had succeeded in returning to the religious and philosophical questions that had long vexed him, and had discovered their solution. As a postscript to his *Autobiography* he wrote:

My interest after making a lifelong *detour* through the natural sciences, medicine and psychotherapy, returned to the cultural problems which had fascinated me long before, when I was a youth scarcely old enough for thinking. At the very climax of my psycho-analytic work, in 1912, I had already attempted in *Totem and Taboo* to make use of the newly discovered findings of analysis in order to investigate the origins of religion and morality . . . I perceived ever more clearly that the events of human history, the interactions between human nature, cultural development and the precipitates of primaeval experiences (the most prominent example of which is religion) are no more than a reflection of the dynamic conflicts between the ego, the id, and the super-ego, which psycho-analysis studies in the individual – are the very same processes repeated upon a wider stage (1935).[95]

For all of these lofty aims, at the time, however, Freud's most immediate aim (apart, perhaps, from actually disinterring Freud himself from the material) was to foster the rupture between himself and Jung. To Ferenczi in the last days of writing it he wrote: 'I am working on . . . the Totem which comes at the right moment to deepen the gap [between himself and Jung] by fathoms . . . I have not written anything with so much conviction since *The Interpretation of Dreams*, so I can predict the fate of the essay' (1913).[96] Similarly to Abraham he wrote that the final essay 'would serve to make a sharp division between us and all Aryan religiosity. For that will be the result of it' (1913).[97] When it was finally finished he wrote again to Ferenczi:

Since *The Interpretation of Dreams* I have not worked at anything with such certainty and elation. The reception will be the same: a storm of indignation except among those near to me. In the dispute with Zurich it comes at the right time to divide us as an acid does a salt. (1913)[98]

Later in the summer Freud did have doubts about the work, and even suggested to Abraham that 'Jung is crazy, but I don't really want a split; I should prefer him to leave of his own accord. Perhaps my Totem work will hasten the break against my will' (1913).[99] The truth of the matter is that Freud did seek to make the break with Jung (just as he had done with Fliess earlier), and he played out the drama of the secession on the stage of the origins of religion. The issues between them, however, ranged far wider than just differences over origins: they covered everything from personal relations to basic conceptions of the neuroses. When the break finally occurred Freud interpreted it as being for the same reason as his original break with Breuer: '[I have been] struck by the complete analogy' he wrote to Abraham, 'that can be drawn between the first running away from the discovery of sexuality behind the neuroses by Breuer and the latest one by Jung. That makes me more certain that this is the core of psychoanalysis' (1913).[100]

There can be little doubt though that Freud's elation with *Totem and Taboo* was related to his being able to demonstrate the psychological origins of religion, to further his cause against his enemy, religion itself. What precisely did his theory say? Although the four essays range over a wide variety of topics, certain themes and subjects reoccur frequently. In the first ones Freud examined ideas about incest and the taboos which surround them. Since, for Freud, the world was a totally closed system these taboos had to be generated from the same source as any other aspect of human experience (dreams, parapraxes, symptoms) hence 'a comparison between the psychology of primitive peoples . . . and the psychology of neurotics . . . will be bound to show numerous points of agreement' (1913).[101] Specifically, Freud believed that the point of agreement was that both 'the horror of incest displayed by savages' and the 'mental life of neurotic patients' exhibited 'essentially an *infantile* feature' which was that the 'incestuous fixations of libido . . . play . . . the principle part in . . . unconscious mental life' (1913).[102] This discovery – which as he said he knew already – both confirmed his views on the importance of infantile sexuality, and helped explain – if there was any doubt amongst the analysts – that any rejection of the thesis was not based on rational grounds but upon 'primitive fears'. In Freud's own words:

> We are driven to believe that this rejection is principally a product of the distaste which human beings feel for their early incestuous wishes, now over-taken by repression. It is therefore of no small importance that we are able to show that these same incestuous wishes, which are later destined to become unconscious, are still regarded by savage people as immediate perils against which the most severe measures of defence must be enforced. (1913)[103]

This convenient conclusion, which effectively denies the possibility of rational argument about Freud's conclusions, is only warrantable if one accepts the notion that mental life is a product of, or has at its source, infantile desires and wishes. On the basis of the evidence in the dream book, and in the parapraxis book, such a supposition is not supported. Indeed, the evidence there points to precisely the same thing that Jung was arguing at the time: namely that it was the conflicts of the *present* which were the determining factors in dreams, parapraxes, and neuroses. Jung had stated this quite categorically in a series of lectures he was giving in the USA in 1912. In those Jung stated that he was 'very suspicious . . . that patients often have a pronounced tendency to account for their ailments by some long-past experience, ingeniously drawing the analysts' attention away from the present to some false trace in the past'.[104] This tendency he noted was to 'lure us as far away as possible from the critical present' and it was the present which held the clue to the neurosis: 'the cause of the pathogenic conflict lies mainly in the present moment'.[105] It is small wonder then that Freud at the time, saw the refutation of Jung's position as vital – since acceptance would cast so much doubt on the whole edifice of psychoanalysis – and, when once he had achieved this through essentially a political move of excluding him from psychoanalysis, he later saw 1912 as the 'climax' of his psycho-analytic work.

The corollary of this is that in Freud's seeking to point out the parallels between contemporary neuroses and primitive thought he may well have been seeking a justification for, and rationalization of, his own feelings over the question of incest. The second essay in the book is an attempt to explain the notion of taboo further by drawing upon the analogy that exists between taboos and 'obsessional prohibitions of neurotics'.[106] The main consequence of this was that Freud felt that, through this discussion he had thrown 'light on the nature and origin of *conscience*'. In other words, Freud maintained:

> It may begin to dawn on us that the taboos of the savage Polynesians are after all not so remote from us as we were inclined to think at first, that the moral and conventional prohibitions by which we ourselves are governed may have some essential relationship with these primitive taboos and that an explanation of taboo might throw a light upon the obscure origin of our own 'categorical imperative'. (1913)[107]

The net effect of this was to suggest that 'neither taboos nor prohibitions are psychologically superfluous' (1913)[108] but that they were just *psychological* products that only sought to curb and control 'the oldest and most powerful of human desires'.[109] As such they were relative and thus open to very serious question. Of course, Freud argued, they were different, in that taboos were maintained through social control and through social institutions, moral imperatives and the conscience were maintained internally and psychologically. Conscience, in this scheme, produces a sense of guilt and that sense of guilt 'has about it much of the nature of anxiety'. Freud then explained that:

> . . . the anxiety points to unconscious sources. The psychology of the neuroses has taught us that, if wishful impulses are repressed, their libido is transformed into anxiety. And this reminds us that there is something unknown and unconscious in connection with the sense of guilt, namely the reasons for the act of repudiation. The character of anxiety that is inherent in the sense of guilt corresponds to this unknown factor. (1913)[110]

Since this sense of guilt is universal Freud maintained that 'psycho-analysis is no more than confirming the habitual pronouncement of the pious: we are all miserable sinners' (1913).[111] However, in contradiction to both a Judaic understanding and the Christian understanding of this statement, Freud affirmed it only to deny its fundamental meaning. True, said Freud, everyone experiences this 'sense of guilt' (we are all, in a psychological sense, sinners), but this 'sense of guilt' does not stem from the infringement of any objective, eternal moral code, as in Judaism and orthodox Christian theology, but from the unsuccessful resolution of natural, psychological, mechanisms which have internalized social conventions and prohibitions. Freud thus relativized guilt to become just another inappropriate defence mechanism just like the neuroses. Accordingly one consequence of this picture of guilt is that it helps to explain why there is so much feeling of guilt around, but it also denies guilt of its ontological status. On this view guilt engendered by incest is seen as understandable but unnecessary – a convenient conclusion for Freud if he had indeed had an incestuous relationship with Minna.

For Freud the way to be free of guilt was to *recognize it* as what it is – a psychological phenomenon – and thus to gain freedom through the understanding. It was part of Freud's whole philosophy to see understanding a phenomenon (by which he meant explaining it in natural terms) as the answer to it: 'our first purpose' he wrote in one of his lectures, 'was to understand the disorders of the human mind, because a remarkable experience had shown us here understanding and cure almost coincide, that a traversable road leads from one to the other' (1933).[112] In this context Freud sought to *understand* guilt and in understanding alone to remove its potency. The mechanism becomes very clear from a discussion he had with his Swiss pastor friend, Pfister, in 1928. Having first stated that in his view the subject of God and Christ were 'logically untenable but psychologically only too intelligible irrationalities of life' he explained what positive value could be gained from a study of Christ and his life:

> In contrast to utterances as psychologically profound as 'Thy sins are forgiven thee; arise and walk' there are a number of others which are conditioned exclusively by the time, psychologically impossible, useless for our lives. Besides, the above statement calls for analysis. If the sick man had asked: 'How knowest thou that my sins are forgiven?' The answer could only have been 'I, the Son of God, forgive thee . . .' And now, just suppose I said to a patient 'I, Professor Sigmund Freud, forgive thee thy sins'. What a fool I should make of myself. (1928)[113]

Here Freud made a very significant admission: he concurred with the idea that physical ailments could be caused by sin or some sort of aberrant behaviour and the consequent sense of guilt just as Christ did in the case of this paralytic patient. Christ tackled the problem by offering forgiveness – forgiveness backed up, as far as we can gather, by a real right to offer it (at least the paralytic man thought so). Freud recognized that he did not have such a right, and so he attempted to remove the need to feel guilty by undermining the objective validity of the guilt. Jesus said in forgiveness you will find healing and freedom. Freud said in recognizing that you are feeling guilty inappropriately as a result of your having an understandable but necessary internalized set of values you will find freedom. If guilt has a function and a reality that goes beyond the fact that it can be the psychological product produced when a social convention is broken, if that is, as well as guilt feelings there is genuine guilt then Freud's solution is merely palliative. The analysis of guilt as a human experience although having some validity is not exhausted by Freud's reduction of it to a response evoked when a social code is violated.[114]

Freud went further in his book though. He was not just concerned to undermine the basis for guilt about social transgressions such as murder and incest, he sought to undermine the ontological status of guilt itself, and to root the existence of guilt in humanity not just in his psychology but also in his history. This was the focus of the last essay, 'The Return of Totemism in Childhood'. In that essay Freud explained that in order to understand the universality of totemism an explanation is required which 'should be at once an historical and a psychological one. It should tell us under what conditions this peculiar institution developed and to what physical needs in men it has given expression' (1913).[115] In other words Freud wanted to provide an account of the psychology of the 'sense of guilt' and a history.

'The Return of Totemism in Childhood' was the attempt to do just that. Jones described it as 'by far the most important of all [the essays]' and 'the one to which the rest of the book led up'.[116] The arguments of the essay are complicated. The first premise of the theory was that the psychology of the neuroses was a 'given' – psychoanalysis, asserted Freud, has discovered the true nature of the neuroses. Freud was categorical on this point: 'The findings of psycho-analysis . . . have shown . . . that the earliest sexual excitations of youthful human beings are invariably of an incestuous character and that such impulses when repressed play a part that can scarcely be over-estimated as motive forces of neuroses in later life' (1913).[117] Secondly, he stated that Totemism was a universal phenomenon which, though demonstrated by anthropologists to exist universally, had not been satisfactorily explained by them. The third supposition Freud introduced at this point was that originally, way back in prehistory 'men . . . lived in comparatively small groups or hordes within which the jealousy of the oldest and strongest male prevented sexual promiscuity' (1913).[118] This idea Freud adopted from Darwin. A few years later, in 1921, he explained the significance of this horde:

> In 1912 I took up a conjecture of Darwin's to the effect that the primitive form of human society was that of a horde ruled over despotically by a powerful male. I attempted to show that the fortunes of this horde have left indestructable traces upon the history of human descent; and especially, that the development of totemism, which comprises in itself the beginnings of religion, morality, and social organization, is connected with the killing of the chief by violence and then transformation of the paternal horde into a community of brothers. To be sure, this is only a hypothesis, like so many others with which archeologists endeavour to lighten the darkness of prehistoric times – a 'Just-So-Story', as it was amusingly called by a not unkind English critic; but I think it is creditable to such a hypothesis if it proves able to bring coherence and understanding into more and more new regions. (1921)[119]

Put in these terms Freud sounds so reasonable – it's just a hypothesis, a 'just-so-story', a 'scientific fairy-tale' – however, the air of reasonableness belies an underlying intransigence – the theory was crucial to his viewpoint. Freud's premises were thus: the Oedipus complex exists and is the root of all neuroses ('the nuclear complex of the neuroses'); totemism exists as a phase in all cultures and is the most primitive form of religion; prehistoric men lived in primal hordes. The argument then stated that: since every aspect of man is governed by natural laws and processes, then something must have happened in prehistory to generate totemism and, that something must have had a psychical structure akin to the Oedipus complex. Accordingly, Freud postulated, the sons, jealous of their father, committed parricide: 'one day the brothers who had been driven out came together, killed and devoured their father and so made an end of the patriarchal horde. United, they had succeeded in doing what would have been impossible for them individually . . . Cannibal savages as they were, it goes without saying that they devoured their victim as well as killing him' (1913).[120] Having performed this act – Freud genuinely believed that he was describing an historical event (he concluded his essay with a quotation from Goethe – 'in the beginning was the Deed')[121] the principles of psychoanalytic psychology came into play once again:

> In order that [this] may seem plausible . . . we need only suppose that the tumultuous mob of brothers were filled with the same contradictory feelings which we can see at work in the ambivalent father-complexes of our children and of our neurotic patients. They hated their father, who

presented such a formidable obstacle to their craving for power and their sexual desires; but they loved and admired him too. After they had got rid of him, had satisfied their hatred and had put into effect their wish to identify themselves with him, the affection which had all this time been pushed under was bound to make itself felt. It did so in the form of remorse. A sense of guilt made its appearance, which in this instance coincided with the remorse felt by the whole group. The dead father became stronger than the living one had been . . . . (1913)[122]

In order to bolster the cogency of this argument about the origins of religion, Freud had to adopt a version of evolutionary thought, at variance with the conventional Darwinian perspective. Freud had somehow to explain how this 'primal deed', the parricide of the sons, came to assume a place in the psyches of all subsequent generations that caused them to create a palliative system. He thus resurrected the discredited, Lamarckian, doctrine of the 'inheritance of acquired characteristics', and postulated, in contradiction to Darwinian evolutionary theory that 'a child . . . fills in the gaps in individual truth with prehistoric truth; he replaces occurrences in his own life by occurrences in the life of his ancestors' (1918).[123] The *Totem* argument only holds water if you accept that ideas and phantasies can be inherited from one generation to another. Freud recognized their pivotal place in his arguments and became a staunch defender of Lamarckian inheritance throughout the rest of the century.

So important did Freud deem the work of Lamarck, that he suggested to Ferenczi early in the Great War, that he should write a book specifically on the subject of the relationship of Lamarckism and psychoanalysis. It was not until 1916 that he pursued the matter further. He was hoping to collaborate on a book with Ferenczi to 'leave a visiting card on biologists'.[124] The book never materialized although he expressed his intentions with it to Abraham in 1917:

The idea is to put Lamarck entirely on our ground and to show that the 'necessity' that according to him creates and transforms organisms is nothing but the power of unconscious ideas over one's own body, of which we see the remnants in hysteria, in short the 'omnipotence of thoughts'. This would actually supply a psycho-analytic explanation of adaptation; it would put the coping stone on psycho-analysis. There would be two linked principles of progressive change, adaptation, of one's body and subsequent transformation of the external world. (1917)[125]

Although the book was never written, Lamarckism remained, as it was in the *Totem* essay a key element in his thought: 'Lamarck's theory of evolution coincides with the final outcome of psychoanalytic thinking' he wrote to Groddeck in 1917.[126] While at the end of his life, when the

theory was once again revived to bolster his argument against Judaism –
this time with reference to their 'excessive consciousness of guilt – he again
staunchly maintained a Lamarckian position even in the face of overt
criticism from Jones. Jones recalled that all he would say about this was
that everyone else was wrong. Thus, his last book, *Moses and
Monotheism*, contains an argument buttressed at the crucial point by an
untenable evolutionary theory – a fact known, but not accepted by Freud:

> My position, no doubt, is made more difficult by the present attitude of
> biological science, which refuses to hear of the inheritance of acquired
> characteristics by succeeding generations. I must, however, in all modesty
> confess that nevertheless I cannot do without this factor in biological
> evolution. (1939)[127]

To Jones this reiteration 'over and over again', in an 'obstinate' manner
of a discredited theory was almost inexplicable. 'It is not easy' Jones noted,
'to account for the fixity with which Freud held this opinion and the
determination with which he ignored all the biological evidence to the
contrary . . . it almost looks as if he himself shared [an] illusion when
it came to Lamarckism'.[128] In the end he had to offer a rather lame
excuse, 'an ineffaceable mark left on his mind' from his oppressive
religious upbringing. To my mind, the place that it occupies in the
arguments of the *Totem* book, and that book's place as a refutation of
Jung and the strictures of religion – the climax of his psychoanalytic
work – provide a better explanation of the tenacity with which he held
on to Lamarckism. Without the reinforcement provided by 'primal history'
Freud's arguments in favour of the *infantile* origins of adult behaviour
fell flat, and Jung's position arguing for a 'current conflict' model of
neuroses became more tenable. Similarly without the 'primal history' the
critique of religion is decidedly shallow. The primal history also provided
an answer to the 'stranger than fiction' problem of phantasies – anything
unaccountable for in the individual's history could be accounted for as
a manifestation of a primal, ancestral, memory. The introduction of a
phylogenetic answer in 1912 to the question he posed in 1897 about the
origins of 'the horrible perverse details which are . . . as alien to their
experience as to their knowledge' (1897) provided Freud, for the first time,
with an answer (see chapter 2). He was not going to abandon this lightly.

Out of his morass of speculative, phantasy history Freud suggested that
society, religion, and morality arose: 'Society was now based on complicity
in the common crime; religion was based on the sense of guilt and the
remorse attaching to it; while morality was based partly on the exigencies
of this society and partly on the penance demanded by the sense of guilt'
(1913).[129] Freud then, compounded his erroneous picture of the origin

of religion by providing an account of the development of religion in which the 'sense of guilt and remorse' became the motive force to generate a 'father-God' outside themselves and the world, to whom the sons could make atonement. The transformation of the dead primal-father into a father God is no problem if the principles of psychoanalysis are adhered to:

> The psycho-analysis of individual human beings . . . teaches us with quite special insistence that the God of each of them is formed in the likeness of his father, that his personal relation to God depends on his relation to his father in the flesh and oscillates and changes along with that relation, and that at bottom God is nothing other than an exalted father . . . if psycho-analysis deserves any attention, then . . . the paternal element in that concept must be the most important one. (1913)[130]

Freud's account of religion, and its origin, in *Totem and Taboo* were replete with erroneous suppositions and discredited anthropological data. He took these, and using the dubious logic of psychoanalysis which related everything to *infantile* conflicts, he concocted a theory which palliated his own conscience, and attempted to undermine the whole basis of a belief in a real God who created man. On Freud's conjectures God is nothing but a transformed big-daddy in the sky: he is created in the image of man. Now, while it is patently obvious that our understanding of God as a father is coloured by our experiences of our human fathers, it by no means follows, unless you believe in Freud's 'fairy-tales' and 'just-so-stories', that God does not exist, or that he cannot be known except in relation to our understanding of human fatherhood.

The fact is that while this account of religion does accord with psychoanalysis it does not accord with any account of any religion other than the ideas of Frazer on 'savages', and on a version of the history of Judaism which totally ignores the richness and variety of that heritage. None of the great non-revelatory religions of the world, Taoism, Hinduism, Buddhism, conform to this picture of the genesis of religion except by a tortuous logic. Similarly, the religions which claim a revelatory character, Judaism, Christianity, and Islam, have so many essential features which contradict this account as to render it useless as a guide to understanding any of them. Of course, one can, just as in the case studies (see chapter 4) adopt a logic which accepts affirmation as negative, absence as secret presence, and alternative elements as inessential, but such a logic does more harm to its proponent than to its target. On the basis of Freud's own theories we may regard his sentiments with respect to religion as mere wish-fulfilments: 'I regard myself as one of the most dangerous enemies of religion' (1926).[131]

Having written *Totem and Taboo* Freud felt that he had effected the destruction of his enemy religion and shown that the true origin of man's sense of guilt was in the primal deed. Thus in 1927 he was to affirm his own thesis: 'Parricide, according to a well known view, is the principal and primal crime of humanity as well as of the individual. (See my *Totem and Taboo* . . .) It is in any case the main source of the sense of guilt, though we do not know if it is the only one: researches have not yet been able to establish with certainty the mental origin of guilt and the need for expiation. But it is not necessary for it to be the only one' (1927).[132] He did return to the question of religion again in his writings, but never with as fundamental venom as in *Totem and Taboo*. Indeed, he was to continue to try to demonstrate that religion was 'in conflict with reason' and that it was a sign of the human need to be 'irrational',[133] even devoted his last years to a last attempt to attack the old enemy' *Moses and Monotheism* (published in 1939). The book deserves consideration but much more as a product of his last years in the next section. At the very end of his life, in the face of his impending death he was even more unequivocal about the pathological nature of religion, and religious questions. To Marie Bonaparte he wrote:

> The moment one enquires about the sense or value of life one is sick, since objectively neither of them has any existence. In doing so one is only admitting a surplus of unsatisfied libido, and then something else must happen, a sort of fermenting, for it to lead to grief and depression. These explanations of mine are certainly not on a grand scale, perhaps because I am too pessimistic. There is going through my head an advertisement which I think is the boldest and most successful American one I know of. 'Why live, when you can be buried for ten dollars?' (1937)[134]

If there was any reality to the phenomena of religion it was only the reality of the discovery of some hitherto, unacknowledged aspect of the mind. The phenomena of religion were the phenomena of the mind – 'mysticism', he wrote in 1938, 'is the obscure self-perception of the realm outside the ego, of the id'.[135] It is to the last years that we now must turn.

MEETING DEATH: THANATOS, CANCER AND THE EXODUS

> If I could I should gladly do as others do and bestow on mankind a rosy future, and I should find it much more beautiful and consoling if we could count on such a thing. But this seems to me to be yet another instance of illusion (wish-fulfilment) in conflict with truth. The question is not what belief is more pleasing or more comfortable or more advantageous to life, but of what may approximate more closely to the puzzling reality that lies outside us. (1930)[136]

Plate 12. Freud in London in 1939

Unusually for men who have made a significant impact on a field Freud was not young when he published his monumental work. In other fields – mathematics, physics, philosophy – it is frequently the case that the most important contributions made to the theories are made by men who have not had the chance to stultify in the field too long. When Freud published his *Interpretation of Dreams* he was over 40; when he published *Totem and Taboo*, at the time he called the climax of his psychoanalytic work, he was 57: and yet his fertile mind continued to throw out novel ideas and insights. I have already outlined how his theoretical model of the mind changed throughout this century, but I have deliberately not outlined one of his most controversial adaptations of his theory since it is so obviously part of his last years, namely his development of the idea that there is a death instinct in human beings.

Although I have said that the idea of the death instinct was a product of his last years, there is a sense in which the problem of death had always been of very profound significance to him. His adaptation of the old saying about preparing oneself for life by preparing oneself for death really was the motto of his life. This theme was linked to his ideas on the importance of numbers, which formed a part of even his earliest speculations. To Silberstein he had once proposed, even if half-jokingly, a number mythology. By noting that 'everything in the real world has its equal, or equivalent, in the world of numbers' (1873)[137] he went on to say 'numbers even have a mythology and a God' (ibid.). He hoped that Silberstein would find that this new theory was 'marvellous proof of human perspicacity in general and of your friend, its creator, in particular' (ibid.).

With this interest in numerology there was little doubt that when, in 1887 he met Wilhelm Fliess, who was at that time developing a theory of periodicity, the two men developed an instant intellectual rapport. Throughout their friendship, as shown by their letters, numbers, periodicity, dates and their connections were the constant preoccupation of both of them. In particular the notion that one's key dates were biologically determined (birth, illness, death, etc.) became almost an obsession with them. This interest was exacerbated by Freud's own curious medical history of the time – he suffered, from 1893 onwards, from a heart condition which appeared to be potentially lethal. Freud sought help over this condition from both Fliess and Breuer who offered conflicting advice about the cause of the problem – with Breuer maintaining it was relatively benign and Fliess positing it to be more serious. The two older doctors disagreed on their recommendations to Freud, notably on whether he could, or should, smoke. Freud, who undoubtedly had an addiction to nicotine played the two off against each other, basically because he could not give up his beloved cigars. Freud's physician of his later years, on the basis of examining the symptoms reported in the letters to Fliess, has concluded that Freud had had a mild coronary thrombosis in 1894. This diagnosis was tentative, and is rendered even more so by the fact that Freud may well have been suffering from the effects of cocaine addiction, since he had been using cocaine regularly since 1884. Whatever the cause of the problem the effects were to render the ideas of Fliess on periodicity and the timing of death fascinating. Here we see the origins of Freud's pessimistic forecast about the new century – as containing, for certain, the dates of their deaths (see chapter 4, p. 144). Freud himself later revealed to Jung that this interest was a manifestation of 'the specifically Jewish nature of my mysticism' (1909).[138]

The question of death and its relation to life was obviously highlighted by the carnage of the Great War – a war in which three of his sons were involved directly. In 1919 he began working on an essay in which he was to radically reformulate his ideas on the instincts. To his Hungarian friend, Ferenczi, who was working along similar lines, he wrote in March: 'much of what I am saying in it is pretty obscure, and the reader must make what he can of it' (1919).[139] The essay, entitled *Beyond the Pleasure Principle*, was published in 1920. In it Freud postulated a new theory of instincts in which life became governed not by a single instinct as he had earlier assumed but by two opposing instincts, Eros and the death instinct. Initially, as first proposed this was a 'speculation, often far-fetched speculation, which the reader will consider or dismiss according to his individual predilection' (1920).[140] As with many of his speculations, as time progressed he began to regard it as increasingly fundamental – as he confessed to Robert Fliess, Wilhelm's psychoanalyst son: 'When, originally, I had this idea I thought to myself: this is either something altogether erroneous, or something very important . . . lately I have found myself more inclined toward the second alternative'.[141] Indeed, equally candidly in his *Civilization and its Discontents* 10 years later he wrote:

> To begin with, it was only tentatively that I put forward the views I have developed here, but in the course of time they have gained such a hold upon me that I can no longer think in any other way. To my mind, they are far more serviceable from a theoretical standpoint than any other possible ones; they provide that simplification, without either ignoring or doing violence to the facts, for which we strive in scientific work. (1930)[142]

Despite this obvious position of importance for Freud, the idea of a death instinct was not enthusiastically received by his supporters, nor has it been since. The British psychologist, William McDougall, called it 'the most bizarre monster of all his gallery of monsters',[143] while one American writer, writing recently, has written 'Freud's tortuous formulations on the death instinct can now securely be relegated to the dust bin of history'.[144] Clearly, in the light of the fact that biologically there appears to be a contradiction in the idea of a death instinct governing life, Freud's use of the idea requires some further explanation.

Freud outlined the theory in the following way. He began by noting that in his previous papers he had hitherto assumed that all mental life was

> . . . automatically regulated by the pleasure principle . . . that is to say, that the course of those events is invariably set in motion by an unpleasurable tension, and that it takes a direction such that its final outcome coincides with a lowering of that tension – that is, with an avoidance of unpleasure or a production of pleasure. (1920)[145]

This was the model he had propounded in the 1890s; however, during the course of his subsequent analytic work it slowly proved itself to be inadequate as an explanation of *all* psychic phenomena. In particular the theoretical ideas he had introduced into the system of metapsychology between 1910 and 1920 – narcissism, the compulsion to repeat, and regression – provided a contradiction to this idea. Thus, observations on the war-neuroses in which soldiers would relive in their dreams repeatedly the first traumatic encounter with death, clearly showed that some other principle could be operative in the mental life. Similarly, patients and children recalled both their pleasureable memories *and* those which generated unpleasure. Accordingly, Freud felt compelled, under the weight of the biological problems posed by his original theory of instincts, to modify his monism to dualism: 'biological considerations seemed to make it impossible to remain content with assuming the existence of only a single class of instincts' (1925).[146] These problems then generated a new definition of instincts, not a 'striving forward' – rather a regressive compulsion:

> At this point we cannot escape a suspicion that we may have come upon the track of a universal attribute of instincts and perhaps of organic life in general which has not hitherto been clearly recognized or at least not explicitly stressed. *It seems then, that an instinct is an urge inherent in organic life to restore an earlier state of things* which the living entity has been obliged to abandon under the pressure of external disturbing forces; that is, it is a kind of organic elasticity or, to put it another way, the expression of the inertia inherent in organic life. (1920)[147]

This regressive nature of the instincts provides the sense in which this new theory is 'beyond the pleasure principle' in as much as it constitutes the reason why the organism seeks to repeat *all* previous psychical states, not just the pleasurable ones. Freud's earlier theory became just a special case of this latter one. He supported this new definition of instincts by citing examples of 'the spawning migrations of fishes, the migratory flights of birds'[148] where there is an innate propensity to return to some former state. He also cited the example of the growing embryo 'obliged in the course of its development to recapitulate . . . the structures of all the forms from which it has sprung' in other words 'the whole of embryology is an example of the compulsion to repeat' (ibid.). For Freud the instincts were rooted in the biology of the species, and indeed in the physics of the universe.

This supposed biological fact of the 'conservative nature of the instincts' in which 'from the moment in which a state of things that has once been attained is upset, an instinct arises to create it afresh' (1933),[149] had a logical consequence which Freud pursued. Since life arose ultimately from inanimate matter there must be, argued Freud, a tendency present in life to return to that state:

The attributes of life were at some time evoked in inanimate matter by the action of a force of whose nature we can form no conception. It may perhaps have been a process similar in type to that which later caused the development of consciousness in a particular stratum of living matter. The tension which then arose in what had hitherto been an inanimate substance endeavoured to cancel itself out. In this way the first instinct came into being: the instinct to return to the inanimate state. (1920)[150]

In short, given his definition of instincts, Freud could do nothing else but conclude that 'the aim of all life is death'.[151] Life then became a constant struggle between the life instincts and this regressive death instinct. Freud seemed to be able to provide ample examples of this new, dualistic, conception of life even from the animal world. Thus, he saw the interplay of these instincts in the fact that some insects die after copulation: 'These creatures die in the act of reproduction because after Eros has been eliminated through the process of satisfaction, the death instinct has a free hand for accomplishing its purposes' (1923).[152] Such a struggle was in keeping with his general propensity, like some other continental theorists, to posit, in dialectical fashion, opposing pairs of forces within his system. This sense of the dialectical nature of reality may not have generated the concept of the death instinct specifically but it certainly helped Freud to accept the idea. He introduced the idea that 'the aim of all life is death' out of a sense of the logic of his biology. Indeed it is largely on the basis of this biological determinism, that one modern commentator on Freud, Frank Sulloway, claims that, despite what he said about only being concerned with *psychological* questions, Freud was, and always remained a *biologist* – and that psychoanalysis was not so much a 'depth-psychology' as a 'crypto-biology'.[153]

Although I have followed Sulloway in presenting Freud's introduction of this new development as one constrained by biological logic, there are grounds for noting that other more subjective factors may have had their part. No science is conducted in a vacuum; it always takes shape in the context of other people and their ideas. Freud himself acknowledged other sources for his ideas on the death instinct. One source, worth mentioning briefly is one of his women pupils, Sabina Spielrein. Freud wrote in his *Beyond the Pleasure Principle*: 'a considerable portion of these speculations have been anticipated by Sabina Spielrein . . . in an instructive and interesting paper which, however, is unfortunately not entirely clear to me' (1920).[154] This slightly obscure reference to a pupil demands attention, for Freud never readily conceded priority for ideas to others, indeed there is evidence to suggest that it irked him considerably when he had to acknowledge the ideas of others. Sabina Spielrein was an emigrée from Russia, who had first encountered psychoanalysis when she was taken by her parents in 1904 to the Bürgholzli mental hospital. She became one of the first patients Jung tried to treat with psychoanalysis. As a result it is most probable that she and Jung became lovers. By 1911 she had completed a doctoral thesis on schizophrenia. Jung discussed her case with Freud, without revealing that they were lovers. In 1909 Jung abandoned her when his relationship with her became too fraught with complications with his wife and with Sabina's mother. He claimed that she had phantasized the relationship and that he was being misrepresented.

She subsequently went to Freud in 1911 informing him of Jung's behaviour, and as a result became a psychoanalyst. Far from Freud taking only a passing interest in her and her ideas, given her role as an intimate of Freud's now dethroned 'crown-prince', Freud cultivated her work and encouraged her. Sabina must be credited then with having supplied Freud with the concept (the death instinct) that was to resolve the problems of his system, and dominate the last two decades of his life (it is thought that she contributed even more ideas to Jung during their brief romance).[155]

Others had suggested similar ideas including the nineteenth-century founder of psychophysics, Gustav Fechner of whom Freud wrote in his autobiography: 'I was always open to [his] ideas and have followed that thinker upon many important points' (1925).[156] Similarly, other analysts had written in a cursory way about a 'death instinct', including Wilhelm Stekel who claimed that Freud borrowed the idea from him. Whether Freud did or not is immaterial for our purposes but it is interesting that though he often used as a shorthand designation of his sexual instincts the term Eros, he never adopted the equivalent label, Thanatos, for his death instinct. Thanatos had been the name given to the death instinct by Stekel.[157]

Freud introduced his death instinct as a 'far-fetched speculation' but as time progressed he came to view it as an indispensable, fundamental, postulate of his system. This transition was so marked that in 1930 he could declare: 'I can no longer understand how we can have overlooked the ubiquity of non-erotic aggressivity and destructiveness and can have failed to give it its due place in our interpretation of life' (1930).[158] This hardening of his attitude to the idea may well have been effected as a result of the, often near tragic, circumstances of his life. He himself noted the linkage between his own circumstances and his ideas; writing to one of his close friends in 1919, he wrote 'for my old age I have chosen the theme of death . . .' (1919).[159] It was later charged against him that the *only* reason for its introduction was his distressing personal circumstances. Not only did he develop a severe, debilitating form of cancer but he also experienced a number of profound and significant losses of friends and relations. Once having introduced the idea it seemed as though each year brought a sad confirmation of the struggle of Eros and Thanatos, but also of the ultimate victory of Thanatos.

The first of these blows, which Freud later suggested was an important factor in his ageing, was the loss of Anton von Freund on 20 January 1920. Von Freund was a Hungarian brewer who became interested in psychoanalysis and who, after the war, had given a great deal of money to 'the cause' in order to establish a publishing house for psychoanalysis. Freud had earlier written to Abraham that 'a good share of my better spirits' was attributable to the intervention of von Freund whom he described as 'not merely a wealthy man, but a man of sterling worth and highly intellectual gifts . . . in fact the sort of person whom one would have to invent if he did not already exist' (1918).[160] Freud felt the loss keenly, not least because it threw the finances of the cause onto his own shoulders again. With his increasing international reputation, notably in the USA, however, his personal financial circumstances were never as perilous as in the early days of his marriage. To one of his disciples he wrote in 1922 that 'I find myself relieved of material cares, with the hubbub on all sides of a popularity that I find repellent, and involved in undertakings that take away time and energy from tranquil scientific work' (1922).[161] Whilst to Ferenczi he confessed:

My capacity for interest is so soon exhausted: that is to say it turns away so willingly from the present in other directions. Something in me rebels against the compulsion to go on earning money which is never enough, and to continue with the same psychological devices that for thirty years have kept me upright in the face of my contempt of people and the detestable world. Strange secret yearnings rise in me – perhaps from my ancestral heritage – for the East and the Mediterranean and for a life of quite another kind: wishes from late childhood never to be fulfilled, which do not conform to reality as if to hint at a loosening of one's relationship to it. (1922)[162]

The second blow, which followed quickly on the heels of the first, was the unexpected death of his daughter, Sophie – his 'Sunday child' as he called her.[163] On 25 January 1920 Sophie died from an infection of influenza. She was 26, and had previously been in perfect health, she left behind her two children one of whom was only 13 months old. Freud, as anyone would be, was devastated by the news. Unable to attend the funeral he immediately wrote to his son-in-law affirming: 'it was a senseless, brutal stroke of fate that took our Sophie from us, in the face of which it is useless to recriminate or brood; we can only bow our heads under the blow like the poor helpless creatures we are, mere playthings for the higher powers (1920).[164] To his close friends he was equally resigned and bitter: 'I do not know what more there is to say' he wrote to one, 'it is such a paralysing event, which can stir no afterthoughts when one is not a believer and so is spared all the conflicts that go with that. Blunt necessity, mute submission' (1920).[165] To Ferenczi he wrote that 'the fatal event, however painful, has not been able to overthrow my attitude towards life . . . since I am profoundly irreligious there is no one I can accuse, and I know there is nowhere to which any complaint could be addressed' (1920).[166] For all that, within 3 weeks of her death Freud had introduced the term 'the death instinct' for the very first time in his writing – it was meaningless to address a complaint to an instinct; all one could do was to submit to its necessity. The loss of these two very significant figures in his life affected him deeply for some time – to von Freund's sister he remarked once at this time: 'I don't know whom I am mourning more for now, Toni [von Freund] or our Sophie'.[167]

The discovery of Freud's own cancer was the next event in his life that was to help confirm his belief in the inevitabiliy of Thanatos. In April 1923 Freud went to his doctor and told him to prepare for a shock; on opening his mouth the doctor saw 'an obvious advanced cancer'. The doctor quickly arranged for surgery, but kept the full extent of the news from him. There was a brief period of uncertainty in which the Committee tried to collude with the doctor, fearing that the seriousness of the cancer and its continued growth, would daunt him too greatly. As he was recovering from the first operation, apparently believing it to have been a success, Freud received another, devastating piece of news. In May, Sophie's son Heinz, of whom he was very fond, and who had come to live in Vienna with Mathilde, Freud's oldest daughter, fell ill. Freud, writing to two friends, recalled the:

> ... slow but sure realization that he has a miliary tuberculosis in fact that the child is lost ... I find this loss very hard to bear. I don't think I have ever experienced such grief; perhaps my own sickness contributes to the shock. I work out of sheer necessity; fundamentally everything has lost its meaning for me. (1923)[168]

This gross triumph of Thanatos seems to have put a bitter steel in his soul. Three years later, when consoling his colleague, Binswanger, on the death of his eldest son, Freud remarked that Heinz had stood to him for all children and grandchildren, and that since his death he had not been able to enjoy life; he concluded: 'it is the secret of my indifference – people call it courage – towards the danger to my own life' (1926).[169] So profound was the loss that to another friend he wrote that he was suffering depression for the first time in his life. Indeed to Max Halberstadt, the boy's widower father, he wrote:

> I have spent some of the blackest days of my life in sorrowing about the child. At last I have taken hold of myself and can think of him quietly and talk of him without tears. But the comforts of reason have done nothing to help; the only consolation for me is that at my age I would not have seen much of him. I doubt if you realize how much we all loved him. (1923)[170]

Jones noted that this is the only occasion recorded in Freud's life where he is known to have shed tears.[171]

Having faced that terrible loss, Freud was then faced with his own cancer. A second operation was necessary, this time involving far more radical surgery. The cancer had spread, and an operation was required which removed the whole of his upper jaw and palate on the right side thus turning the mouth and nasal cavity into a single organ. Such a remedy required him to use a metal prosthesis to act as an artificial roof of the mouth. The prosthesis was uncomfortable and needed to be removed, with great pain ensuing, at regular intervals. Freud christened it 'the monster', becoming a source of constant distress and pain for him for the rest of his life. Eating became difficult, as did speaking. Consequently he had to abandon one of his most fertile mediums of expression – the public lecture. (During 1916–17 he had given a series of twenty eight, 2-hour long lectures, mostly without notes, to doctors and laymen at the Vienna Psychiatric Clinic. Although he dismissed them as 'crude stuff meant for the masses'[172] these *Introductory Lectures on Psycho-Analysis* were some of his most successful and persuasive rhetoric. In 1933, when asked to repeat the exercise, he was able only to write a series, not deliver them.) He did manage to retain his ability to do clinical work, despite his difficulty with speech. The last 16 years of his life, however, were dominated by the slow progression of the cancer that eventually killed him.

Between 1923 and 1939, when he died, Freud underwent thirty-one surgical interventions (not to mention the extraction of teeth). His life became a personal battle against the inevitable arrival of death. In November 1923, in the depression following the death of Heinz he attempted to arrest the inevitable and inexorable march of the cancer and agreed to undergo an operation on his testicles. The operation had been devised by a Viennese endocrinologist, Eugen Steinach. Steinach's experimental work on animals on the effects of castration and sex-gland transplantation had been used by Freud in his *Essays* of 1905 in support of his own theses. In 1918 this work had been extended to humans with the claim that it arrested ageing and aided rejuvenation. By the 1930s the surgical procedure was a popular, well-established, but totally unsubstantiated technique which had been carried out on numerous patients. Its popularity – with those who could afford it – only subsequently declined following the isolation of purified sex-hormones later in the century. To Freud, in 1923, grappling within himself over the relationship between life and death – both in his theoretical concerns and within his body – the operation seemed to offer some hope. He found no lasting benefits from the treatment. To his confidant, Lou Andreas-Salomé, he wrote in 1925:

> A crust of indifference is slowly creeping up around me; a fact I state without complaining. It is a natural development, a way of beginning to grow inorganic. The 'detachment of old age', I think it is called. It must be connected with a decisive turn in the relationship of the two instincts postulated by me. The change taking place is perhaps not very noticeable; everything is as interesting as it was before, neither are the ingredients very difficult; but some kind of resonance is lacking; unmusical as I am, I imagine the difference to be something like using the pedal or not. (1925)[173]

As Freud began to realize the consequences of this 'decisive turn' he resolved to make the most use of his time. Thus 1925 was also the year in which he revealed that 'the conditions under which I work have undergone a change . . . Formerly, I was not one of those who are unable to hold back what seems to be a new discovery until it has been either confirmed or corrected . . . But in those days I had unlimited time before me, "oceans of time", . . . now everything has changed. The time before me is limited' (1925).[174] In 1932 he wrote that over the years 'psychoanalysis had become my whole life';[175] as his life ebbed slowly away psychoanalysis became his whole death – all his ideas became pervaded with this sense of death. His earlier theories thus became revised to incorporate this new biological pessimism, and his new theories became expressions of his own struggle with death. Although he died in 1939 he was already meeting death from 1923 onwards.

As if in direct response to the change in conditions Freud admitted that he gave free-rein to his propensity to speculate. Thus the old enemy, religion, became the focus of his speculation once more, as did his theory of the mind (it was in the early 1920s that he introduced his ego, id, super ego model). His new theory of instincts had other consequences too which Freud sought to expound in his last years. Thus, the dream theory (dreams as a means of obtaining pleasure for unconscious infantile sexual desires) had to be revised. The traumatic dreams of those suffering from war neuroses seemed to be a violation of the idea of dreams as wish-fulfilments. Freud modified his theory accordingly to suggest that such traumatic dreams represented unsuccessful attempts to convert the trauma into manageable proportions, and that they were an example of the compulsion to repeat. The dream became then not a wish-fulfilment but 'an *attempt* at the fulfilment of a wish' (1933).[176] Similarly, the 'discovery' of the death instinct posed problems for his theory of psycho-sexual development, problems which he resolved by suggesting that development and regression represented signs of the fusion and defusion of the primal instincts – growth came from the constructive harnessing of the institutional energy of both instincts while neurosis represented their opposition.

Anxiety too became the focus of a revision as a result of Freud's new theory of the instincts and his new theory of the mind. In 1926 he published what has been called 'the last major revision to his beliefs' in the pamphlet *Inhibitions, Symptoms and Anxiety*. To a friend he was candid in his estimation of the revision:

> It shakes up so much that was established and puts things which seemed fixed into a state of flux again . . . But it would be rash to believe that I have now succeeded in finally solving the probem with which the association of anxiety with neurosis confronts us. (1926)[177]

Basically, Freud reverted to the theory of anxiety that he had espoused in his *Project* of 1895 but this time recouched in the language of the ego, the id and the super-ego. The ego faced with the threat of approaching danger situations arising from the instincts requires a means of defence to warn it of the impending danger situation:

> Anxiety is a reaction to a situation of danger. It is obviated by the ego's doing something to avoid that situation or to withdraw from it. It might

be said that symptoms are created so as to avoid the generating of anxiety. But this does not go deep enough. It would be truer to say that symptoms are created so as to avoid a *danger situation* whose presence has been signalled by the generation of anxiety. (1926)[178]

The 'discovery' of the death instinct distinctly coloured his belief in psycho-analysis as a therapy. He was never an optimist about the therapeutic success of psychoanalysis (in the 1890s he had constantly bemoaned his lack of success). In 1906 he had written to Jung saying: 'I should not even claim that every case of hysteria can be cured by [psycho-analysis], let alone all the states that go by that name . . . It is not possible to explain anything to a hostile public; accordingly I have kept certain things that might be said concerning the limits of therapy and its mechanism to myself, or spoken of them in a way that is intelligible only to the intimate' (1906).[179] With the awareness of the death instinct, this therapeutic indifference became a biological 'given' so that he could declare in the 1930s 'my discoveries are not primarily a heal-all'[180] although he had confessed to a friend as early as 1909 'half in jest but really quite seriously . . . the optimum conditions for [psycho-analysis] exist where it is not needed – i.e. among the healthy'.[181] Freud embodied this therapeutic nihilism in one of his last essays 'Analysis Terminable and Interminable' in which he specifically cited the problem of the death instinct as making therapeutic success illusory. However, by this time, while patients provided a source of income, they were not his primary concern, psychoanalysis, which had been born out of 'medical necessity', had become a 'new science of the mind' – it had transcended its humble origins.

By far the most important effect of the 'decisive turn' in Freud's own struggle against Thanatos was his dedication to the goal of securing 'the cause' for the future. Having recognized his own finitude in the face of the encroaching biological necessity of death, Freud was faced with the problem of finding a helmsman for the cause. Jung, earlier groomed by Freud to be the Crown Prince of the movement ('When the Empire I founded is orphaned, no one but Jung must inherit the whole thing' Freud had declared)[182] had deserted him. The Committee was riven with petty personal rivalries rendering it ineffective, particularly in the person of Ernest Jones who disliked many of the other Committee members, notably Otto Rank. Rank himself had been a prime candidate; being called by Freud 'a son and nothing but a son'.[183] Freud, concerned about his health prior to his discovery that he had cancer, had confided his concern to Rank '[because] you are still the youngest and freshest among us' (1922).[184] Rank, however, fell foul of the Committee for developing and publishing, without their consent, an idea, originally Freud's, concerning the importance of birth as a source of neurosis.

Rank had long enjoyed such a closeness to Freud that they shared ideas. In 1909 Freud added a footnote to a revision of *The Interpretation of Dreams* stated that 'the act of birth is the first experience of anxiety, and thus the source and prototype of the affect of anxiety' (1909).[185] Indeed in 1923 he had called birth 'the first great anxiety state'.[186] Rank took that idea and expounded it in a book entitled *The Trauma of Birth* in which he extended the logic of Freud's own position (which said that infantile problems caused neuroses in adults) to suggest that birth itself was the cause of many neuroses. Initially Freud was enthusiastic about the work writing to Ferenczi: 'I don't know whether 66 or 33 percent of it is true, but in any case it is the most important progress since the discovery of psychoanalysis' (1923).[187] Freud even recognized early on the implications of this new theory: 'everything falls into place around this point that you [Rank] are the dreaded David who with his *Trauma of Birth* succeeds in depreciating my work . . .' (1923).[118] Such benign openness to being deposed could not last long, particularly under the pressure of the various Committee members who saw 'signs of an ominous development concerning vital issues of psychoanalysis'.[189] Accordingly, Freud set out to gain a capitulation and a return to the fold of orthodoxy for Rank; in July 1924 he wrote to Rank:

> In the months since our separation [Rank had travelled to the USA], I am even further from agreeing with your innovations. I have seen nothing in two of my cases that have been completed that confirms your views and generally nothing that I did not know before. The final birth phantasy seems to me still to be the child that one gives, analytically, to the father. I am often much concerned about you. The exclusion of the father in your theory seems to reveal too much the result of personal influences in your life which I think I recognize, and my suspicion grows that you could not have written this book had you gone through an analysis yourself. Therefore I beg you not to become fixed but to leave open a way back. (1924)[190]

In a letter to Lou Andreas-Salomé Freud was indeed candid over his concern about developments with Rank; 'for fifteen years' he wrote, 'he was an irreproachable assistant and faithful son to me. Now since he thinks he has made a great discovery, he is behaving so refractorily that I can only look forward to his return from America with great apprehension . . . the situation is perhaps more serious than on any other of the previous occasions' (1924).[191]

Rank did return briefly to the fold, repentant at his aberrations which he confessed had been born out of 'a state which I now recognize as neurotic, I have suddenly returned to myself'.[192] His return was short lived, and by 1926 he had returned to the USA to develop a despised, shortened form of analysis. There, in contrast to Freud's 'long drawn-out psycho-analysis', he developed a system entitled Will Therapy which sought to effect a quick therapeutic intervention. 'I do not believe in spending too much time exploring the past, delving into it . . .' he wrote, 'The past is a labyrinth. One does not have to step into it and move step by step through every turn and twist'.[193] Freud in turn disparaged such superficiality claiming it was 'bold and ingenious; but it did not stand the test of critical examination. Moreover it was a child of its time, conceived under the stress of the contrast between the post-war misery of Europe and the 'prosperity' of America, and designed to adapt the tempo of analytic therapy to the haste of American life' (1937).[194] In fact Rank's ideas have had a considerable resurgence of interest in recent years in America in the form of the Primal Therapy of Arthur Janov.[195] Janov's primal therapy which is derived from the Rankian idea of the birth trauma has in turn been adopted by a Christian counselling movement, known as Clinical Theology' in Britain.[196] While these novel adaptations of these ideas do claim to have had some remarkable successes (clearly many births are difficult and traumatic for all involved) the universality of their claims is disputable, as is their analytic assumption that adult behaviour is *causally* determined by these early life events. Through espousing such an analytically heterodox doctrine as the 'birth trauma' Rank became disinherited from the cause. Freud had to search elsewhere for a successor.

Strangely, in the light of his constant efforts to appoint men pupils to the succession, it was not a man who ultimately came to be both the most important person in the last years of his life, and the one on whom the mantle fell when once he had died, it was his youngest daughter Anna. Anna was the daughter that had arrived at that crucial period of his life in 1895 – it was Anna that Martha was carrying when, in his frustration, he had dreamed the specimen dream of Irma's injection (indeed, she was even named after the Anna of the dream). Although Freud occasionally used material from his children's life to illustrate his theories he was not particularly actively concerned with their growth and development. Anna grew up a serious, retiring and austere girl. As she grew Freud's affection for her grew too, and she gradually began to assume an importance over and above his other children. She began to accompany him on his trips (see plate 10). In 1913 he wrote to Ferenczi: 'My closest companion will be my little daughter, who is developing very well at the moment (you will long ago have guessed the subjective condition for the "Theme of the Three Caskets")' (1913).[197] The paper referred to here is, perhaps, more accurately entitled 'The Motives for the Choice of a Casket', and considered the theme of a choice between three in literature (the choice of Portia's three suitors from among three caskets in the *Merchant of Venice*). The study was replete with the familiar concerns of Freud – the love of a mother; old men facing death and having to choose between women; the use of dreams and their mechanisms as the key to decoding myths and literature. The study went on to consider *King Lear* and his daughters, and here Freud made a very significant admission. He wrote of Lear: 'Is not this once more the scene of a choice between three women, of whom the youngest one is the best, the most excellent one?' (1913).[198] The reference is a clear allusion to the process which we have suggested was taking place in Freud's life whereby he was replacing Minna in his affections with Anna (that is, on the assumption that Minna had already replaced Martha).

Anna became not just the favoured daughter, but Freud's closest confidante and aid – it was she who cared for Freud during his illness, she who represented him at Congresses, she whom Freud asked should be told about his intention at the very end of his life to undergo euthanasia. She became for him all that Martha, and Minna had been, but also all that Jung and Rank should have been to him. Freud had long ago, in the *Interpretation of Dreams*, maintained that 'a girl's first affection is for her father',[199] in the case of Anna, despite her having had a number of suitors from Freud's circle (Freud frequently 'discovered' wishes in his patients and pupils to marry one of his daughters), it was the case that her first and *last* affection was for him. Her role in Freud's life at the end was pivotal, as has been her role in psychoanalysis since his death, not least because she has been the guardian of the holy writ itself.

However, before she could assume that position two things had to happen: she had first to qualify, analytically, and the analytic movement had to qualify for her, namely it had to be in a position whereby it could accept as a leader a person who was not medically qualified. The first condition was met in 1918, or thereabouts. Although it is not precisely clear about the exact relationship between Anna, and her father, and Lou Andreas-Salomé at this time (they were all very close, and Freud sometimes wrote of Anna being 'in analysis' with Lou, and even described Anna as Lou's 'shadow')[200] it is very probable that Freud began to psycho-analyse Anna too. In flagrant violation of all the precepts he had laid down about psychoanalysis, and aware that the complications inherent in a father analysing a daughter were almost insurmountable he conducted her analysis. By this time Anna was a school teacher, she eventually taught for 5 years in an elementary school. When she had been through her analysis (whatever that may mean when it is with your father, and when it results in a life-long devotion to your analyst) she naturally turned to work with children. To his English half nephew, Samuel, he wrote in about 1925 that Anna 'of whom we may well be proud . . . has become a pedagogic [teaching] analyst'. He continued:

> [She] is treating naughty American children, earning a lot of money of which she disposes in a very generous way, helping various poor people. She is a member of the International Psycho-Analytic Association, has won a good name by literary work, and demands the respect of her co-workers. Yet she has just passed her 30th birthday, does not seem inclined to get married, and who can say if her momentary interests will render her happy in years to come when she has to face life without her father?[201]

Child analysis, at least in its orthodox Freudian form, was her field, but Freud had designs on her having a hold over the whole field of analysis.

It was not without significance that Freud in his *New Introductory Lectures* of 1933, in the lecture on the applications of analysis, chose not to expound any of the applications which he himself had pioneered – to ethnology, to mythology, to religion – even though such applications 'are always confirmations of it' (1933).[202] The one topic he chose to expound was child analysis. Freud's estimate of it is most revealing:

> There is one topic which I cannot pass over so easily – not, however, because I understand particularly much about it or have contributed very much to it. Quite the contrary: I have scarcely concerned myself with it at all. I must mention it because it is so exceedingly important, so rich in hopes for the future, perhaps the most important of all the activities of analysis. What I am thinking of is the application of psychoanalysis to education, to the upbringing of the next generation. I am glad that I am at least able to say that my daughter, Anna Freud, has made this study her life-work and has in that way compensated for my neglect. (1933)[203]

She it was who not only helped to legitimate child analysis in the movement, but also consolidate the later emphasis in Freud's work on the importance of the 'ego'. Freud's tentative speculations about the ego and its defences, were capitalized in Anna Freud's theoretical work. Her classic work, *The Ego and the Mechanisms of Defence*, presented to Freud on his eightieth birthday, provided an official sanction for the development of psychoanalysis as ego-psychology. Others had developed a psychoanalysis of the 'ego' before her, but through her endorsement a whole school of 'ego psychology' gained ground in the movement particularly in America. Heinz Hartmann and Erik Erikson were but two of the most important contributors to this bourgeoning school of psychoanalytic thought.[204] However, before Anna was able to effect any of this, there was some considerable preparation required for it to be possible.

From the very beginning of psychoanalysis, Freud, steeped in the biology and medicine of the nineteenth century, had conceived of analysis as an enterprise that was at core a medical enterprise. True, he had nurtured non-physicians such as Rank, and had encouraged both Rank and Jung to venture out into the 'colonies' of biography, literature, and mythology. For all of his desire to construct a 'new science of the mind' he was aware that the home territory of analysis was the neuroses and the clinical sphere. We find his work thus peppered with references to the psychoanalyst as the 'physician' even at late as 1918. In his *Introductory Lectures* he had written 'psycho-analysis is a procedure for the medical treatment of neurotic patients' (1916/1917).[205] In 1924, 2 years after his, by now, psycho-analysed, but medically untrained, daughter, Anna, had become a member of the Vienna Society, Freud wrote that 'it is no longer possible to restrict the practice of psychoanalysis to doctors and to exclude laymen from it' (1925).[206] Without, at that time mentioning his daughter (although he added a footnote in 1935 to mention her) he cited as an example of how this may be the case 'a non-doctor who has been suitably trained can, with occasional reference to a doctor, carry out the analytic treatment not only of children but also of neurotics' (1925).[207] Freud was later to suggest that the widening of analysis to enable laymen to use it was almost directly caused by medicine's inability to recognize the importance of psychoanalysis: 'Doctors have no historical claim to the sole possession of analysis. On the contrary, until recently they have met it with everything possible that could damage it, from the shallowest ridicule to the gravest calumny' (1926).[208]

The matter could hardly rest at that point for with the increasing popularity of psychoanalysis (including an offer for a film on the subject by Sam Goldwyn which Freud refused, and one which he reluctantly let be made by Abraham and Sachs) 'the question of lay analysis' became a focal point of dissention in the movement. There was a marked polarity between the Viennese analysts – who followed Freud's line – and the American analysts – who, much to Freud's annoyance, refused to endorse lay analysis. Ernest Jones in London, and Max Eitingon in Berlin, vacillated between the two poles believing in theory in lay-analysis, but wanting some sort of practical control and safeguard which having psychoanalysis being recommended by a doctor afforded. By this time, given that psycho-analysis was so popular considerations of a pecuniary nature might have played upon their thoughts – far from having to win converts at any cost, there were considerable advantages in accruing the benefits of specialist status. In 1926 Freud was forced to confront the issue more squarely as a result of one of his non-medical pupils, Theodor Reik, being prosecuted under an ancient Austrian law against 'quackery'. The trial of Theodor Reik was thus an opportunity for Freud to expound and defend psychoanalysis against being subsumed by medicine. Reik's trial was the proximate cause of the defence, but Anna's position in the movement may well have been the ultimate cause. In the end it became a battle over orthodoxy with Freud having to battle against the American position – a powerplay for the future of the cause.

Freud having intervened with a Viennese official over Reik's case (which was dropped anyway due to the paucity of the evidence against him), took up the cudgel on behalf of lay analysis. He produced a 22 000-word defence of the subject in the form of a booklet entitled 'The Question of Lay Analysis' together with a shortened version entitled 'Psycho-Analysis and Quackery'. Here was Freud fighting for the very future of the cause; he would not let it rest. To the acting chairman of the Viennese Psychoanalytical Society he wrote: 'The battle for lay analysis must, at one time or the other, be fought to the finish. Better now than later. As long as I live I shall resist that psychoanalysis be swallowed up by medicine' (1926).[209] As ever Freud interpreted dissention from his view as an indication of aberrancy – the opposition to lay-analysis was 'the last mask of the resistance against psycho-analysis, and the most dangerous of all' (1929).[210] The battle rumbled on with the Americans still refusing to accept lay-analysis; the movement was threatened with a split. In 1927 a compromise was accepted which did not reject the Americans from the movement. It was a compromise effected through Anna's intervention. Jones recording the incident remarked: 'it was an historic moment in the dispute between the two continents, and it meant that for the time being the crisis was over'.[211] Freud, who had never really liked America, wrote: 'I feel hurt by the behaviour of American analysts in the matter of Lay-Analysis. They, it seems, are not very fond of me'.[212] Even as late as 1938 he wrote that he had 'never repudiated' his views on the subject and that he insisted 'on them even more intensely than before, in the face of the obvious American tendency to turn psycho-analysis into a mere house-maid of psychiatry' (1938).[213]

That Freud's concerns were not strictly scientific in this matter are shown by his letter to Pfister in Zurich. In 1928, having recently published *The Future of an Illusion*, his latest critique of religion he wrote to Pfister saying:

> I do not know if you have detected the secret link between the 'Lay-Analysis' and the 'Illusion'. In the former I wish to protect analysis from the doctors and in the latter from the priests. I should like to hand it over to a profession which does not yet exist, a profession of *lay* curers of souls who need not be doctors and should not be priests. (1928)[214]

Having, to his mind, destroyed the basis of religion, he felt he had to provide something in its place – lay (secular) soul cure. Given that analysis was only suitable for the healthy Freud's legacy was hardly to have been any comfort to anyone. Some weeks later after Pfister, a Protestant pastor, had remonstrated with him over his negative evaluation of priests Freud took up the theme again. He wrote: 'my remark that the analysts of my phantasy of the future should not be priests does not sound very tolerant, I admit. But you must consider that I was referring to a very distant future. For the present I put up with doctors, so why not priests too?' (1929).[215] Freud's vision for the cause was the long-term establishment of an alternative to the consolations of religion; the persistence of religion and its attempt to offer a 'cure for souls' was but an example of a 'pious illusion' which people could retain on the grounds that he could not deny 'the human right to be irrational'.[216] Freud's alternative, dressed in the garb of rationality, was of a grim biological destiny with humanity poised on the edge of extinction by the power of Thanatos. To Pfister he expounded his conclusions:

> I doubt man's destiny to climb by way of civilization to a state of greater perfection, if I see in life a continual struggle between Eros and the death instinct, the outcome of which seems to me to be indeterminable, I do not believe that in coming to those conclusions I have been influenced by innate constitutional factors or acquired emotional attitudes . . . The death instinct is not a requirement of my heart; it seems to me to be only an inevitable assumption on both biological and psychological grounds. The rest follows from that. Thus to me pessimism seems a conclusion, while the optimism of my opponents seems an *a priori* assumption. I might also say that I have concluded a marriage of reason with my gloomy theories, while others live with theirs in a love-match. I hope they will gain greater happiness from this than I. (1930)[217]

As the 1930s progressed Freud was to find even more confirmations for his theories in the events in the wider world. They were difficult times indeed, as the theologian Paul Tillich has observed the 1930s in Central Europe were a time indelibly stamped 'first of all with a feeling of fear, or, more exactly, of indefinite anxiety . . . not only the economic and political, but also the cultural and religious, security seemed to be lost. There was nothing on which one could build, everything was without foundation'.[218] The post-First World War settlement effected after Versailles with its crippling reparations and its humiliations on the Central Powers, had a profound effect upon Freud. He held America responsible, and the American President, Woodrow Wilson, virtually personally liable for the deprivations and the disasters. To one American he is supposed to have said: 'Your Woodrow Wilson was the silliest fool of the century, if not of all centuries . . . And he was also probably one of the biggest criminals – unconsciously, I am sure'.[219] Freud wreaked

his psychoanalytic revenge on Wilson, though, in the form of a biography
of the man, written in collaboration with William C. Bullitt, an American
diplomat who had attended the Paris Peace Conference of 1919. Both
men had an axe to grind against Wilson: Freud, for the ravages the post-
war settlement did to the Austro-Hungarian Empire, and Bullitt, for
Wilson's refusal to consider his advice at the conference. The two of them
thrashed out the ideas of the book, Bullitt later recalled it was 'the result
of much combat. Both Freud and I were extremely pig-headed: somewhat
convinced that each one of us was God'.[220] They did not agree a final
draft until 1938, by which time Bullitt was the American Ambassador
in Paris, but the book could not be published on the grounds that it was
quite possibly libellous. Freud's assessment of Wilson stands at the front
of this book. In many ways it stands as a fitting assessment of Freud
himself.

One of the consequences of the post-Paris settlement which was to have
an enduring effect upon Freud was the disintegration of the Weimar
Republic in Germany and the subsequent rise of Hitler and the Nazis.
As he surveyed the scene in Europe in 1930, with Hitler's National Socialist
Germany Worker's Party already the second largest in Germany, he wrote,
prophetically: 'we are moving towards dark times: the apathy of old age
ought to enable me to rise above it all, but I cannot help the fact that
I am sorry for my seven grandchildren' (1930).[221] In 1932 Freud was
asked by an organization originally founded by the League of Nations
(the pre-Second World War, impotent, equivalent of the United Nations)
to contribute to an exchange of letters between himself and Einstein on
the subject of war and its avoidance. The exchange, eventually published
as a pamphlet, *Why War?* in English, French and German contained
Freud's assessment of mankind's prospects. Freud's conclusion was: 'the
upshot of observations . . . is that there is no likelihood of our being
able to suppress humanity's aggressive tendencies' (1932).[222] The book
was banned in Germany where Adolf Hitler had just become Chancellor
of Germany, and the Third Reich had been inaugurated.

Banning his books was only the beginning of the anti-Semitic Nazis.
In 1933 Freud's works were publicly consigned to the flames along with
those of Einstein, Thomas Mann, and other, Jewish, writers in Berlin.
The books were thrown in with the declamation: 'Against the soul-
destroying over estimation of the sex life – and on behalf of the nobility
of the human soul – I offer to the flames the writing of one, Sigmund
Freud!'[223] Freud is said to have commented: 'at least I burn in the best
of company';[224] and with tragic irony: 'What progress we are making!
In the Middle Ages they would have burnt me; nowadays they are content
with burning my books'[225] (little did Freud know then that four of his
five sisters were to die in German concentration camps – the Holocaust

was yet to come). As Hitler gained confidence and the Third Reich grew so too did the harassment of psychoanalysis. Since most analysts were Jews their position became increasingly untenable, many were forced to emigrate – Eitingon to Palestine, Sachs to the USA and many others. Freud, though pessimistic about the general outlook, continued to believe that in Vienna he was relatively safe and did not need leave.

One event during this period hurt Freud particularly. To Pfister he wrote in 1933 that 'there has been little occasion for me to change my opinion of human nature, particularly the Christian Aryan variety' (1933).[226] Most cutting of all the manifestations of so-called Christian ideas and people was the appointment in 1933 of Jung to the International General Medical Society for Psychopathology, virtually the only officially recognized organ in Germany for any form of psychotherapy including psychoanalysis. To Freud, this looked like the ultimate betrayal, especially when Jung began publishing articles proclaiming the 'fact' that 'the Aryan unconscious has a higher potential than the Jewish'.[227] Indeed, privately Jung was quite specific in his denigration of Freud's views and certainly seems to endorse the official Nazi line on their value:

> As is known, one cannot do anything against stupidity, but in this instance the Aryan people can point out that with Freud and Adler, specific Jewish points of view are publicly preached and, as can be proved likewise, points of view that have an essentially corrosive character. If the proclamation of this Jewish gospel is agreeable to the government, then so be it. Otherwise, there is also the possibility that this would not be agreeable to the government . . . .[228]

Jung's words and actions, in being there at all, confirmed to Freud the centrality of Jung's anti-Semitism. Jung was to continue to work for the New society until his resignation in 1940, and was to claim that he had only taken the post in order to help his (mainly Jewish) psychotherapeutic colleagues. There is no doubt, though, that for all that he helped individuals, Jung's message, and his interpretation of Freud's limitations, did resonate with the prevailing orthodoxy of Germany at the time – an orthodoxy which required all psychotherapists to read *Mein Kampf* to obtain their psychological beliefs.

Freud hung on in Vienna,[229] trusting that his, by now, world-wide reputation would protect him and his immediate family and friends. On 9 March 1938 the Austrian Chancellor announced a plebiscite to discover whether Austria should remain independent. Two days later on Hitler's orders he called off the plebiscite and resigned. On learning this news Freud went to his diary and penned the words 'Finis Austriae'. The new Chancellor promptly invited the German Army in, and on 12 March Hitler himself was in Austria where he decided to incorporate Austria into the German Reich. The speed of events overtook the Freud family, and it became impossible for them to emigrate without official permission. It is possible that Freud could have remained in Vienna, he certainly felt inclined to meet the final indignities of German occupation head on . . . but for Anna he felt a move judicious. To Jones he later wrote: 'the advantage the emigration promises Anna justifies all our little sacrifices. For us old people . . . emigrating wouldn't have been worthwhile'. (1938)[230]

It was only possible for Freud to emigrate thanks to the intervention of William Bullitt with President Roosevelt, and Ernest Jones with the Lord Privy Seal and with the Home Secretary, both personal friends. Eventually, after much harassment from the Gestapo, the payment of gross financial penalties, the dissolution and partial destruction of Freud's library and papers, and the confiscation of many of his publications, Freud and his close family (Martha, Minna, Anna, Martin, Mathilde and her husband) were permitted to leave on 4 June 1938. To his son Ernst, already in England he wrote:

> Two prospects keep me going in these grim times, to rejoin you all and – to die in freedom. I sometimes compare myself with the old Jacob who, when a very old man, was taken by his children to Egypt . . . Let us hope that it won't also be followed by an exodus from Egypt. It is high time that Ahasuerus came to rest somewhere. (1938)[231]

After a brief stop in Paris, Freud continued his journey to London where Jones had prepared a home for him.

Freud lived in London for just over a year. It was a year filled with poignancy – the events on the continent, his deteriorating physical condition contrasted with the almost constant stream of prestigious visitors to his home (Salvador Dali, H. G. Wells, the Secretaries of the Royal Society and others). Freud responded in the way he knew best – he turned once more to writing. He quickly began work on a text, which ultimately he never finished, entitled *An Outline of Psycho-Analysis*. He opened the book with a declaration of his aim:

> The aim of this brief work is to bring together the tenets of psycho-analysis and to state them, as it were dogmatically – in the most concise form and in the most unequivocal terms. The intention is naturally not to compel belief or to arouse conviction. (1938)[232]

Not an easy book to read, it does, however, provide a succinct summary of Freud's final ideas on psychoanalysis, the system he had created. These were not the only subjects of his last years – his last creative energies were directed at the old enemy, religion; *Moses and Monotheism* published in 1939. It has been called a 'chaotic composition' since Freud took *two* previously published articles, two prefaces (one of which was written in Vienna, one in London), and he fused them together in a confused 'bricolage' of a book. The ideas for it had been swimming round in his head for some few years; he wrote 'it tormented me like an unlaid ghost' (1939).[233] Whilst it was at the printer's Freud wrote to a correspondent describing his perception of it:

> It contains an investigation based on analytical assumptions of the origin of religion, specifically Jewish monotheism, and is essentially a sequel to and an expansion of another work which I published 25 years ago under the title of *Totem and Taboo*. New ideas do not come easily to an old man; there is nothing left for him to do but repeat himself. It can be called an attack on religion only in so far as any scientific investigation of religious belief presupposes disbelief. Neither in my private life nor in my writings have I ever made a secret of my being an out-and-out unbeliever. (1938)[234]

When eventually it was published, at such a time of darkness for Jewry, Freud confessed that he regretted the fact that the book set out 'to deprive a people of the many whom they take pride in as the greatest of their sons' (1939).[235] Despite that regret he stood his ground: 'Needless to say' he wrote to a friend 'I don't like offending my own people either. But what can I do about it? I have spent my whole life standing up for what I have considered to be scientific truth, even when it was uncomfortable and unpleasant for my fellow men. I cannot end up with an act of disavowal' (1938).[236]

His thesis, though not departing from that outlined in *Totem and Taboo* went further than that earlier work inasmuch as it was a specific attack on the origins of the Jewish religion and its Christian off-shoot. Whereas *Totem and Taboo* had posited the origins of religion in some sort of vague, unspecified, prehistory, *Moses and Monotheism* sought to undermine the origins of mono-theism and show its natural roots. As with his earlier work the book has a logic behind it. First, on the basis of his name, Freud announced that Moses was an Egyptian not a Jew. Secondly, he suggested that this Egyptian Moses then imposed upon the Jews the religion of the Pharaoh Akenaton, the religion of the one god Aten. Thirdly, the special sign of Jewishness, circumcision, the sign of the covenant, was imposed by the Egyptian Moses on the Jews. As a consequence of these three theses the whole of the Mosaic epic from the exodus and Sinai through to his death on the edge of the promised land is seen as a struggle between Moses trying to force his alien god, Aten, on the people, and the Jews wedded to their tribalistic god Jahweh opposing this. The conflict, Freud maintained, ended with the revolt of the Jews against Moses and their killing him on the mountain outside the promised land. From then on the familiar logic of *Totem and Taboo* replete with Lamarckism took over.

What are we to make of this thesis, which Freud himself called a 'novel' which he admitted was based 'on psychological probabilities alone' and that 'objective evidence . . . had not been obtainable' (1939).[237] Indeed, it is a study about which Freud disarmingly wrote:

> I am very well aware that in dealing so autocratically and arbitrarily with Biblical tradition – bringing it up to confirm my views when it suits me and unhesitatingly rejecting it when it contradicts me – I am exposing myself to serious methodological criticism and weakening the convincing force of my arguments. But this is the only way in which one can treat material of which one knows definitely that its trustworthiness has been severely impaired by the distorting influence of tendentious purposes. . . . Certainly is in any case unattainable and moreover it may be said that every other writer on the subject has adopted the same procedure. (1939)[238]

To Hans Sachs he described the *Moses* book as 'quite a worthy exit, I believe' (1939).[239] The passage I have just quoted may be said to be an appropriate final word about the whole of Freud's work – 'it's trustworthiness has been severely impaired by the distorting influence of tendentious purposes'. As he himself wrote in the study: 'the implications to which I am now leading . . . need only be accepted if the theories on which they are based turn out to be correct' (1939).[240]

By January 1939 the cancerous growths in his mouth were so established again that it became impossible to operate – Thanatos could only now be palliated. Though in constant pain he refused all drugs until the very end when in September, shortly after the Second World War had started, in keeping with a pact he had made with Max Schur, his physician, he requested morphine. He died at 3.00 a.m. 23 September, 1939. He had achieved what he had once called 'the longed-for rest . . . eternal nothingness' (1929).[241] He was cremated at Golders Green 3 days later in the presence of a large number of his closest friends.

Conclusion

For one who'd lived among enemies so long:
If often he was wrong and, at times absurd,
To us he is no more a person
Now but a whole climate of opinion. (W. H. Auden)

It gives some measure of the importance and influence of Freud to recollect the words of Auden written *in memoriam* shortly after Freud's death in 1939. From the days of loneliness and despair in the late 1890s and early 1900s Freud's fortunes, and those of his 'new science of the mind', had gradually increased and spread to the point where they undergirded many facets of our culture. The world could no longer understand itself without coming to terms with this multi-faceted, all-pervasive atmosphere of belief – Freud had, quite literally, found the frame of reference, not just for Auden's generation, but also for all subsequent ones. The psychoanalytic perspective on life has become one of the permanent features of the intellectual milieu of the twentieth-century.[1]

In coming to terms with psychoanalysis we are confronted with three separate issues which demand our attention: (a) What do we think of the new science of the mind? (b) What do we think of the new general psychoanalytic perspective, the 'whole climate of opinion'? (c) What do we think of the man himself? Many have tried to answer each of these questions without reference to the others. Debate abounds in philosophy of science over whether Freud's theories are genuinely scientific – batteries of tests are applied from the canons of the philosophy of science to Freud's individual theories as the Oedipal origins of the neuroses are compared to the law of universal gravitation. Frequently, though not always, Freud's theories are deemed to have failed and psychoanalytic theory is judged to be pseudo-scientific – lacking the 'real' stamp of science, mere theology masquerading as scientific truth.[2] Similarly, debate abounds about the importance of Freud for our culture, about his fluctuating fortunes in the market place of opinion – about whether he ushered in the 'triumph of the therapeutic', to use one commentator's description of his impact.[3] Finally, interest in the man himself continues unabated with new biographies, novels, television dramas each presenting their various conceptions of 'the development of the hero'.[4]

It is my contention, implicit throughout the book that it is impossible

Plate 13. Freud's study at number 19 Berggasse, Vienna

to answer adquately any of the three questions posed above without reference to the other two. It is only as we become fully aware of the extent to which Freud's own subjective experiences, and his personal life impinged upon, and coloured his theories that we can be in any position to determine answers to the more general questions. It is not a question of reducing a scientific argument, or a philosophical argument to an *ad hominum* attack – Freud used the evidence he gained from his own life and experience to construct his system. We have to come to terms with it – as Freud himself said 'a more intimate knowledge of a man [leads] to a more exact estimate of his achievements'.

Accordingly, if my point is valid, then only those studies which blend the biographical material with the psychological material have any hope of coming to an 'exact estimate' of Freud and psychoanalysis. Studies of psychoanalysis which merely take the *Complete Psychological Works of Sigmund Freud* and study them in isolation from their biographical context miss the point – Freud himself, when referring to an array of Goethe's complete works, is reported to have said, 'all this was used by him as a means of self-concealment'.[5] Similarly, biographies and portraits of Freud which ignore the theoretical context within which he lived again miss the point – Freud acted out the dramas of his theories. One-sided pictures of Freud abound – from the hagiographical to the derogatory – a 'more exact estimate' can only emerge from the careful juxtapositioning of biography and theory. A vivid symbol of the intimacy of these two integral elements of a complete understanding of Freud – the personal reality and the world he investigated – is depicted in the arrangement of his study (see plate 13). Surrounded by his beloved books and archaeological treasures, his desk was overlooked by a window, and there in the middle of the window he set a mirror so that whenever he looked up, and out to the world, his vision of that world included a vision of himself. No adequate understanding of Freud and psychoanalysis can ignore the inviolate intricacy of the two.[6] Of course, given that we still have volumes of Freud's letters yet to be revealed in either their unexpurgated, or, in many cases, in any form, the particular blend I have presented in this book may yet be wrong. Kurt Eissler, 'defender of the faith' and 'royal archivist' has recently suggested that material apertaining to Freud's life should be embargoed till the next century on the grounds that in the future there will be 'more distance' so that people 'will be more objective'[7] – a defence premised upon the idea that the world cannot yet abide the truth Freud revealed.

It was Thomas Carlyle who once warned 'let men beware when God lets loose a great thinker in the world'. Freud was, beyond a doubt, a great thinker, even a genius – the system he created, and the movement he initiated and sustained, are testimony to that. However, in the light

of the width of his vision, and its all-encompassing logic, we should retain
our respect, indeed our caution. Freud himself would not have cavilled
at that sense of wariness, though he would at many of our conclusions –
he once complained to a pupil 'first they call me a genius and then they
proceed to reject all my views'.[8] He recognized the precariousness of
those who venture into new, uncharted areas of human experience, and
to Fliess announced the spirit with which he ventured forth:

> I am actually not at all a man of science, not an observer, not an
> experimenter, not a thinker. I am by temperament nothing but a
> *conquistador*, an adventurer, if you wish to translate this term – with all
> the inquisitiveness, daring, and tenacity characteristic of such a man. Such
> people are apt to be treasured if they succeed, if they have really discovered
> something; otherwise, they are thrown by the wayside.[9]

But just as Schliemann, one of Freud's favourite *conquistador* mentors,
in his enthusiasm for the mythical Troy of Homer's *Iliad*, was unconcerned
with the finer points of the site, and even, excavated the site along the
lines of his preset notions, so too, we may suggest, did the *conquistador*
of the mind uncover his material. The plasticity of the material can be
conformed to any number of explanatory accounts.

Towards the end of his life Freud suggested that, whatever else he may
have done, he had felt himself to have laid a good foundation (or, to
continue the archaeological metaphor, had excavated some sure recesses).
Interestingly, in the light of the centrality I have suggested of religion
in Freud's thought, he felt that his theories had well and truly grounded
the old enemy, religion. To Ludwig Binswanger he explained it thus:

> I have always lived on the ground floor and in the basement of the
> building – you maintain that on changing one's view point one can also
> see an upper floor housing such distinguished guests as religion, art and
> others. You are not the only one; most cultivated specimens of *homo natura*
> think likewise. In this respect you are the conservative, I the revolutionary.
> If I had another life of work ahead of me, I would dare to offer even those
> high-born people a home in my lowly hut. I already found one for religion
> when I stumbled on the category 'neurosis of mankind'. But we are
> probably talking at cross purposes and it will be centuries before our dispute
> is settled. (1936)[10]

I suspect that the proper juxtaposition of biography and theory will
lead to a re-evaluation of the form and status of the 'lowly hut', and
to a 'changing [of] one's viewpoint'. Despite Freud's predictions that
it might take centuries to resolve the question, to my mind, the evidence
exists, to help effect a change in viewpoint which is long overdue.[11]

Chronological Notes

[NB In this chronology I have given more attention to the dates around the 1880s, and 1900s as the particular timing of cases and events is usually crucial to understanding their significance.]

1856	Sigismund Freud was born at Freiberg in Moravia.
1860	Freud family settled in Vienna in a poor, Jewish quarter, Leopoldstradt.
1865	Freud entered the Sperl Gymnasium, Leopoldstradt.
1872	He visited Freiberg with two school friends and experienced his 'first calf love' for Gisela Fluss and her mother.
1873	He graduated from the Gymnasium *summa cum laude*. In the Autumn he entered the University of Vienna in the Medical department but studied widely.
1874, 1875	He continued his studies, notably philosophy, under Franz Brentano, and physiology under Ernst Brücke.
1875	He changed his name to Sigmund and visited his half-brothers in England. Whilst there he determined to become a physician.
1876	He received a small travel and research scholarship to work in Trieste on the anatomy of male eels. In the autumn he joined Brücke's Institute of Physiology working on nerve histology. He met von Fleischl who was ultimately (in 1891) to die from the effects of addiction to morphine and cocaine.
1877, 1878	Researched the histology of the spinal ganglia of a particular genus of fish, the results of which were presented to the Vienna Academy in July 1878 by Brücke. Freud began developing a friendship with Joseph Breuer at this time – the two were to develop a 'theory of hysteria' which was published later in 1893 and in 1895.
1879, 1880	Freud continued at the Brücke Institute but also fulfilled his military service. In 1880 Breuer began his treatment of 'Anna O'.
1881	Freud graduated as a Doctor of Medicine, and was appointed as demonstrator at the Brücke Institute.
1882	He met, and became engaged to Martha Bernays. Breuer discussed his 'Anna O' case with him for the first time. He joined the Vienna General Hospital first in the Department of Surgery, then in the Department of Internal Medicine with Professor Nothnagel.

1883   He transferred to the Psychiatric Clinic of the General
             Hospital to work with professor Meynert. He visited
             Gmunden in July with Breuer – his first experience of Alpine
             scenery.
1884   He joined the Department of Nervous Diseases. He began
             to study, and use, the drug cocaine. He was particularly
             interested in its relationship to sexual potency and sexuality,
             for various reasons he failed to capitalize on the *one* safe use
             of the drug – for local anaesthesia in ophthalmology – for
             which his friend Carl Koller is accorded the discovery.
             Evidence exists to suggest that Freud went on using, and
             recommending the use of, cocaine by nasal application, until
             sometime in the mid 1890s.
1885   He was Appointed *Privatdozent* in Neuropathology. In April
             Freud destroyed all of his earlier papers and notes.
1885, 1886 He obtained a travel grant to study in Paris under Professor
             Charcot, whilst there he began the translation of some of
             Charcot's lectures, and although maintaining his neurological
             work, began to consider specializing in the neuroses.
1886   On returning from Paris he set up a private practice in neuro-
             pathology, and a further brief period of military service before
             marrying Martha Bernays in September. He delivered two
             papers on hypnotism and one on 'male hysteria' to audiences
             in Vienna – they were not well received. In February, Minna
             Bernays' former fiancé, Ignaz Schönberg, died.
1887   His first child, Mathilde was born (of his subsequent children:
             Martin was born in 1889; Oliver in 1891, Ernst in 1892; Sophie
             in 1893; and Anna in 1895). He first made the acquaintance
             of Wilhelm Fliess in this year. His relationship to Fliess, which
             by 1892 was the most important and intimate of all his
             friendships, went through various phases, it lasted until 1904
             when it was irrevocably broken over a dispute about
             plagiarism. Freud used hypnosis extensively on his patients.
1889   Freud went to Nancy to study Bernheim's hypnotic techniques
             (he also translated two volumes of Bernheim's work). Freud
             began to treat Emmy von N. by a new method 'to a large
             extent' and began to treat Frau Cäcilie M.
1891   Freud published, jointly with his friend Oskar Rie, a
             monograph on cerebral paralyses in children, and his very
             first book *On Aphasia* which he dedicated to Breuer. The
             Freud family moved to 19, Berggasse, the apartment he was
             not to vacate until 1938.
1892   Freud treated Elizabeth von R. – 'the first full length analysis
             of hysteria'.

1893   Katharina 'case'. 'Preliminary Communication' published
            with Breuer – this paper was subsequently reproduced as
            chapter 1 of *Studies of Hysteria*. Monograph on cerebral
            diplegia in children published.
1894   Increased tensions in the Freud/Breuer relationship.
1895   February – Emma Eckstein given surgery by Fliess – an
            operation on her nose which was bungled and precipitated
            her near death in April.
            April – Freud announced that he was working on his
            'Psychology for Neurologists' – Freud worked on the ideas
            throughout the summer.
            May – *Studies on Hysteria* published.
            July – 'Dream of Irma's Injection' reportedly the first dream
            'thoroughly analysed'.
            September – after having visited Fliess in Berlin Freud wrote
            'Project for a Scientific Psychology' – two unpublished
            notebooks – he was variously elated and depressed by its
            content and gave up work on it by the end of the year.
            October – Freud wrote of his conviction that he had 'solved
            the riddle of the neuroses'. He lectured on hysteria to the
            Vienna Physicians Society.
1896   January – Freud wrote a brief, unpublished paper on 'the
            neuroses of defence' and called it a 'Christmas fairy tale'.
            April – Freud announced the 'seduction theory' to the Vienna
            Society for Psychiatry and Neurology.
            May – Delivered his first lecture on dream interpretation. He
            described his position as 'isolated . . . because a void is
            forming round me'.
            October – Death of Jacob Freud an event which he later
            described as having 'revolutionized his soul' – only Minna
            Bernays, by now living as a member of the household (a
            position she was to maintain until her death in 1941) was
            present in the house to console him.
            December – Freud was still working on the seduction theory
            but developing an interest in Krafft-Ebing's theories on
            perversions and Weier's ideas on demonology and witchcraft.
1897   January – Freud steeped in both his seduction theory and
            material from his studies in the accounts of witchcraft
            suggested to Fliess that much of his clinical material was
            phantasy but *based* upon actual seductions. He also completed
            his last neurological treatise – *Infantile Cerebral Paralysis*.
            February – Professor Nothnagel and Krafft-Ebing informed
            Freud of their intention to put his name forward for a

Professorship. In February and March two other relatives died (Freud's disgraced uncle Josef and Martha's uncle Michael Bernays). Vienna finally got its anti-Semitic mayor, Karl Leuger, appointed, the city was awash with anti-Semitism.

April – Freud and Fliess had one of their 'congresses' in Nuremberg where they studied 'the Middle Ages'.

July – Freud went on a walking holiday with Minna Bernays.

August – Freud informed Fliess of the neurosis which was prompting him to consider himself as his chief patient.

September – after a brief stay in Venice with his wife, Freud, his brother, Alexander, and a colleague and patient, Felix Gattl, undertook an extensive tour of Tuscany and Umbria in Central Italy. The tour was specifically connected with Freud's resolve to re-examine the themes of Italian art which hitherto he had found otiose because of their predominantly Christian themes. The tour was to evoke a number of important ideas and images in his mind (these were to find expression in his dream book which was conceived at roughly this time). Of particular note was his encounter with the frescos at Orvieto of the Last Judgement by Signorelli – the 'finest' he had ever seen. The frescos were later to be the focus of one of his studies in *The Psychopathology of Everyday Life*. In his confrontation with Signorelli's picture we may suggest he found the spark which was to ignite his imagination and provoke the exercise known as his 'self-analysis'. Freud also visited another place of great personal significance to him – Lake Trasimeno – scene of his hero, Hannibal's encampment.

On return from Italy Freud announced to Fliess the rejection of his seduction theory. He also joined the B'nai B'rith Society, and travelled to Berlin to consult Fliess.

October – Freud, in the throes of his 'self-analysis', reported to Fliess the very first 'infantile' material and eventually outlined the Oedipus complex. He also revealed to Fliess the news of 'sexual excitation' being of no more use to him.

December – announced to Fliess that he had created his own 'endopsychic myths' about immortality etc.

1898   February – Freud published a paper 'Sexuality in the Aetiology of the Neuroses' which despite the radical changes in his views during 1897 gave little hint of any change from his published views of 1896. During the year Freud was engaged in much of the preliminary work for his dream book, a number of his important dreams (later described in his dream book) occurred during this year – Count Thun; the Botanical Monograph; 'Non Vixit'; Goethe's attack on Herr M'; 'My Son the Myops'; 'The Three Fates'.

June – Freud sent Fliess his first 'psychoanalytic study' of a piece of literature – C. F. Meyer' story *Die Richterin*.

July – Freud began an extensive tour of the Alps with Minna. He then followed this with a trip to Bosnia with his wife. Martha, having fallen ill, Freud continued alone. On this trip he met a lawyer from Berlin, they discussed 'death and sexuality' – this was the occasion of his famous 'Signorelli parapraxis'. The paper, 'Signorelli Parapraxis', was published in December.

1899   May – Freud sent off his 'Screen Memories' paper – a disguised autobiographical paper.

Summer – Freud rented a large farmhouse in Bavaria. It was here that he wrote most of *The Interpretation of Dreams*. This was published in November (but with an imprint dated 1900).

1900   Freud was very disappointed at the reception of his dream book. He began a lecture course on dreams at the university. August – Freud's congress with Fliess at Achensee proved to be their final meeting together. The two fell out (although they continued to correspond until 1904). After the congress Freud took Martha and Minna to the Tyrol. At the end of August and first half of September Freud and Minna travelled through northern Italy. Minna was taken to the spa at Merano and Freud returned to Vienna. During his tour with Minna there is evidence to suggest that he consummated his desires for her. The 'aliquis parapraxis' dates from this time. On his return to Vienna Freud heard of the appointment of his friend Königstein to a professorship. Freud set about writing a short introduction to his dream book entitled *On Dreams* (it was published in 1901). He also took on a new patient, an 18-year-old girl whose case study was later written up as the Dora case (and published eventually in 1905). He continued to collect material for his book on the psychopathology of everyday life (the text of which was completed in mid-February 1901). Minna had not recovered from her complaint.

1901   Some of the fruits of his endeavours of 1900 were published – notably *On Dreams* and the papers which were eventually to be collated into the book, *The Psychopathology of Everyday Life* (published in 1904). In late summer Freud visited Rome with his brother Alexander – it was 'the high-point of my life'. On returning from Rome Freud resolved to lobby for his professorship which was granted early in 1902.

1902   Freud was granted the title *Professor Extraordinarius*. The 'Psychological Wednesday Society' began as a weekly meeting of Freud, Stekel, Adler and a few others. Freud went to Italy in the summer with Alexander. Freud and Fliess ended their regular correspondence (they exchanged letters over a matter of plagiarism in 1904).

1904   The papers concerning the pathology of everyday life which had previously been published in journal form were published as the book *The Psychopathology of Everyday Life*. Freud went with his brother Alexander to Greece in the summer. On the Acropolis, in Athens, Freud experienced a 'disturbance of his memory' which he was later to analyse in some depth. He became engaged in an acrimonious exchange of letters with Fliess. Freud had passed on information about Fliess' theories to a patient/pupil Swoboda who had in turn passed it on to Weininger who had published them as his own theories in 1903 – the subject under dispute was bisexuality. Freud, at first, denied that he had been guilty of doing this, but later recounted and accepted his role in the affair, but suggested to Fliess that it was unimportant. Weininger committed suicide shortly after publishing his book, but Swoboda on receiving his papers after his death added insult to injury in 1904 by publishing yet more of Fliess' views without giving credit to Fliess. Fliess eventually decided that the only course of action open to him was to publish some of his most recent correspondence with Freud in order to establish his claim for priority. He did this in 1906, sparking off a public debate in the Viennese press and prompting Freud to offer public denials of his culpability.

1905   Freud published three important studies: *A Fragment of a Case Study* (the Dora Case begun and largely completed in 1901 but left unpublished); *Jokes and their Relation to the Unconscious*; and *Three Essays on the Theory of Sexuality* (his first public repudiation of the seduction theory and his first treatise on the subject of infantile sexuality).

1906   Freud's private practice was by now well established and patients were beginning to come to him from far afield. Fliess published details of Freud's complicity in the Swoboda affair. In April Freud began to exchange letters with C. G. Jung in Zurich.

1907   Freud's fame abroad was spreading. In Zurich E. Bleuler was encouraging his pupils to become involved with Freud. During the year Max Eitingon, Carl Jung and Karl Abraham all visited him from Zurich. Sandor Ferenczi from Budapest visited him. Freud published his first extended psychoanalytic study of literature – the study of Jensen's *Gradiva*. The Zurich group formed a Freud society. Freud destroyed much of his earlier correspondence for the second time in his life. The 'Rat Man' first came to Freud. Freud published his first paper on religion: 'Obsessive actions and Religious Practices'.

1908   In April the Psychological Wednesday Society was transformed into the Vienna Psychoanalytical Society. April was also the month of the very first International Congress in Salzburg. Freud lectured on the 'Rat Man'. During the summer Freud went to Holland and England and Zurich (where he met with Jung). A Psychoanalytic Society was founded in Berlin with Karl Abraham. The group was to prove an influential one as it was here that Melanie Klien developed some of her ideas on child-analysis. Blueler introduced Freud to the memoires of Schreber – the two discussed the case.

1909   In February Freud's eldest daughter, Mathilde, married. In the summer Freud, Ferenczi and Jung were invited to the USA by Stanley Hall, the President of Clark University, Worchester, Massachusetts. They delivered lectures on psychoanalysis as part of the tenth anniversary of the University. Freud was awarded an honorary doctorate. Freud met William James on this trip and James Putnam, who was to be very influential in introducing psychoanalysis to the USA (Putnam and Freud corresponded regularly until 1916). Freud published his case history 'Little Hans' and his 'Rat Man' study.

1910   In February Freud had his first encounter with the 'Wolf-Man'. The second International Psychoanalytical Congress was held at Nuremberg in March. In May the American Psychopathological Association was founded – Freud and Jung were honorary members. Freud published his Worcester lectures, *Five Lectures on Psychoanalysis* and his study of *Leonardo*. In the summer Freud toured Southern Italy and Sicily with Ferenczi.

1911   Freud broke with one of the founder members of the Vienna group, Alfred Adler. The Third International Congress was held at Weimar in September. Freud founded a journal, *Imago*, to serve as a forum for the development of psychoanalytic study of culture. Freud published his study of Schreber. Sabina Spielrein, having been intimately involved with Jung and abandoned by him, came to work with Freud.

1912	Freud founded another journal, *Zeitschrift*. Stekel, another founder of the Viennese group broke with Freud. Freud spent much of the year working on the ideas for his book *Totem and Taboo*. This was in part designed to widen the gulf which was apparent between himself and Jung. Freud visited Rome in the summer, where he wrote his preface for *Totem and Taboo*. Freud called this year the 'very climax of my psychoanalytic work'.

1913	January – Freud's daugher, Sophie, married.
Totem and Taboo was published. Freud began to write the paper 'Moses of Michaelangelo', which was published in 1914. Ferenczi founded the Budapest Psychoanalytic Society in May. Jones founded the London Psychoanalytic Society in October. The final break with Jung occurred, and the Seven Rings Committee was formed.

1914	Sophie produced Freud's first grandchild.
Freud wrote *On the History of the Psychoanalytic Movement* in part to vindicate his views rather than Jung's. With the outbreak of war Freud's sons, Martin and Ernst enrolled, Oliver was involved with engineering work. Freud completed his Wolf Man Case though it was not published until 1918.

1915	Freud wrote his 'Thoughts for the Times on War and Death'. The first of the lectures which became his *Introductory Lectures* were delivered.

1916	Freud contemplated writing a book on Lamarck 'to leave a visiting card on biologists'. The second set of 'Introductory Lectures' were delivered.

1917	The *Introductory Lectures* now complete, were published in full.

1918	After the war had finished, the Fifth International Psychoanalytic Congress was held in Budapest. There was increased interest expressed in psychoanalysis as a means of treating the war neuroses. The suggestion was raised at the Congress concerning the possibility of establishing a training analysis, a didactic analysis. Freud raised the question of creating analytic clinics at this Congress. The publishing side of psychoanalysis was secured through the generosity of Anton von Freund, a brewer from Budapest. The Wolf Man Case was published.

1919	Freud began the work on the reformation of his theory of instincts which eventually led to the postulation of the 'death instinct'. One of his important followers Victor Tausk committed suicide. In October Freud was given the title of Professor of the University – he remained excluded from the Faculty Board, however.

Sophie gave birth to her second son, Heinz Rudolf.

1920   January saw the death of two people that Freud felt very keenly. Anton von Freund and his 'Sunday Child', Sophie. The idea of the 'death instinct' was first mentioned in his writing. This was published in *Beyond the Pleasure Principle*. The Berlin Policlinic was opened making Berlin one of the most important psychoanalytic centres in the world. Freud was invited to contribute to a study on the treatment of war neuroses by the Commission of the Austrian Military Authorities. In September the Sixth International Psychoanalytical Congress was held at The Hague.

1921   Freud published *Group Psychology and the Analysis of the Ego*. Georg Groddeck sent Freud five chapters of his study in which he introduced the term '*das Es*', the 'id' or the 'it'. Freud began to work on the revisions of his theory of the mind – the transformation from the topographical to the structural model.

1922   Freud continued to work on his reformation of his model of the mind – his 'speculation' as he called it.

In May Anna Freud was made a member of the Vienna Society delivering her first analytic paper to the Society in June. Berlin hosted the Seventh International Psychoanalytical Congress in September.

1923   Early in the year it was discovered that Freud had cancer of the jaw. In April he had the first of thirty-three operations to stem the cancer, including a major one in October which removed half his mouth and necessitated the use of an uncomfortable prosthesis. The Committee was riven with dissention about how to manage Freud's cancer.

In June Freud's favouite grandson, Heinz Rudolf, died – Freud declared that life had lost all meaning.

Freud published *The Ego and the Id*, the 'speculation' which revealed his new model of the mind. Rank published his views on *The Trauma of Birth* – they were hailed initially by Freud.

1924   Freud was too ill to attend the Eighth International Psychoanalytical Congress in Salzburg. Freud worked on preparing his autobiography. Under pressure from the Committee Freud sought to reprimand Rank for heterodoxy.

Rank initially capitulated. Signs of a rift with Ferenczi were appearing too.

1925   Freud was again too ill to attend the International Congress (held this year in Hamburg).

In June Freud's early mentor, Josef Breuer died, Freud wrote an obituary for him. Princess Marie Bonaparte came to him for analysis. Freud published his *Autobiography*.

In December Freud lost his close friend Karl Abraham who died on Christmas Day.

Freud began work on his reformation of his theory of anxiety.

1926   On his seventieth birthday Freud received many telegrams and tributes indicating his world-wide influence and reputation. The Committee was dissolved. Freud's reformulated theory of anxiety was published as *Inhibitions, Symptoms and Anxiety*. Theodor Reik was prosecuted for 'quackery', Freud used this as an opportunity to write a defence of a non-medical psychoanalysis, *The Question of Lay Analysis*. Rank made his final break with Freud and emigrated to the USA.

1927   Freud wrote *The Future of an Illusion* his critique of 'ordinary religion' and his attempt to defend psychoanalysis against possible adoption by priests.

1928   Freud's interpretations of literature extended to Dostoyevsky in an essay entitled 'Dostoyevsky and Parricide'.

1929   Freud worked on his book on 'civilization, guilt feeling, happiness, and similar matters' which was eventually published as *Civilization and Its Discontents*. Max Schur was appointed as Freud's Physician.

1930   In July Freud was awarded the Goethe prize which gave him a considerable degree of satisfaction.

In September Amalie Freud died aged 95.

Despite having yet another operation in October and pneumonia Freud was still able, by the end of the year, to resume work with patients.

1931   Freud published a paper 'On Female Sexuality'.

1932   The estrangement with Ferenczi became almost complete. Freud had to endure five operations on his jaw.

Freud worked with William Bullitt on their study of Thomas Woodrow Wilson.

Freud also prepared a further set of introductory lectures.

1933   The *New Introductory Lectures* were published as a sequel and supplement to the earlier ones.

In May Ferenczi died.

May also saw the burning of Freud's books in Berlin, and

the infiltration of the German Society for Psychotherapy by Nazis. C. G. Jung was appointed as the editor of its journal. Freud's exchange of letters with A. Einstein was published as a book entitled *Why War?* – at Freud's insistence it appeared in French, English and German editions.

1934   Freud began working on a new study of Moses eventually to appear as *Moses and Monotheism.*

1936   With the cancer spreading Freud faced four operations in this year. He also celebrated his eightieth birthday – an event acknowledged by Einstein, Thomas Mann, Virginia Woolf, H. G. Wells and many others. Freud was made an honorary member of the Royal Society. Freud also celebrated his golden wedding anniversary.

1937   Freud published an important paper 'Analysis Terminable and Interminable'.

1938   Following the Nazi *Anschluss* of Austria, through the good offices of Ernest Jones, Marie Bonaparte, William Bullitt and President Roosevelt, Freud eventually managed to leave Vienna with his wife and family. The exodus brought him to London. *Moses and Monotheism* was published in German. Even after yet more operations he was able to begin work on *An Outline of Psychoanalysis* which he never finished.

1939   In March, an English edition of *Moses and Monotheism* was published.

Freud's health gradually deteriorated.

Shortly after the start of the Second World War Freud requested morphine. He died at 3.00 a.m. September 23. He was cremated 3 days later.

Suggestions for Further Reading

INTRODUCTORY

Freud was a prolific writer as his published works and the various volumes (either published or projected) attest. For English readers the prime source of his ideas must be the *Standard Edition of the Complete Psychological Works of Sigmund Freud* translated from the German under the general editorship of James Strachey, in collaboration with Anna Freud, assisted by Alix Strachey, Alan Tyson and Angela Richards (London: Hogarth Press and Institute of Psycho-Analysis, 1953–74). German readers may wish to refer to *Gesammelte Werke* edited by Anna Freud with the collaboration of Marie Bonaparte (Vols. 1–17, London: Imago Publishing Co., 1940–52; Vol. 18, Frankfurt am Main: S. Fischer, 1968). The usefulness of the *Standard Edition* has been further enhanced by the publication of *The Concordance to the Standard Edition of the Complete Psychological Works of Sigmund Freud* edited by S. A. Guttman, R. L. Jones and S. M. Parrish (6 vols., Boston: G. K. Hall, 1980).

More readily available than the *Standard Edition*, but based upon it, is the Pelican Freud Library edited by Angela Richards. The first thirteen volumes are in print, there are a further three volumes planned.

There have been numerous criticisms levelled at the English translations of Freud, notably at Strachey's *Standard Edition*. The criticisms suggest that there is a consistent tendency in this work to obscure some of the common-sense meanings of Freud's original words by introducing 'technical' terms in their place. Rycroft (see below) mentions this in his dictionary, but its most recent proponent has been Bruno Bettleheim in his book *Freud and Man's Soul* (New York: Alfred A. Knopf, 1982; and London: Chatto and Windus and Hogarth Press, 1983). Both Rycroft and Bettleheim provide an important corrective to this tradition.

Personally, I have found that for all the insight Freud's psychological writings provide into the man himself, a more balanced portrait only emerges from the study of his correspondence. In the volumes of his letters, even though some of these have not been published in full, one sees a picture of Freud's complexity and of the many conflicts which continue to exist in his mind. Reading Freud's letters one comes into a closer intimacy with Freud the man which, arguably, the psychological works were designed to hide. Of the volumes of letters which have already been published I suggest that the betrothal letters to Martha Bernays be studied first, and then, given their strategic place in the genesis of Freud's ideas, the Fliess letters; the Jung correspondence be considered next (not least because of the completeness of the published edition); the dialogue with Karl Abraham would come next on my list of priorities. These may be obtained in the following editions.

The Origins of Psycho-Analysis. Letters to Wilhelm Fliess, Drafts and Notes: 1887–1902. Edited by Marie Bonaparte, Anna Freud, Ernst Kris; translated by Eric Mosbacher and James Strachey. Introduction by Ernst Kris (London: Imago, 1954); The complete unexpurgated version of these letters has now been published: *The Freud/Fliess Correspondence* edited by Jeff Masson (Cambridge, Mass: Harvard University Press, 1985); *The Freud/Jung Letters: The correspondence between Sigmund Freud and C. G. Jung.* Edited by William McGuire. Translated by Ralph Manheim and R. F. H. Hull (London: Hogarth Press and Routledge and Kegan Paul, 1974; Princeton, N. J.: Bollingen Series XCIV, Princeton University Press, 1974); *A Psycho-Analytic Dialogue: The Letters of Sigmund Freud and Karl Abraham, 1907–1926.* Edited by Hilda Abraham and Ernst Freud. Translated by Bernard Marsh and Hilda Abraham (London: Hogarth Press and the Institute of Psycho-Analysis, 1965). The compilation of selections from his correspondence entitled: *The Letters of Sigmund Freud, 1873–1939.* Edited by Ernst Freud (London: Hogarth Press, 1961 and New York: Basic Books) is particularly useful for the glimpses provided there into some of his important correspondence (notably the betrothal letters to Martha Bernays, and some letters to Minna Bernays). Publication of unexpurgated versions of Freud's correspondence with other key figures in his life (Silberstein, Ferenczi, Jones) is an ongoing project which should be encouraged and welcomed.

Some of the vicissitudes of Freud scholarship in this field have been explored by Janet Malcolm in the *New Yorker:* 'Annals of Scholarship: Trouble in the Archives – I' and 'Annals of Scholarship: Trouble in the Archives – II' (*New Yorker*, 5 December 1983, p. 59–152, 12 December 1983, p. 60–119, now published as a book *In the Freud Archives*, New York: Alfred Knopf, 1983; London: Jonathan Cape, 1984).

A useful reference work to have available when reading Freud is Charles Rycroft's *A Critical Dictionary of Psychoanalysis* (Harmondsworth: Penguin, 1972).

BIOGRAPHICAL MATERIAL

The standard, important biographical sources which should be consulted if greater detail of Freud's life is required are as follows.

Clark, R. W. *Freud: The Man and the Cause* (London: Jonathan Cape Ltd/Weidenfeld and Nicholson Ltd, 1980; paperback edition: Paladin/Granada, 1982).

Ellenberger, H. F. *The Discovery of the Unconscious: The History and Evolution of Dynamic Psychiatry* (New York: Basic Books; Harmondsworth: Allen Lane Press, 1970).

Jones, E. *Sigmund Freud: Life and Work Vol. I, The Young Freud, 1856–1900; Vol. II, Years of Maturity, 1901–1919; Vol. III, The Last Phase, 1919–1939* (London: Hogarth Press; New York: Basic Books, 1953; 1955; 1957. Abridged, single-volume paperback edition edited by L. Trilling, Harmondsworth: Pelican Books, 1964).

Roazen, P. *Freud and His Followers* (New York: Alfred A. Knopf; Harmondsworth: Penguin Books, 1975).

Ruitenbeek, H. M. (ed). *Freud as We Knew Him* (Detroit: Wayne State University Pres, 1973).

Schur, M. *Freud: Living and Dying* (London: Hogarth Press and Institute of Psycho-Analysis; New York: International Universities Press, 1972).

Sulloway, F. J. *Freud, Biologist of the Mind: Beyond the Psychoanalytic Legend* (London: Burnett Books in association with André Deutsch Ltd.; New York: Basic Books, 1979; paperback edition London: Fontana Books, 1980).

Of immense value, in terms of the sense of Freud and his context, is the volume depicting his life in pictures and words: *Sigmund Freud: His Life in Pictures and Words* compiled by Ernst Freud; Lucie Freud and Ilse Grubrich-Simitis. With a biographical sketch by K. R. Eissler (London: André Deutsch, 1978 and Harmondsworth: Penguin Books, 1985).

In addition to the above the work of Peter Swales has been indispensable to my understanding of Freud. Swales has published his findings into Freud, for the most part, only privately. I am most grateful to him for providing me with copies of his papers. They may be obtained from him (at an appropriate charge of $25 or £15) from 285, Mott Street, B14, New York, N.Y. 10012, USA or from 2, High Street, Haverfordwest, Pembrokeshire, UK. They are also available in most of the major psychoanalytic libraries of the world and the world copyright libraries. I have made use of the following papers

Swales, P. J. 'Freud, Minna Bernays, and the Conquest of Rome: New light on the Origins of Psychoanalysis', *The New American Review*, Spring/Summer 1982.

—— 'Freud, Minna Bernays, and the Intimation of Christ' (unpublished lecture delivered at the New School for Social Research, New York City May 20, 1982).

—— 'Freud, Johann Weier, and the Status of Seduction; The Role of the Witch in the Conception of Fantasy' (privately published monograph, 1982, 2 High Street, Haverfordwest, Pembrokeshire, UK).

—— 'Freud, Fliess, and Fratricide; The Role of Fliess in Freud's Conception of Paranoia' (privately published monograph, 1982, 2 High Street, Haverfordwest, Pembrokeshire, UK).

—— 'Freud, Martha Bernays, and the Language of Flowers, Masturbation, Cocaine, and the Inflation of Fantasy' (privately published monograph, 1982).

—— 'Freud, Cocaine, and Sexual Chemistry; The Role of Cocaine in Freud's Conception of the Libido' (privately published monography, 1983).

—— 'Freud, Krafft-Ebing, and the Witches; The Role of Krafft-Ebing in Freud's Flight into Fantasy' (privately published monograph, 1983).

—— Wilhelm Fliess: Freud's OTHER-A Biography (in press, New York: Random House Books).

ON READING FREUD

To anybody wanting to begin reading Freud the sheer volume of his papers can be daunting – Where does one start? What is the most suitable *entrée* to the corpus? Which studies should be avoided until a foundation has been laid? To some extent the answer to these questions will vary according to the particular interests of the potential reader – someone with an interest in art history, for example, might want to pitch in with the studies of art while someone whose chief interests are in the field of anthropology may feel that the studies in prehistory are the most appropriate. That said, since the level of many of the papers varies – sometimes Freud was addressing a technical audience, sometimes a lay audience – clearly some starting points are better than others.

I would like to suggest that Freud's disguised, autobiographical paper of 1899 'Screen Memories' (*S.E.* III, pp. 301–22) makes a good place to start (not least for the insight it gives into the self-analysis). Then I suggest reading three other products from this period – the first two chapters of *The Psychopathology of Everyday Life*, 'The Forgetting of Names' (the account of the Signorelli parapraxis) and 'The Forgetting of Foreign Words' (the *aliquis* parapraxis) (*S.E.* VI, pp. 9–24); and *On Dreams*, Freud's summary of his big dream book (*S.E.* V, pp. 631–86).

Next I suggest that '"Civilized" sexual morality and modern nervous illness' (*S.E.* IX, pp. 179–204) is a concise summary of the theory of sexuality born out of his studies. I would then go on to read 'The Claims of Psycho-Analysis to Scientific Interest' (*S.E.* XIII, pp. 164–90); a succinct statement of Freud's aspirations for psychoanalysis. This last paper bears direct comparison with his later *The Question of Lay Analysis: Conversations with an Impartial Person* (*S.E.* XX, pp. 179–250).

Freud's lectures are certainly worth reading – in particular his Clark Lectures 'Five Lectures on Psycho-Analysis' (*S.E.* XI, pp. 3–55), and his *Introductory Lectures on Psycho-Analysis* (*S.E.* XV and XVI).

Of the case studies the story of Little Hans, 'Analysis of a Phobia in a Five Year-Old Boy' (*S.E.* X, p. 3–147) is the most accessible, though feminists might find the Dora case, 'Fragment of an Analysis of a Case of Hysteria' (*S.E.* VII, pp. 3–122) most interesting from their perspective.

Many of his later views are best explored in the *New Introductory Lectures on Psycho-Analysis* (*S.E.* XXII, pp. 3–182).

SECONDARY LITERATURE

The following books may be used to supplement and expand upon the information contained in the works already cited.

Chapter 1

Amacher, P. *Freud's Neurological Education and Its Influence on Psychoanalytic Theory, Psychological Issues*, **4**, 4 (Monograph 16) (New York: International Universities Press, 1965).
Andersson, Ola *Studies in the Prehistory of Psychoanalysis: The Etiology of Psychoneuroses and some Related Themes in Sigmund Freud's Scientific Writings and Letters, 1886–1896* (Stockholm: Svenska Bokforlaget/Norstedts, 1962).
Bakan, D. *Sigmund Freud and the Jewish Mystical Tradition* (Princeton: D. Van Nostrand Co.: paperback edition Boston: Beacon Press, 1975).
Freud, S. *Cocaine Papers* Edited and Introduced by R. Byck. Notes by Anna Freud (New York: Stonehill Publishing Co., 1974).
Thorton, E. M. *Freud and Cocaine, The Freudian Fallacy* (London: Blond and Briggs, 1983).

Chapter 2

Anzieu, Didier *L'Auto-analyse: Son Rôle dans la decouverte de la psychoanalyse par Freud, sa fonction en psychoanalyse* (Paris: Presses Universitaires de France, 1959).

Ellenberger, H. F. The story of 'Anna O': A critical review with new data, *Journal of the History of the Behavioural Sciences,* **8,** 267–79 (1972).

Ellenberger, H. F. L'histoire d' 'Emmy von N', *L'Evolution Psychiatrique,* **42,** 519–40 (1977).

Forrester, J. *Language and the Origins of Psychoanalysis* (London: Macmillan 1979; New York: Columbia University Press, 1980).

Kanzer, M. and Glenn, J. (eds) *Freud and his Self-Analysis* (New York: Aronson, 1979).

Levin, K. *Freud's Early Psychology of the Neuroses: A Historical Perspective* (Pittsburgh: University of Pittsburgh Press, 1978).

Masson, J. M. *The Assault on Truth: Freud's suppression of the Seduction Theory* (London: Faber 1984; New York: Farrar, Straus and Giroux).

Stewart, W. S. *Psychoanalysis: The First Ten Years, 1888–1898* (London: Allen and Unwin, 1969).

Chapter 3

Elms, A. C. Freud, Irma, Martha: Sex and marriage in the dream of Irma's Injection, *Psychoanalytic Review,* **67,** 83–108 (1980).

Grinstein, A. *On Sigmund Freud's Dreams* (Detroit: Wayne State University Press, 1968; second edition under the title of *Sigmund Freud's Dreams* – New York: International Universities Press Inc., 1980).

Hartman, F. A reappraisal of the Emma episode and the specimen dream, *Journal of the American Psychoanalytic Association* (in press) (1984).

Mahony, P. J. Towards a formalist approach to dreams, *International Review of Psycho-Analysis,* **4,** 83–98 (1977).

Timpanaro, S. *The Freudian Slip: Psycho-Analysis and Textural Criticisms* translated by Kate Soper (London: New Left Books, 1976).

Chapter 4

Brome, V. *Freud and His Early Circle: The Struggle of Psycho-Analysis* (London: Heinemann, 1967) now reissued, slightly abridged as *Freud and His Disciples: The Struggle for Supremacy* (London: Caliban Books, 1984).

Brome, V. *Ernest Jones: Freud's Alter Ego* (London: Caliban Books, 1983).

Carotenuto, A. *A Secret Symmetry: Sabina Spielrein between Jung and Freud* translated by Arno Pomerans, John Shepley and Krishna Winston (New York: Pantheon Books, 1982; London: Routledge and Kegan Paul, 1984).

Decker, H. S. *Freud in Germany: Revolution and Reaction in Science 1893–1907, Psychological Issues,* **11**, 1. (Monograph 41) (New York: International Universities Press, 1977).

Eisler, K. R. *Talent and Genius: The Fictitious Case of Tausk contra Freud* (New York: Grove Press Inc., 1971).

Eisler, K. R. On mis-statements of would-be Freud biographers with special reference to the Tausk controversy, *International Review of Psycho-Analysis,* **1**, 391–414 (1974).

Eisler, K. R. *Victor Tausk's Suicide* (New York: International Universities Press, 1983).

Gardiner, M. (ed.) *The Wolf-Man by the Wolf-Man* (London: Hogarth Press and Institute of Psycho-Analysis, 1971; New York: Basic Books).

Gay, P. *Freud, Jews and Other Germans: Masters and Victims in Modernist Culture* (New York: Oxford University Press, 1978).

Hale, N. G. Jr. *Freud and the Americans.* Vol. I: *The Beginnings of Psychoanalysis in the United States, 1876–1917* (New York: Oxford University Press, 1971).

Hale, N. G. Jr. (ed.) *James Jackson Putnam and Psychoanalysis. Letters between Putnam and Sigmund Freud, Ernest Jones, William James, Sandor Ferenczi, and Morton Prince, 1877–1917.* Translated by Judith Bernays Heller (Cambridge, Mass.: Harvard University Press, 1971).

Jones, E. *Free Associations: Memories of a Psycho-Analyst* (London: Hogarth Press, 1959).

Kanzer, M. and Glenn, J. (eds) *Freud and His Patients* (New York: Aronson, 1980).

Neiderland, W. G. *The Schreber Case: Psychoanalytic Profile of a Paranoid Personality* (New York: The New York Times Book Company, 1974).

Nunberg, H. and Fedlern, E. (ed.) *Minutes of the Vienna Psychoanalytic Society* Volumes I–IV (New York: International Universities Press, Inc., 1962–1975).

Obholzer, K. *The Wolf-Man, Sixty Years Later* translated by Michael Shaw (London: Routledge and Kegan Paul, 1982).

Roazen, P. *Brother Animal: The Story of Freud and Tausk* (New York: Alfred A. Knopf 1969; Harmondsworth: Penguin, 1973).

Roazen, P. Reflections on ethos and authenticity in psychoanalysis, *Human Context,* **4**, 577–587 (1972).

Sachs, H. *Freud: Master and Friend* (London: Imago, 1945; Cambridge: Harvard University Press, 1944).

Schatzman, M. *Soul Murder: Persecution in the Family* (London: Allen Lane Press, 1973).

Chapter 5

Klein, D. B. *Jewish Origins of the Psychoanalytic Movement* (New York: Praeger, 1981).

Marcuse, H. *Eros and Civilization* (Boston: Beacon Press, 1956; London: Abacus Books, 1972).

Robert, M. *From Oedipus to Moses; Freud's Jewish Identity* (New York: Anchor Books, 1976).

Notes and References

INTRODUCTION

1 Letter to Martha Bernays 2:2:1886 (no. 94). *Letters of Sigmund Freud, 1873–1939* (edited by Ernst Freud, translated by Tania and James Stern, London: Hogarth Press, 1961) p. 215. (Afterward referred to as *Letters* – the American and British editions of this book have a different pagination therefore I have referred to the date and the number of each letter to aid identification.)
2 'Introduction' to *Thomas Woodrow Wilson, Twenty-eighth President of the United States: A Psychological Study* (Freud and Bullitt; London: Weidenfeld and Nicolson, 1967) p. XVI.
3 For a recent attempt to work through this sort of perspective in the human sciences see *Sociology and the Human Image* (D. Lyon; Leicester: IVP, 1983).
4 Letter to A. Zweig 31:5:36 (no. 285) *Letters*, p. 426. Also in *The Letters of Sigmund Freud and Arnold Zweig* edited by Ernst Freud. Translated by Professor and Mrs W. D. Robson Scott (London: The Hogarth Press and the Institute of Psycho-Analysis) p. 127. (Afterward referred to as *Zweig Letters*.)
5 Letter to F. Wittels 18:12:23 (no. 205), *Letters*, p. 350.
6 *An Autobiographical Study* from the *Standard Edition of the Complete Psychological Works of Sigmund Freud* Vol. XX, p. 73. (Afterward referred to as just *S.E.* with the particular volume in Roman numerals following.)
7 Letter to Martha Bernays 28:4:1885 (no. 61), *Letters*, pp. 152–3.
8 'Address delivered to the Goethe House at Frankfort' (1930) quoted by Ernst Kris in *The Origins of Psycho-Analysis; Letters to Wilhelm Fliess, Drafts and Notes: 1887–1902* (Freud; edited by Marie Bonaparte, Anna Freud and Ernst Kris, translated by Eric Mosbacher and James Strachey, London: Imago, 1954), p. 237, note 3. (Afterward referred to as *Origins*).
9 Quoted in a letter to Wilhelm Fliess 3:12:97 (no. 77), *Origins*, p. 236.
10 Cf. F. J. Sulloway, *Freud, Biologist of the Mind: Beyond the Psychoanalytic Legend* (London: Fontana, 1980), pp. 445–95. (Afterward referred to as *Freud, Biologist.*)

CHAPTER 1

1 Letter to the Burgomaster of Pribor 25:10:1931, *S.E.* XXI, p. 259.
2 'Screen Memories', *S.E.* III, p. 312.
3 *The Interpretation of Dreams*, *S.E.* IV, p. 192.
4 'A childhood recollection from *Dichtung und Wahreit*', *S.E.* XVII, p. 156.
5 Quoted by Ernest Jones in *Sigmund Freud: Life and Work* Vol. I *The Young Freud, 1856–1900*, p. 3. (Afterward I shall refer to the various volumes of

Jones' biography as Jones I, II and III.) (N.B.: The English and American versions of these volumes have a different pagination.)

6 Letter to Ferenczi 16:9:1930 (no. 256), *Letters*, p. 399.
7 Letter to Fliess 3:10:97 (no. 70), *Origins*, p. 219.
8 Ibid.
9 *The Interpretation of Dreams*, S.E. V, p. 424.
10 Ibid., p. 483.
11 Letter to Fliess 3:1:99 (101), *Origins*, pp. 270–1.
12 'The background of Freud's disturbance on the Acropolis', *American Imago* (1969) p. 127. (Reprinted in *Freud and His Self-Analysis* edited by Mark Kanzer and Jules Glenn, New York: Aronson, 1979 pp. 117–34.) (Afterward referred to as *Freud: Self Analysis*.)
13 Letter to Fliess 3:10:97 (no. 70), *Origins*, pp. 219–20.
14 Ibid.
15 Ibid.
16 'Screen Memories', *S.E.* III, p. 312.
17 Quoted by Theodor Reik in *The Inner Experience of a Psychoanalyst* (London: George Allen and Unwin, 1949), p. 16. US Edition: *Listening with the Third Ear: The Inner Experience of a Psychoanalyst* New York: Farrar, Straus, 1948) p. 25.
18 'Screen Memories', *S.E.* III, p. 312.
19 Letter to Martha Bernays 23:7:1882 (no. 7), *Letters*, pp. 39–40.
20 Jones I, p. 21.
21 *An Autobiographical Study*, S.E. XX, p. 7.
22 Letter to Lou Andreas-Salomé 6:1:1935 from *Sigmund Freud and Lou Andreas-Salomé: Letters* (edited by Ernst Pfeiffer and translated by William and Elaine Robson-Scott, London: Hogarth Press and The Institute of Psycho-Analysis, 1972) p. 205. (Afterwards referred to as *Salomé Letters*.)
23 *An Autobiographical Study*, S.E. XX, p. 8. Sentence added in 1935.
24 Jacob Freud quoted by Jones I, pp. 21–2.
25 'Letter to the editor of the Jewish Press Centre in Zurich', *S.E.* XIX, p. 291.
26 Jones I, p. 22.
27 *The Interpretation of Dreams*, S.E. IV, p. 197.
28 'Address to the Society of B'nai B'rith', *S.E.* XX, p. 273.
29 Letter to Morselli 18:2:1926 (no. 219), *Letters*, p. 366.
30 Letters to Pfister 11:4:1926 and 9:10:1918 from *Psycho-Analysis and Faith: The Letters to Sigmund Freud and Oskar Pfister* (edited by Ernst Freud and Heinrich Meng and translated by Eric Mosbacher, London: Hogarth Press and The Institute of Psycho-Analysis) pp. 103 and 63. (Afterward referred to as *Faith Letters*.)
31 Letter to Morselli 18:2:1926 (no. 219), *Letters*, p. 366.
32 'Address to the Society of B'nai B'rith', *S.E.* XX, p. 274.
33 Ibid.
34 Preface to the Hebrew translation of *Totem and Taboo*, S.E. XIII, p. xv.
35 'Obsessive actions and religious practices', *S.E.* IX, pp. 126–7.
36 Letter to Fliess 3:10:97 (no. 70), *Origins*, p. 219.
37 Letter to Fliess 15:10:97 (no.71), *Origins*, p. 221.

38 Letter to Fliess 3:12:97 (no. 77), *Origins*, p. 237.
39 Reported by Laforgne, 'Personal memories of Freud' (1956), from *Freud as We Knew Him* (edited by Hendrik Ruitenbeek, Detroit: Wayne State University Press, 1973) p. 344. (Afterward referred to as *Freud as We Knew Him*.)
40 *The Interpretation of Dreams*, S.E. IV, p. 196.
41 'Some reflections on schoolboy psychology', *S.E.* XIII, pp. 241–2.
42 'Screen Memories', *S.E.* III, p. 312.
43 Letter to Fliess 21:9:99 (no. 119), *Origins*, p. 298.
44 'My brother Sigmund Freud', from *Freud as We Knew Him*, p. 141.
45 Letter to Martha Bernays 14:8:1882 (no. 8), *Letters*, p. 40.
46 'Some reflections on schoolboy psychology', *S.E.* XIII, p. 242.
47 *Freud, His Life and His Mind: A Biography* (London: Grey Walls Press) p. 34.
48 'My brother Sigmund Freud', from *Freud as We Knew Him*, p. 141.
49 *An Autobiographical Study*, S.E. XX, p. 8.
50 'My brother Sigmund Freud', from *Freud as We Knew Him*, p. 141.
51 Letter to Martha Bernays 2:2:1886 (no. 94), *Letters*, p. 215.
52 'My brother Sigmund Freud', from *Freud as We Knew Him*, p. 141.
53 Letter to Julie Braun-Vogelstein 30:10:1927 (no. 232), *Letters*, pp. 379–80.
54 Letter to Martha Bernays 7:2:1884 (no. 37), *Letters*, p. 112. Freud sometimes referred to the *Academia Castellana* (AC) as the *Academia Espagnola* (AE). Cf. the picture of their seal in *Sigmund Freud: His Life in Pictures and Words* (edited by Ernst Freud, Lucie Freud and Ilse Grubrich-Simitis, translated by Christine Trollope, London: André Deutsch, 1978) pp. 67 and 325. (Afterward referred to as *Freud: Pictures*.)
55 Letter to Eduard Silberstein 9:9:1875 (no. 40). Transcription and translation held at Sigmund Freud Copyrights Ltd, Colchester. Translation by Arnold Pomerans.
56 Letter to Martha Bernays 28:10:1883, from 'Some early unpublished letters of Freud', by Ernst Freud, *International Journal of Psycho-Analysis* L pp. 419–27. (1969). (Afterward referred to as 'Early Letters'.)
57 'Screen Memories', *S.E.* III, p. 313.
58 Letters to Emil Fluss 28:9:1872 and 7:2:1873, from Early letters', pp. 421–22.
59 Letter to Silberstein 4:9:1872 (No. 14 1F), from the Colchester transcript.
60 Letter to Emil Fluss 00:00:1872, from Early letters', p. 421.
61 Jones II, p. 456.
62 Jones I, p. 61.
63 Jones in a letter to Bernfield dated 20:2:1952 in the Bernfield Collection of the Library of Congress. Cited by Swales in his paper, 'Freud, Martha Bernays and the Language of Flowers', (privately published paper, 1982) p. 5. (Afterward referred to as Swales, 'Flowers'.)
64 *On the History of the Psycho-Analytic Movement*, S.E. XIV, p. 16.
65 Letter to Silberstein 4:9:1872 (no. 14 1F), from Colchester.
66 Letter to Emil Fluss 16:6:1873 (no. 1, *Letters*, P. 22.
67 *An Autobiographical Study*, S.E. XX, p. 8.
68 Letter to Emil Fluss 17:3:1873, from 'Early letters', p. 423.
69 Letter to Emil Fluss 1:5:1873, from 'Early letters', p. 424.

70 *An Autobiographical Study*, S.E. XX, p. 8.

71 Ibid, p. 9.

72 Letter to E. Silberstein 11:7:1873 (no. 2B and 2C), at Colchester.

73 *An Autobiographical Study*, S.E. XX, p. 8.

74 *Introductory Lectures on Psycho-Analysis*, S.E. XVI, p. 284.

75 *The Interpretation of Dreams*, S.E. IV, p. 212.

76 Letter to E. Silberstein 8:11:1874 (no. 3G), at Colchester.

77 Letter to Fliess 2:4:96 (no. 44), *Origins*, p. 162.

78 Letter to Martha Bernays 15:11:1883 (no. 28), *Letters*, p. 90.

79 Letter to E. Silberstein 7:3:1875 (no. 4F), at Colchester.

80 *The Unconscious Before Freud* (London: Tavistock, 1962), p. 169.

81 Quoted by Jahoda from *Freud and the Dilemmas of Psychology* (London: Hogarth Press, 1977), p. 16. (Afterward referred to as *Freud: Dilemmas*.)

82 Curriculum vitae from *Freud: Pictures*, p. 82.

83 Letter to Martha Bernays 18:10:1883, cited by Jones I, p. 45.

84 Cited by Anna Freud Bernays in *Freud as We Knew Him*, p. 144.

85 Letter to E. Silberstein 9:9:1875 (no. 4O), at Colchester.

86 Anna Freud Bernays in *Freud as We Knew Him*, p. 145.

87 *An Autobiographical Study*, S.E. XX, p. 9.

88 Cited by Sulloway in *Freud, Biologist*, p. 14.

89 *An Autobiographical Study*, S.E. XX, p. 9.

90 *The Interpretation of Dreams*, S.E. V, p. 450.

91 *An Autobiographical Study*, S.E. XX, p. 10.

92 Ibid.

93 Letter to Martha Bernays 19:6:1884 (no. 45), *Letters*, p. 128.

94 Letter to Martha Bernays 2:1:1884, from *Freud: Pictures*, p. 103.

95 Letter to Martha Bernays 5:10:1882 (no. 12) *Letters*, p. 48.

96 Letter to Martha Bernays 14:2:1884 (no. 38) *Letters*, p. 114.

97 Cited by Levin, K. *Freud's Early Psychology of the Neuroses: A Historical Perspective* (Pittsburgh: University of Pittsburgh Press), p. 25.

98 Letter to Martha Bernays 9:10:1883 (no. 24), *Letters*, p. 82.

99 Letter to Minna Bernays 21:2:1883 (no. 13), *Letters*, p. 53.

100 Letter to Martha Bernays 7:2:1884 (no. 37), *Letters*, p. 112.

101 Letter to Martha Bernays 10:1:1884 (no. 32), *Letters*, p. 103.

102 Letter to Martha Bernays 16:1:1884 (no. 33), *Letters*, p. 104.

103 Letter to Martha Bernays 7:1:1884 (no. 31), *Letters*, p. 99.

104 *The Interpretation of Dreams*, S.E. V, p. 437.

105 *An Autobiographical Study*, S.E. XX, p. 11.

106 Cited by Freud in a Letter to Martha Bernays 25:10:1883 (no. 27), *Letters*, p. 87.

107 *An Autobiographical Study*, S.E. XX, p. 12.

108 Letter to Martha Bernays 17:5:1885 (no. 65), *Letters*, pp. 156–7.

109 Letter to Martha Bernays 29:5:1884 (no. 44), *Letters*, p. 126.

110 *An Autobiographical Study*, S.E. XX, p. 11.

111 Letter to Martha Bernays 21:4:1884 (no. 43), *Letters*, pp. 122–3.

112 Letter to Martha Bernays, 2:6:1884. Cited by Jones I, p. 93.

113 Cited by Hans Sachs in *Freud: Master and Friend* (London: Imago, 1945) p. 69. (Afterward referred to as *Freud: Master*.)

114 *An Autobiographical Study*, *S.E.* XX, p. 14.
115 Ibid.
116 Letter from Jones to Bernfield 28:4:1952 cited by Harry Trosman and Ernest Wolf 'The Bernfield collaboration in the Jones biography of Freud' *International Journal of Psycho-Analysis*, **54**, pp. 227–33, p. 231 (1973).
117 Cf. E. M. Thornton's interesting, but somewhat idiosyncratic book, *Freud and Cocaine, The Freudian Fallacy* (London: Blond and Briggs, 1983) and P. Swales 'Freud, cocaine, and sexual chemistry: The role of cocaine in Freud's conception of the libido' (privately published, 1983). (Afterward referred to as Swales 'Cocaine'.)
118 Cf. This thesis has been most cogently advocated by Swales cf. in particular 'Cocaine'.
119 'Fragment of an analysis of a case of hysteria', *S.E.* VII, p. 113.
120 *Three Essays on the Theory of Sexuality*, *S.E.* VII, p. 216.
121 Letter to C. G. Jung 19:4:1908 from *The Freud/Jung Letters: The Correspondence between Sigmund Freud and C. G. Jung* (edited by William McGuire, translated by Ralph Manheim and R. F. C. Hull. Bollingen Series XCIV, London: Routledge and Kegan Paul, 1974) pp. 140–1. (Afterward referred to as *Freud/Jung Letters*.)
122 *Introductory Lectures on Psycho-Analysis*, *S.E.* XVI, p. 389. I am using Swales' translation from Swales 'Cocaine', p. 1.
123 Letter to Martha Bernays 29:3:1884 (no. 40), *Letters*, p. 118.
124 Cited in *Freud: Pictures*, p. 327.
125 *An Autobiographical Study*, *S.E.* XX, p. 11.
126 Letter to Martha Bernays 20:6:1885 (no. 70), *Letters*, pp. 166–7.
127 Letter to Martha Bernays 31:3:1885 (no. 60), *Letters*, p. 151.
128 Letter to Martha Bernays 19:10:1885 (no. 81), *Letters*, p. 183.
129 Letter to Martha Bernays 21:10:1885 (no. 82), *Letters*, p. 186.
130 Letter to Martha Bernays 24:11:1885 (no. 86), *Letters*, p. 196.
131 'Report on my studies in Paris and Berlin', *S.E.* I, p. 5.
132 Cited by Freud, ibid., p. 10.
133 Letter to J. Breuer 16:1:1884, from *Freud: Pictures*, p. 102.
134 Letter to Martha Bernays 13:7:1883 (no. 14), *Letters*, p. 56.
135 Letter from Breuer to Fore, 21:11:1907 cited by Cranefield, 'Josef Breuer's evaluation of his contribution to psycho-analysis', *International Journal of Psycho-Analysis* **XXXIX**, pp. 319–22 (1958). (Afterward referred to as 'Breuer's contribution'.)
136 'Five lectures on psycho-analysis', *S.E.* XI, p. 9.
137 'Charcot', *S.E.* III, p. 22.
138 'On the psychical mechanism of hysterical phenomena: Preliminary communication', *S.E.* III, p. 27.
139 Cf. Sulloway, *Freud, Biologist*, pp. 28–42.
140 Letter to Martha Bernays 12:12:1885 (no. 88), *Letters*, p. 201.
141 Letter to Martha Bernays 20:1:1886 (no. 92), *Letters*, p. 208.
142 Letter to Martha Bernays 2:2:1886 (no. 94), *Letters*, p. 214.
143 Letter to Martha Bernays 10:2:1886 (no. 96), *Letters*, p. 221.
144 Letter to Koller 13:10:1886, cited by Clark, *Freud: The Man and the Cause* (London: Granada, 1982) p. 74. (Afterward referred to as *Freud: The Cause*.)

145 Letter to Rosa Freud 8:3:1886, cited in *Freud: The Cause*, p. 76.
146 'Report of my studies in Paris and Berlin', *S.E.* I, p. 10.
147 'Autobiographical note', *S.E.* III, p. 325.
148 'Report of my studies in Paris and Berlin', *S.E.* I, p. 5.

CHAPTER 2

1 *An Autobiographical Study*, *S.E.* XX, p. 60.
2 Cited by Jahoda, *Freud: Dilemmas*, p. 16.
3 'Freud in his historical context', from *Freud: Modern Judgements* (edited by Frank Cioffi, London: Macmillan, 1973) pp. 52–3. (Afterward referred to as *Freud: Modern Judgements*.)
4 Letter to Martha Bernays 2:2:1886 (no. 94), *Letters*, p. 214.
5 *An Autobiographical Study*, *S.E.* XX, p. 18.
6 From the Introduction to *Origins*, p. 10.
7 Letter to Fliess 24:11:1887 (no. 1), *Origins*, p. 52.
8 Letter to Carl Koller 13:10:1886, from *Freud: Pictures*, p. 131.
9 Letter to Martha Bernays 13:5:1886 (no. 101), *Letters*, p. 230.
10 'Charcot', *S.E.* III, p. 19.
11 Ibid., p. 19.
12 Ibid., p. 22.
13 'Some points for a comparative study of organic and hysterical motor paralyses', *S.E.* I, p. 171.
14 Ibid., p. 169.
15 Wagner-Jauregg *Lebenserinnerungen*, cited by Kurt Eisler in *Talent and Genius: The Fictitious Case of Tausk contra Freud* (New York: Quadrangle Books) p. 354. (Afterward referred to as *Talent*.)
16 Jones I, p. 230.
17 Reported by Schnitzler (1886), cited by Sulloway in *Freud, Biologist*, p. 39.
18 Freud later suggested in *The Interpretation of Dreams* that Meynert had confessed to him that his opposition was prompted by the fact that he had a palsy in his arm, i.e., that he was a case of male hysteria. *S.E.* V, p. 438.
19 *Freud, Biologist*, p.37.
20 *An Autobiographical Study*, *S.E.* XX, p. 15ff.
21 Cited in *Freud: Pictures*, p. 153. It should be noted that the term 'psychic' refers to that aspect of the mind we would now call 'psychological' it does not refer to that which is now customarily termed 'psychic'.
22 Cf. *Freud, Biologist*, pp. 445–95.
23 Letter to Fliess 28:12:1887 (no. 2), *Origins*, p. 53.
24 Ibid.
25 Cited by Sulloway in *Freud, Biologist*, p. 42.
26 Cited by Eisler in *Talent*, p. 355.
27 Ibid., p. 355.
28 Ibid., p. 353–4.
29 That is not to suggest that Meynert was a model scientist in his behaviour. It is worth noting that Wagner-Jauregg, a contemporary of Freud's has

suggested that in many of the great debates in which Meynert was a protagonist 'with Meynert, the guilt was usually on Meynert's side'. Cited by Sulloway in *Freud, Biologist*, p. 45, note 17.

30 'Review of August Forel's *Hypnotism*', *S.E.* I, p. 97.
31 Letter to Fliess 29:8:1888 (no. 5), *Origins*, p. 58.
32 Ibid., pp. 58–9.
33 *An Autobiographical Study*, *S.E.* XX, p. 17.
34 'Charcot', *S.E.* III, pp. 22–3.
35 'Preface to Theodor Reik's *Ritual* (1919)', *S.E.* XVII, p. 259.
36 *An Autobiographical Study*, *S.E.* XX, p. 16.
37 Footnote added in 1924 to *Studies on Hysteria*, *S.E.* II, p. 105.
38 *Introductory Lectures of Psycho-Analysis*, *S.E.* XVI, p. 462.
39 *On the History of the Psycho-Analytic Movement*, *S.E.* XIV, p. 16.
40 *An Autobiographical Study*, *S.E.* XX, p. 19.
41 Ibid., pp. 19–20.
42 Ibid., p. 20.
43 Ibid., p. 19.
44 Letter to Martha Bernays, cited by Jones I, p. 245.
45 Letter from Breuer to Forel 21:11:1907, cited in 'Breuer's Contribution', p. 320.
46 Ibid., pp. 319–20.
47 *Studies on Hysteria*, *S.E.* II, p. 48.
48 Ibid., p. 85.
49 Ibid., p. 7.
50 Ibid., p. 123.
51 Ibid., p. 11.
52 Ibid., p. 6.
53 Ibid., p. 305.
54 Letter to Fliess 18:12:1892 (no. 11), *Origins*, p. 64.
55 Letter to Fliess 22:6:1894 (no. 19), *Origins*, p. 95.
56 *An Autobiographical Study*, *S.E.* XX, p. 21ff.
57 Letter to Fliess 2:5:1891 (no. 8), *Origins*, p. 61.
58 *Freud: Pictures*, p. 136.
59 Letter to Minna Bernays 13:7:1891 (no. 107), *Letters*, p. 239.
60 Figures cited by Stengel in his Introduction to *On Aphasia: A Critical Study* (translated by E. Stengel, London: Imago, 1953) p. xiv.
61 With the renewed interest in language and psychoanalysis particularly on the continent following the work of J. Lacan, *On Aphasia* has been increasingly viewed as a crucial text for understanding the whole of psychoanalysis–'the talking cure' cf. John Forrester's *Language and the Origins of Psychoanalysis* (London: Macmillan, 1980).
62 *Studies on Hysteria*, *S.E.* II, p. 21. Freud maintained that Breuer had concealed the complicated erotic elements in his relationship with 'Anna O' and suggested that the treatment was terminated when Anna supposedly presented Breuer with a phantom pregnancy and hysterical birth. The story perpetuated by Jones in the light of more recent research by Ellenberger 'cannot be confirmed and does not fit into the chronology of the case'. (Ellenberger, H. 'The story of 'Anna O': A critical review with new data', *Journal of the History of the Behavioural Sciences* 8, pp. 267–79 (1972).

63 'The neuro-psychosis of defence: (An attempt at a psychological theory of acquired hysteria, of many phobias and obsessions and of certain halucinatory psychoses)', *S.E.* III, p. 52. (Afterward referred to as 'The neuro-psychoses of defence'.)

64 *Studies on Hysteria, S.E.* II, p. 15.

65 Ibid., p. 110.

66 Ibid., p. 266.

67 Ibid., pp. 302–3.

68 'On beginning the treatment (further recommendations on the technique of psycho-analysis, I)', *S.E.* XII, p. 135.

69 'The neuro-psychoses of defence', *S.E.* III, p. 57.

70 *Studies on Hysteria, S.E.* II, p. 274.

71 Cited by Freud in *On the History of the Psycho-Analytic Movement, S.E.* XIV, p. 13.

72 Letter to Fliess 6:10:1893 (no. 14), *Origins*, p. 77.

73 Letter to Fliess 17:11:1893 (no. 15), *Origins*, p. 79.

74 *Studies on Hysteria, S.E.* II, p. 133.

75 Ibid., p. 176.

76 Ibid., p. 69, note 1. cf. Swales 'Freud, his teacher, and the birth of psychoanalysis' (unpublished paper, 1984).

77 Letter to Fliess 7:2:1894 (no. 16), *Origins*, p. 81. Emphasis mine.

78 Letter to Fliess 21:5:1894 (no. 18), *Origins*, p. 83.

79 Unpublished comment cited by Ralph Blumenthal in, 'Scholars seek the hidden Freud in newly emerging letters: Subtleties in origins of master's theories sought in documents', *The New York Times* [*Science Times*] 18 August 1981, pp. C1 and C2. (Afterward referred to as Blumenthal 'Scholars'.)

80 *On the History of the Psycho-Analytic Movement, S.E.* XIV, p. 21.

81 Letter from Breuer to Forel 21:11:1907, cited in 'Breuer's Contribution', p. 320.

82 Letter to Fliess 8:12:1895 (no. 38), *Origins*, p. 137.

83 *Studies on Hysteria, S.E.* II, p. xxix.

84 All cited by Clark in *Freud: the Cause*, pp. 135–6.

85 *An Autobiographical Study, S.E.* XX, p. 23.

86 Letter to Fliess 1:4:1896 alluded to by Jones in Jones I, p. 280 and 281 but published in full in Blumenthal, Scholars p. C1.

87 'My views on the part played by sexuality in the aetiology of the neuroses', *S.E.* VII, p. 271.

88 *Studies on Hysteria, S.E.* II, p. 260.

89 Letter to Fliess 26:4:1896 (unpublished in *Origins*, cited by Schur, M. *Freud: Living and Dying* (London: Hogarth Press and the Institute of Psycho-Analysis, 1972), p. 104. (Afterward referred to as *Freud: Dying*.)

90 Letter to Fliess 26:4:1896 (unpublished in *Origins*), cited by David Gelman in 'Finding the Hidden Freud' (*Newsweek*, 21 December 1981, pp. 44–51), p. 46.

91 *Memories, Dreams and Reflections* (recorded and edited by Aniela Jaffe, translated from the German by Richard and Clara Winston, London: Collins and Routledge and Kegan Paul, 1963). My edition Fontana books, p. 172. (Afterward referred to as *Memories, Dreams and Reflections*.)

92 Ibid., pp. 173, 174, 176. It is worth noting that at this time Jung himself was being less than candid about his own sexual involvement with one of his patients, Sabina Spielrein. Cf. Aldo Carotenuto, *A Secret Symmetry: Sabina Spielrein between Jung and Freud* (translated by Arno Pomerans, John Shepley and Krishna Winston; New York: Pantheon Books, 1982); and Bruno Bettleheim, 'Scandal in the Family' *New York Review of Books*, **30**, 11, 30 June 1983, pp. 39–44.

93 *Memories, Dreams and Reflections*, P. 174.

94 Cf. Jacques Ellul, *The New Demons* (Oxford: Mowbray, 1975).

95 Letter to Fliess 8:10:1895 (no. 29), *Origins*, p. 126.

96 Letter to Fliess 15:10:1895 (no. 30), *Origins*, p. 127.

97 'Heredity and the aetiology of the neuroses', *S.E.* III, p. 149.

98 Ibid., p. 149.

99 'Further remarks on the neuro-psychoses of defence', *S.E.* III, p. 164.

100 Letter to Fliess 27:4:1895 (no. 23), *Origins, S.E.*, p. 118.

101 Letter from Breuer to Fliess 5:7:1895, cited by Jones I, p. 266.

102 Strachey, *S.E.* IV, p. xviii.

103 Strachey, *S.E.* I, p. 293.

104 Strachey, *S.E.* I, p. 290.

105 Sulloway *Freud, Biologist*, p. 123. I have followed Sulloway's reconstruction of the context of the *Project* closely in what follows.

106 Letter to Fliess 25:5:1895 (no. 24), *Origins*, pp. 119–20.

107 *Project for a Scientific Psychology, S.E.* I, p. 295. (*Origins*, p. 355.)

108 Letter to Fliess 16:8:1895 (no. 27), *Origins*, p. 123.

109 *Project for a Scientific Psychology, S.E.* I, p. 352. (*Origins*, p. 410.)

110 Letter to Fliess 20:10:1895 (no. 32), *Origins*, p. 129.

111 Letter to Fliess 29:11:1895 (no. 36), *Origins*, p. 134.

112 Letter to Fliess 8:12:1895 (no. 38), *Origins*, p. 137.

113 Letter to Fliess 30:6:1896 (no. 48), *Origins*, p. 169.

114 Letter to Fliess 26:10:1896 (no. 49), *Origins*, p. 170.

115 Letter to Fliess 2:11:1896 (no. 50), *Origins*, p. 170.

116 Letter to Fliess 2:11:1896 (no. 50), *Origins*, p. 171.

117 Letter to Fliess 4:12:1896 (no. 51), *Origins*, P. 172.

118 Letter to Fliess 12:6:1897 (no. 65), *Origins*, pp. 210–11.

119 Letter to Fliess 7:7:1897 (no. 66), *Origins*, p. 212; also Jones I, p. 337.

120 Letter to Fliess 14:8:1897 (no. 67), *Origins*, pp. 213–14.

121 Jones I, p. 334.

122 The importance of the following development in Freud's thought has been brought out by Peter Swales in two of his papers, I am following Swales' argument here. Cf. Swales 'Freud, Johann Weier, and the status of seduction: The role of the witch in the conception of fantasy' (privately published, 1982) and 'Freud, Krafft-Ebing, and the witches: The role of Krafft-Ebing in Freud's flight into fantasy' (privately published, 1983). (Afterward referred to respectively as Swales 'Weier' and Swales 'Krafft-Ebing'.)

123 Letter to Fliess 17:7:1897 (no. 56), *Origins*, pp. 187–8. I have used the translation of Swales in Swales 'Weier,' p. 8.

124 Letter to Fliess 24:1:1897 (no. 57), *Origins*, p. 188.
125 Ibid., p. 189.
126 Letter to Fliess 28:4:1897 (no. 60), *Origins*, p. 195.
127 Letter to Fliess 7:7:1897 (no. 66), *Origins*, p. 213. Cf. Sulloway *Freud, Biologist* Appendix C 'Dr. Felix Gattel's scientific collaboration with Freud (1897/98)', pp. 513–15.
128 Letter to Fliess 14:11:1897 (no. 75), *Origins*, p. 231.
129 Letter to Fliess 21:9:1897 (no. 69), *Origins*, p. 215.
130 Ibid., pp. 215–16.
131 *On the History of the Psycho-Analytic Movement, S.E.* XIV, p. 17.
132 *An Autobiographical Study, S.E.* XX, p. 34.
133 Unpublished portions of letters dated 12:12:1897 and 22:12:1897 cited by Blumenthal 'Did Freud's isolation lead him to reverse theory on neurosis?' *New York Times* [*Science Times*] 25 August 1981, pp. C1–2. (Afterward referred to as Blumenthal 'Isolation'.)
134 Jones I, p. 367, Jones II, p. 374.
135 H. Gardner in *Art through the Age* (7th ed) (New York: Harcourt Brace Javanovich, 1977), p. 518.
136 The passages quoted from the letters of Gomperz to his wife are translated and cited by Peter Swales in an important unpublished lecture given at the New School for Social Research, New York, 20 May 1982 'Freud, Minna Bernays and the Imitation of Christ'. (Afterward referred to as Swales 'Imitation'). This whole section follows Swales' argument. I am indebted to him for the use of this material.
137 Cf. letter to Fliess 15:10:1897 (no. 71), *Origins*, pp. 221–5.
138 Cf. letter to Fliess 12:12:1897 (no. 78), *Origins*, pp. 237–8.
139 Swales even suggests in his 'Imitation' paper that the 'discovery' of infantile sexuality – that children are polymorphously-perverse sexual beings with incestuous desires for their parents – may also have been generated by consideration of the images of Italian art. In the transformed secular religion Freud was constructing, the religious image of the madonna and child became denuded of religious significance and infused with sexual meaning.
140 Letter to Fliess 3:10:1897 (no. 70), *Origins*, pp. 218–19.
141 Letter to Fliess 15:10:1897 (no. 71), *Origins*, p. 221.
142 Ibid., p. 221.
143 Letter to Fliess 27:10:1897 (no. 72), *Origins*, pp. 225–6.
144 Letter to Fliess 31:10:1897 (no. 73), *Origins*, p. 7.
145 Letter to Fliess 14:11:1897 (no. 75), *Origins*, p. 234.
146 Letter to Fliess 3:12:1897 (no. 77), *Origins*, p. 236.
147 Ibid.
148 *'On the History of the Psycho-Analytical Movement, S.E.* XIV, p. 18.
149 Letter to Fliess 21:9:1897 (no. 69), *Origins*, p. 217.
150 'That first great error' is from a letter to Abraham 5:7:1907 from *A Psycho-Analytic Dialogue: The Letters of Sigmund Freud and Karl Abraham, 1907–1926* (edited by Hilda Abraham and Ernst Freud translated by Bernard Marsh and Hilda Abraham, London: Hogarth Press and the Institute of Psycho-Analysis, 1965) p. 2. (Afterward referred to as *Analytic Dialogue*.) The passage from the Löwenfeld book is taken from *Freud: The Assault on*

truth Freud's suppression of the seduction theory (London: Faber, 1984), p. 121. (Afterward referred to as *Freud: Assault*.)

151 Cf. Sulloway *Freud, Biologist*, chapter 6, pp. 171–237.

152 *Three Essays on the Theory of Sexuality, S.E.* VII, p. 135.

153 Ibid., p. 191.

154 Ibid., p. 175.

155 Letter to A. Zweig 15:7:1934 cited by Jones III, p. 203.

156 'My views on the part played by sexuality in the aetiology of the neuroses', *S.E.* VII, p. 271.

157 Letter to Ferenczi 9:7:1913, cited in Freeman, L. and Stream, H. S., *Freud and Women* (New York: Unger 1981), p. 3. (Afterward referred to as *Freud and Women*.)

158 *New Introductory Lectures on Psycho-Analysis, S.E.* XXII, p. 133.

159 Letter to Fliess 15:10:1897 (no. 71), *Origins*, pp. 223–4.

160 *The Interpretation of Dreams, S.E.* IV, p. 262.

161 *Introductory Lectures of Psycho-Analysis, S.E.* XVI, p. 337.

162 'An outline of psycho-analysis', *S.E.* XXIII, p. 192.

163 All of these quotations are cited by Freeman and Stream in *Freud and Women*, p. 38.

164 Eisler *Talent*.

165 Cf. Wilhelm Reich in *Reich Speaks of Freud* (Harmondsworth: Penguin) p. 115.

166 Cf. Swales 'Flowers' and Swales 'Freud, Minna Bernays, and the conquest of Rome: New light on the origins of psycho-analysis', *The New American Review*, Spring/Summer, 1982, pp. 1–23. (Afterward referred to as Swales 'Conquest'.)

167 Cf. in particular Swales 'Flowers'.

168 'Civilized sexual morality and modern nervous illness', *S.E.* X, p. 200.

169 Letter from Jones to Bernfield 20:2:1952, cited by Swales 'Flowers', p. 17.

170 'Screen Memories', *S.E.* III, p. 316. Swales translation from Swales 'Flowers', p. 9.

171 Swales reaches the conclusion that by carefully putting Freud's ideas and dreams in their proper chronological sequence 'we are now compelled to conclude that, in truth, the infantile fantasy was produced during his self-analysis precisely in compliance with a wish to prove and promote his doctrine of an unconscious involving related psychosexual phenomena; also by way of indulging, nostalgic, romantic, and psychosexual fancies of his own – in short, then, wish fulfillment' (Swales 'Flowers', p. 52).

172 Jones II, p. 431.

173 This last sentence is a hint that Freud's sexuality was directed at another person close to him, viz. Minna Bernays, his sister-in-law. Cf. Swales 'Conquest', 'Imitation' and 'Flowers'.

174 Letter to Max Halberstadt 27:7:1912 (no. 155), *Letters*, p. 300.

175 Maryse Choisy *Sigmund Freud: A New Appraisal* (London: Peter Owen, 1963), p. 49.

176 Letter to Marie Bonaparte 17:12:1936, cited in Jones III, p. 224.

177 Letter to Fliess 30:7:1898 cited in Jones I, p. 334.

178 Unpublished letter to Fliess cited by Masson in an unpublished manuscript (an early draft of his introduction to the complete Freud/Fliess letters) at Colchester.
179 Letter to Fliess 25:5:1895 (no. 24), *Origins*, p. 120.
180 Cf. Roazen *Brother Animal: The Story of Freud and Tausk* (London: Allen Lane, 1969), p. 40. (Afterward referred to as *Brother Animal*.)
181 *Introductory Lectures on Psycho-Analysis, S.E.* XVI, p. 316.
182 Jones II, p. 431.
183 Letter to Fliess 31:10:1897 (no. 73), *Origins*, p. 227.
184 Letter from Emma Jung 6:11:1911, from *Freud/Jung Letters*, p. 456.
185 Letter to E. Jones 12:2:1920 cited by Jones III, p. 21.
186 'Some neurotic mechanisms in jealousy, paranoia and homosexuality', *S.E.* XVIII, p. 228.
187 Unpublished letter to Marie Bonaparte 3:1:1937 cited by Schur *Freud: Dying*, p. 487.
188 Clark *Freud: The Cause*, p. 21.
189 Hans Sachs *Freud: Master*, p. 7.
190 Clark *Freud: The Cause*, p. 21.
191 'Screen Memories', *S.E.* III, p. 317.
192 Masson's comment comes from *Freud: Assault*, p. 73. Strachey's and Jones' from unpublished letters cited by Masson *Freud: Assault*, p. 208, n. 17. Masson's reflections on the Freud/Fliess relationship will presumably constitute the core of his Introduction to the complete Freud/Fliess correspondence. Just what he will say given his fall from grace with the protectors of the Freud image, is an open question. Janet Malcolm has recently written an extensive account of the recent traumas of the Freud Archives, cf. 'Annals of scholarship: Trouble in the archives – I, *New Yorker*, 5 December 1983, pp. 59–152) and 'Annals of scholarship: Trouble in the archives – II, *New Yorker,* 12 December 1983, pp. 60–119 also published as a book *In the Freud Archives* (New York: Alfred Knopf, 1983; London: Jonathan Cape 1984). (Afterward referred to as 'Trouble I' and 'Trouble II'.)
193 '"Civilized" Sexual Morality and Modern Nervousness', *S.E.* IX, p. 200.
194 Letter to Ferenczi 6:10:1910 cited Jones II, p. 93 and Masson *Freud: Assault*, p. 207, n.15.
195 The remarks about Adler and Stekel are from a letter to Ferenczi cited by Brome *Freud and His Disciples: The Struggle for Supremacy* (London: Caliban Books, 1984), p. 41. (Afterward referred to as *Freud: Disciples*.) The passage about Freud's success compared to the paranoic comes from a letter to Ferenczi 6:10:1910 cited Jones II, p. 92 and Masson *Freud: Assault*, p. 154.
196 Letter to Ferenczi 12:10:1910 cited by Masson in his Introduction to the Freud/Fliess Correspondence.
197 Unpublished letter to Ferenczi 17:10:1910 cited Masson *Freud: Assault*, p. 208.
198 'Psycho-analytic notes on an autobiographical account of a case of paranoia (dementia paranoides)', *S.E.* XII, p. 72.
199 Letter to E. Jones 8:12:1912 cited by Jones I, p. 334.

200 Letter to Anon. 9:4:1935 (no. 277), *Letters*, pp. 419–20.
201 'A child is being beaten: A contribution to the study of the origin of sexual perversion', *S.E.* XVII, pp. 200–201.
202 Letter to Fliess 4:1:1898 (no. 81), *Origins*, p. 242. I have used Swales' translation from his paper 'Freud, Fliess, and fratricide: The role of Fliess in Freud's conception of paranoia' (privately published, 1982), p. 8. (Afterward referred to as Swales 'Fratricide'.)
203 Letter to Fliess 1:8:1899 (no. 113), *Origins*, p. 289.
204 *Three Essays on the Theory of Sexuality*, *S.E.* VII, p. 22.

CHAPTER 3

1 *The Interpretation of Dreams, S.E.* V, p. 608 (sentence added in 1909 to the 2nd Edition).
2 Cf. Strachey's Introduction to *The Interpretation of Dreams, S.E.* IV, p. xx.
3 *Introductory Lectures on Psycho-Analysis', S.E.* XV, p. 83.
4 'Five Lectures on Psycho-Analysis', *S.E.* XI, p. 33.
5 Ibid., pp. 33.
6 Bellevue was a house situated on a hill in one of the suburbs of Vienna. Freud and his family used the house during the summer holidays. It was while he was there this summer, after the publication of his *Magnum opus*, that his mind wandered to the events surrounding his specimen dream.
7 Letter to Fliess 12:6.1900 cited by Max Schur in 'Some additional "Day Residues" of the specimen dream of psychoanlysis' from Loewenstein, R. M., Newman, L. M., Schur, M. and Solnit, A. J. (eds) *Psychoanalysis–A General Psychology Essays in Honor of Heinz Hartmann* (New York: International Universities Press, 1966) pp. 45–85. (Afterward referred to as Schur 'Day Residues'.) The letter can be found in *Origins* (letter no. 137), pp. 321–22. Schur's article is reproduced in *Freud: Self Analysis*, pp. 87–116.
8 *The Interpretation of Dreams, S.E.* IV, p. 120. Though Freud obviously set great store on this dream (as shown by his speculation about a plaque) it was not Freud's first account of a dream and its interpretation–there is an account of a dream of a 'young man' of Freud's acquaintance dated 1894 – he did draw particular attention to this dream as the *first* he had *thoroughly* analysed.
9 *On the History of the Psycho-Analytic Movement, S.E.* XIV, p. 20.
10 *New Introductory Lectures on Psycho-Analysis, S.E.* XXII, p. 7.
11 *On the History of the Psycho-Analytic Movement, S.E.* XIV, p. 20.
12 'Preface' to the Second Edition of *The Interpretation of Dreams, S.E.* IV, p. xxvi.
13 Letter to Fliess 28:5:1899 (no. 107), *Origins* p. 281.
14 'Preface' to the third English edition of *The Interpretation of Dreams, S.E.* IV, p. xxxii.
15 Letter to Fliess 12:2:1900 (no. 137), *Origins*, p. 322. Freud's letters of the 1890s show frequent concern about who else might know 'the secret', cf. letter of 10:3:1898 (no. 84), *Origins*, p. 247.
16 Letter to Fliess 29:8:1894 (no. 21), *Origins*, p. 101.

17 *An Autobiographical Study*, S.E. XX, p. 47.
18 Cf. Sulloway *Freud, Biologist*, pp. 448–64.
19 Letter to Fliess 23:3:1900 (no. 131), *Origins*, p. 313. It was at this time that Freud explained to Fliess that his best consolation was for his children (letter of 7:5:1900, no. 134) which is quoted at the beginning of this book.
20 Letter to C. G. Jung 16:4:1909 (no. 139F), *Freud/Jung Letters*, p. 219.
21 Letter to Fliess 11:9:1899 (no. 118), *Origins*, pp. 296–7.
22 Preface to the first edition of *The Interpretation of Dreams*, S.E. IV, p. xxiii.
23 *The Interpretation of Dreams*, S.E. IV, p. 105.
24 *The Interpretation of Dreams*, S.E. IV, p. 107.
25 Ibid., S.E. V, p. 359, note 1911.
26 Foulkes, D., *A Grammar of Dreams* (Hassocks, Sussex: Harvester Press, 1978), p. 36.
27 *The Interpretation of Dreams*,, S.E. IV, p. 118.
28 'Project for a scientific psychology', S.E. I, p. 340. Also in *Origins*, p. 402.
29 *The Interpretation of Dreams*,, S.E. IV, p. 160.
30 Ibid., p. 165.
31 Ibid., S.E. V, p. 561.
32 Ibid., S.E. IV, p.198.
33 Letter to Fliess 10:3:1898 (no. 84), *Origins*, pp. 246–7.
34 *The Interpretation of Dreams*,, S.E. IV, p. 12.
35 Ibid., S.E. V, p. 589.
36 *On Dreams*,, S.E. V, p. 671.
37 Letter to André Breton from 'Three Letters from Sigmund Freud to André Breton', (Davis, F. B.) *Journal of the American Psychoanalytic Association* **54**, pp. 127–134, 1973.
38 Letter from Jung to Freud 14:2:1911 (no. 235J), *Freud/Jung Letters*, p. 392.
39 Ibid., pp. 392–3.
40 Letter from Freud to Jung 17:2:1898 (no. 236F), *Freud/Jung Letters*, p. 394.
41 Ibid., p. 395.
42 Ibid.
43 Ibid.
44 Letter from Freud to Jung 12:5:1911 (no. 255F), *Freud/Jung Letters*, p. 422.
45 Letter to Fliess 24:3:1898 (no. 86), *Origins*, p. 249.
46 Letters to Fliess 6:9:1899 (no. 117), *Origins*, p. 295.
47 Letter to Fliess 9:2:1898 (no. 83), *Origins*, p. 244.
48 Letter to Fliess 22:7:1899 (no. 112), *Origins*, p. 287.
49 Letter to Fliess 23:10:1898 (no. 99), *Origins*, p. 269 I have used Schur's translation from Schur 'Day Residues', p. 74.
50 Letter to Fliess 9:6:1898 (unpublished portion of letter 90) cited by Schur in 'Day Residues', pp. 74–5.
51 Letter to Fliess 20:6:1898 (unpublished portion of letter 91) cited by Schur in 'Day Residues', p. 75.
52 Letter to Fliess 1:8:1899 (no. 113), *Origins*, pp. 288–9.
53 Letter to Fliess 4:3:1895 cited by Schur in 'Day Residues', p. 55.
54 Letter to Fliess 8:3:1895 cited by Schur in 'Day Residues', pp. 56–7.
55 Ibid., p. 57.
56 Ibid., p. 58.

57 Letter to Fliess 28:3:1895 cited by Schur in 'Day Residues', p. 62.
58 Letter to Fliess 11:4:1895 cited by Schur in 'Day Residues', pp. 63–64.
59 Letter to Fliess 20:4:1895 cited by Schur in 'Day Residues', pp. 65–6.
60 Letter to Fliess 16:4:1896 cited by Schur in 'Day Residues', p. 80.
61 Letter to Fliess 26:4:1896 cited by Schur in 'Day Residues', p. 80.
62 Letter to Fliess 17:1:1897 (unpublished portion of letter 56) cited by Schur in 'Day Residues', p. 83.
63 Cf. Blumenthal 'Isolation' and Masson, J. M. *Freud: Assault*
6´ Clark *Freud: The Cause*, p. 152.
65 *The Interpretation of Dreams,*, S.E. IV, p. 293.
66 Letter from Karl Abraham to Freud 8:1:1908, in *Analytic Dialogue*, p. 18.
67 Letter to Abraham 9:1:1908, in *Analytic Dialogue*, p. 20.
68 Jacques Lacan and Didier Anzieu discerned this sexual aspect in the dream, cf. Anzieu *L'Auto-Analyse* (Paris: Presses Universitaires de France, 1959).
69 The latent sexual aspects of the dream have also been analysed by Mahony in 'Towards a formalist approach to dreams', *International Review of Psycho-Analysis* **4**, pp. 83–98 (1977).
70 *The Interpretation of Dreams*, S.E. IV, p. 218.
71 Ibid., p. 1.
72 Cf. for example the recent work of Crick and Mitchison, 'The function of dream sleep', *Nature* **304**, 14 July 1983, pp. 111–114, and Morton Schatzman, 'Solve your problems in your sleep', *New Scientist* **98**, 9 June 1983, pp. 692–3. pp. 692–3.
73 Letter to Roback 20:2:1930, cited in Jones III, Appendix A, p. 480 (letter 15).
74 *The Psychopathology of Everyday Life*, S.E. VI, p. xii, note 1. There are a number of objections to Strachey's habit of coining neologisms when translating words which in the German have a relatively well-defined meaning but which have no English equivalent. Cf. Rycroft in his Introduction to his *Critical Dictionary of Psychoanalysis* (Harmondsworth: Penguin Books, 1972) and Bettleheim in his *Freud and Modern Man's Soul* (London: Chatto and Windus and Hogarth Press, 1983).
75 *The Psychopathology of Everyday Life*, S.E. VI, p. 59.
76 Ibid., pp. 78–9.
77 A. A. Brill's insertion into his translation of Freud's text, *The Psychopathology of Everyday Life* from *The Basic Writings of Sigmund Freud* (translated by A. A. Brill, New York: Random House, The Modern Library, 1938), p. 57.
78 *The Psychopathology of Everyday Life*, S.E. VI, pp. 79–80.
79 Letter to Fliess 26:8:1898 (no. 94), *Origins*, pp. 261–2. There is evidence that Freud had already formulated the beginnings of a theory of parapraxes by as early as 1882 for in a letter written to Martha during that year, there is a blot of ink which Freud begs Martha 'not to trouble yourself with an interpretation'. There is a picture of the blot in *Freud: Pictures*, p. 95.
80 Letter to Fliess 26:8:1898 (no. 94), *Origins*, pp. 261–2.
81 Letter to Fliess 31:8:1898 (no. 95), *Origins*, p. 262.
82 Lipps 1885, cited as note 1 of letter 94 of *Origins*, p. 261.
83 Letter to Fliess 27:9:1898 (no. 97), *Origins,* p. 267.
84 Letter to Fliess 22:9:1898 (no. 96), *Origins*, p. 265.

85 For an extensive discussion, to my mind persuasive, of the significance of this parapraxis see Swales 'Imitation'.
86 Letter to Fliess 14:10:1900 (no. 139), *Origins*, p. 325.
87 Jones I p. 180.
88 Paul Roazen *Freud and His Followers* (London: Allen Lane, 1976), p. 83. (Afterward referred to as *Freud: Followers*.)
89 Letter to Minna Bernays 7:2:1886 (no. 95), pp. 216–17.
90 Cited by Freeman and Stream *Freud and Women*, p. 47.
91 Jones II, p. 432.
92 Jones II, p. 469. How Jones could maintain this view in the light of the evidence he had in his possession is staggering.
93 Letter to Putnam 8:7:1915 from *James Jackson Putnam and Psychoanalysis. Letters between Putnam and Sigmund Freud, Ernest Jones, William James, Sandor Ferenczi and Morton Price, 1877–1917* (edited by Nale, N. G., translated by Judith Bernays Heller, Cambridge, Massachusetts; Harvard University Press, 1971) p. 189. (Afterward referred to as *Putnam Letters*.)
94 Letter to Jung 27:4:1911 (no. 253F), *Freud/Jung Letters*, p. 419.
95 Letter to Fliess 3:1:1911 (no. 101), *Origins*, pp. 270–1.
96 The case is reported in *The Psychopathology of Everyday Life*, S.E. VI, pp. 8–14.
97 Swales 'Conquest'. I have followed Swales argument here.
98 *The Psychopathology of Everyday Life*, S.E. VI, p. 8.
99 'Screen Memories', *S.E.* III, p. 309.
100 Cited by Gillie after Swales in 'The Secret Love Life of Sigmund Freud', *Sunday Times*, 3 January 1982, pp. 25–7. Cf. 'Trouble II'.
101 All reported by John Billinsky 'Jung and Freud (The end of a romance)', *Andover Newton Quarterly* 10, pp. 39–43 (1961).
102 Ibid., p. 42.
103 *The Psychopathology of Everyday Life*, S.E. VI, p. 219.
104 Clark *Freud: The Cause*, p. 52.
105 I believe that Swales has provided a reasonable set of alternative interpretations of many of these in his various writings, e.g., 'Flowers', 'Conquest', 'Imitation', 'Fratricide'.
106 *The Interpretation of Dreams*, S.E. IV, p. 215.
107 Letter to Fliess 20:6:1898 (no. 91), *Origins*, p. 256.
108 *Jokes and their Relation to the Unconscious*, S.E. VIII, p. 109.
109 Jones I, p. 370.
110 Jones I, p. 370.
111 Cf. Swales 'Conquest', the evidence for which is drawn from his studies in Merano and the area.
112 *On Dreams*, S.E. V, p. 636.
113 *On Dreams*, S.E. V, pp. 638, 648, 650, 655–7. Cf. Swales 'Conquest'.
114 *The Psychopathology of Everyday Life*, S.E. VI, p. 119.
115 *On Dreams*, S.E. V, pp. 640, 671.
116 *The Interpretation of Dreams*, S.E. V, p. 196–7. Swales' translation from Swales 'Conquest'.
117 Swales 'Conquest' and 'Imitation' have made out a case for this identification.

118 'On the universal tendency to debasement in the sphere of love (Contributions to the psychology of love II)', *S.E.* XI, p. 186.
119 Letter to Max Halberstadt 7:7:1912 (no. 152), *Letters*, p. 297.
120 Even if the interpretation of this period of Freud's life as it is presented in full by Swales turns out to be erroneous in the light of fresh revelations from the Freud Archives (which I suspect it will not), the material Swales presents renders the orthodox interpretations of this time in need of considerable revision. For myself, I conclude this section with some of Freud's words to Jung: 'just let five or ten years pass and the analysis of the "aliquis" which today is not regarded as cogent, will have become cogent, though nothing in it will have changed', letter to Jung 26:5:1907 (no. 27F), *Freud/Jung Letters*, p. 54.
121 *Jokes and their Relation to the Unconscious, S.E.* VIII, p. 89.
122 *An Autobiographical Study, S.E.* XX, pp. 65–6.
123 Cited by Freud in *The Interpretation of Dreams, S.E.* IV, p. 297, note 1.
124 Cited by Strachey in his Introduction to *Jokes and their Relation to the Unconscious, S.E.* VII, p. 4. Cf. letter to Fliess 12:6:1897 (no. 65), *Origins*, p. 211.
125 Letter to Fliess 11:9:1899 (no. 118), *Origins*, p. 297.
126 *The Interpretation of Dreams, S.E.* IV, p. 298, note 1.
127 Cited in *Origins*, p. 260, note 1.
128 *Jokes and their Relation to the Unconscious, S.E.* VIII, p. 28, note 1.
129 Ibid., p. 161.
130 Ibid., p. 117.
131 *The Interpretation of Dreams, S.E.* IV, p. 298, note 1.
132 *An Autobiographical Study, S.E.* XX, p. 66.
133 *The Psychopathology of Everyday Life, S.E.* VI, p. 219.
134 *Jokes and their Relation to the Unconscious, S.E.* VIII, p. 110.
135 Ibid., p. 111.
136 Preface to Theodor Reik's *Ritual, S.E.* XVII, p. 259.

CHAPTER 4

1 Jones II, pp. 3–4.
2 Letter to Fliess 15:10:1897 (no. 71), *Origins*, p. 223.
3 Letter to Fliess 8:1:1900 (no. 127), *Origins*, p. 307.
4 Incident cited by Vincent Brome in *Freud: Disciples*, p. 31.
5 Letter to Fliess 4:4:1900 (no. 132), *Origins*, p. 316.
6 *An Autobiographical Study, S.E.* XX, p. 48.
7 Sulloway in *Freud, Biologist* effectively refutes these interpretations, cf. pp. 445–95.
8 *On the History of the Psycho-Analytic Movement, S.E.* XIV, p. 22.
9 'Review of *The Psychopathology of Everyday Life*', *Journal of Abnormal Psychology*, 1, 2, June 1906, p. 103.
10 'Shibboleth' of orthodoxy comes from a letter to Pfister 27:5:19 cited by Jones III, p. 15. 'Debauching' quote cited by Cioffi in *Freud: Modern Judgements*, p. 10.

11 Cited by Clark in *Freud: The Cause*, p. 191.
12 Cited by Jones in a lecture entitled 'Our Attitude Towards Greatness' published as *Sigmund Freud: Four Centenary Addresses* (New York: Basic Books) p. 46.
13 Letter to Fliess 11:3:1902 (no. 152), *Origins*, p. 342.
14 Ibid., pp. 343–4.
15 Ibid., p. 344.
16 'Fragment of an analysis of a case of hysteria', *S.E.* VII, p. 7.
17 Letter to Fliess 14:10:1900 (no. 139), *Origins*, p. 325.
18 Letter to Fliess 25:1:1901 (no. 140), *Origins*, pp. 325–6.
19 Letter to Fliess 25:1:1901 (no. 140), *Origins*, p. 326 and unpublished letter 9:6:1901 cited by Strachey in his Introduction to 'Fragment of an analysis of a case of hysteria', *S.E.* VII, p. 4.
20 Unpublished letter to Fliess 3:3:1901 cited by Blumenthal in 'Isolation'.
21 Cited by Toril Moi 'Representation of Patriarchy: Sexuality and Epistemology in Freud's Dora' *Feminist Review* 9, pp. 60–74, p. 67, 1981.
22 'Fragment of an analysis of a case of hysteria', *S.E.* VII, pp. 114–15.
23 Ibid., p. 9.
24 Ibid., p. 12.
25 Ibid., p. 28.
26 Ibid., p. 78.
27 Ibid., p. 78.
28 Ibid., p. 48.
29 Ibid., p. 79.
30 Ibid., p. 59.
31 From *Studies on Hysteria, S.E.* II, quoted by Thomas, cf. note 32.
32 'A Fine Romance' review of *A Secret Symmetry*, by Carotenuto, *New York Review of Books*, 13 May 1982, p. 3.
33 'Fragment of an analysis of a case of hysteria', *S.E.* VII, p. 120, note 1.
34 Ibid., p. 13.
35 Ibid., p. 13.
36 Ibid., p. 116.
37 Ibid., p. 117.
38 Reported in the *Minutes of the Vienna Psycho-Analytic Society*, Vol. I, *1906–1908* (New York: International Universities Press, 1962) pp. 100–102.
39 'The dynamics of transference', *S.E.* XII, p. 104.
40 *New Introductory Lectures on Psycho-Analysis, S.E.* XXII, p. 132.
41 'Fetishism', *S.E.* XXI, p. 154.
42 *Sigmund Freud's Mission: An Analysis of His Personality and Influence* (New York: Harper and Brothers, 1959), p. 31.
43 Letter to Silberstein 27:2:1875 (no. 4E), at Colchester.
44 *Three Essays on the Theory of Sexuality, S.E.* VII, p. 191.
45 *New Introductory Lectures on Psycho-Analysis, S.E.* XXII, p. 135.
46 Letter to Marie Bonaparte cited by Jones II, p. 468. In recent years feminists have sought to redress this distortion in Freud's thought, with varying degrees of criticism to Freud himself. Cf. Miller, *Psycho-Analysis and Women* (Harmondsworth: Penguin, 1973) and Mitchell, J. *Psychoanalysis and Feminism* (Harmondsworth: Penguin, 1974).

47 Letter to Abraham 3:3:1911, *Analytic Dialogue*, p. 103.
48 Letter to Abraham 18:12:1910, *Analytic Dialogue*, p. 97.
49 From Schreber, Daniel Paul, *Memoirs of my Nervous Illness* (translated and edited by Ida Macalpine and Richard A. Hunter with Notes and Discussion, London: Dawson, 1955), p. 342.
50 'Psycho-analytic notes on an autobiographical account of a case of paranoia (dementia paranoides)', *S.E.* XII, pp. 62–3.
51 Cf. William Niederland, *The Schreber Case: Psychoanalytic Profile of a Paranoid Personality* (New York: Quadrangle/New York Times Book Co.) and Morton Schatzman *Soul/Murder: Persecution in the Family* (London: Allen Lane, 1973).
52 The following account of this last congress is based upon Peter Swales' paper 'Fratricide'.
53 Letter to Fliess 23:3:1900 (no. 131), *Origins*, p. 314.
54 *The Interpretation of Dreams, S.E.* V, p. 483.
55 Ibid., p. 459.
56 Letter to Jung 17:2:1908 (no. 70F), *Freud/Jung Letters*, p. 121. For a detailed account of this whole incident see Brome *Freud: Disciples*, pp. 1–13.
57 Letter to Abraham 13:2:1911, *Analytic Dialogue*, pp.100–1.
58 Letter from Abraham to Freud 26:2:1911, Ibid., p. 102.
59 Letter to Abraham 3:3:1911, Ibid., p. 103.
60 Postscript added in 1923 to 'Notes upon a case of obsessional neurosis, *S.E.* X, p. 249, note 1.
61 Foreword to *The Wolf-Man by the Wolf-Man* (edited by Muriel Gardiner, London: Hogarth Press and Institute of Psycho-Analysis, 1971).
62 Freud Ibid., p. 150.
63 Jones II, p. 308.
64 Letter to Ferenczi 13:2:1910, from J. Masson's review of *Gesprache mit dem Wolfsmann* (Obholzer), *International Review of Psycho-Analysis* pp. 116–19 (1981).
65 'From the history of an infantile neurosis', *S.E.* XVII, p. 104.
66 'Review of *The Wolf-Man by the Wolf-Man*' (edited by Muriel Gardiner), *International Journal of Psycho-Analysis* 53, pp. 419–22 (1972) p. 420.
67 'From the history of an infantile neurosis', *S.E.* XVII, p. 103, note 1.
68 Foreword to *The Wolf-Man by the Wolf-Man* (edited by Muriel Gadiner, London: Hogarth Press and Institute of Psycho-Analysis, 1971).
69 Cf. Karin Obholzer *The Wolf-Man, Sixty Years Later* (translated by Michael Shaw, London: Routledge and Kegan Paul, 1982).
70 Cited by Ellenberger *The Discovery of the Unconscious: The History and Solution of Dynamic Psychiatry* (London: Allen Lane, 1970) p. 458.
71 Letter to Fliess 8:2:1897 (no. 58), *Origins*, p. 192.
72 'Analysis of a phobia in a five-year-old boy', *S.E.* X, p. 6.
73 Ibid., p. 7.
74 *Three Essays on the Theory of Sexuality, S.E.* VII, pp. 193, note 4.
75 'Analysis of a phobia in a five-year-old boy', *S.E.* X, p. 104.
76 Cf. postcript to Ibid., p. 148.
77 Letter from Jung to Jones 1:6:1909, cited by Clark in *Freud: The Cause*, p. 236.

78 For an account of the acrimonious nature of the development of psycho-analysis in England see Melitta Schmideberg, 'A contribution to the history of the psycho-analytic movement in Britain', *Brit. J. Psychiatry* **118**, pp. 61–68 (1971).
79 'Contributions to a discussion on masturbation', *S.E.* XII, p. 250.
80 Letter to Silberstein 11:4:1875 (no. 4I), at Colchester.
81 Ibid.
82 *Introductory Lectures on Psycho-Analysis, S.E.* XVI, pp. 244.
83 *The Future of an Illusion, S.E.* XXI, p. 36.
84 *An Autobiographical Study, S.E.* XX, p. 58.
85 Ibid., p. 32.
86 'On narcissism: an introduction', *S.E.* XIV, p. 77.
87 'Freud in his historical context', from Cioffi *Freud: Modern Judgements*, p. 54.
88 *The New Demons* (Oxford: Mowbray, 1975), p. 65.
89 I am following the suggestions contained in an important series of papers by Joseph Sandler, Christopher Dare and Alex Holder in the *British Journal of Medical Psychology* over the period from 1972–1982 under the general title 'Frames of reference in psychoanalytic psychology. Cf. 'Frames of reference in psychoanalytic psychology I – Introduction', and 'II – The historical context and phases in the development of psychoanalysis' and 'III – A note on basic assumptions', *British J. Med. Psychol.* **45**, pp. 127–47 (1972). The series has continued through to 'XII – The characteristics of the structural frame of reference', *Brit. J. Med. Psychol.* **55**, pp. 203–7 (1982). I have used three diagrams from these papers.
90 *An Autobiographical Study, S.E.* XX, p. 55.
91 *Three Essays on the Theory of Sexuality, S.E.* VII, pp. 190–1. cf. *Freud: Assault*, pp 119–134.
92 *An Autobiographical Study, S.E.* XX, p. 34.
93 Cited in Blumenthal 'Isolation'. Masson says the same thing, except that he makes his application wider than just psychoanalysis in *Freud: Assault*, p. 144.
94 *An Autobiographical Study, S.E.* XX, pp. 32–3.
95 *Introductory Lectures on Psycho-Analysis, S.E.* XV, p. 295.
96 Adapted from 'Frames of reference in psychoanalytic psychology V – The topographical frame of reference: the organization of the mental apparatus', *Brit. J. Med. Psychol.* **46**, pp. 29–36 (1973).
97 *An Outline of Psycho-Analysis, S.E.* XXIII, p. 158.
98 'The resistances to psycho-analysis', *S.E.* XIX, p. 217.
99 *The Ego and the Id, S.E.* XIX, p. 17.
100 Ibid., p. 12.
101 *An Autobiographical Study, S.E.* XX, pp. 57–59.
102 Letter to Groddeck 17:4:1921, cited by Clark *Freud: The Cause*, p. 434.
103 Letter to Ferenczi 21:7:1922, Jones III, p. 104, cited by Ibid. p. 435.
104 Letter to Groddeck 25:3:1923 (no. 201), *Letters*, p. 347.
105 Letter from Groddeck to his wife 15:5:1923, cited by Clark *Freud: The Cause*, p. 435.
106 Both figures are adapted from 'Frames of reference in psychoanalytic psychology XII – The characteristics of the structural frame of reference', *Brit. J. Med. Psychol.* **55**, pp. 203–7 (1982).

107 *New Introductory Lectures on Psycho-Analysis, S.E.* XXII, pp. 73–4.
108 Ibid., p. 77.
109 Ibid., p. 77.
110 Ibid., p. 79.
111 *The Ego and the Id, S.E.* XIX, p. 56.
112 *New Introductory Lectures on Psycho-Analysis, S.E.* XXII, p. 80.
113 Cited by Maryse Choisy in *Sigmund Freud: A New Appraisal* (London: Peter Owen, 1963), p. 5.
114 Letter to Silberstein 28:4:1910 (no. 5N), at Colchester.
115 On the History of the Psycho-Analytic Movement, *S.E.* XIV, p. 12.
116 Letter to Abraham 22:8:1910, *Analytic Dialogue*, p. 92.
117 *On the History of the Psycho-Analytic Movement, S.E.* XIV, pp. 12–13.
118 'Address to the B'nai B'rith', *S.E.* XX, p. 273.
119 Letters to Fliess 3:12:1897 (no. 77) and 19:9:1901 (no. 146), *Origins*, pp. 236, 335.
120 Letter to Fliess 19:9:1901 (no. 146), *Origins*, pp. 335–6.
121 *Sigmund Freud's Mission: An Analysis of His Personality and Influence* (New York: Harper and Brothers, 1959), p. 94.
122 Letter from Ferenczi to Freud 26:12:1918, Jones III, p. 7.
123 *The Interpretation of Dreams, S.E.* IV, pp. 196–7.
124 Ibid., p. 194.
125 Letter to Werner Achelis 30:1:1927 (no. 228), *Letters*, p. 376.
126 Letter from Arnold Zweig to Freud 2:12:19130, *Zweig Letters*, p. 23 cited by Swales 'Imitation'. Swales presents a convincing case for this identification. David Bakan in his *Sigmund Freud and the Jewish Mystical Tradition* (Princeton: D. Van Nostrand Co., 1958), has also suggested this link.
127 Letter to Fliess 9:12:1899 (no. 125), *Origins*, p. 304.
128 Letter to Fliess 11:3:1900 (no. 130), *Origins*, p. 311.
129 Cited by Sulloway *Freud, Biologist*, p. 450–1.
130 From Stekel's *Autobiography*, cited by Clark *Freud: The Cause*, p. 182.
131 Cited by Clark *Freud: The Cause*, p. 183.
132 Cited by Clark *Freud: The Cause*, p. 213.
133 Ibid., p. 214.
134 Cited by Roazen in *Brother Animal*, p. 134 and Brome in *Freud: Disciples*, p. 19.
135 Cited by Sulloway *Freud, Biologist*, p. 486.
136 *Freud: Master*, p. 11.
137 'Freud as a Leader' from Cioffi *Freud: Modern Judgements*, p. 146.
138 The description of Rank as 'research worker, proof reader, adopted son' is that of Anaïs Nin, a confidant and colleague of Rank, the later commentator is Paul Roazen. Roazen *Freud: Followers*, pp. 390–2.
139 One of the most infamous of the suicides of those in Freud's circle was that of Victor Tausk in 1919. Paul Roazen has presented the events around this suicide in *Brother Animal*, his conclusions have been disputed by Kurt Eisler in his two books *Talent and Genius* and in his *Victor Tausk's Suicide* (New York: International Universities Press, 1983).
140 Cited by J. Wortis 'Fragments of a Freudian analysis', *American Journal*

of Orthopsychiatry, X pp. 843–9 (1940). c.f. Brome *Freud: Disciples* for accounts of the defections.

141 Letter to Oskar Pfister 26:2:1911, from *Faith Letters*, p. 26.
142 Cited by Sulloway *Freud, Biologist*, p. 481.
143 From *Thirty Years with Freud* (London: Hogarth Press and Institute of Psycho-Analysis, 1940) pp. 44–5. (Afterward referred to as *Freud: Thirty Years*.)
144 *Freud: Master*, pp. 1–2.
145 Cited by Sulloway *Freud, Biologist*, p. 481 and by Roazen *Freud: Followers*, p. 225.
146 *Memories, Dreams, and Reflections*, p. 173.
148 Jones II, p. 37.
149 Letter to Jung 17:1:1909 (no. 125F), *Freud/Jung Letters*, pp. 6–7.
150 Cited by Jones in *Free Associations: Memories of a Psycho-Analyst* (London: Hogarth Press, 1959), p. 167.
151 Letter to Abraham 26:12:1908 and 3:5:1908, *Analytic Dialogue*, pp. 64, 34.
152 Letter to Jung 2:9:1907 (no. 42F), *Freud/Jung Letters*, p. 82.
153 Cited by Roazen *Freud: Followers*, p. 374.
154 Letter to Putnam 19:6:1914, *Putnam Letters*, p. 176.
155 *On the History of the Psycho-Analytic Movement, S.E.* XIV, p. 43.
156 Letter to Eugen Bleuler 28:9:1910, from Franz Alexander and Sheldon Selesnick 'Freud–Bleuler correspondence', *Archives of General Psychiatry* 12, pp. 1–9 (1965), p. 2. (Afterward referred to as 'Bleuler Correspondence'.)
157 Letter to Bleuler 16:10:1910, 'Bleuler Correspondence', p. 4.
158 Letter to Bleuler 27:10:1910, 'Bleuler Correspondence', p. 4.
159 Letter from Bleuler to Freud 11:3:1911, 'Bleuler Correspondence', p. 5.
160 Letter to Putnam 19:6:1914, *Putnam Letters*, p. 176.
161 Letter to Jung 17:10:1909 (no. 158F), *Freud/Jung Letters*, p. 255.
162 Letter to Putnam 8:7:1909, *Putnam Letters*, p. 189.
163 Cited by L. Binswanger, *Sigmund Freud: Reminiscences of a Friendship* (New York and London: Grune and Stratton, 1957), p. 9.
164 Letter to Abraham 18:7:1914, *Analytic Dialogue*, p. 184.
165 Letter to Jones 1:8:1912, cited Jones II, p. 173.
166 *Free Associations: Memories of a Psycho-Analyst* (London: Hogarth Press), p. 228.
167 Letter to Samuel Freud 21:2:1921, cited by Clark *Freud: The Cause* p. 427.
168 'Lines of advance in psycho-analytic therapy', *S.E.* XVII, p. 167.
169 Letter to Wilfred Lay 13:12:1920, cited by Clark *Freud: The Cause*, p. 427.
170 Cited in Roazen *Freud: Followers*, p. 329.
171 *New Introductory Lectures on Psycho-Analysis, S.E.* XXII, p. 69.
172 *An Autobiographical Study, S.E.* XX, p. 53.
173 Cited by Roazen *Freud: Followers*, p. 309.
174 Letter from Abraham to Freud 6:2:1925, *Analytic Dialogue*, p. 380.
175 Cited by Roazen *Freud: Followers*, p. 411.

CHAPTER 5

1 Letter to Fliess 5:11:1897 (no. 74), *Origins*, p. 228.
2 *Delusions and Dreams in Jensen's Gradiva, S.E.* IX, p. 8.

3 Cf. letter to Silberstein 2:10:1875 (no. 4O), at Colchester.
4 Letter to Martha Bernays 1:4:1884, from Jones III, p. 448.
5 Letter to Martha Bernays written in 1884 Jones I, p. 123.
6 Letter to Fliess 4:10:1897 (no. 70), *Origins*, p. 221.
7 Cf. Blumenthal 'Isolation' and Masson *Freud: Assault.*
8 Letter to Fliess 15:10:1897 (no. 71), *Origins*, p. 224.
9 Letter to Fliess 20:6:1898 (no. 91), *Origins*, p.256.
   Cf. Swales 'Imitation' for a detailed examination of Freud's interest in and knowledge of Meyer.
10 Letter from Jung to Freud 24:5:1907 (no. 26J), *Freud/Jung Letters*, p. 49.
11 Letter to Jung 26:5:1907 (no. 27F), *Freud/Jung Letters*, pp. 51–2.
12 Ibid., p. 52.
13 Letter to Jung 17:10:1909 (no. 158F), *Freud/Jung Letters*, p. 255.
14 Translators introduction to *Leonardo Da Vinci and a Memory of His Childhood, S.E.* XI, p. 61.
15 Ibid., p. 82.
16 Ibid., pp. 85–6.
17 Letter to Lou Andreas-Salomé 9:2:1919, *Salomé Letters*, p. 90.
18 Letter to Pfister 6:3:1910, *Faith Letters*, p. 34.
19 *Leonardo Da Vinci and a Memory of His Childhood, S.E.* XI, p. 132.
20 Freud in 1910, cited Jones III, p. 444.
21 *Leonardo Da Vinci and a Memory of His Childhood, S.E.* XI, p. 101.
22 Ibid., p. 136.
23 Postcard to Martha Freud 6:9:1901, cited by Jones II, p. 409.
24 Letter to Eduardo Weiss 12:4:1933, *Freud: Pictures*, p. 205.
25 'Moses of Michaelangelo', *S.E.* XIII, p. 229.
26 Letter to Ferenczi 17:10:1912, cited by Jones II, p. 411.
27 'Moses of Michelangelo', *S.E.* XIII, p. 233.
28 Letter to Putnam 17:5:1914, *Putnam Letters*, p. 174.
29 Letter from Putnam to Freud 2:6:1914, *Putnam Letters*, p. 174.
30 'A short account of psycho-analysis', *S.E.* XIX, p. 202.
31 Editor's introduction to *On the History of the Psycho-Analytic Movement, S.E.* XIV, pp. 4–5.
32 *Beyond the Pleasure Principle, S.E.* XVIII, p. 22.
33 Letter to Abraham 26:7:1914, *Analytic Dialogue*, p. 186.
34 Letter to Abraham 25:8:1914, *Analytic Dialogue*, p. 193.
35 Letter to Lou Andreas-Salomé 25:11:1914, *Salomé Letters*, p. 21.
36 Letter to Abraham 22:9:1914, *Analytic Dialogue*, p. 197.
37 Letter to Abraham 4:3:1915, from *Sigmund Freud 1856–1939: Forty Years After* (catalogue prepared the Goethe Institute Exhibition available from Sigmund Freud Copyright Ltd, Colchester), p. 24. (Afterward referred to as *Freud: Forty Years*.)
38 'Thoughts for the times on war and death', *S.E.* XIV, p. 300.
39 Letter to Van Eeden 28:12:1914, *S.E.* XIV, pp. 301–2.
40 *Why War?* (with A. Einstein), *S.E.* XXII, p. 215.
41 'The claims of psycho-analysis to scientific interest', *S.E.* XIII, p. 186.
42 Letter to Lou Andreas-Salomé 28:7:1929, from *Freud: Forty Years*, p. 35.
43 Letter to Pfister 9:10:1918, *Faith Letters*, p. 61.

44 Cited by Reik in *Freud: Thirty Years*, p. 16. In 1930 he echoed these words publically exploring the nature of aggression: '*Homo homini lupus* [a phrase from Plautus] man is wolf to man. Who in the face of all his experience of life and history, will have the courage to dispute this assertion?' *Civilization and its Discontents, S.E.* XXI, p. 111.

45 *Civilization and its Discontents, S.E.* XXI, pp. 144–5.

46 'The resistances to psycho-analysis', *S.E.* XIX, p. 219.

47 *New Introductory Lectures on Psycho-Analysis, S.E.* XXII, p. 179.

48 Ibid., p. 181.

49 *The Future of an Illusion, S.E.* XXI, p. 49.

50 Cited by Jones III, p. 377.

51 *Civilization and its Discontents, S.E.* XXI, pp. 81–2.

52 Letter to Putnam 8:7:1915, *Putnam Letters*, p. 189.

53 'Freud 1956' An address delivered to the Grolier Club 21:2:1956 (New York: privately printed, 1956), p. 15.

54 Letter to Fliess 12:12:1897 (no. 78), *Origins*, p. 237.

55 Letter to Fliess 3:12:1897 (no. 77), *Origins*, p. 236.

56 Letter to Fliess 4:7:1901 (no. 144), *Origins*, p. 333 I have used Strachey's version from, *S.E.* XIII, pp. x–xi.

57 *The Psychopathology of Everyday Life, S.E.* VI, p. 259.

58 Cf. Donald Mackay *The Clockwork Image* (Leicester, IVP, 1974).

59 Jones III, p. 387.

60 *Moses and Monotheism: Three Essays, S.E.* XXIII, p. 122.

61 *Leonardo Da Vinci and a Memory of His Childhood, S.E.* XI, p. 123.

62 Letter to Jung 2:1:1910 (no. 171F), *Freud/Jung Letters*, pp. 283–4.

63 *The Future of an Illusion, S.E.* XXI, p. 31.

64 *Civilization and its Discontents, S.E.* XXI, pp. 74–5.

65 The words quoted come from a letter to Lou Andreas-Salomé 11:12:1927, *Salomé Letters*, p. 172, while the other examples are cited by Clark *Freud: The Cause*, pp. 467–71.

66 Letter to Ferenczi 23:10:1927, Jones III, p. 147.

67 Cf. the correspondence between the two of them in the *Faith Letters*.

68 Cited by Clark *Freud: The Cause*, p. 469.

69 Letter to Werner Achelis 30:1:1927 (no. 228), *Letters*, p. 375.

70 'The claims of psycho-analysis to scientific interest', *S.E.* XIII, p. 186.

71 *The Future of an Illusion, S.E.* XXI, p. 54.

72 Cited by Brandell in *Freud: Child of his Century* (London: Routledge and Kegan Paul, 1979), p. 19.

73 Letter to Fliess 16:10:1895 (no. 31), *Origins*, p. 128.

74 Letter to Ferenczi 13:5:1913, cited by Brome in *Freud: Disciples*, p. 132.

75 *New Introductory Lectures on Psycho-Analysis, S.E.* XXII, p. 160.

76 Ibid., p. 168.

77 *The Psychopathology of Everyday Life* (1907 Additions to the text), *S.E.* VI, p. 48.

78 Letter to Oppenheim 28:10:1909 from Freud and Oppenheim *Dreams in Folklore* (translated by A. M. O. Richards edited with an introduction by Strachey, New York: International Universities Press, 1958), p. 13.

79 Ibid.

80 *New Introductory Lectures on Psycho-Analysis, S.E.* XXII, p. 146.
81 'The claims of psycho-analysis to scientific interest', *S.E.* XIII, pp. 185–6.
82 Ibid., p. 186.
83 Letter to Jung 12:11:1911 (no. 280F), *Freud/Jung Letters*, p. 459.
84 Letter from Jung to Freud 14:11:1911 (no. 280J), Ibid. p. 460.
85 Letter to Pfister 27:5:1919, cited by Jones III p. 15.
86 *On the History of the Psycho-Analytic Movement, S.E.* XIV, p. 37.
87 Letter to Jung 20:8:1919 (no. 268F), *Freud/Jung Letters*, p. 438.
88 Letter from Jung to Freud 29:8:1911 (no. 269J), Ibid, p. 439.
89 Letter to Jung 1:9:1911 (no. 270F), Ibid., p. 441.
90 Cf. letter from Emma Jung to Freud 30:10:1911, Ibid., pp. 452–3.
91 Letter to Jung 2:11:1911 (no. 278F), Ibid., p. 453.
92 Letter to Ferenczi 30:11:1911, Jones II, p. 394.
93 Letter to Jones 9:4:1913, Ibid., p. 396.
94 Letter to Ferenczi 1:5:1913, Ibid., p. 396.
95 Postscript to *An Autobiographical Study, S.E.* XX, p. 72.
96 Letter to Ferenczi 8:5:1913, Jones II, p. 396.
97 Letter to Abraham 13:5:1913, Ibid., p. 396.
98 Letter to Ferenczi 13:5:1913, Ibid., p. 396.
99 Letter to Abraham 1:6:1913 Ibid., pp. 396–7.
100 Letter to Abraham 26:10:1913, *Analytic Dialogue*, p. 151.
101 *Totem and Taboo, S.E.* XIII, p. 1.
102 Ibid., p. 17.
103 Ibid.
104 *The Theory of Psychoanalysis* (The Fordham Lectures 1912) from *The Collected Works of C. G. Jung* (edited by Gerhard Adler, Michael Fordham and Herbert Read; William McGuire, Executive Editor; translated by R. F. C. Hull, New York and Princeton (Bollingen Series xx) and London: Routledge and Kegan Paul), Vol. 4, p. 132. (Afterward referred to as *Fordham Lectures.*)
105 Ibid., p. 166.
106 *Totem and Taboo, S.E.* XIII, p. 67.
107 Ibid., p. 22.
108 Ibid., p. 70.
109 Ibid., p. 32.
110 Ibid., p. 69.
111 Ibid., p. 72.
112 *New Introductory Lectures on Psycho-Analysis, S.E.* XXII, p. 145.
113 Letter to Pfister 25:11:1928, *Faith Letters*, p. 125.
114 Those interested in this argument may like to consider the matter further through the study of a work such as Paul Tournier *Guilt and Grace* (London: Hodder and Stoughton, 1969).
115 *Totem and Taboo, S.E.* XIII, p. 108.
116 Jones II, pp. 401–2.
117 *Totem and Taboo, S.E.* XIII, pp. 123–4.
118 Ibid., p. 125.
119 *Group Psychology and the Analysis of the Ego, S.E.* XVIII, p. 122.

120 *Totem and Taboo, S.E.* XIII, pp. 141–2.
121 Ibid., p. 161.
122 Ibid., p. 143.
123 'From the history of an infantile neurosis', *S.E.* XVII, p. 97.
124 Letter to Ferenczi 25:1:1917, cited Jones III, p. 334.
125 Letter to Abraham 11:11:1917, *Analytic Dialogue*, pp. 261–2.
126 Letter to Georg Groddeck 5:6:1917 (no. 176), *Letters*, p. 323.
127 *Moses and Monotheism, S.E.* XXIII, p. 100.
128 Jones III, p. 336.
129 *Totem and Taboo, S.E.* XIII, p. 146.
130 Ibid., p. 147.
131 Letter to Marie Bonaparte 21:4:1926, Jones III, p. 131.
132 'Dostoevsky and Parricide', *S.E.* XXI, p. 183.
133 Letter to Pfister 16:2:1929, *Faith Letters*, p. 129.
134 Letter to Marie Bonaparte 13:8:1937, cited Jones III, p. 495.
135 'Findings, ideas, problems', *S.E.* XXIII, p. 300.
136 Letter to Pfister 7:2:1930, *Faith Letters*, p. 133.
137 Letter to Silberstein 1873, (no. 2G), at Colchester.
138 Letter to Jung 16:4:1909 (no. 139F), *Freud/Jung Letters*, p. 220.
139 Letter to Ferenczi 31:3:1919, Jones III, p. 42.
140 *Beyond the Pleasure Principle, S.E.* XVIII, p. 24.
141 Cited by Sulloway *Freud: Biologist*, p. 412.
142 *Civilization and its Discontents, S.E.* XXI, p. 119.
143 Cited by Sulloway, *Freud: Biologist*, p. 393.
144 Ibid., p. 394.
145 *Beyond the Pleasure Principle, S.E.* XVIII, p. 7.
146 *An Autobiographical Study, S.E.* XX, p. 57.
147 *Beyond the Pleasure Principle, S.E.* XVIII, p. 36 (Freud's emphasis).
148 The first example is taken from *New Introductory Lectures on Psycho-Analysis, S.E.* XXII, p. 106, the second from *Beyond the Pleasure Principle, S.E.* XVIII, p. 37, and from *New Introductory Lectures on Psycho-Analysis, S.E.* XXII, p. 106.
149 Ibid., p. 106.
150 *Beyond the Pleasure Principle, S.E.* XVIII, p. 38.
151 Ibid., p. 38.
152 *The Ego and the Id, S.E.* XIX, p. 47.
153 Cf. *Freud: Biologist*.
154 *Beyond the Pleasure Principle, S.E.* XVIII, p. 55.
155 Details of the important place of Sabina Spielrein in the thinking of both Jung and Freud at this time are contained in Carotenuto's *A Secret Symmetry: Sabina Spielrein between Jung and Freud* (translated by Arno Pomerans, John Shepley and Krishna Winston, New York: Pantheon Books, 1982; London: Routledge and Kegan Paul, 1984), cf. also Bruno Bettleheim 'Scandal in the Family' *New York Review of Books* 30, 11, 30 June 183, pp. 39–44. Unfortunately, Jung's literary guardians refused permission for Jung's letters to Spielrein to be published. She died in Russia in the Stalin purges.
156 *An Autobiographical Study, S.E.* XX, p. 59.

… Cause, p. 432 and Roazen *Freud: Followers*, p. 231.
… contents, S.E. XXI, p. 120.
… alomé 1:8:1919, *Salomé Letters*, p. 99.
… :8:1918, *Freud: Pictures*, p. 217.
… 21:5:1922, Jones III, p. 88.
… czi 30:3:1922, Jones III, p. 88.
… . 20.
… Max Halberstadt 25:1:1920, *Freud: Pictures*, p. 220.
… to Eitingon 3:2:1920, Jones III, p. 20.
… etter to Ferenczi 4:2:1920, Jones III, pp. 20–1.
… Cited by Roazen *Freud: Followers*, p. 362.
168 Letter to the Levy sisters 11:6:1923, *Freud: Pictures*, p. 229.
169 Letter to Binswanger 15:10:1926, Jones III, p. 97.
170 Letter to Max Halberstadt 7:7:1923, cited by Clark *Freud: The Cause*, p. 441.
171 Jones III, p. 96.
172 Letter to Lou Andreas-Salomé 14:7:1916, *Salomé Letters*, p. 48.
173 Letter to Lou Andreas-Salomé 10:5:1925, *Salomé Letters*, p. 154.
174 'Some psychical consequences of the anatomical distinction between the sexes', *S.E.* XIX, pp. 248–9.
175 'My contact with Josef Popper-Lynkeus', *S.E.* XXII, p. 224.
176 *New Introductory Lectures on Psycho-Analysis, S.E.* XXII, p. 29.
177 Letter to Pfister 3:1:1926, *Freud: Pictures*, p. 238.
178 *Inhibitions, Symptoms and Anxiety, S.E.* XX, p. 128.
179 Letter to Jung 6:12:1906 (no. 8F), *Freud/Jung Letters*, p. 12.
180 Cited by Sulloway *Freud: Biologist.*
181 Letter to Pfister 18:1:1909, *Faith Letters*, p. 15.
182 Jones II, p. 32.
183 Cited by Roazen *Brother Animal*, p. 62.
184 Letter to Rank 4:8:1922, cited by Clark *Freud: The Cause*, p. 450.
185 *The Interpretation of Dreams, S.E.* V, p. 400.
186 *The Ego and the Id, S.E.* XIX, p. 58.
187 Letter to Ferenczi 24:3:1924, Jones III, p. 61.
188 Letter to Rank 26:11:1923, cited by Grosskurth in 'In the throes of separation' (Review of *Otto Rank: A Rediscovered Legacy*), *Times Literary Supplement* 6 May 1983, p. 451.
189 Letter from Abraham to Freud 21:2:1924, *Analytic Dialogue*, p. 349.
190 Letter to Rank 23:7:1924, cited by Clark *Freud: The Cause*, p. 453.
191 Letter to Lou Andreas-Salomé 11:8:1924, *Salomé Letters*, p. 138.
192 Letter from Rank to the Committee 26:12:1924, cited by Clark *Freud: The Cause*, p. 455.
193 Cited by Clark *Freud: The Cause*, p. 457.
194 'Analysis terminable and interminable', *S.E.* XXIII, p. 216.
195 Cf. A. Janov *The Primal Scream, Primal Therapy: The Cure for Neurosis* (New York: Dell Publishing, 1970).
196 Cf. Frank Lake *Clinical Theology* (London: Darton, Longman and Todd, 1966).
197 Letter to Ferenczi 9:7:1913, *Freud: Pictures*, p. 207.
198 'The theme of the three caskets', *S.E.* XII, p. 293.

199 *The Interpretation of Dreams, S.E.* IV, p. 257.
200 Cf. letters to Lou Andreas-Salomé 3:7:1922 and 11:8:1924, *Salomé Letters,* pp. 117, 137.
201 Unpublished letter to Samuel Freud cited by Clark *Freud: The Cause,* p. 480.
202 *New Introductory Lectures on Psycho-Analysis, S.E.* XXII, p. 146.
203 Ibid., p. 146.
204 Cf. David Rappaport's 'A Historical Survey of Psychoanalytic Ego Psychology' *Psychological Issues* 1, 1, 5–17 (1958).
205 *Introductory Lectures on Psycho-Analysis, S.E.* XV, p. 15.
206 *An Autobiographical Study, S.E.* XX, p. 70.
207 Ibid.
208 *The Question of Lay Analysis, S.E.* XX, p. 229.
209 Letter to Paul Federn 27:3:1926 from Ernst Federn 'How Freudian are the Freudians? Some remarks on an unpublished letter', *Journal of the History of the Behavioural Sciences* III, 3, pp. 269–81 (1967) p. 269.
210 Letter to Ferenczi 27:4:1929, Jones III, p. 320.
211 Jones III, p. 318.
212 Cited by Roazen *Freud: Followers,* pp. 386–7.
213 Letter to Schnier 5:7:1938, Jones III, p. 323.
214 Letter to Pfister 25:11:1928, *Faith Letters,* p. 126.
215 Letter to Pfister 16:2:1929, *Faith Letters,* pp. 128–9.
216 Ibid., p. 129.
217 Letter to Pfister 7:2:1930, *Faith Letters,* pp. 132–3.
218 P. Tillich *The Courage to Be,* (London: Fontana, 1957).
219 Comment to Eastman cited by Clark *Freud: The Cause,* p. 476.
220 Cited by Clark *Freud: The Cause,* p. 476.
221 Letter to Arnold Zweig 7:12:1930, *Zweig Letters,* p. 25.
222 Letter to Einstein, September 1932, published as, *Why War!, S.E.* XXII, p. 202.
223 Cited in *Freud: Pictures,* p. 282.
224 Cited by Reik in *Freud: Thirty Years,* p. 36.
225 Cited in *Freud: Pictures,* p. 283.
226 Letter to Pfister 28:5:1933, *Faith Letters,* p. 140.
227 Cited by Brome in *Freud: Disciples,* p. 143. c.f. the evenhanded discussion of chapter 11, 'Was Jung Pro-Nazi or Anti-Semitic?', pp. 142–153.
228 Letter from Jung to Wolfgang Kranefeldt 9:2:1934, *International Review of Psycho-Analysis* 4, p. 377 (1977).
229 Cf. the excellent chapter by Clark in *Freud: The Cause* for the last days in Vienna and of how Freud managed to escape, pp. 502–30.
230 Cited by Clark *Freud: The Cause,* p. 507.
231 Ibid., p. 511.
232 *An Outline of Psycho-Analysis, S.E.* XXIII, p. 139.
233 *Moses and Monotheism: Three Essays, S.E.* XXIII, p. 103.
234 Letter to Singer 31:10:1938, from *Freud: Forty Years,* p. 39.
235 *Moses and Monotheism: Three Essays, S.E.* XXIII, p. 110.
236 Letter to Singer 31:10:1938 (no. 307), *Letters,* p. 448.
237 *Moses and Monotheism: Three Essays, S.E.* XXIII, p. 119.
238 Ibid., p. 27 note 2.

239 *Freud: Master*, p. 182.
240 *Moses and Monotheism: Three Essays*, S.E. XXIII, p. 78.
241 Letter to Max Eitingon 1:12:1929 (no. 245), *Letters*, p. 391.

CONCLUSION

1 That is not to say that within any given discipline or field Freud's fortunes have not fluctuated, in most they have dramatically — as even a cursory study of the history of psychiatry demonstrates. Interest in, and respect for, psychoanalysis has waxed and waned and sometimes waxed again in many areas.

2 One of the classic treatments of this subject is Karl Popper in his *Conjectures and Refutations* (London: Routledge and Kegan Paul, 1963). Frank Cioffi has pursued this logic in his 'Freud and the Idea of a Pseudoscience' from Borger, R. and Cioffi, F. *Explanation in the Behavioural Sciences* (Cambridge: Cambridge University Press, 1970). More recently, there has been a fascinating debate in the *British Journal of Medical Psychology*. This was initiated by Harry Gumtrip's posthumous paper, 'Psychoanalysis and some scientific and philosophical critics (Dr Eliot Slater, Sir Peter Medawar and Sir Karl Popper)' **51**, pp. 207–24 (1978); sustained by David Will 'Psychoanalysis as a human science' **53**, pp. 201–11 (1980); and by Keith Oatley's 'Refraction and the appropriation of truth in Psychoanalysis' **55**, pp. 1–11 (1982). The debate continues with Michael Radford's 'Psychoanalysis and the Science of Problem-Solving Man: An Appreciation of Popper's Philosophy and a Response to Will, 1980' **56**, 1983 pp. 9–26 and with Will's 'Transcendental realism and the scientificity of psychoanalysis: A reply to recent criticism' **56**, pp. 371–8 (1983). Cf. also B. A. Farrell's *The Standing of Psychoanalysis* (Oxford: Oxford University Press, 1982) and Adolf Grünbaum's *The Foundations of Psychoanalysis: A Philosophical Critique* (USA: University of California Press, 1984).

3 Cf. Philip Rieff *The Triumph of the Therapeutic* (Harmondsworth: Penguin, 1969).

4 D. M. Thomas, *The White Hotel* (London: Gollancz, 1978) is an example of a recent novelist's interest in Freud. Carey Harrison's *Freud: a Novel* (London: Weidenfeld and Nicholson, 1984) is another example. It is based upon the BBC Television series on Freud, starring David Suchet as Freud — BBC 1984.

5 Cited by Sachs *Freud: Master*, p. 103.

6 My thanks to Peter Swales for this interesting vignette on Freud's world.

7 Cited by Janet Malcolm 'Trouble II', p. 78.

8 Cited by Joseph Wortis *Fragment of an Analysis with Freud* (New York: Simon and Schuster, 1954), p. 142.

9 Letter to Fliess 1:2:1900, *Freud: Dying*, p. 201.

10 Letter from Freud to Binswanger 8:10:1936 (no. 286), *Letters*, p. 427.

11 To those who object to my analysis of Freud's life and work I suggest that the response of King Boabdil to his news not be taken too literally in my case.

Permissions Acknowledgements

The author and publishers would like to thank Celia Hurst at Sigmund Freud Copyrights Ltd and John Charlton at The Hogarth Press Ltd for giving assistance with the location of rights holders. They are grateful to Sigmund Freud Copyrights Ltd for granting permission to quote extracts from unpublished Freud letters to Silberstein and Ferenczi and would also like to thank the organizations and publishers listed below for their permission to reprint material for which they hold either US, World or UK rights.

A Basic Books Inc. for:
1 Extracts from *Collected Papers* vol. 1, by Sigmund Freud. Authorized translation under the supervision of Joan Riviere.
2 Extracts from *Collected Papers* vols 2 and 4, by Sigmund Freud.
3 Extracts from *Collected Papers* vol. 3, by Sigmund Freud. Authorized translation by Alix and James Strachey.
4 Extracts from *Collected Papers* vol. 5, by Sigmund Freud. Edited by James Strachey.

Items A1–4 are published by Basic Books Inc. by arrangement with The Hogarth Press Ltd and The Institute of Psychoanalysis, London.

5 Extracts from *Three Essays on the Theory of Sexuality* by Sigmund Freud. Translated and newly edited by James Strachey. © 1962 by Sigmund Freud Copyrights Ltd.
6 Extracts from *The Interpretation of Dreams* by Sigmund Freud. Translated from the German and edited by James Strachey. Published in the USA by Basic Books Inc., by arrangement with George Allen & Unwin Ltd and The Hogarth Press Ltd.
7 Extracts from *Studies on Hysteria* by Josef Breuer and Sigmund Freud. Translated from the Geman and edited by James Strachey. Published in the USA by Basic Book Inc. by arrangement with The Hogarth Press Ltd.
8 Extracts from *The Origins of Psycho-Analysis: Letters to Wilhelm Fliess, Drafts and Notes 1887–1902* by Sigmund Freud. Edited by Marie Bonaparte, Anna Freud and Ernst Kris. Authorized translation by Eric Mosbacher and James Strachey. © 1954 by Basic Books Inc.
9 Extracts from *The Letters of Sigmund Freud, 1873–1939* selected and edited by Ernst L. Freud. Translated by Tania and James Stern. © 1960 by Sigmund Freud Copyrights Ltd. Introduction © 1975 by Steven Marcus.
10 Extracts from *The Life and Work of Sigmund Freud* by Ernest Jones MD Volume 1 © 1953 by Ernest Jones, © 1981 by Mervyn Jones. Volume 2 © 1955 by Ernest Jones. Volume 3 © 1957 by Ernest Jones.
11 Extracts from *Psycho-Analysis and Faith: The Letters of Sigmund Freud*

and Oskar Pfister. Edited by Ernest Freud and Heinrich Meng. Translated by Eric Mosbacher. © 1963 by Ernest Freud.

12 Extracts from *A Psycho-Analytic Dialogue: The Letters of Sigmund Freud and Karl Abraham, 1907–1926*. Edited by Hilda Abraham and Ernst Freud. Translated by Bernard Marsh and Hilda Abraham.

13 A diagram from *A Grammar of Dreams* by David Foulkes. © 1978 by Basic Books Inc. Publishers.

B Basic Books Inc. and the Mary Evans Picture Library for plate 13. Photo by Edmund Engelman.

C The British Psychological Society and Prof. J. Sandler for diagrams first published in the *British Journal of Medical Psychology* vols 46 and 55.

D The Hogarth Press Ltd for:

1 Extracts from *The Life and Work of Sigmund Freud* by Ernest Jones MD Copyright as in A10.

2 Extracts from *The Freud/Jung Letters: The Correspondence between Sigmund Freud and C. G. Jung*. Edited by William McGuire, translated by Ralph Manheim and R. F. C. Hull. Bollingen Series 94, © 1974 by Sigmund Freud Copyrights Ltd and Erbengemeinschafe Prof. Dr C. G. Jung.

3 Extracts from *Letters of Sigmund Freud*. Details as in A9.

4 Extracts from *The Origins of Psycho-Analysis*. Details as in A8.

5 Extracts from *Psycho-Analysis and Faith*. Details as in A11.

E The Hogarth Press Ltd and the Institute of Psychoanalysis for:

1 Extracts from *A Psycho-Analytic Dialogue*. Details as in A13.

2 Extracts from *Sigmund Freud and Lou Andreas-Salome: Letters*. Edited by Ernst Pfeiffer. Translated by William and Elaine Robson-Scott.

3 Extracts from *The Letters of Sigmund Freud and Arnold Zweig*. Edited by Ernst Pfeiffer. Translated by William and Elaine Robson-Scott.

4 Extracts from *Freud: Living and Dying* by Max Schur.

5 Extracts from *Thirty Years with Freud* by Reik.

6 Extracts from *Freud: Master and Friend* by Hans Sachs.

F Sigmund Freud Copyrights Ltd for permission to reprint previously published Freud quotations from a large number of works for which they hold copyright.

G Sigmund Freud Copyrights Ltd, The Institute of Psychoanalysis and The Hogarth Press Ltd for permission to quote from *The Standard Edition of the Complete Psychological Works of Sigmund Freud*. Translated and edited by James Strachey.

H Sigmund Freud Copyrights Ltd and the Mary Evans Picture Library for plates 1–9, 11 and 12.

I Sigmund Freud Copyrights Ltd and the Mary Evans Picture Library for plate 10. Photo by Max Halberstadt.

J Harcourt Brace Jovanovich Inc. for:

1 Extracts from *Sigmund Freud and Lou Andreas-Salome: Letters*. Details as in E2.

2 Extracts from *The Letters of Sigmund Freud and Arnold Zweig*. Details as in E3.

K Princeton University Press for extracts from *The Freud/Jung Letters*. Details as in D2.

L George Allen & Unwin (Publishers) Ltd for:
  1 Extracts from *The Interpretation of Dreams*. Details as in A7.
  2 Extracts from *Introductory Lectures on Psycho-Analysis* and *Delusions and Dreams in Jensen's Gradiva* by Sigmund Freud.
M Routledge and Kegan Paul PLC for extracts from *Leonardo da Vinci and a Memory of his Childhood*, *Totem and Taboo* and *Jokes and their Relation to the Unconscious*, all by Sigmund Freud.
N Adam and Charles Black Publishers for extracts from *The Psychopathology of Everyday Life* by Sigmund Freud. Originally published by Ernest Benn Ltd.
O International Universities Press Inc. for extracts from *Freud: Living and Dying*. Details as in E4.
P W. W. Norton Inc. for extracts from the following, all by Sigmund Freud: *Leonardo da Vinci and a Memory of his Childhood*, *Totem and Taboo*, *Jokes and their Relation to the Unconscious*, *Introductory Lectures on Psycho-Analysis*, *On Dreams*, *The Psychopathology of Everyday Life*, *Beyond the Pleasure Principle*, *Group Psychology and the Analysis of the Ego*, *The Ego and the Id*, *The Question of Lay Analysis*, *New Introductory Lectures on Psycho-Analysis*, *Civilization and its Discontents*, *The Future of an Illusion*, *An Autobiographical Study* and 'An Outline of Psycho-analysis'.

Index

sexuality *(continued)*
  and dreams, 98, 100, 107–8, 119–20,
    134–6
  guilt and, 70, 119
  homosexuality, 91–4, 120, 146, 153,
    156–8
  hysteria and, 35–6, 57, 61–2, 64–70
  instincts and, 169
  of SF, 67–70, 84–5, 87–96, 119, 129,
    157–8
  sublimated, 87, 199, 200, 204
  theory and practice, 67–96
  of women, 146, 153–5
'Sexuality in Aetiology of Neuroses', 260
Shakespeare, William, 195, 243
Signorelli, Luca, 78–9, 126, 129, 131,
  260–1
Silberstein, Eduard, 21–3, 25–7, 154, 164,
  176, 230, 269
sisters of SF, 13, 17, 20, 27, 41, 248
sleep, states of, 121
  see also dreams
slips of tongue, 101, 122–38, 141
  *see also Psychopathology of Everyday
    Life*
Social Darwinism, 43
somnabulism, 57
sons of SF *see* Freud: Ernst; Martin; Oliver
Sophocles, 85
speech *see* slips of tongue
Spielrein, S., 234, 264
Steinbach, Eugen, 238
Stekel, Wilhelm, 93, 107, 180–2, 202,
  23–5, 264
  photograph of, 162
Strachey, Alix, 268
Strachey, James, 92, 122, 202, 268
structural model of mind, 170–4
Studies on Hysteria, 45, 59–67 *passim*,
  70–1, 86, 152, 259
sublimation, 87, 199, 200, 204, 212
suicide, 182
Sulloway, Frank, 50, 51, 83, 233–4, 270
super-ego, 170, 172–4
superstition about death, 101
Swales, Peter, 131, 270–1
Swoboda, H., 262
symbolism in dreams, 104
symptoms: dreams, slips and jokes, 97–
  142
Szasz, Thomas, 181

taboo, 218–21, 225–8, 230, 251–2
'talking cure' for hysteria, 56, 58
Tausk, Victor, 188–9, 265
Thanatos, 235
  see also death instinct
'Theme of Three Caskets', 242
theories of psychoanalytic movement,
  164–75
Thomas, D. M., 151
'Thoughts for Times on War and Death',
  264
Three Essays on Theory of Sexuality, 36,
  82, 161, 262
Tillich, Paul, 247
time, lack of, 238–9
Tolstoy, Count Leo, 208
topographical model of mind, 168–70,
  172
Totem and Taboo, 218–20, 225–8, 230,
  251–2
training, psychoanalytic, 189, 245
transference, 62, 63, 152–3
transitionphases in sexuality, 86–7
Tyson, Alan, 268

'Über Coca', 34–5
unconscious, 95, 164
  Brentano on, 26
  and dreams, 106–7, 113
  and guilt, 221
  and jokes *see Jokes* etc
  in model of mind, 168–9, 172–3
  and war, 203
United States, 244–8
Utilitarianism, 43
utopianism, 205–6

Van Gogh, V., 44
Vienna
  academic society, 47–51, 65, 69
  early life in, 17–37, 41–2
Vienna Psychoanalytic Society, 51,
  181–91 *passim*, 175, 245–6
Virchow, R., 26
Virgil, 130–1, 178–9

Walter, Bruno, 146
war, 202–3, 214, 231, 239, 247–50, 264
Weier, Johann, 76, 195, 259
Weininger, O., 262
Wells, H. G., 250